QUESTIONS THAT MATTER

AN INVITATION TO PHILOSOPHY

SECOND SHORTER EDITION

QUESTIONS THAT MATTER

AN INVITATION TO PHILOSOPHY

SECOND SHORTER EDITION

Ed. L. Miller
University of Colorado

OVERTURE
BOOKS

Boston, Massachusetts   Burr Ridge, Illinois   Dubuque, Iowa
Madison, Wisconsin   New York, New York   San Francisco, California
St. Louis, Missouri

McGraw-Hill

A Division of The McGraw·Hill Companies

QUESTIONS THAT MATTER: AN INVITATION TO PHILOSOPHY

Acknowledgments appear on pages 440–444, and on this page by reference.

This book is printed on acid-free paper.

4 5 7 8 9 0 DOC/DOC 0

ISBN 0–07–042264–8

Editorial director: *Phillip A. Butcher*
Sponsoring editor: *Sarah Moyers*
Marketing manager: *Daniel M. Loch*
Project manager: *Paula M. Buschman*
Project supervisor: *Scott Hamilton*
Designer: *Larry J. Cope*
Compositor: *Shepherd Incorporated*
Typeface: *10.5/13.5 Janson*
Printer: *R. R. Donnelley & Sons Company*

Library of Congress Cataloging-in Publication Data

Miller, E. L. (Ed. LeRoy), (date)
    Questions that matter: an invitation to philosophy/Ed. L.
Miller.—2nd shorter ed.
        p. cm.
    Condensation of Questions that matter, 4th ed.
    Includes bibliographical references and index.
    ISBN 0–07–042264–8 (alk. paper)
    1. Philosophy—Introductions. I. Title.
BD21.M46 1997
100—dc21   97–1299

http://www.mhcollege.com

For
the fair
Cynthia

Preface

Questions That Matter: An Invitation to Philosophy, Second Shorter Edition, is intended as an introductory text in philosophy, for courses lasting from eight to fifteen weeks. It is a condensation of *Questions That Matter*, Fourth Edition, and retains the general organization and special features that have been so popular with readers.

Most of the students using this text will have no prior background in philosophy, and this first encounter is likely to be the students' best opportunity to master a subject that really does pose the questions that matter. Thus I have been guided throughout by a concern to represent and discuss the issues in a concise, clear, and stimulating style. Furthermore, I have attempted to organize the content so that the student will be able to appreciate that there is coherence and direction amid the twists and turns in the history of philosophical ideas. I have also been guided by a conviction that explanatory aids can promote understanding of an often challenging subject.

This book has grown out of many years of teaching beginning philosophy courses. I am grateful to untold numbers of students, who have shown me what works and what doesn't in the attempt to confront, engage, and instruct.

ORGANIZATION

Each part of the book represents a major branch of philosophy—metaphysics, epistemology, philosophy of religion, ethics, and social and political philosophy. Within each branch or problem area, students are introduced to the key issues, positions, and thinkers and are given (whenever possible) historical contexts, connections, and developments. A two-chapter introduction has been prefixed to the whole. The first chapter explains the nature of philosophy and includes a discussion of issues and problems involved in the philosophical enterprise. The second chapter provides a brief discussion of logic in order to help students analyze philosophical arguments. While the text has been designed so that topics flow logically from one to another, instructors will also find that it is flexible enough to allow them to structure the course in any order they deem appropriate.

FEATURES

Because it is important to be introduced to the arguments of the major thinkers in their own words, the text contains frequent and usually copious quotations from primary sources. These passages, from both historical and contemporary writers, are carefully introduced and summarized in order to aid comprehension. A list of primary sources can be found within the chapter listings in the table of contents.

Boxed inserts appear in the text at those points where basic terms, concepts, or positions need to be explained, summarized, or emphasized. Still other boxes contain relevant material—for example, biographical sketches and brief readings from literature of the period.

Artwork provides explanations of concepts, portraits of philosophers, facsimile documents, and the like.

Each chapter concludes with a review section containing a brief summary, a list of basic ideas, questions for reflection and discussion, and an annotated bibliography geared especially to research and writing projects.

A glossary at the end of the book offers a handy reference for definitions of key terms found within the text.

ED. L. MILLER

Contents

About the Author

Ed. L. Miller holds a Ph.D. in Philosophy from the University of Southern California and a Doctorate of Theology from the University of Basel, Switzerland. Professor Miller's philosophical interests encompass both the history of philosophy and philosophical theology. In addition to numerous articles and reviews, his other books include: *Believing in God, Philosophical and Religious Issues, God and Reason,* and *Salvation History in the Prologue of John.* He has taught at California Lutheran University, St. Olaf College, and, for the last thirty years, at the University of Colorado, Boulder. In addition to being a member of the philosophy faculty, he also teaches for the Religious Studies Department and is Director of the Theology Forum, A Center for Theological/Philosophical Discussion. He is a member of the American Academy of Religion, the Society of Christian Philosophers, and Studiorum Novi Testamenti Societas. He is listed in *The Directory of American Scholars* and *Contemporary Authors.* Professor Miller plays several musical instruments, and spare time is often spent on the plains doing research on the Colorado Indian War, in the mountains skiing, or on his boat on Lake Dillon.

THE
NATURE
OF
PHILOSOPHY

P HILOSOPHICAL REFLECTION is not an activity indulged in only by specialists called philosophers who allegedly live in architectural monstrosities known as ivory towers. Just as each of us at times engages casually in horticulture or medicine or carpentry without special training, so practically all of us on certain occasions spontaneously occupy ourselves with philosophical questions.

"We may, for example, read in the newspapers of a child born hopelessly malformed and defective, but who, if operated upon at once, might nonetheless be kept alive. And we may read further that the physician in charge, realizing that the child's life could not be other than a grievous burden to himself, to his parents, and to society, refrained from operating and allowed the child to die. Then, in letters from readers to the editors of newspapers all over the country, controversy rages about whether the physician's action was morally right or morally wrong. And even if we do not ourselves take active part in them, we too form opinions on the question.

"In such a controversy the participants do not merely state their moral appraisal of the physician's course. They also give reasons of one kind or another to support the validity of their judgment. And if these reasons are in turn challenged, each participant brings forth considerations he believes adequate to vindicate the validity of his reasons.

"The reasons, and the reasons for the reasons, that are thus appealed to as grounds for endorsing or condemning the physician's action, constitute a moral philosophy, or a least a fragment of one. And the mental activity of searching for those reasons, and of then so editing them as to purge them of the inconsistencies of exaggerations or errors that opponents were able to point out, constitute philosophizing, or philosophical reflection.

"In this example the issue is a moral one, and the philosophy constructed on the spur of the occasion by a participant is therefore, as far as it goes, a moral philosophy: that is, a theory of the nature of the difference between moral right and wrong, and of the nature of the situations to which appraisal in terms of morality and immorality is congruous. But similar controversies, or indeed doubts within one person's mind, arise about issues of other kinds: about the merits of certain works of art, for example, or about educational issues, or about the sufficiency of the evidence offered as basis for a given assertion, and so on. The fragmentary philosophies similarly improvised on such occasions are then a philosophy of art, a philosophy of education, or a philosophy of knowledge. And there can be no doubt that, on the occasions impelling us to engage in such reflection, a judgment shaped by the conclusions reached in that reflective manner is likely to be wiser than would be one made without it."

C. J. Ducasse, *The Key Reporter* 23 (1958), p. 3.

CHAPTER 1

What
Is
Philosophy?

I NASMUCH AS this text seeks to introduce the reader to philosophy, it may seem appropriate to begin by defining the term. We will indeed try to define and characterize philosophy, but the reader should have no illusions that this is how one comes to understand it. The only way to understand what philosophy is about is to *participate* in it. This means to be confronted with philosophical questions, to use philosophical language, to become acquainted with differing philosophical positions and maneuvers, to read the philosophers themselves, and to grapple with the issues for oneself. Therefore it is not at the beginning but rather at the *end* of such a book as this that one might really understand something of philosophy. Nevertheless, we must begin somewhere, and it may be useful to have at least *some* idea of the subject before us, right at the start.

"Philosophy is like the measles. It must be caught from someone who is already infected. To learn to philosophize, you must try your luck arguing with a live philosopher."

Elmer Sprague, *What Is Philosophy?* (New York: Oxford University Press, 1961), p. 3.

THE WORD ITSELF

Four ways of getting at the meaning and nature of philosophy may be proposed. *First*, let us look at the word itself. "Philosophy" comes from a Greek word which means "love of wisdom. It was first used by the ancient Greek thinker Pythagoras (about 600 B.C.), who likened philosophers—pursuers of wisdom—to spectators at ancient games:

> . . . when Leon the tyrant of Philius asked him who he was, he said, "A philosopher," and that he compared life to the Great Games, where some went to compete for the prize and others went with wares to sell, but the best as spectators; for similarly, in life, some grow up with servile natures, greedy for fame and gain, but the philosopher seeks for truth.[1]

To be sure, something of the spirit and character of philosophy is suggested in this way by the very meaning of the word—but not much. We must know more about this "pursuit of wisdom."

THE FIELDS OF PHILOSOPHY

Let us then, *second*, approach the meaning of philosophy from a different standpoint, namely, from the standpoint of its several fields or areas of investigation. Not all lists of the fields of philosophy would agree, but most of them would almost certainly include six: *metaphysics, epistemology,*

---

[1]Diogenes Laertius, *Lives of Eminent Philosophers*, VIII, 8, tr. R. D. Hicks (Cambridge, MA: Harvard University Press, 1925), II.

value-theory, ethics, aesthetics, and *logic.* Some of these terms may seem to be taken from a foreign language, but they are not as difficult as they sound.

Metaphysics means, usually, the study or theory of reality. The question of metaphysics is: What is reality? What is real? This involves, of course, many related questions, such as, Is reality some kind of "thing"? Is it one or is it many? If it is one, then how is it related to the many things around us? Can ultimate reality be grasped by the five senses, or is it supernatural or transcendent? And so on. It should be mentioned that sometimes the word "metaphysics" is used in a narrower way to concern only *transcendent* reality, that is, reality which lies beyond the physical world and cannot therefore be grasped by means of the senses. Therefore, supernaturalists do metaphysics in the first sense because they raise the question of reality, and they do metaphysics also in the narrower sense because they believe in supernatural or transcendent reality, say, God. On the other hand, materialists do metaphysics in the first sense because they too raise the question of reality, but their belief is not metaphysical in the narrower sense because they deny that anything is real except matter.

Epistemology is the study or theory of knowledge. The question of epistemology is: What is knowledge? What does it mean "to know"? This too implies many other questions, such as, How is knowledge acquired? What, if anything, do the senses contribute to knowledge? What does reason contribute? Can we be really certain of anything? What is truth? Some philosophers think that the fields of metaphysics and epistemology are, in a way, the pillars of all the rest. Why would one say this? Are the questions, What is real? And how can I know it? in some sense the most basic questions of all? Is it possible that how you answer these questions will determine your whole philosophical outlook?

Value-theory is, obviously, the study of value. The question here is: What is value? It should be noted that this question does not involve any particular sort of value, but value of *all* sorts—the value of tables, steaks, political ideologies, laws, actions—with value in any and all of its manifestations. *Ethics,* on the other hand, is concerned with a *particular* sort of value, namely, value as it applies to personal actions, decisions, and relations; it is concerned with *moral* value. It raises the question, What is morally good? What is right? Here again a whole cluster of questions suggest themselves, such as, Are there any absolute or universal moral principles? Does the end ever justify the means? Am I my brother's keeper? *Aesthetics* is also the study of a particular sort of value, namely, the values involved in art and our experience of beauty. It raises the question, What is art? It addresses such issues as the relation of beauty to art, whether there can be any objective standards by which artistic works may be judged (or is beauty in the eye of the beholder?), and the connections among art, reality, and truth. (It should be noted that ethics, which studies moral value, and aesthetics, which studies aesthetic values, are properly sub-fields of value-theory, which raises the question of value as such.)

Logic is the formulation of the principles of right reasoning. We have saved logic for last, since traditionally it stands in a somewhat different relation to the philosopher than the other fields do. The other fields suggest something that is studied by the philosopher—reality, knowledge, value, etc. Logic is a *tool* which philosophers employ as they set about to investigate these issues. This was recognized already in antiquity. Aristotle was the first to formulate in a systematic way the principles of right reasoning, and the writings in which he did this (his "logical" writings) came to be called the *Organon*, which in Greek means "instrument" or "tool." This view of logic as a tool has, however, changed somewhat in recent years. With the rise of mathematical and symbolic logic, logic itself has become for many a proper *object* of philosophical study.

When we distinguish in this way the several fields of philosophy, we suggest something of the diversity of philosophical questions: the question of reality, the question of knowledge, the question of morality, etc. But the questions posed by these various fields cannot, after all, be so neatly separated. In many ways these questions (and their answers) rise and fall together. Do not the questions of value-theory bear directly upon ethics,

The Fields of Philosophy

- *Metaphysics:* The study of reality (sometimes also the study of transcendent reality).
- *Epistemology:* The study of knowledge.
- *Value-theory:* The study of value.
- *Ethics:* The study of moral value, right and wrong.
- *Aesthetics:* The study of beauty and art.
- *Logic:* The principles of right reasoning.

SECOND-ORDER INQUIRIES

An ordinary question such as "What is X?" is called a *first-order* question. A question about a first-order question is called a *second-order* question—for example, "What is the meaning of the question, 'What is X?'" Second-order questions are also called *meta* questions, or "talk about talk." Sometimes whole studies can be oriented in the direction of second-order concerns. Thus *meta*ethics is talk about ethical talk. Philosophical areas such as philosophy of religion, philosophy of science, philosophy of law, and philosophy of education tend to be second-order inquiries. On the other hand, it is often difficult to separate talking about talk from the primary talking itself. Why would you raise a second-order issue unless you were interested in the primary issue in the first place?

aesthetics, and metaphysics itself? Would not one's theory of reality (for example one's affirmation or denial of God) probably hold implications for one's view of morality, knowledge, and reality? Would not the opinion that there is no certain knowledge whatsoever cast a certain light—or darkness—over all questions of reality, value, or anything else? In this way we must emphasize also the *unity* of philosophical questions.

In addition to the standard fields of philosophy some further areas should be mentioned, namely, where philosophical concern relates itself to other disciplines: The "philosophy of _____" category. Examples are the philosophy of religion, philosophy of science, philosophy of education, and philosophy of law. Here a particular discipline is viewed and treated *philosophically;* the philosopher is concerned with such issues as the nature of that discipline's subject matter, the adequacy of its methodology, the meaning and clarification of its concepts, its logical coherence, and its relation to and implications for other fields. In the "philosophy of _____" studies, it is sometimes difficult to separate the *primary* subject (religion, science, education, law) from the *secondary* questions raised by the philosopher (questions concerning methodology, concepts, logic, relations). Nonetheless, it should be clear that the philosophy of _____" studies are largely "second-order" studies, that is, studies *about* studies. If, for example, you ever take a course in the philosophy of science, you

SOCRATES

Socrates was born in Athens about 470 B.C. He must have come from a fairly well-to-do family (there is some evidence that his father was a stonecutter), since as a young man he was a fully armed hoplite (foot soldier) in the army.

His appearance and character are notorious. He is said to have resembled a satyr (mythological creature, half human and half goat), we know that he had a pug nose, and the comic dramatist Aristophanes represented him as strutting like a waterfowl and rolling his eyes. We also know that he was a man of considerable physical endurance: He could spend long hours in meditation (once, a whole day and night) uninterrupted by the need for food; he once went barefoot on a wintry military expedition; and he could consume vast amounts of wine without becoming the least bit tipsy. More than once he distinguished

(continued on next page)

won't light any Bunsen burners, collect any specimens, or dissect any frogs. What you will do is think and talk *about* science. That is, you will analyze the meaning of science, scientific language and concepts, scientific procedures, conclusions, and implications.

It should be noted, though, that in actual usage the distinction between the fields of philosophy and the "philosophy of _____" areas is not hard and fast. Aesthetics, for example, could accurately be represented as the philosophy of art, whereas philosophy of religion would certainly raise, say, the metaphysical issue of God's existence and nature.

himself for bravery during the Peloponnesian War, during which time he married Xanthippe, who, according to tradition, was one of the world's outstanding shrews. In Plato's *Symposium*, Socrates represents himself as having been instructed by Diotima, a prophetess-philosopher, who—if she actually existed—was an important thinker indeed.

In the *Apology* (Plato's account of Socrates' trial) Socrates relates the origin of his philosophical mission: Once a friend of Socrates asked the Delphic Oracle who the wisest of men was, to which the Oracle responded, "Socrates." Socrates himself was much perplexed by this answer and concluded that if indeed he was the wisest it could only be because he was aware of his *ignorance*. Much turned off by the Sophists, who seemed to him to be more interested in the appearance of truth than in truth itself (and even charged for their instruction), Socrates pursued abiding and fixed truth. In fact, Aristotle credits him with being the first to seek *definitions*, especially of moral ideas such as justice and piety. Socrates utilized *dialogue* as the method of this pursuit, confronting, interrogating, and wheedling his adversaries into clearer thinking.

Eventually, he was found on the wrong side politically and was tried and found guilty of trumped-up charges of teaching strange gods and corrupting the youth. He scorned the opportunity of escaping prison and willingly drank the poisonous hemlock. The year was 399 B.C.

Although universally regarded as the model of the philosophic spirit, and in some ways as the founder of Western philosophy, Socrates never published a word—and thus today would have been denied tenure at any major university.

A RATIONAL CRITICAL ENTERPRISE

In our *third* attempt to characterize philosophy we propose something more illuminating than giving the root meaning of the word and something less cumbersome than spelling out its several fields. And we come to the heart of the matter when we suggest that whatever else it may be, philosophy is a *rational* and *critical* enterprise.

The word "rational" is important. Sometimes in philosophical discussion the words "rational," "rationalist," and "rationalism" are used with a rather technical meaning, as we shall see later. But here we intend these words in a more ordinary and loose sense. They have to do with *reason* and *reasonableness*. A rational argument, for example, is one that makes sense, is coherent, and is well founded. A rationalist is a person who is given to argument, investigation, and evaluation. And rationalism is the position which affirms reason as one of the highest authorities—maybe even *the* highest authority—in matters of belief and conduct. There is, in all of this, a certain *critical* activity that must not be missed. In being a *rational* enterprise, philosophy seeks to eradicate from our perspectives every taint and vestige of ignorance, superstition, prejudice, blind acceptance of ideas, and any other form of irrationality. It challenges our ideas, analyzes them, and tests them in light of evidence and arguments. It presses us to coherent and valid expressions of our ideas.

The early Greek philosopher Socrates (ca. 470–399 B.C.) has always been regarded as a kind of *symbol* of philosophical activity, especially its rational and critical nature. It is no wonder. Socrates was constantly pressing himself and everyone else for clarity and answers. His method was to engage someone over the meaning of some term or idea, usually a moral concept, and then to cross-examine his opponent mercilessly until some progress or clarity was achieved. According to Plato's *Apology* (an account of Socrates' defense at his trial), Socrates likens himself to a gadfly which incessantly stings and disturbs and challenges the citizenry:

> If you put me to death, you will not easily find anyone to take my place. It is literally true, even if it sounds rather comical, that God has specially appointed me to this city, as though it were a large thoroughbred horse which because of its great size is inclined to be lazy and needs the stimulation of some stinging fly. It seems to me that God has attached me to this city to perform the office of such a fly, and all day long I never cease to settle here, there, and everywhere, rousing, persuading, reproving every one of you. You will not easily find another like me, gentlemen, and if you take my advice you will spare my life. I suspect, however, that before long you will awake from your drowsing, and in your annoyance you will take Anytus' advice and finish me off with a single slap, and then you will go on sleeping till the end of your days, unless God in his care for you sends someone to take my place. . . .[2]

---

[2]Plato, *Apology*, 29D–31A, 33B–C, tr. Hugh Tredennick, in *Plato: The Collected Dialogues*, eds. Edith Hamilton and Huntington Cairns (New York: Pantheon Books, 1961).

It is from this same context that perhaps the most famous line of all philosophical literature comes: "The unexamined life is not worth living":

> I tell you that to let no day pass without discussing goodness and all the other subjects about which you hear me talking and examining both myself and others is really the very best thing that a man can do, and that life without this sort of examination is not worth living. . . .[3]

As in Socrates, the accent in all philosophy clearly falls on reason and criticism. But can *everything* be reasoned? Must *every* proposition, idea, and belief be exposed to the searchlight of critical reflection? Some philosophers would answer with a loud Yes. Others would not be so optimistic, insisting that there are *limits* to the rational and critical enterprise. If true, then this in itself is an important fact about philosophy and must be reckoned with constantly. Many philosophers do in fact recognize that reality and our experience of it are, after all, bigger than philosophy: Not everything can be grasped intellectually; not everything can be reduced to an argument; not everything can be expressed in language. But what happens at the point where reason gives out? Do we simply draw a blank? Some would say that it is at this point that the *nonrational* too plays a role, and even an inevitable role. But it is important here that we do not confuse "nonrational" with "irrational." That which is *ir*rational is incompatible with general experience or reason itself, whereas that which is *non*rational is simply different from and maybe even higher than experience or reason.

If we *do* believe in nonrational knowledge, what forms might it take? Certainly philosophers disagree among themselves about the possible significance of the claims of intuition in the sense of an immediate and direct apprehension of truth, mystical experience as a transcendent and ecstatic union with ultimate reality, various forms of religious and inner illumination, poetic visions or feelings, and the like. On the other hand, many would agree at least on the inevitable presence of *ultimate presuppositions* (also called basic assumptions, faith assertions, etc.) which are known with certainty as the foundations of all of our other ideas but which themselves cannot be proved. This view is known as *foundationalism*. Probably the

---

[3]Ibid., 38A.

THE INEVITABILITY OF PHILOSOPHY

In his *A Preface to Philosophy*, Mark B. Woodhouse provides a nice set of examples of the inescapability of philosophical issues.*

1. A neurophysiologist, while establishing correlations between certain brain functions and the feeling of pain, begins to wonder whether the "mind" is distinct from the brain.

2. A nuclear physicist, having determined that matter is mostly empty space containing colorless energy transformations, begins to wonder to what extent the solid, extended, colored world we perceive corresponds to what actually exists, and which world is the more "real."

3. A behavioral psychologist, having increasing success in predicting human behavior, questions whether any human actions can be called "free."

4. Supreme Court justices, when framing a rule to distinguish obscene and nonobscene art works, are drawn into questions about the nature and function of art.

(continued on next page)

most common defense of this view is the claim that from a purely logical standpoint not everything can be argued or there would never be an end to the arguing. A long time ago Aristotle pointed out that every argument finally rests on something that cannot be proved, and that it is the mark of an uneducated person not to realize that. There must be, as it were, a last outpost or final court of appeal. Do you believe with foundationalists that every philosophical system or position or argument necessarily rests at some point or other on some idea or ideas which are certain and basic and undemonstrable? If so, then you must believe that here, if no place else, the *non*rational too makes a contribution.

5. A theologian, in a losing battle with science over literal descriptions of the universe (or "reality"), is forced to redefine the whole purpose and scope of traditional theology.

6. An anthropologist, noting that all societies have some conception of a moral code, begins to wonder just what distinguishes a moral from a nonmoral point of view.

7. A linguist, in examining the various ways language shapes our view of the world, declares that there is no one "true reality" because all views of reality are conditioned and qualified by the language in which they are expressed.

8. A perennial skeptic, accustomed to demanding and not receiving absolute proof for every view encountered, declares that it is impossible to know anything.

9. A county commissioner, while developing the new zoning ordinances, begins to wonder whether the *effect* or the *intent* (or both) of zoning laws makes them discriminatory.

10. An IRS director, in determining which (religious) organizations should be exempted from tax, is forced to define what counts as a "religion" or "religious group."

*Mark B. Woodhouse, *A Preface to Philosophy* (Belmont, CA: Wadsworth, 1980), pp. 25–26.

DIFFERING CONCEPTIONS

So far, so good. Nearly everyone would agree with what has been said here about the meaning and origin of the word "philosophy," about the several standard fields and areas of philosophy, and about its rational and critical nature. Beyond that it is not so easy to say what philosophy is. In fact, the definition and meaning of philosophy is itself one of the big issues in contemporary philosophy! In our *fourth* way of getting at the meaning and nature of philosophy, it will be useful to suggest something of the very different forms which philosophy as a rational and critical enterprise has taken.

We will limit ourselves to four: The speculative, the analytic, the existential, and the phenomenological conceptions of philosophy.

The *speculative* approach is probably the most familiar. In this view, philosophy is the grandest of all disciplines. The speculative philosopher raises and tries to answer the most ultimate and far-ranging questions of all (what is reality)? what is the ultimate good? what is the total meaning of things?) and to make sense of reality and experience as a whole. Advocates of this conception of philosophy insist that it is faithful to the broad sweep and character of our philosophical tradition and to what the giants of that tradition were really up to. In the beginning, Plato had, in fact, described the philosopher as a "spectator of time and eternity," and many philosophers since (such as Aristotle, St. Thomas, Descartes, Spinoza, Kant, Hegel) saw their philosophical task as a sort of cosmic one. The American philosopher Alfred North Whitehead (1861–1947) is a modern example of this view. Whitehead himself employed the expression "speculative philosophy" and defined it as

> the endeavor to frame a coherent, logical, necessary system of general ideas in terms of which every element of our experience can be interpreted. By this notion of "interpretation" I mean that everything of which we are conscious, as enjoyed, perceived, willed, or thought, shall have the character of a particular instance of the general scheme.[4]

Certainly less flamboyant is the *analytic* approach to philosophizing. This view of philosophy (which is not called "analytic" for nothing) takes *linguistic analysis,* or the analysis of language, as the proper and legitimate task of the philosopher. Although these philosophies also see their forerunners among the traditional philosophers, analytic philosophy as a clearly defined approach to the philosophical issues is essentially a recent and contemporary movement. What is the driving conviction behind this approach? These thinkers, or at least the "ordinary language" analysts, lay the muddles, mistakes, and dead ends which characterize the history of philosophy to *linguistic confusion.* The proper task of the philosopher, at least for now, is therefore to unravel and to clarify philosophical language. When this is done, it will be seen that many or most of the traditional problems of philosophy turn out to be not real problems at all, but

---

[4]Alfred North Whitehead, *Process and Reality* (New York: Macmillan, 1929), p. 4.

If you go to a doctor or dentist, you will expect him or her to proceed with the utmost precision, employing the very latest techniques which doctors and dentists agree to be the most effective. But look at the disagreement, argument, and variety of opinion that prevails among philosophers. What does this say about the philosophical enterprises? Is it a good or bad sign? What are the important differences between, say, the medical profession and the philosophical profession?

*pseudo*problems, problems not of reality but of language. One of the best-known of these philosophers is the English philosopher G. E. Moore (1873–1958), who provides an excellent statement of the analytic view of philosophy:

> It appears to me that in Ethics, as in all other philosophical studies, the difficulties and disagreements, of which its history is full, are mainly due to a very simple cause: namely to the attempt to answer questions, without first discovering precisely what question it is which you desire to answer. I do not know how far this source of error would be done away, if philosophers would try to discover what question they were asking, before they set about to answer it. . . . But I am inclined to think that in many cases a resolute attempt would be sufficient to assure success; so that, if only this attempt were made, many of the most glaring difficulties and disagreements in philosophy would disappear.[5]

With the *existential* approach the pendulum swings back in the opposite direction. For the existentialist philosopher, traditional philosophy has been too occupied with abstractions and trivialities. The primary object of philosophical reflection is, rather, the human being as concretely existing reality—this approach isn't called "existentialism" for nothing. Authentic philosophizing will, for these thinkers, reflect the sense of urgency and crisis of contemporary human existence and experience. A good example of this view of the philosophical enterprise is the late French writer and

---

[5]George Edward Moore, *Principia Ethica* (Cambridge University Press, 1903), p. vii.

FEMINIST PHILOSOPHY

It has often been observed that women are, by and large, conspicuous by their absence from the history of philosophy. It is true, for example, that in the massive *Encyclopedia of Philosophy* one searches in vain for women in philosophy, except for the most incidental references. Some have felt that there may be more going on here than meets the eye.

Feminist philosophers argue that a male bias has been at work in our philosophical tradition, resulting not only in the exclusion of important contributions by women but even controlling some of our basic philosophical concepts. In the following extracts from an article in the *American Philosophical Association Newsletter on Feminism and Philosophy*, Alison Jaggar emphasizes the first, briefly develops "dualistic thinking" as an example of the second, and concludes that, if real, the male bias in philosophy betrays some of the ideals of philosophy itself.

> The western philosophical tradition at first sight appears to be almost exclusively the creation of male minds. No woman is listed among the great names of philosophy, and those women whose names are mentioned in a philosophical context usually are presented as having made at best minor contributions. Harriet Taylor, for instance, is admitted to have helped J. S. Mill, but Mill's strong assertion that she was his main philosophical inspiration invariably is discounted. Other women in the history of philosophy fare even worse: Socrates' wife, Xanthippe, was a nag, seeking to divert her husband from his philosophical midwifery, while Queen Christina of

(continued on next page)

thinker Albert Camus (1913–1960), who focuses the existentialists' understanding of the most fundamental question of philosophy:

> Judging whether life is or is not worth living amounts to answering the fundamental question of philosophy. All the rest—whether or not the world has three dimensions, whether the mind has nine or

Sweden was so immoderate in her demands that she caused Descartes' death by making him get up too early in the morning.

The apparent absence of women from the western tradition is far from entirely illusory. There is no doubt that women's opportunities to enter into philosophical discourse have been curtailed severely by lack of education and by other social constraints. Nevertheless, some feminists believe that a few women did manage to make a philosophical contribution, but that this contribution has been overlooked because of bias against work by women. . . .

One persistent theme in both French and Anglo-American feminist philosophy is a criticism of dualistic modes of conceptualization. Feminist philosophers frequently claim that the western tradition typically presents reality as structured by polar oppositions, pairs of entities or qualities that are defined in contrast to each other. Examples of such dichotomous categorizations include private/public, nature/culture, body/mind, particular/universal, concrete/abstract, object/subject, subjective/objective, emotion/reason. Feminists have asserted that these dichotomies evidence male bias at least in the sense that the first term in each pair historically has been associated with femininity and conceived as inferior to the second term, which is associated with masculinity. A considerable amount of feminist philosophy responds to these dualisms in various ways. Some feminists seek to free the dichotomies from their gendered associations; some retain the gendered connotations, but seek to invert the hierarchical ordering; others still claim that dualistic thinking itself is masculine and endeavor to rethink the distinctions in ways that will avoid the problems supposedly engendered by rigid dichotomies. . . .

(continued on next page)

twelve categories—come afterwards. These are games. . . . I have never seen anyone die for the ontological argument . . . the meaning of life is the most urgent of questions.[6]

---

[6]Albert Camus, *The Myth of Sisyphus and Other Essays,* tr. Justin O'Brien (New York: Knopf, 1955), pp. 3–4.

Showing that claims of male bias in philosophy are possible does not establish, of course, that any such claims in fact can be substantiated. It may be that some claims can be substantiated and others cannot. The commitment to investigate male bias, however, springs from an impulse that is simultaneously philosophical and feminist. It is philosophical in so far as it seeks to understand the world in terms of categories and ideals that do not reflect and promote merely the interests of a few, and it is feminist in so far as it is inspired by a determination that women's achievements and capacities, concerns and interests, should receive full and fair appreciation and evaluation. If feminists are correct in even some of their claims, it is the western tradition rather than feminist philosophy that, perhaps unknowingly, has subordinated truth to politics and that therefore constitutes a highly sophisticated form of propaganda.*

Well, what about this? What do you make of the idea that concepts and ways of philosophizing might be male-biased? Be that as it may, the traditionally male-dominated philosophical world is on notice. Feminist philosophy is achieving increased visibility and importance as is evident from the number of courses being offered on the topic of philosophy and women, the appearance of the APA *Newsletter on Feminism and Philosophers*, the appearance of *Hypatia: A Journal of Feminist Philosophy*, and, of course, the increased numbers of women teaching philosophy and otherwise contributing to contemporary philosophical work. Can you imagine ways in which this may bear on the direction of future philosophizing?

---

*Alison Jaggar, "How Can Philosophy Be Feminist?" *American Philosophical Association Newsletter on Feminism and Philosophy* (April 1988), pp. 4, 6, 8.

There is still another broad conception of the major task of philosophy. This approach to philosophical issues may seem to lie somewhere between the analytic and existential, with an emphasis on description. Again, one should pay attention to the word. Phenomenology is named from the Greek passive participle *phenomenon*, which literally means something *seen* or *observed*. In a nutshell, phenomenology, as a general philosophical perspective, stresses that whatever is *given* to consciousness—what is directly

"Life without philosophy is inconceivable."

—Socrates

"Philosophy is a silent dialogue between the soul and itself."

—Plato

"All men by nature desire to know."

—Aristotle

experienced or "seen"—is the proper point of departure for, and the proper subject matter of, philosophical reflection. Once it is recognized that consciousness is always "consciousness-*of* something," or is "intentional," this reflective focus upon consciousness does not limit the phenomenologist to some "inner states," for it embraces all the traditional topics of philosophy. This, too, is essentially a twentieth-century perspective, and, in contrast to British-inspired analytic philosophy, has been loosely characterized as "continental" philosophy. It originated with German philosopher Edmund Husserl (1895–1938). Its interest in undercutting our habitual, distorting beliefs and theories *about* experiences and their objects is apparent in the following from Husserl's *Ideas:*

> . . . *a new way of looking at things* is necessary, one that contrasts *at every point* with the natural attitude of experience and thought. To move freely along this new way without ever reverting to the old viewpoints, to learn to see what stands before our eyes, to distinguish, to describe, calls, moreover, for exacting and laborious studies.[7]

It is one thing to distinguish in this way between broadly different conceptions of the philosophical enterprise, and something else to apply the distinctions to actual cases of philosophizing. Sometimes a philosopher's approach may be easily identified in these terms, but sometimes not. The speculative, analytic, existential, and phenomenological interests have a way of melting together in a given philosopher's work, and this reminds us

[7]Edmund Husserl, "Introduction," in *Ideas,* tr. Boyce Gibson (London: George Allen & Unwin, 1931), p. 43.

that here, as with much else in this book, one cannot simply ruse in with "hammer and tongs" where the employment of subtler and more nuanced tools is called for.

A WORKING DEFINITION

Perhaps, finally, we may pose a working definition of philosophy, one that does some justice to what we have seen to be both its theme and its variations: *Philosophy is the attempt to think rationally and critically about the most important questions.*

The *theme* is that philosophy is a rational and critical activity. Philosophizing in all forms seeks to think and to think hard about something. But about what? Here we have the *variation.* Our references to the speculative, analytic, and existential approaches in philosophy should provide sufficient evidence that there are quite differing ideas as to what philosophy should be rational and critical *about.* Still, even here philosophers have in common that they see themselves as addressing the really important questions, questions which are fundamental to everything.

PROFESSOR MILLER'S
FOUR PRINCIPLES

It will be apparent soon enough that this book has a decidedly historical cast. To be sure, we want to pay attention to current developments. But we want also to know about those thinkers, movements, and broad perspectives, strewn over 2500 years, that have brought us where we are today and otherwise confront us with so many—yes—philosophical options. There are, however, pitfalls in the study of historical philosophy. As warnings against these pitfalls I have formulated Four Principles for the Study of the History of Philosophy. Heeding these principles may save you lots of misunderstanding and other troubles. The principles are:

- The Clarification Principle.
- The Deculturalization Principle.
- The Modified Sergeant Friday Principle.
- The Smartness Principle.

The *Clarification Principle* asserts that it is always easier to appreciate the clarity of an idea once the idea has been clarified. The point here is that we should not judge too harshly those who have not benefited from long years of critical reflection and consequent clarification of ideas. Some distinctions are hard to see until they are seen; then they are *easy* to see. Also, some claims are *obviously* true, once the competing claims have been shown to be impossible; and so on.

According to the *Deculturalization Principle*, the real substance of philosophy should never be confused with the cultural elements necessarily involved in its expression. Any philosophy, in an attempt to express itself, must resort, for example, to a certain language. And is it a surprise that a philosophy may reflect a prevailing view of the physical universe, or draw upon standard ideas about the soul, or employ examples from conventional morality or images from popular religion? The important point is to recognize that these may be purely incidental to the real point, and not to throw out the baby with the bathwater. What is called for is, rather, a setting free of the real philosophy from these purely accidental features inevitably involved in its expression for a particular audience at a particular time and place.

The *Modified Sergeant Friday Principle* seeks to instill a healthy respect for the text, that is, what the philosopher actually wrote: "Just the text, ma'am, just the text."[8] It may, of course, sometimes be necessary or useful to speculate on what a philosopher might have said, should have said, or could have said, or to try to fill in some gaps or draw some inferences, but one must never lose sight of what is actually there in the text. That, in the end, is all we have.

Finally, the *Smartness Principle:* Always assume that the philosopher is smarter than you are. The danger here is that a philosopher may say something that seems to you to be silly, stupid, or absurd, so you give up on it, whereas if you had stayed with it you might have learned that, in the larger context or with further explanation, it wasn't stupid at all. It may, of course, turn out that you were right—"That really *was* dumb!"—but that too is something you may not be sure of if you throw in the towel too soon.

---

[8]For those readers who are too young to know, Sergeant Friday was the main character in the radio, and then TV, program *Dragnet*. He often responded to overly enthusiastic witnesses with a pointed, "Just the facts, ma'am, just the facts."

ὁ δὲ ἀνεξέταστος βίος οὐ βιωτὸς ἀνθρώπῳ

"For man, the unexamined life is not worth living."
—Socrates

I don't pretend that these are the only principles relevant for the study of the history of philosophy, but I do claim that they're good ones, and that they're suggestive of the sorts of concerns that make for solid study.

CHAPTER 1 IN REVIEW

Summary

The best way to appreciate what philosophy is about is to *philosophize*. This book will make it possible to be actually confronted with basic philosophical issues and to engage many important philosophers on their own ground.

In the meantime, though, something important can be learned about philosophy through a consideration of the word itself (the "love of wisdom"), its several branches (metaphysics, epistemology, ethics, etc.), and differing styles of philosophizing (such as the speculative, analytic, and existential). In an attempt to emphasize both the essence and the breadth of philosophical activity, we proposed a working definition: Philosophy is the attempt to think rationally and critically about the most important questions. One should always remember Socrates and his challenge. "The unexamined life is not worth living," as embodying the ultimate philosophical concern. On the other hand, it must be admitted that reason has its limits, and what role is to be played by the nonrational (say, ultimate presuppositions) is itself a good philosophical question.

Everyone is more or less engaged in the philosophical enterprise, and though philosophical issues may seem at times rather remote, a moment's reflection will reveal that they really are basic and, whether one realizes it or not, they deeply affect our daily lives. Let us, then, make the most of our philosophical impulses by beginning where we are and, by critical reflection, analysis, and clarification, progress if possible to someplace even better.

Basic Ideas

- The problem of understanding philosophy.
- "Philosophy": the love of wisdom.
- The fields of philosophy.
  Metaphysics.
  Epistemology.
  Ethics.
  Value-theory.
  Aesthetics.
  Logic.
- The unity of philosophical questions.
- The nature of the "philosophy of _____" areas.
- Second-order studies.
- Rationalism (the loose sense).
- Socrates as a model of the philosophical spirit.
- The limits of reason.
- The nonrational and the irrational.
- Foundationalism.
- Four conceptions of philosophy.
  The speculative.
  The analytical.
  The existential.
  The phenomenological.
- Professor Miller's Four Principles.
  The Clarification Principle.
  The Deculturalization Principle.
  The Modified Sergeant Friday Principle.
  The Smartness Principle.

Questions for Reflection

- In spite of their stress on the use of reason, some philosophers readily concede that reason has its limits. Do you believe that it is possible, nonetheless, to know something in a *non*rational way? Why do some even maintain that this is crucial to philosophizing itself? How might the appeal to the nonrational be abused?

- Is the ideal of reasoning in a purely objective way (that is, uninfluenced by biases and the like) really possible? If not, then what? And what about the difference in intellectual "temperaments"? Is that good or bad? What's to be done about it?
- How might it be argued that the borderlines between philosophy and *all* other disciplines may often be very blurred? Why might philosophers look upon their own discipline as the biggest and best?

For Further Reading

Mortimer J. Adler. *The Conditions of Philosophy: Its Checkered Past, Its Present Disorder, and Its Future Promise.* New York: Atheneum, 1965. A well-known philosopher examines the nature of philosophy and its relation to other disciplines, and reflects on the past, present, and future of the philosophical enterprise.

H. Johnstone (ed.). *What Is Philosophy?* New York: Macmillan, 1965. An anthology of pieces reflecting a variety of views on the nature of philosophy.

Stephan Körner. *What is Philosophy? One Philosopher's Answer.* London: Penguin Press, 1969. A treatment (which aims to be "intelligible to laymen and useful to beginners") of the several branches of philosophy, including reflections on its past and its contemporary situation.

Mark B. Woodhouse. *A Preface to Philosophy.* 3rd ed. Belmont, CA: Wadsworth, 1984. A useful and readable account of the subject matter of philosophy as well as the doing, reading, and writing of philosophy.

*In addition, see several relevant articles in *The Encyclopedia of Philosophy*, ed. Paul Edwards. New York: Macmillan, 1967: "Philosophy." "Philosophy of Law," "Philosophy of Religion," "Metaphysics," "Epistemology," etc.

CHAPTER 2

A
Little
Logic

E HAVE seen that philosophers, more than most people, strive to make their arguments, positions, and pronouncements *rational*, that is, well conceived, well evidenced, well stated, and persuasive. To ensure this goal philosophers pay attention to the philosophical discipline of *logic*, which we have already defined as the study of right reasoning. Not that there is any choice about it. The philosopher can no more do without logic than the physicist can do without mathematics. It is the tool or, as someone has suggested, the "key" to philosophizing.

From the traditional logic first formulated by Aristotle to the various forms of contemporary symbolic and mathematical logic (which would seem to many like a foreign language), the science of logic has become a very complicated and sophisticated business. A real course in logic would have to take up many matters: the nature and uses of language, problems of definition, types of propositions, types of arguments, the construction and use of symbolic languages, probability theory, the nature of hypotheses and theories, etc. We cannot do much in the space of a single chapter, but a beginner in philosophy should be introduced at least to some of the bare elements of logic. An acquaintance with these is relevant not only for our thinking about the ideas and positions represented in this book, but also for our thinking about everything, every day.

THE THREE LAWS OF THOUGHT

We might appropriately begin with the Three Laws of Thought, for in a sense they are the beginning of all thinking. Traditionally, these principles have been perceived as the rock-bottom principles of all thought and discourse, the principles that make thought and discourse even *possible*. It is important, therefore, to pay attention to these laws. They are:

1. *The Law of Non-Contradiction*
   Nothing can both be and not be at the same time and in the same respect.
2. *The Law of the Excluded Middle*
   Something either is or is not.
3. *The Law of Identity*
   Something is what it is.

It is important to see that if these principles are not accepted as true, then nothing we think or say makes any sense, not even this very sentence. They make our ideas and words and language *stand still*, as it were, while we deal with them. Try to imagine making any claim about anything if any one of these principles did not hold. Go ahead, try!

Some comments on the Three Laws. First, at a technical level these principles actually turn out to be identical. Even so, you should try to appreciate that at the level of ordinary and practical discourse they get at very different issues. Next, as stated above, these principles have a kind of metaphysical cast, expressing as they do what can or cannot *be*. They could just as easily be given an epistemological cast, expressing what can or cannot *be true:* A statement cannot be both true and false at the same time and in the same respect; a statement is either true or false; a true statement is true. Also, concerning the Law of Non-Contradiction the qualifying phrase, "at the same time and in the same respect," must be emphasized. A table, for example, may indeed be red and not red at *different* times; or it may be rectangular and not be four-legged at the same time in these *different* respects; but it cannot both be and not be (anything) at the *same* time and in the *same* respect.

Further, as *fundamental* principles these cannot be shown to be true, since they are the principles by which all *other* claims may be shown to be true. It was, in fact, the Law of Non-Contradiction that Aristotle was speaking of when he said that it is the mark of an uneducated person not to realize that some things cannot be proved; otherwise *nothing* could be proved.

> Some, indeed, demand to have the law proved, but this is because they lack education; for it shows lack of education not to know of what we should require proof, and of what we should not. For it is quite impossible that everything should have a proof; the process would go on to infinity, so that even so there would be no proof.[1]

Do you see that there must be some "anchors" for our thinking and discoursing if our thinking and discoursing are to be ultimately meaningful? And that these anchors must be undemonstrable? Think of geometry. All its reasoning depends finally on its axioms. But there is no way to prove the axioms.

Finally, various objections to the Three Laws are inevitably raised, but they usually involve misunderstandings. *Against the Law of Non-Contradiction:* Aren't there situations which involve inherently self-contradictory factors? Answer: No. Factors in a situation may stand in *tension* with one another or in *opposition* with one another, but such conflicts do not constitute *self-contradictory* situations in which one and the same thing both is and is-not at the same time and in the same respect. *Against the Law of the Excluded Middle:* Is everything either black or white with nothing in between? Answer: That isn't a good example, for something may be *neither* black nor white; it may be gray. What the principle states is that either something is *X* or it is not-*X*, white or not-white, gray or not-gray, etc. *Against the Law of Identity:* Things change, don't they? Answer: Yes, but the principle has reference to *whole* ideas, including any change they might involve. Thus the fact that tables are always changing doesn't detract a bit from the truth that a table is a table.

---

[1]Aristotle, *Metaphysics*, 1006a, tr. W. D. Ross, in *Basic Works of Aristotle*, ed. Richard McKeon (New York: Random House, 1941).

Contemporary logicians sometimes question the exalted position that in the past has been bestowed on the Three Laws of Thought. It is now seen, for example, that the logical territory mapped out by these principles is only a part of the total territory. Nonetheless, they may be accepted as basic to the world of everyday discourse that most of us live in, and often crucial to philosophical reasoning as well. They still stand as important anchors of thought and discourse.

WHAT IS AN ARGUMENT?

When you see the word "argument" you might think of disagreements or quarrels, often accompanied by shouting, clenched fists, tears, and the like. Well, an argument might or might not involve these things. Consider the following interchange:

A: Capital punishment is immoral.

B: No it isn't!

A: Yes it is!

B: Well, what do *you* know about it?!

A: I know more about it than you do!

B: Oh yeah? You're an idiot!

There is plenty of disagreement and lots of noise here but no *argument*. An argument is an attempt to show that something is true by providing evidence for it. More technically, it is a group of propositions in which one is said to follow from at least one other. The proposition which follows from the others, that is, the "something to be shown," is called the *conclusion;* the propositions from which the conclusion follows, that is, the evidence, are called *premises.* Thus we have the argument

> It is immoral to kill persons.
> Capital punishment is the killing of persons.
> _____
> Therefore, capital punishment is immoral.

in which the first two propositions are the premises of the argument and the third is the conclusion. Naturally, in an argument not just any old propositions can serve as premises and conclusion, as in

In fourteen hundred and ninety-two,
Columbus sailed the ocean blue.
Switzerland exports many cuckoo-clocks.

Therefore, capital punishment is immoral.

but there must be some *connection* between them. This connection, by which the conclusion is said "to follow" from the premises, is called an *inference*, or, more technically, an *entailment*.

In ordinary discourse, arguments may be presented in a variety of ways. Usually, though, there are certain words or expressions that introduce premises, and another set of words that introduce conclusions. We list here just a few of them:

Premise-signals	Since, because, for, as, inasmuch as, otherwise, in view of the fact that, for the reason that
Conclusion-signals	Therefore, thus, accordingly, we may infer, which shows that, points to the conclusion that, as a result

Can you separate the premises from the conclusion in the following argument?

. . . for a producer to convince the institutions which finance movies that his film will be profitable, he has to line up a "bankable" star; and if he has a project for a political movie, the star is unlikely to sign on if he doesn't agree with the film's politics. Which means that the political movies the public is getting from Hollywood today represent, by and large, the political thinking of actors.[2]

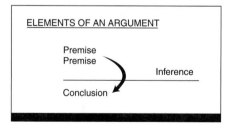

ELEMENTS OF AN ARGUMENT

Premise
Premise
Inference
Conclusion

---

[2]Richard Grenier, "Jane Fonda & Other Political Thinkers," *Commentary*, June 1979.

What is the nature of the connection between premises and conclusion—the inference—that results in arguments? Here the important distinction between *deductive* and *inductive* arguments comes into play. What is important is the kind of connection that exists between premises and conclusion in deductive and inductive arguments. In a valid deductive argument the premises ensure, or *guarantee*, the conclusion: If the premises are true, the conclusions *must* be true also. It is a matter of necessity. In a good inductive argument, on the other hand, the premises *suggest* the conclusion ("to induce" means "to influence" or "to persuade"): If the premises are true, the conclusion is *probably* true. It is a matter of *probability*.

INFORMAL FALLACIES

A fallacy is a mistake in reasoning. *Formal* fallacies are mistakes in the form of an argument rather than the content. That is, no matter what the premises may assert, no valid conclusion can be drawn—the argument misfires—because the premises are not related according to the rules of logical validity. Can you identify the formal fallacy in this "argument"?

> If it rained last night the streets will be wet.
> The streets are wet.
> _____
> Therefore, it rained last night.

Informal fallacies, on the other hand, have everything to do with the content of an argument. They are mistakes which arise from carelessness with respect to the relevance of ideas or carelessness with respect to the clarity and consistency of our language. In fact, informal fallacies are usually classified as *fallacies of relevance* and *fallacies of ambiguity*. There are many such fallacies. We give here only some of the most common ones of each type. Mastery of them will not only provide a chance to learn a little Latin, but will prevent many unnecessary blunders in philosophical discussion, and, for that matter, any discussion whatsoever.

Fallacies of Relevance

1. *Argumentum ad Baculum* ("appeal to force") employs threat, intimidation, pressure, etc., as tools of persuasion. Example: "I notice

LOGICAL FALLACIES

Formal fallacies
Mistakes in reasoning due to a failure in following the rules for the formal structure of valid arguments. These fallacies do not concern truth or falsity but validity.

Informal fallacies
Mistakes in reasoning due to carelessness regarding relevance and clarity of language. These fallacies bear directly on issues of truth and falsity.

---

that you work part-time for the campus police. I will expect you to fix my parking ticket in order to assure yourself a good grade in my course."

2. *Argumentum ad Hominem* ("appeal to the man") *Abusive* irrelevantly attacks the person making a claim rather than attacking the claim itself. Example: "You pro-choice people are selfish, godless, and immoral—probably communists too!"

3. *Argumentum ad Hominem* ("appeal to the man") *Circumstantial* seeks to undermine a claim by calling attention to the (irrelevant) circumstances of the one making the claim. When it specifically cites the origins or causes of someone's opinion, it is known as the *Genetic Fallacy*. Example: "Coach McCartney's view on abortion can be discounted since he's a Christian."

4. *Argumentum ad Ignorantiam* ("appeal to ignorance") affirms the truth of something on the basis of the lack of evidence to the contrary. Example: "The superb quality of her character can be demonstrated by the fact that I have never heard a word spoken against her."

5. *Argumentum ad Populum* ("appeal to the crowd") seeks to strengthen a claim by an emotional appeal to the passions and prejudices of the listeners. Example: "This bill has been written in the spirit of the founding fathers of this great nation and upholds all

that is sacred. To vote against it would be to cast both tradition and God's will to the wind!"

6. *Argumentum ad Misericordiam* ("appeal to pity") directs attention from relevant evidence by arousing pity and sympathy for the plight of someone. Example: If O. J. Simpson is reduced to penury, just think what that would mean for his poor children!"

7. *Argumentum ad Verecundiam* ("appeal to authority") appeals to an unqualified expert or irrelevant authority. Example: "I can tell you that I have the same confidence in my A-C Delco spark plugs for my car that I had in my plane when I was the first person to break the sound barrier."

8. *Petitio Principii* ("begging of the question") occurs when the conclusion of an argument is already present, usually disguised, in one of its premises. Also called circular reasoning. Example: "You can't expect eighteen-year-olds to vote intelligently, because they are too young to have good judgment about the issues."

9. *Accident* is the fallacy of applying a general rule to a specific situation in which some accidental condition makes it an exception to the rule. Example: "This is the Sabbath, a day of rest. So I don't intend to check on the animals in the pasture, storm or no storm."

10. *Converse Accident* consists in generalizing on the basis of an inadequate number of instances or on the basis of atypical instances, and thus moves in the opposite direction from the Fallacy of Accident. Example: "Professor Tweed canceled our appointment. Boy, that guy sure doesn't care about his students."

11. *False Cause* is the fallacy consisting in either (1) confusing an effect or feature of a condition with the cause of that condition (*non causa pro causa*, "taking what is not the cause for the cause") or (b) identifying X as the cause of Y merely on the grounds that X occurs before Y (*post hoc ergo propter hoc*, "after this, therefore, because of this"). Example: "The feminist movement has failed disastrously. Ever since it began to attract followers, the incidence of child abuse has increased dramatically."

12. *Complex Question* consists of posing a question which can be answered only on the basis of an answer to a prior and unasked question. Example: "Where did you hide the money you stole?" (The unasked question is, "Did you steal the money?")

Fallacies of Ambiguity

1. *Equivocation* occurs when a word or expression changes its meaning in the course of an argument. Example: "Everyone says she has good *taste* so I would love to nibble on her ear."

2. *Amphiboly* (literally, "thrown on both sides") involves an ambiguous grammatical construction that can be understood in two ways. Example: "Henry went out on the porch on the Fourth of July and watched the fireworks in his pajamas."

3. *Misplaced Accent* consists of so emphasizing a word or expression, or omitting relevant information, as to yield a misleading sense. Example:

AIR FARES REDUCED 50%
some restrictions apply

4. *Composition* results from attributing the characteristics of the parts of a whole to the whole itself. Example: "If every player on the team is good, then it's a good team."

5. *Division* (the reverse of the Fallacy of Composition) attributes the characteristics of the whole to its parts: It's a very good team, so each of its players must be very good."

Can you identify some of these, or yet other, informal fallacies in your day-to-day experience? A good place to look might be editorial pages in your local newspapers, or letters to the editor in magazines, or television commercials.

CHAPTER 2 IN REVIEW

Summary

Whatever else philosophers might be interested in, they are surely interested in coherent and persuasive reasoning. Laying down the rules and providing some techniques is the task of logic.

For a long time the Three Laws of Thought (Non-Contradiction, Excluded Middle, Identity) were regarded as the ultimate principles of all being and thinking. These principles do not now usually enjoy such an exalted status, but they still serve as important guides for ordinary as well as philosophical discourse. Is it not the case that failure to honor them would result in the greatest confusion? Can you imagine holding a meaningful conversation with someone who will not honor any one of them?

Still more relevant is the nature of *arguments*. If philosophers aren't good at arguing, what *are* they good at? A real argument is a carefully devised piece of reasoning involving premises (what is reasoned *from*), a conclusion (what is reasoned *to*), and an inference (the connection which yields the conclusion from the premises). But does the conclusion follow from the premises necessarily or probably? This is the difference between a valid *deductive* argument, where the conclusion is *guaranteed* by the premises, and an *inductive* argument, where the conclusion is *supported* by the premises.

Among the most important things to be learned from an introduction to logic are the informal fallacies. As opposed to *formal* fallacies, mistakes with respect to the formal structure of an argument, *informal* fallacies arise from inattention to the relevance or clarity of language. In fact, the several specific informal fallacies divide into the *fallacies of relevance* and the *fallacies of ambiguity*. Mastery of the informal fallacies will prove rewarding time and time again.

Basic Ideas

- Logic as the tool or key to philosophizing
- The Three Laws of Thought
  Non-Contradiction
  Excluded Middle
  Identity
- The nature and elements of an argument
- Deductive reasoning
- The distinction between formal and informal fallacies
- Informal fallacies
  Fallacies of relevance (twelve of them)
  Fallacies of ambiguity (five of them)

Questions for Reflection

- Why is it often said that logic is the primary tool of philosophers? Why has it been called the "key" to philosophizing?

- Even though we have distinguished between deductive and inductive reasoning, how might they both play a part in a single argument? The conclusion may follow validly from the premises, but how might we come by the premises?

- Everyday talk is sometimes full of fallacies, especially informal fallacies. Can you spot and identify any in today's newspaper? You might pay special attention to the editorial pages and letters to the editor.

For Further Reading

John Burbidge. *Within Reason: A Guide to Non-Deductive Reasoning.* Kenmore, NY: Broadview Press, 1990. An introductory treatment of nondeductive reasoning regularly employed by most people with an emphasis on analogical reasoning.

Morris R. Cohen and Ernest Nagel. *An Introduction to Logic and Scientific Method.* New York: Harcourt, Brace & Co., 1934. An old but still standard treatment of both formal logic and applied logic and the scientific method.

Irving M. Copi. *Introduction to Logic.* 7th ed. New York: Macmillan, 1990. The most widely used logic text, covering all aspects of the subject under the topics of language, deduction, and induction.

S. Morris Engel. *With Good Reason: An Introduction to Informal Fallacies.* 4th ed. New York: St. Martin's Press, 1990. Full and often humorous discussion (cartoons, etc.) of the informal fallacies, prefaced by discussion of the nature of logic, language, arguments, etc.

C. L. Hamblin. *Fallacies.* London: Methuen, 1970. Excellent treatment (at points technical) of both informal and formal fallacies as well as other topics such as the concept of argument and Indian logic.

Ronald Jager (ed.). *Essays in Logic from Aristotle to Russell.* Englewood Cliffs, NJ: Prentice Hall, 1963. A collection of classical statements dealing with various aspects of logic such as induction and deduction, formal and informal logic, methods of experimental inquiry, etc.

David Kelley. *The Art of Reasoning.* New York: Norton, 1988. A useful, readable text, designed for courses in critical thinking and elementary logic.

Lionel Ruby. *The Art of Making Sense: A Guide to Logical Thinking.* 2nd ed. Philadelphia: Lippincott, 1968. A well-known, lively, and nontechnical discussion of all aspects of everyday logic.

PART ONE

THE
QUESTION
OF
REALITY

W | HAT IS reality? What are things made of? What is ultimate?
What is it that everything depends on for its existence? What is
really real?

There are many ways of posing the question of reality. However you
pose the question, you *do* have an answer—don't you? Your idea of reality
may be only half-conscious (and it may be only half-baked), but you do
have some answer of your own to the question: What is really real? The
point is to have a *good* answer, an answer that is well conceived and well
evidenced. Why is this so important?

Some philosophers would say that in some ways the metaphysical question, or the question of reality, is the basis of all the other questions that
matter. Whether or not this is strictly true, no one would deny that the
metaphysical question is at least a *basic* one. Will not what you believe
about reality determine to some degree what you believe about all sorts of
other things? If, for example, someone told you that he or she believes

that all that exists is matter in motion, governed by fixed and unalterable laws, then couldn't you predict pretty much what that person thinks about some other important things? If, on the other hand, you were informed that he or she believes in a supernatural and absolute being, couldn't you immediately guess that his or her views on those matters would probably be quite different?

In this way, then, the question of reality is a fundamental one. How we answer it will determine in a big way our perspectives on many issues, as well as our perspective on the universe and our experience *generally*. Let us, then, have a care with respect to the question of reality.

The
Idea
of
Form

P HILOSOPHY REALLY came of age with Plato (427–347 B.C.). Here we encounter the first full-fledged philosophical *system*. By a philosophical system we mean a fundamental idea or theory that is worked out for all aspects of experience. Thus Plato's philosophy addresses everything from reality, to knowledge, to ethics, to art, to religion, to cosmology, etc. So encompassing and magnificent is Plato's philosophy that Alfred North Whitehead called all subsequent philosophy a series of footnotes to it!

PLATO AND SOCRATES

Plato, who is sometimes called the finest writer of ancient Greece, expressed his philosophy in numerous "dialogues." In the earlier of these dialogues Plato develops the ideas of his teacher Socrates through portrayals of Socrates' discussions with his contemporaries, discussions which proceed by questions and answers. Socrates is usually represented as asking in one way or another, "What is *X*?" His respondent's answer is then subjected to a searching analysis which generates still more and better answers. A representative passage from one of these early dialogues is the following from the *Euthyphro:*

EUTHYPHRO: . . . I would indeed affirm that holiness is what the gods all love, and its opposite is what the gods all hate, unholiness.

SOCRATES: Are we to examine this position also, Euthyphro, to see if it is sound? Or shall we let it through, and thus accept our own and others' statement, and agree to an assertion simply when somebody says that a thing is so? Must we not look into what the speaker says?

EUTHYPHRO: We must. And yet, for my part, I regard the present statement as correct.

SOCRATES: We shall soon know better about that, my friend. Now think of this. Is what is holy holy because the gods approve it, or do they approve it because it is holy?

EUTHYPHRO: I do not get your meaning.

SOCRATES: Well, I will try to make it clearer. We speak of what is carried and the carrier, do we not, of led and leader, of the seen and that which sees? And you understand that in all such cases the things are different, and how they differ?

EUTHYPHRO: Yes, I think I understand.

SOCRATES: In the same way what is loved is one thing, and what loves is another?

EUTHYPHRO: Of course.

SOCRATES: Tell me now, is what is carried "carried" because something carries it, or is it for some other reason?

EUTHYPHRO: No, but for that reason.

SOCRATES: And what is led, because something leads it? And what is seen, because something sees it?

EUTHYPHRO: Yes, certainly.

SOCRATES: Then it is not because a thing is seen that something sees it, but just the opposite—because something sees it, therefore it is seen. Nor because it is led, that something leads it, but because something leads it, therefore it is led. Nor because it is carried, that something carries it, but because something carries it, therefore it is carried.

Do you see what I wish to say, Euthyphro? It is this. Whenever an effect occurs, or something is effected, it is not the thing effected that gives rise to the effect; no, there is a cause, and then comes this effect. Nor is it because a thing is acted on that there is this effect; no, there is a cause for what it undergoes, and then comes this effect. Don't you agree?

EUTHYPHRO: I do.

SOCRATES: Well then, when a thing is loved, is it not in process of becoming something, or of undergoing something, by some other thing?

EUTHYPHRO: Yes, certainly.

SOCRATES: Then the same is true here as in the previous cases. It is not because a thing is loved that they who love it love it, but it is loved because they love it.

EUTHYPHRO: Necessarily.

SOCRATES: Then what are we to say about the holy, Euthyphro? According to your argument, is it not loved by all the gods?

EUTHYPHRO: Yes.

SOCRATES: Because it is holy, or for some other reason?

EUTHYPHRO: No, it is for that reason.

SOCRATES: And so it is because it is holy that it is loved; it is not holy because it is loved.

EUTHYPHRO: So it seems.

SOCRATES: On the other hand, it is beloved and pleasing to the gods just because they love it?

EUTHYPHRO: No doubt of that.

SOCRATES: So what is pleasing to the gods is not the same as what is holy, Euthyphro, nor, according to your statement, is the holy the same as what is pleasing to the gods. They are two different things.

EUTHYPHRO: How may that be, Socrates?

SOCRATES: Because we are agreed that the holy is loved because it is holy, and is not holy because it is loved. Isn't it so?

EUTHYPHRO: Yes.

SOCRATES: Whereas what is pleasing to the gods is pleasing to them just because they love it, such being its nature and its causes. Its being loved of the gods is not the reason of its being loved.

EUTHYPHRO: You are right.

SocRATES: But suppose, dear Euthyphro, that what is pleasing to the gods and what is holy were not two separate things. In that case if holiness were loved because it was holy, then also what was pleasing to the gods would be loved because it pleased them. And, on the other hand, if what was pleasing to them pleased because they loved it, then also the holy would be holy because they loved it. But now you see that it is just the opposite, because the two are absolutely different from each other, for the one [what is pleasing to the gods] is of a sort to be loved because it is loved, whereas the other [what is holy] is loved because it is of a sort to be loved. Consequently, Euthyphro, it looks as if you had not given me my answer—as if when you were asked to tell the nature of the holy, you did not wish to explain the essence of it. You merely tell an attribute of it, namely, that it appertains to holiness to be loved by all the gods. What it is, as yet you have not said. So, if you please, do not conceal this from me. No, begin again. Say what the holy is, and never mind if gods do love it, nor if it has some other attribute; on that we shall not split. Come, speak out. Explain the nature of the holy and unholy.

EUTHYPHRO: Now, Socrates, I simply don't know how to tell you what I think. Somehow everything that we put forward keeps moving about us in a circle, and nothing will stay where we put it.[1]

In the *Dialogues*, which were composed over many years, Plato gradually introduced his own (and more developed) ideas in place of those of the historical Socrates, though he continued to employ Socrates as the mouthpiece of these ideas. It is, of course, a problem to know where the real Socrates leaves off and Plato's own ideas begin. This is called the Socratic Problem. For the purpose of our discussion here we will not concern ourselves with this problem and will simply speak of the philosophy embodied in the *Dialogues* as Plato's philosophy.

THE TWO WORLDS: APPEARANCE AND REALITY

Many philosophers have found it necessary to conceive of reality in two spheres or levels: what *appears* to be real and what *is* real. Already in the beginning stages of the history of philosophy Plato introduced this two-layer

---

[1]Plato, *Euthyphro*, 9E–11B, tr. Lane Cooper, in *Plato: The Collected Dialogues*, eds. Edith Hamilton and Huntington Cairns (New York: Pantheon Books, 1961).

PLATONIC DIALOGUE

"Plato presented philosophy in an entirely spontaneous form, not as ponderous treatises but in dramatic dialogues between friends, in which Socrates figured as the presiding genius. He invented the form to make his concepts intelligible to the layman, and never was philosophy graced with more beauty; this first attempt to humanize knowledge was warm, personal, fresh, and frequently humorous, an intoxicating mixture of poetry and hard thought."

Felix Marti-Ibanez, *Tales of Philosophy* (New York: Potter, 1964), p. 31.

---

view of reality. For Plato, too, it is the difference between Appearance and Reality, though he expressed it also by means of the terms *Becoming* and *Being*. With such talk Plato affirms his conviction that in addition to the ever-changing world around us (Becoming), there is another world, an external and unchanging reality (Being). Why would one believe in an *additional* world such as this?

Plato had many reasons for believing in a transcendent world, that is, a reality lying beyond space and time. We will limit ourselves to two of these reasons, but perhaps the two most important.

First, Plato's view of reality is a reaction to that of his predecessor, Protagoras. Protagoras, a Sophist[2] who was active about 425 B.C., was responsible for one of the most famous lines ever uttered: "Man is the measure of all things." His meaning is clear from a more accurate and complete quotation:

A man is the measure of all things; of the things that are, that they are, and of the things that are not, that they are not.[3]

---

[2] The Sophists (literally, "wise men") were the first to teach wisdom for a fee, something that irked Socrates. Actually, the Sophists may not have been as wise as they were clever with words, and they were accused of "making the stronger argument appear to be the weaker, and the weaker argument appear to be the stronger." But in the days of Athenian democracy, when an individual was required to defend himself in the law courts, the Sophists' "wisdom" was, understandably, much in demand!

[3] Protagoras, *Fragment I*, tr. Ed. L. Miller.

TRANSCENDENT REALITY

. . . in philosophy usually means reality which transcends or lies beyond *space* and *time*. Thus God, as represented in classical theology, is a transcendent being, and true Reality, for Plato, is transcendent. Can you imagine a transcendent being in the sense of forming a mental image? The answer is No, for images are bound by spatio-temporal conditions, such as size, color, shape, motion, etc. Can you *conceive* of a transcendent being? The answer is Yes, if by that you mean that you can have an idea or concept of that being. Thus you cannot *imagine* God, though you may have an *idea* of him.

This means that the individual—each and every person—is the criterion unto himself or herself as to what exists and what doesn't. The thought was expanded, of course, to include truth and morality. Whatever you perceive as true or false *is* true or false, and whatever you think is good or bad *is* good or bad. This is known as relativism or subjectivism because it makes the most important things *relative* to and dependent upon the individual (or community, society, etc.), or because it asserts that the subject (either an individual, community, society, etc.) is the source and standard of being, truth, and goodness.

For Plato (and for most philosophers since) it was absurd to say that being, truth, and morality are "up for grabs" and can be or mean whatever an individual wishes! This would mean the immediate collapse not only of all serious talk about what's real and unreal, and what's true and false, but also all talk about moral responsibility, praise, blame, punishment, and so on. No, says Plato. Our understanding of being, truth, and goodness must—if it is to be really meaningful—be anchored in some *objective* (that is, it exists outside of our own minds), *independent* (it is not dependent on anything else for its existence), and *absolute* (it does not come or go or otherwise change) Reality. There must then exist above our minds and beyond this world another world, a world of Reality (Being).

Second, Plato's view of reality is a reaction to still another of his predecessors, the Pre-Socratic philosopher Heraclitus. Heraclitus went about saying things like, "The sun is new every day," and "We are and we are not." These are ways in which Heraclitus expressed his view—a very famous view—that everything is constantly changing, nothing stands still for a moment, the world and everything in it is in a ceaseless movement, activity, coming and going, ebbing and flowing. In fact, "All things flow" caught on as a Heraclitean slogan, and Heraclitus himself appears to have likened the fluctuating universe to a river: "You can't step twice into the same river." The idea is that by the time you have put a foot into the water, different water is flowing there.

What did this colorful and dynamic view of the world have to do with the development of Plato's conception of reality? Just as Protagoras' relativism, says Plato, leads to impossible conclusions, so does Heraclitus' doctrine of flux: If all reality is constantly changing, then all discourse is impossible, and the same is true for knowledge itself. Why is this? For the answer, read on.

Plato inherited from still another Pre-Socratic philosopher, Parmenides, the idea that genuine knowledge and discourse must be about what *is*, not what *is not*—after all, you can't think about, talk about, or have any knowledge of what *isn't*, can you? (The word "nothing" does not denote something, but rather the negation or absence of something.) Furthermore, what *is* (Being) must be *one* and *unchanging*. Do you see why being must be one and unchanging? Do not multiplicity and change involve difference, absence, relativity, and degrees? And do not these in turn involve various sorts of nonbeing? Now since a thing cannot both be and not be (the Law of Non-Contradiction), it is *logically* impossible that what *is* could also be what *is not*. How then could that which *is* involve multiplicity and change? True being is therefore one and unchanging. And only this can be an object of knowledge and discourse.

Now consider again Heraclitus' world of flux. What is it that you refer to when you comment on that table over there in the corner? "Why," you say, "just that table over there in the corner." But on the Heraclitean view there *is* no table over there in the corner: By the time you say "that table" it is no longer *that* table, but has already become a *different* table. Likewise for everything in the Heraclitean world of flux. If then, says Plato, knowledge and talk about tables, chairs, dogs, cats, justice, and anything else, is about anything *real*, it must be because there is more to reality than the sensible world of multiplicity and change. There must be a world of *Being* in addition to the world of *Becoming*.

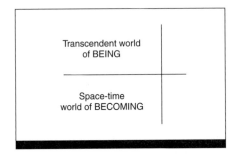

In his dialogue *Timaeus*, Plato himself poses the distinction between the two worlds, the worlds of Being and Becoming, and the corresponding difference between knowledge and opinion, as clearly as one could hope for:

> . . . we must make a distinction and ask, What is that which always is and has no becoming, and what is that which is always becoming and never is? That which is apprehended by intelligence and reason is always in the same state, but that which is conceived by opinion with the help of sensation and without reason is always in a process of becoming and perishing and never really is.[4]

The same distinction is strikingly posed in the *Republic*, where Plato clearly represents the world of Becoming as a "twilight" zone or "half-way region" between reality and unreality:

> . . . we have discovered that the many conventional notions of the mass of mankind about what is beautiful or honourable or just and so on are adrift in a sort of twilight between pure reality and pure unreality.
>
> We have.
>
> And we agreed earlier that, if any such object were discovered, it should be called the object of belief and not of knowledge. Fluctuating in that half-way region, it would be seized upon by the intermediate faculty.
>
> Yes.

---

[4]Plato, *Timaeus*, 27D–28A, tr. Benjamin Jowett, in *Plato: The Collected Dialogues*.

So when people have an eye for the multitude of beautiful things or of just actions or whatever it may be, but can neither behold Beauty or Justice itself nor follow a guide who would lead them to it, we shall say that all they have are beliefs, without any real knowledge of the objects of their belief.

That follows.

But what of those who contemplate the realities themselves as they are forever in the same unchanging state? Shall we not say that they have, not mere belief, but knowledge?

That too follows.

And, further, that their affection goes out to the objects of knowledge, whereas the others set their affections on the objects of belief; for it was they, you remember, who had a passion for the spectacle of beautiful colours and sounds, but would not hear of Beauty itself being a real thing.

I remember.

So we may fairly call them lovers of belief rather than of wisdom—not philosophical, in fact, but philodoxical. Will they be seriously annoyed by that description?

Not if they will listen to my advice. No one ought to take offence at the truth.

The name of philosopher, then, will be reserved for those whose affections are set, in every case, on the reality.

By all means.[5]

THE THEORY OF THE FORMS

Grasping the distinction between the two worlds is the first step toward an understanding of Plato's theory of reality. The next step is to grasp that for Plato the transcendent world, the world of Being, is populated by realities called Forms, which are the causes of the particular things that exist beneath them, like tables, chairs, dogs, cats, circles, human beings,

---

[5]Plato, *The Republic*, 479D–480A, tr. Francis MacDonald Cornford (New York: Oxford University Press, 1941).

PLATO

PLATO WAS born in Athens in 427 B.C. According to one tradition he was originally named Aristocles but came to be called Plato (from the Greek *platus*, "wide") because of his broad shoulders. He came from an aristocratic family and no doubt received a very cultured education. He was at first bent upon a career in politics, but was soon captivated by Socrates and his philosophy, and the fate of Socrates at the hands of the Athenian democracy (he was present at Socrates' trial) further sealed Plato's revulsion at such politics. From Socrates Plato learned to fix his attention not on the fluctuating objects of sense experience, but on the fixed and abiding *essence* of things as the only possible objects of true knowledge.

(continued on next page)

instances of beauty, examples of justice, and so on, for every different kind of thing there is.

We are ready, then, to consider Plato's *theory of the Forms*. At least that is what it is usually called. It is also sometimes called the *Theory of Ideas*. But here we must be on guard not to confuse *these* Ideas (capital *I*) with the ideas (small *i*) that exist merely in our minds. It will be seen that while our ideas have no existence apart from our minds, the Platonic Ideas exist objectively and absolutely: They would exist even if everything else were to disappear. In any case, it is useful to employ a capital *F* and *I* to remind us of the unique status of the Platonic Forms or Ideas.

Why the word "Form"? It translates the Greek word *eidos*, which does, in fact, mean "form" in the ordinary, usual sense: shape, structure, appearance. As will shortly be seen, Plato certainly does *not* mean something visible. Still, it is easy to see why Plato took over this word for his

When he was about 40, Plato visited Italy, possibly to engage the Pythagoreans there and to see the volcanoes. In Italy he became friends with Dion, the brother-in-law of Dionysus I, tyrant of Syracuse. Dionysus I, however, disliked Plato and had him sold as a slave. He was recognized by an acquaintance who ransomed him and had him sent back to Athens. There, in 388 B.C., he founded his school, the Academy, sometimes called the first European university. At the Academy Plato produced many elegant dialogues and lectured on many different topics (the lectures are lost), including rhetoric, biology, mathematics, astronomy, and, of course, philosophy—the pursuit of the highest reality and truth. Plato was intensely interested in political philosophy, and it was his desire to experiment with his ideal of the Philosopher-King that led him to return to Syracuse, where Dionysus I had been succeeded by his nephew, Dionysus II. Intrigues within the court spoiled Plato's philosophical education of Dionysus II, and the project was a failure.

Plato presided over the Academy until his death in 347 B.C. In the meantime, however, a pupil had matriculated at the Academy by the name of Aristotle.

Plato is universally regarded as one of the finest writers of Greek literature. His numerous and polished dialogues include the *Apology, Euthyphro, Phaedo, Phaedrus, Meno, Republic, Symposium, Theaetetus, Sophist, Timaeus, Statesman, and Laws.*

own purpose. After all, a Platonic Form does have everything to do with what a thing *is*, and thus even with its physical structure, shape, or appearance. But if it helps, there are many expressions one could substitute for the word "Form": essence, nature, essential structure, object of a definition, etc. Again, what they all designate is what a thing *is*, its "whatness."

It may be helpful, further, to outline the main features of Forms. They may be characterized as:

- *Objective.* They exist "out there" as objects, independently of our minds or wills.
- *Transcendent.* Though they exist "out there," they do not exist in space and time; they lie, as it were, above or beyond space and time.

- *Eternal.* As transcendent realities they are not subject to time and therefore not subject to motion or change.
- *Intelligible.* As transcendent realities they cannot be grasped by the senses but only by the intellect.
- *Archetypal.* They are the models for every kind of thing that does or could exist.
- *Perfect.* They include absolutely and perfectly all the features of the things of which they are the models.

Perhaps now we are ready for a more explicit statement of the theory of the Forms: It is the belief in a transcendent world of eternal and absolute beings, corresponding to every kind of thing that there is, and causing in particular things their essential nature.

More generally: For every particular and imperfect thing in the world of Becoming (a table, a chair, an instance of justice, an example of beauty, a circle) there is a corresponding reality which is its absolute and perfect essence or Form in the world of Being (Table, Chair, Justice, Beauty, Circle). The particular and imperfect thing, though imperfect, is what it is by virtue of its corresponding Form, which imparts to it, or causes in it, its essence or general nature. Because something has an essence or general nature, it is an imperfect *something*. On the other hand, it is an *imperfect* something because while it reflects being from above, it is invaded and contaminated by nonbeing from below: The changeless is set in motion, the one is multiplied into many, the absolute is relativized, the universal is particularized.

In view of all this, the following passage from Plato's *Euthyphro* should make a lot of sense. Here Socrates has asked Euthyphro about the meaning of holiness. Euthyphro responded with examples of holiness.

SOCRATES: . . . try to tell me more clearly what I asked you a little while ago, for, my friend, you were not explicit enough before when I put the question. What is holiness? You merely said that what you are now doing is a holy deed—namely, prosecuting your father on a charge of murder.

EUTHYPHRO: And, Socrates, I told the truth.

SOCRATES: Possibly. But, Euthyphro, there are many other things that you will say are holy.

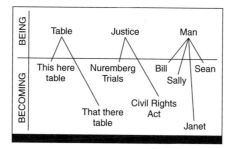

EUTHYPHRO: Because they are.

SOCRATES: Well, bear in mind that what I asked of you was not to tell me one or two out of all the numerous actions that are holy; I wanted you to tell me what is the essential form of holiness which makes all holy actions holy. I believe you held that there is one ideal form by which unholy things are all unholy, and by which all holy things are holy. Do you remember that?

EUTHYPHRO: I do.

SOCRATES: Well, then, show me what, precisely, this ideal is, so that, with my eye on it, and using it as a standard, I can say that any action done by you or anybody else is holy if it resembles this idea, or, if it does not, can deny that it is holy.[6]

This brief passage expresses or embodies many of the things we have just explained. Notice for example, (1) Plato's use of words or phrases like "essential form" and "ideal" for the essence in the world of Being; (2) the contrast between the *one* essence in the world of Being (in this case Holiness) and the *many* instances of it in the world of Becoming (numerous holy acts); (3) the way in which the Form is said to be the cause of its many sensible instances; (4) the Form referred to as a standard for judgment; and (5) the way in which the particular instance is said to resemble the model.

This last point leads us further. We have said above that particular things have a nature or essence because they stand in some sort of relation to their Forms. But what, exactly, is this relation? How does the Form impart essence to the particular thing? This is a troublesome question, and

---

[6]Plato, *Euthyphro*, 6C–E.

Plato seems to have been bothered by it, though he never resolved it. Until now, we have been representing the Form as the model, and the sensible instance of the Form as a copy or imitation of it. This is the most common way of representing Plato's theory at this point. But Plato actually resorts to *two* explanations (really, *metaphors*) of how the Form gives essence to particular things. Sometimes, as in the above passage in the *Euthyphro*, he talks as if sensible things are *copies* or *imitations* of the Forms, and at other times he talks of a *participation* of the sensible thing in its Form. Thus a table is a table because it imperfectly reflects or is an imperfect copy of its pattern or model, the Form Tableness, or it is a table because it participates in the Form Tableness. The following passage from the *Phaedo* is useful not only because it makes explicit (though ambiguous) reference to a Form's relation to its sensible instances—he speaks of the Form's "presence in it" or "association with it"—but also because it shows that Plato did not concern himself with a rigorous explanation of this point:

> It seems to me that whatever else is beautiful apart from absolute beauty is beautiful because it partakes of that absolute beauty, and for no other reason. Do you accept this kind of causality?
>
> Yes, I do.
>
> Well, now, that is as far as my mind goes; I cannot understand these other ingenious theories of causation. If someone tells me that the reason why a given object is beautiful is that it has a gorgeous color or shape or any other such attribute, I disregard all these other explanations—I find them all confusing—and I cling simply and straightforwardly and no doubt foolishly to the explanation that the one thing that makes that object beautiful is the presence in it or association with it, in whatever way the relation comes about, of absolute beauty. I do not go so far as to insist upon the precise details— only upon the fact that it is by beauty that beautiful things are beautiful. This, I feel, is the safest answer for me or for anyone else to give, and I believe that while I hold fast to this I cannot fall; it is safe for me or for anyone else to answer that it is by beauty that beautiful things are beautiful. Don't you agree?[7]

---

[7]Plato, *Phaedo*, 100C–E, tr. Hugh Tredennick, in *Plato: The Collected Dialogues.*

We will see later that Plato's failure to be precise on the nature of the Form's relation to the particular is exactly what Aristotle seized as the Achilles' heel of Plato's whole theory.

Another important matter: Things can participate in more than one Form. This can happen in two ways. *First,* Forms themselves "blend" with one another, so that by imitating or participating in one Form a thing may actually be sharing in many Forms. Is this not necessary, since the Forms both of *X* and *Y* may hold some essential feature in common? For example, if it is the essence of trees, dogs, cats, and humans to live, then however their Forms may otherwise differ, they must at least all blend with the Form Life; if apples, cherries, bananas, and oranges are all by nature sweet, then whatever else each of their Forms involves, they must all encompass Sweetness. Plato does not, however, believe that blending can go on forever as if we could just keep throwing in new ingredients to explain more and more specialized kinds of things. There must be a last, most specific definition in order to account for the ultimate difference of things.

But what about a feature which is not properly part of a thing's essence? Ink does not have to be blue in order to be ink, does it? This brings us to the *second* way things can imitate or participate in more than one Form. The Form Ink involves whatever it means to be *ink*, including having color. Now if this happens to be blue, then in addition to imitating or participating in the essential Form of Ink, including color, this ink must also participate in the Form Blue. Ask yourself: Is a certain feature of a thing part of that thing's very essence? If so, then that feature is one of the Forms that blend to make up the Form of that thing. If not, then that thing participates in this particular feature or Form accidentally or "on its own," as it were.

DEGREES OF REALITY AND KNOWLEDGE

So far we have been speaking as if Plato distinguished between two layers or levels of reality: *Being* and *Becoming,* Forms and their sensible copies. But Plato's theory of reality is somewhat more complicated than that. Here his famous image of the Divided Line, from the *Republic,* is helpful—Plato must have known that a picture is worth a thousand words.

> . . . take a line divided into two unequal parts, one to represent the visible order, the other the intelligible; and divide each part again in the same proportion, symbolizing degrees of comparative clearness

or obscurity. Then (*A*) one of the two sections in the visible world will stand for images. By images I mean first shadows, and then reflections in water or in close-grained, polished surfaces, and everything of that kind, if you understand.

Yes, I understand.

Let the second section (*B*) stand for the actual things of which the first are likenesses, the living creatures about us and all the works of nature or of human hands.

So be it.

Will you also take the proportion in which the visible world has been divided as corresponding to degrees of reality and truth, so that the likeness shall stand to the original in the same ratio as the sphere of appearances and belief to the sphere of knowledge?

Certainly.

Now consider how we are to divide the part which stands for the intelligible world. There are two sections. In the first (*C*) the mind uses as images those actual things which themselves had images in the visible world; and it is compelled to pursue its inquiry by starting from assumptions and traveling, not up to a principle, but down to a conclusion. In the second (*D*) the mind moves in the other direction, from an assumption up towards a principle which is not hypothetical; and it makes no use of the images employed in the other section, but only of Forms, and conducts its inquiry solely by their means.

I don't quite understand what you mean.

Then we will try again; what I have just said will help you to understand. (*C*) You know, of course, how students of subjects like geometry and arithmetic begin by postulating odd and even numbers, or the various figures and the three kinds of angle, and other such data in each subject. These data they take as known; and, having adopted them as assumptions, they do not feel called upon to give any account of them to themselves or to anyone else, but treat them as self-evident. Then, starting from these assumptions, they go on until they arrive, by a series of consistent steps, at all the conclusions they set out to investigate.

Yes, I know that.

You also know how they make use of visible figures and discourse about them, though what they really have in mind are the originals of which these figures are images: they are not reasoning, for instance, about this particular square and diagonal which they have drawn, but about *the* Square and *the* Diagonal; and so in all cases. The diagrams they draw and the models they make are actual things, which may have their shadows or images in water; but now they serve in their turn as images, while the student is seeking to behold those realities which only thought can apprehend.

True.

This, then, is the class of things that I spoke of as intelligible, but with two qualifications: first, that the mind, in studying them, is compelled to employ assumptions, and, because it cannot rise above these, does not travel upwards to a first principle; and second, that it uses as images those actual things which have images of their own in the section below them and which, in comparison with those shadows and reflections, are reputed to be more palpable and valued accordingly.

I understand: you mean the subject-matter of geometry and of the kindred arts.

(D) Then by the second section of the intelligible world you may understand me to mean all that unaided reasoning apprehends by the power of dialectic, when it treats its assumptions, not as first principles, but as *hypotheses* in the literal sense, things "laid down" like a flight of steps up which it may mount all the way to something that is not hypothetical, the first principle of all; and having grasped this, may turn back and, holding on to the consequences which depend upon it, descend at last to a conclusion, never making use of any sensible object, but only of Forms, moving through Forms from one to another, and ending with Forms.

I understand, he said, though not perfectly; for the procedure you describe sounds like an enormous undertaking. But I see that you mean to distinguish the field of intelligible reality studied by dialectic as having a greater certainty and truth than the subject-matter of the "arts," as they are called, which treat their assumptions as first principles. The students of these arts are, it is true, compelled to exercise thought in contemplating objects which the senses cannot perceive; but because they start from assumptions without going back to a first principle, you do not regard them as gaining true understanding about those objects, although the objects themselves, when connected with a first principle, are intelligible. And I think you would call the state of mind of the students of geometry and other such arts, not intelligence, but thinking, as being something between intelligence and mere acceptance of appearances.

You have understood me quite well enough, I replied. And now you may take, as corresponding to the four sections, these four states of mind: *intelligence* for the highest, *thinking* for the second, *belief* for the third, and for the last *imagining*. These you may arrange as the terms in a proportion, assigning to each a degree of clearness and certainty corresponding to the measure in which their objects possess truth and reality.

I understand and agree with you. I will arrange them as you say.[8]

There is no end to what could be said about Plato's philosophy on the basis of the Line. Here we will summarize the most important points.

To begin with, note that the Line is not divided into equal parts but *unequal* parts, and likewise the bottom and top segments of the Line are divided in the same ratio. This is Plato's way of suggesting that as we proceed from the bottom to the top of the Line we attain greater and greater degrees of reality and certainty. The first and major division of the Line represents, obviously, the distinction between the world of Being and the world of Becoming. By now we are certainly familiar with this distinction. But now each of the resulting lines, below and above, is in turn divided. This results in a sort of ladder of reality (on the metaphysical side of the Line) and a ladder of knowledge (on the epistemological side). The ladder of reality extends from mere images of sensible things (reflections in pools of water, photographs, paintings, memories, etc.) to the sensible things themselves (actual tables, chairs, humans, instances of justice or beauty, etc.), to the Forms which these sensible things copy. If the Form or essence includes a specific and concrete physical embodiment (Table, Circle, Human), then the Form is a "lower Form"; if the Form has no specific and concrete physical embodiment (Justice, Beauty), then it is a "higher Form." Corresponding to this ladder of reality is the ladder of knowledge.

---

[8]Plato, *The Republic*, 509D–511E.

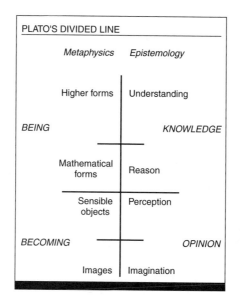

This extends from mere imagination (which grasps images) to perception (which grasps actual sensible things) to reason (which is a rational and deductive way of grasping the lower Forms) to understanding (which grasps the higher Forms in a direct and intuitive way).

THE GOOD, THE SUN, AND THE CAVE

But there is more. It turns out that there is something above even the Forms themselves, something which we must situate at the very top of the Line. In the *Republic* Plato calls it the "essential Form of the Good."[9] Why must we believe in something even above the Forms, a sort of Form of the Forms? The answer is this: Just as the many images, say in a pool of water, must derive their relative being from some one thing above them, like an actual table, and actual tables must derive their relative being from some one thing

---

[9]According to a later form of Platonism, Neo-Platonism, Plato calls this Supreme Reality by various names, depending on the context. In the *Symposium*, where Plato is talking about the soul's quest for the beautiful, it is called *Beauty;* elsewhere, when Plato considers reality in a kind of mathematical light, he appears to have called it the *One*. But in the *Republic* it is called by its most familiar name: the *essential Form of the Good*.

above *them*, the Form Table, so must the Forms (both lower and higher) derive *their* being from a source which is above *them:* the Form of the Good.
And just as it is above all realities and is their ultimate source, so it is above
all knowledge and is its ultimate source. Of course, in order to be the *source*
of being and knowledge, it itself cannot be *a* being or *a* thing known. That is
why Plato says of the Good that it is *beyond being and knowledge.*

In a well-known analogy, Plato likens the essential Form of Goodness
to the sun. The Good is to the intelligible world, or world of Being, as the
sun is to the visible world, or world of Becoming:

> First we must come to an understanding. Let me remind you of the
> distinction we drew earlier and have often drawn on other occasions,
> between the multiplicity of things that we call good or beautiful or
> whatever it may be and, on the other hand, Goodness itself or
> Beauty itself and so on. Corresponding to each of these sets of many
> things, we postulate a single Form or real essence, as we call it.
>
> Yes, that is so.
>
> Further, the many things, we say, can be seen, but are not objects of
> rational thought; whereas the Forms are objects of thought, but
> invisible.
>
> Yes, certainly.
>
> And we see things with our eyesight, just as we hear sounds with our
> ears and, to speak generally, perceive any sensible things with our
> sense-faculties.
>
> Of course.
>
> Have you noticed, then, that the artificer who designed the senses
> has been exceptionally lavish of his materials in making the eyes able
> to see and their objects visible?
>
> That never occurred to me.
>
> Well, look at it in this way. Hearing and sound do not stand in need
> of any third thing, without which the ear will not hear nor sound be
> heard; and I think the same is true of most, not to say all, of the
> other senses. Can you think of one that does require anything of
> the sort?
>
> No, I cannot.

But there is this need in the case of sight and its objects. You may have the power of vision in your eyes and try to use it, and colour may be there in the objects; but sight will see nothing and the colours will remain invisible in the absence of a third thing peculiarly constituted to serve this very purpose.

By which you mean—?

Naturally I mean what you call light; and if light is a thing of value, the sense of sight and the power of being visible are linked together by a very precious bond, such as unites no other sense with its object.

No one could say that light is not a precious thing.

And of all the divinities in the skies is there one whose light, above all the rest, is responsible for making our eyes see perfectly and making objects perfectly visible?

There can be no two opinions: of course you mean the Sun.

And how is sight related to this deity? Neither sight nor the eye which contains it is the Sun, but of all the sense-organs it is the most sun-like; and further, the power it possesses is dispensed by the Sun, like a stream flooding the eye. And again, the Sun is not vision, but it is the cause of vision and also is seen by the vision it causes.

Yes.

It was the Sun, then, that I meant when I spoke of that offspring which the Good has created in the visible world, to stand there in the same relation to vision and visible things as that which the Good itself bears in the intelligible world to intelligence and to intelligible objects.

How is that? You must explain further.

You know what happens when the colours of things are no longer irradiated by the daylight, but only by the fainter luminaries of the night: when you look at them, the eyes are dim and seem almost blind, as if there were no unclouded vision in them. But when you look at things on which the Sun is shining, the same eyes see distinctly and it becomes evident that they do contain the power of vision.

Certainly.

Apply this comparison, then, to the soul. When its gaze is fixed upon an object irradiated by truth and reality, the soul gains understanding and knowledge and is manifestly in possession of intelligence. But when it looks towards that twilight world of things that come into existence and pass away, its sight is dim and it has only opinions and beliefs which shift to and fro, and now it seems like a thing that has no intelligence.

That is true.

This, then, which gives to the objects of knowledge their truth and to him who knows them his power of knowing, is the Form or essential nature of Goodness. It is the cause of knowledge and truth; and so, while you may think of it as an object of knowledge, you will do well to regard it as something beyond truth and knowledge and, precious as these both are, of still higher worth. And, just as in our analogy light and vision were to be thought of as like the Sun, but not identical with it, so here both knowledge and truth are to be regarded as like the Good, but to identify either with the Good is wrong. The Good must hold a yet higher place of honour.

You are giving it a position of extraordinary splendour, if it is the source of knowledge and truth and itself surpasses them in worth. You surely cannot mean that it is pleasure.

Heaven forbid, I exclaimed. But I want to follow up our analogy still further. You will agree that the Sun not only makes the things we see visible, but also brings them into existence and gives them growth and nourishment; yet he is not the same thing as existence. And so with the objects of knowledge: these derive from the Good not only their power of being known, but their very being and reality; and Goodness is not the same thing as being, but even beyond being, surpassing it in dignity and power.[10]

It may be useful to spell out exactly the various elements in the analogy: The sun is analogous to the Form of the Good; the visible world is analogous to the intelligible world (the world of Forms); Light is analogous to Truth; the objects of sight are analogous to the objects of knowledge (the

---

[10]Plato, *The Republic*, 507A–509B.

Forms); and sight is analogous to knowledge. Or perhaps a more visual summary will help.[11]

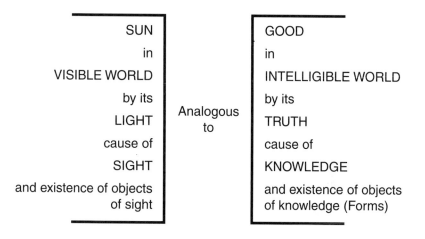

SUN		GOOD
in		in
VISIBLE WORLD		INTELLIGIBLE WORLD
by its	Analogous to	by its
LIGHT		TRUTH
cause of		cause of
SIGHT		KNOWLEDGE
and existence of objects of sight		and existence of objects of knowledge (Forms)

The two main points of the analogy are: *First*, just as the sun lights up the world and makes physical objects visible to our eyes, so does the Good illuminate intelligible objects (Forms) and render them knowable by the mind. *Second*, and closely related, just as the sun actually causes things in the world to exist and sustains them—without the light of the sun, the world would wither away—so does the Good cause in the Forms their very being and truth.

In Plato's theory of reality, the Good is, then, the ultimate principle of reality and truth. Any degree or instance of being, truth, unity, harmony, beauty, or intelligibility found anywhere, either in the world of Becoming or in the world of Being, is traceable finally to the Good. This is, some would say, the closest thing in Plato to traditional conceptions of God, both Western and Eastern.

The Good is also the ultimate object of the soul's progress. And now we are ready for the Allegory of the Cave, one of the most famous passages in all of literature. In this allegory Plato asks us to picture men imprisoned in an underground cavern who mistake the shadowy figures and echoes reflected on the wall facing them for reality. But how deluded they

---

[11]The table is based on R. C. Cross and A. D. Woosley, *Plato's Republic: A Philosophical Commentary* (London: Macmillan, 1966), pp. 202, 231.

are! It is only by forcing them (and that is what it would take to dislodge them from their comfortable and familiar setting) out of the cave and into the upper world that, though temporarily dazzled and blinded by the true light, they would eventually recognize their former delusion. But read it for yourself.

. . . here is a parable to illustrate the degrees in which our nature may be enlightened or unenlightened. Imagine the condition of men living in a sort of cavernous chamber underground, with an entrance open to the light and a long passage all down the cave. Here they have been from childhood, chained by the leg and also by the neck, so that they cannot move and can see only what is in front of them, because the chains will not let them turn their heads. At some distance higher up is the light of a fire burning behind them; and between the prisoners and the fire is a track with a parapet built along it, like the screen at a puppet-show, which hides the performers while they show their puppets over the top.

I see, said he.

Now behind this parapet imagine persons carrying along various artificial objects, including figures of men and animals in wood or stone or other materials, which project above the parapet. Naturally, some of these persons will be talking, others silent.

It is a strange picture, he said, and a strange sort of prisoners.

Like ourselves, I replied; for in the first place prisoners so confined would have seen nothing of themselves or of any other, except the shadows thrown by the fire-light on the wall of the Cave facing them, would they?

Not if all their lives they had been prevented from moving their heads.

And they would have seen as little of the objects carried past.

Of course.

Now, if they could talk to one another, would they not suppose that their words referred only to those passing shadows which they saw?

Necessarily.

And suppose their prison had an echo from the wall facing them? When one of the people crossing behind them spoke, they could only suppose that the sound came from the shadow passing before their eyes.

No doubt.

In every way, then, such prisoners would recognize as reality nothing but the shadows of those artificial objects.

Inevitably.

Now consider what would happen if their release from the chains and the healing of their unwisdom should come about in this way. Suppose one of them were set free and forced suddenly to stand up, turn his head, and walk with eyes lifted to the light; all these movements would be painful, and he would be too dazzled to make out the objects whose shadows he had been used to seeing. What do you think he would say, if someone told him that what he had formerly seen was meaningless illusion, but now, being somewhat nearer to reality and turned towards more real objects, he was getting a truer view? Suppose further that he were shown the various objects being carried by and were made to say, in reply to questions, what each of them was. Would he not be perplexed and believe the objects now shown him to be not so real as what he formerly saw?

Yes, not nearly so real.

And if he were forced to look at the fire-light itself, would not his eyes ache, so that he would try to escape and turn back to the things which he could see distinctly, convinced that they really were clearer than these other objects now being shown to him?

Yes.

And suppose someone were to drag him away forcibly up the steep and rugged ascent and not let him go until he had hauled him out into the sunlight, would he not suffer pain and vexation at such treatment, and, when he had come out into the light, find his eyes so full of its radiance that he could not see a single one of the things that he was now told were real?

Certainly he would not see them all at once.

He would need, then, to grow accustomed before he could see things in that upper world. At first it would be easiest to make out shadows, and then the images of men and things reflected in water, and later on the things themselves. After that, it would be easier to watch the heavenly bodies and the sky itself by night, looking at the light of the moon and stars rather than the Sun and the Sun's light in the daytime.

Yes, surely.

Last of all, he would be able to look at the Sun and contemplate its nature, not as it appears when reflected in water or any alien medium, but as it is in itself in its own domain.

No doubt.

And now he would begin to draw the conclusion that it is the Sun that produces the seasons and the course of the year and controls everything in the visible world, and moreover is in a way the cause of all that he and his companions used to see.

Clearly he would come at last to that conclusion.[12]

The point of the story should be obvious. We, like the prisoners in the cave, are deluded about reality. We mistake the unreal for the real, and only with the greatest difficulty can we be turned, and indeed we might have to be *forced*, in the direction of truth and reality. But we *must* be turned in that direction, and we *must* ascend into the upper regions of truth and reality. Why? Because rationality is the essence of man. Thus our nature is fulfilled in the contemplation and knowledge of reality. And this means happiness or well-being. Even in this life, as much as possible we must be liberated and detached from the darkness of the sensible world of Becoming and opinion and live as much as possible in the enjoyment of Being and knowledge. At death, however, the soul will be freed forever from the distractions and imperfections of Becoming and can enjoy absolutely and without interruption the knowledge of Being. That is why, says Plato, the real philosopher—lover of wisdom—looks forward to death.

---

[12]Plato, *The Republic*, 514A–516C.

ARISTOTLE'S CRITICISM OF PLATO

As Plato was a student of Socrates and developed his ideas, so Aristotle was the student of Plato and developed *his* ideas. Less charitably, Aristotle ruthlessly criticized his master's theory of the Forms and propounded a quite different one.

Toward the beginning of his *Metaphysics*, Aristotle provides his own summary of the Socratic-Platonic theory:

> . . . [Plato], having in his youth first become familiar with Craty-lus[13] and with the Heraclitean doctrines (that all sensible things are ever in a state of flux and there is no knowledge about them), these views he held even in later years. Socrates, however, was busying himself about ethical matters and neglecting the world of nature as a whole but seeking the universal in these ethical matters, and fixed thought for the first time on definitions; Plato accepted his teaching, but held that the problem applied not to sensible things but to enti-ties of another kind—for this reason, that the common definition could not be a definition of any sensible thing, as they were always changing. Things of this other sort, then, he called Ideas, and sensi-ble things, he said, were all named after these, and in virtue of a rela-tion of these; for the many existed by participation in the Ideas that have the same name as they.[14]

Later he criticizes this view with a long string of objections; in fact, some have counted as many as twenty-five or more. Not all of Aristotle's objections are as important as others, as when he twits Plato for creating an additional world of things, as if we did not already have enough to explain!

More important is Aristotle's so-called Third-man Argument. It goes like this. In order to explain the similarity between (1) a first man and (2) a second man, we must posit (3) a third man, the Ideal Man or Form. But then there will have to be a similarity between (1) the first two men and

---

[13]Cratylus was a follower of Heraclitus but pushed the teaching of his master even fur-ther, for he said that one could not step into the same river even *once!*

[14]Aristotle, *Metaphysics*, 987a–b, tr. W. D. Ross, in *Basic Works of Aristotle*, ed. Richard McKeon (New York: Random House, 1941).

(2) the third man posited, the Form of Man. How do we now explain this similarity? We must again posit (3) a third and "higher" man. But then there will be a similarity between (1) all the previous men and (2) *this* third man. How do we explain *this* similarity? According to Aristotle, the process of positing a "third man" will have to go on forever, but in that case, the original similarity is never explained. Is this a fair argument against Plato? Some have countered that the argument will only work if you think the original third man, the Form of Man, is itself actually a *man* and possessing the features which particular men possess. Would Plato agree to this? Is the Form of Man *itself* two-legged and rational? This is a difficult question, and much ink has been spilt trying to explain just how Plato viewed the Forms in this respect. Be that as it may, this is still not Aristotle's main objection to Plato.

The main problem, for Aristotle, is the problem of the *chōrismos*, a Greek word which means "separation." Aristotle correctly represents Plato as having placed the ultimate causes of things (the Forms) in a transcendent world and thus *separated* from the things they are supposed to be the causes of. But this gives rise immediately to two very big questions, as Aristotle shows in the following:

> Above all one might discuss the question what on earth the Forms
> contribute to sensible things, either to those that are eternal or to
> those that come into being and cease to be. For they cause neither
> movement nor any change in them. But again they help in no wise
> either towards the knowledge of the other things (for they are not
> even the substance of these, else they would have been in them), or
> towards their being, if they are not in the particulars which share
> in them; though if they were, they might be thought to be causes,
> as white causes whiteness in a white object by entering into its
> composition. . . .

> But, further, all other things cannot come from the Forms in any of
> the usual senses of "from." And to say that they are patterns and the
> other things share in them is to use empty words and poetical
> metaphors. . . .

> Again, it would seem impossible that the substance and that of which
> it is the substance should exist apart; how therefore, could the Ideas,
> being the substances of things, exist apart? In the *Phaedo* the case is
> stated in this way—that the Forms are causes both of being and of

becoming; yet when the Forms exist, still the things that share in them do not come into being, unless there is something to originate movement.[15]

One question Aristotle poses is, How can the Forms be the causes of the natures or "whatnesses" of things without being *in* those things? His answer: They can't. *Another* question which Aristotle poses is, How do Plato's transcendent and unchanging Forms account for the most evident fact about the things around us, namely, their coming into being and their motion and change? His answer: They don't. In sum, the *chōrismos*, or separation, between the Forms and particular sensible things, like a great gulf fixed, makes it impossible for the Forms to *do* anything for those things at the most critical points. That is bad enough. What is worse, when Plato attempts to explain how the Forms are related to sensible things, he provides no really rigorous philosophical explanation but resorts to "empty words and poetical metaphors" such as *participation* and *imitation.*

In fairness to Plato, it should be noted that many of Aristotle's specific criticisms (for example, the Third-man Argument) were anticipated and discussed by Plato himself. More generally, in the *Timaeus* Plato did account for motion and change in the world, and as for his attempts to bridge the two worlds with "empty words and poetical metaphors," we saw in an earlier passage from the *Phaedo* that Plato freely granted the difficulty of language at this point.

ARISTOTLE'S VIEW OF FORM

One must not conclude from the above that Aristotle rejected Plato's theory of reality for a radically different one. Aristotle too believed absolutely in Forms. As with Plato, so with Aristotle: Only by means of Forms, the objective essences of things, can we account for the order around us, both in nature and in morality, and only because of Forms is knowledge of anything possible. The *difference* lies in their views of how the Forms are related to particular things.

It should be clear from the above quotation that Aristotle rejected Plato's idea of *transcendent* Forms in favor of an idea of *immanent* Forms, that is, a view of Forms as existing *within* particular sensible things. He

---

[15]Ibid., 991a–b.

overcomes Plato's unbridgeable chasm between Forms and sensible things by asserting that Forms can only be causes of things if they are *in* those things. But understand: There is no abstract "tableness" out there any more than there is any unimaginable formless matter or formless "stuff." What *is* out there are particular *tables*—this table, that table, and other tables. The Form or essence Table exists only as individualized or particularized (that is, turned into a concrete, particular thing) by some wood, glue, and varnish. And likewise with everything. The Form (which accounts for the essence or whatness of a thing) combined with matter (which gives that essence a concrete and particular expression) is what is *real.* As one slogan puts it, "No form without matter, and no matter without form." For those who prefer a more technical expression, this view or idea is called *hylomorphic composition* (from the Greek *hylē,* "matter," and *morphē,* "form"): Everything in the natural world is composed of both form and matter; there can be no instances of unformed matter or "unmattered" form.

Thus it is with everything in the *natural* world. With respect to God, the situation is quite different. The matter in a thing provides for its changeability and movement, since matter is the potential in a thing to change or become something different. Think of a table. It can be chopped into bits, burned into ashes, or dismantled and turned into a chair, only because there is *wood* there. But there can be no matter, or potential for change and motion, in God, who is the Unmoved Mover. God, the immutable source of all motion, must himself be utterly devoid of matter. He is Pure Form.

All of this so far may sound rather technical and bland. But the whole show is considerably enlivened when the *teleological* side of this theory of reality is stressed. And it should be stressed because it is a major feature of the Aristotelian perspective.

"Teleology" comes from the Greek word *telos,* "end" or "goal," and means the study of, or the belief in, principles that give rise to the order and purpose that pervades all reality. (We will see momentarily that these principles are otherwise called "final causes.") The conviction that reality is infused and governed by teleological principles is not new with Aristotle, though he thought it was. It is an obvious feature of the Platonic philosophy too, and is clearly discernible in some of the Pre-Socratics. Still, it received with Aristotle perhaps the strongest expression in the whole history of philosophy. For Aristotle, there is, so to say, both an "inside" and an "outside" story. The inside story concerns the way in which anything, say,

Plato and Aristotle, from "The School of Athens" (detail)
by Raphael. In this representation, Plato and Aristotle are
distinguishable from one another in several respects. How
many of them can you identify?

an acorn, is propelled naturally, by the form within, into a full-fledged, giant oak tree. What is important, then, is more than a static form—it includes a power that develops the thing into its full reality. As for the outside story: The oak tree is nourished by the nutrients in the ground, is dependent on the change of seasons, and otherwise stands in a complex relation to the rest of nature—using it for its own purposes, maintaining its own structure in the face of perturbances, and producing more acorns. The whole of nature is, in fact, a network of intimately related things, conspiring, as it were, upon the production of the efficient, harmonious, beautiful, and value-laden universe that confronts our sense at every turn.

The real difference between Plato's idea of *transcendent* Forms and Aristotle's idea of *immanent* Forms shows up very vividly in their discussions of art. In the last parts of the *Republic*, Plato argued that art is "thrice removed" from reality: A painting is an imperfect representation or copy of a man who himself is an imperfect copy of the real thing, Man; likewise a drama imperfectly represents people and things which are themselves imperfect copies of their Forms. For these reasons Plato advocated banishing the arts—at least the *representative* arts—from the ideal society. Aristotle, with his view of immanent Forms, draws exactly the opposite conclusion. It is because the essence and ideal of things are embodied *in* those things that the artistic representation brings us *closer* to reality. As Aristotle says in a helpful passage in his *Poetics*, what the artist does is represent things in their *universality*, to use Aristotle's term, and that is why the artist's work is more philosophical than, say, the historian's work, which represents things merely in their *particularity*.

> . . . the poet's function is to describe, not the thing that has happened, but a kind of thing that might happen, i.e. what is possible as being probable or necessary. The distinction between historian and poet is not in the one writing prose and the other verse—you might put the work of Herodotus into verse, and it would still be a species of history; it consists really in this, that the one describes the thing that has been, and the other a kind of thing that might be. Hence poetry is something more philosophic and of graver import than history, since its statements are of the nature rather of universals, whereas those of history are singulars. By a universal statement I mean one as to what such or such a kind of man will probably or necessarily say or do—which is the aim of poetry, though it affixes proper names to the characters; by a singular statement, one as to what, say, Alcibiades did or had done to him.[16]

Two final points. First, although we have dwelt upon form and matter, according to Aristotle there are actually *four* principles, or "causes," which are necessarily involved in the constitution or explanation of a thing:

- Material cause
- Formal cause
- Efficient cause
- Final cause

---

[16]Aristotle, *Poetics*, 1451a–b, tr. Ingram Bywater, in *Basic Works of Aristotle*.

The *material cause* is the matter, or "stuff," something is made out of; the *formal cause* is its essence, or whatness: the *efficient* or *moving cause* is what brings the thing into being; and the *final cause* is the end, or purpose, of the thing. Can you identify the four causes of, say, a table? It may be noticed that the last three causes are closely related, and Aristotle himself suggests that they may be lumped together under the formal cause, leaving us with the general twofold distinction: material cause/formal cause. Thus the key terms on the constitution and explanation of things are matter and form. Second, Aristotle stressed even more strongly than Plato the difference between "substantial" Forms and "accidental" Forms. Fido *necessarily* involves the Form Dog; it is of Fido's very nature or substance to be a dog. But it is only an accident that Fido involves the forms Shaggy, Brown, and Shortlegged; it is not part of Fido's essence that he possesses these features—he might or might not, and still be a *dog*.

AFTER PLATO AND ARISTOTLE

Aristotle provides, thus, a criticism of Plato's theory of reality. But his own theory, after all, is not really all that different. For both Plato and Aristotle the true reality of something is identified with its Form. And this general view, often called *realism*, was propagated throughout subsequent centuries, mainly through the Christian thinkers St. Augustine (d. 430), who taught more or less the Platonic version, and St. Thomas Aquinas (d. 1275), who taught more or less the Aristotelian version.

Obviously, this kind of philosophy is radically different from all those approaches which reject Form as sort of philosophically superstitious. It was, in fact, against this very idea that William of Ockham (d. 1349?) formulated the principle known as Ockham's Razor, in an attempt to cut away all unnecessary principles and realities: *Entia non sunt multiplicanda praeter necessitatem*, "Entities are not to be multiplied without necessity." The resulting view was known as *nominalism* (from the Latin *nomen*, "name"), the view that Forms or universals (such as Animal, Whiteness, etc.) have no external or independent existence, but are merely names or words by which we group together things which possess similar features.

Nominalism will perhaps appear to you as a very simple and clean approach: Away with all that silly and needless talk about substantial forms, accidental forms, metaphysical causes, and the like! On the other hand, we must not forget about the problems that spawned the belief in Forms in the first place: Without objective Forms, or essences, how, for example, are real knowledge, rational discourse, and moral judgment possible?

Or perhaps you would like a compromise. A third option is *conceptualism*. This is a philosophical halfway house between realism and nominalism inasmuch as it holds that there *are* universals but they are *mind-made*. Catness, for example, has no existence outside the mind, but it certainly does exist within the mind—a mental entity—and is employed for the sake of meaningful thought and discourse about reality.

It should not be thought that the realist-nominalist debate is just an antiquated piece in the Museum of Philosophical Ideas. The issue yet exercises contemporary thinkers. A good example is Willard V. Quine, one of the most influential English-speaking philosophers of the twentieth century, who relates the issue to mathematics. What is mathematics about? Is it about *anything?* There are three possible answers. First, you can say, as *logicism* does, that mathematics is about mind-independent objects, and this would commit you to a belief in something like Platonic or Aristotelian Forms, or realism. Second, you can say, with *formalism*, that mathematics isn't about anything, really; it is a formal game similar to chess where the pieces have no significance apart from the board, other pieces, the rules, and so on, and this would be to take a nominalist view. Third, there is an intermediate position, *intuitionism*, according to which mathematics is about mental constructs, and this, of course, corresponds to conceptualism. Quine himself (at least the later Quine) is the sort of philosopher who, in trying to answer the question of what exists, tries as much as possible to keep both feet in the physical world and appeals to the least number of abstract entities required to do the job. Nonetheless, he finds himself having to appeal to abstract or mind-independent entities, and thus he turns out to be a kind of mathematical Platonist.

Be that as it may, in the following extract from "On What There Is," Quine states in his own words how the very old problem of universals is alive and well ("ontology" is the theory of what is, and a "bound variable" is a formal logician's equivalent to a pronoun).

"I can see the horse, Plato, but not horseness."
—Antisthenes

Classical mathematics . . . is up to its neck in commitments to an ontology of abstract entities. Thus it is that the great mediaeval controversy over universals has flared up anew in the modern philosophy of mathematics. The issue is clearer now than of old, because we now have a more explicit standard whereby to decide what ontology a given theory or form of discourse is committed to: a theory is committed to those and only those entities to which the bound variables of the theory must be capable of referring in order that the affirmations made in the theory be true.

Because this standard of ontological presupposition did not emerge clearly in the philosophical tradition, the modern philosophical mathematicians have not on the whole recognized that they were debating the same old problem of universals in a newly clarified form. But the fundamental cleavages among modern points of view on foundations of mathematics do come down pretty explicitly to disagreements as to the range of entities to which the bound variables should be permitted to refer.

The three main mediaeval points of view regarding universals are designated by historians as *realism*, *conceptualism*, and *nominalism*. Essentially these same three doctrines reappear in twentieth-century surveys of the philosophy of mathematics under the new names *logicism*, *intuitionism*, and *formalism*.[17]

CHAPTER 3 IN REVIEW

Summary

"Form" is one of the most important words in the history of philosophy. In fact, when the first full-blown philosophies came on the scene, those of Plato and Aristotle, they were built almost entirely around this concept.

In an important sense, the idea of Form is an answer to any philosophies, such as those of Heraclitus (as Plato understood him) and Protagoras, which dissolve everything into a flux of relativity. According to Plato and other Form-philosophers, we must believe in an objective basis for the things existing around us, for knowledge, and for value judgments.

---

[17]Willard Van Orman Quine, "On What There Is," in *From a Logical Point of View: Nine Logico-Philosophical Essays*, second ed., rev. (Cambridge, MA: Harvard University Press, 1980), pp. 13f.

This basis is the Form, or essence, which constitutes the real *being* of a thing. As being, the Form must be one, immutable, ideal, transcendent, etc., and this being is imperfectly represented in particular, sensible things by "participation" or "imitation." Plato conceives all reality as a ladder or scale and, corresponding to this, knowledge too (the image of the Divided Line). But the basic distinction is between the sensible world of Becoming and the transcendent or intelligible world of Being, with the essential Form of Goodness ranging over all (the Analogy of the Sun). The practical point is to make our way, as much as possible in this life, into the higher realm of the intelligible and to enjoy the illumination of reality and truth (the Allegory of the Cave).

Aristotle belongs to this philosophical tradition too, but represents an important variation. He criticized Plato's theory of the Forms in several ways, but mainly because of the gap it leaves between the Forms and the things they are the Forms *of:* the problem of the *chōrismos.* Instead, Aristotle insisted that, while we must believe in the Forms or objective essences of things, they cannot be separated from those things. This is Aristotle's doctrine of *immanent* (rather than transcendent) Forms: The Forms must be *in* things. His conception of matter as potentiality and therefore providing for change and his doctrine of the Four Causes are also important features of his thought.

In subsequent centuries the realist metaphysics of Plato and Aristotle received Christian reinterpretations and restatements, most notably at the hands of St. Augustine and St. Thomas Aquinas. On the other hand, it was also *attacked* by nominalist philosophers, such as Ockham, for whom the Forms were merely general or universal terms which lump similar things into classes. The debate between realism (Forms have objective reality), nominalism (Forms are universal terms), and conceptualism (Forms are mental entities) is a fundamental and continuing one.

Basic Ideas

- "Systematic" philosophy
- The nature of a Platonic dialogue
- The Socratic Problem
- The problem with Protagorean subjectivism
- The problem with Heraclitean flux
- The distinction between the worlds of Becoming and Being
- The meaning of "Form"

- Six features of Platonic Forms:
  Objective
  Transcendent
  Eternal
  Intelligible
  Archetypal
  Perfect
- Platonic metaphors for the Form's relation to the particular:
  Imitation
  Participation
- Two ways in which something can share in more than one Form
- The Divided Line: Degrees of reality and knowledge
- The Good as the Form of Forms
- The Analogy of the Sun
- The Allegory of the Cave
- Aristotle's main criticism of Plato's theory: The problem of the *chōrismos*, "separation"
- Aristotelian teleology
- Aristotle's Four Causes
  Material
  Formal
  Efficient
  Final
- Aristotle's conception of immanent Forms
- Hylomorphic composition
- Substantial and accidental Forms
- Ockham's Razor
- Realism, nominalism, and conceptualism
- Quine: a mathematical Platonist

Questions for Reflection

- Plato's philosophy is sometimes called a rather "poetic" one. What does this mean? Is it good or bad? What is to be made of the fact that Plato anticipated Aristotle's criticisms but did not regard them as decisive?
- If one rejects every philosophy of forms, such as that of Plato or Aristotle, what then? What about the initial problems that sparked such philosophies in the first place?

- Is it necessary to accept, say, Plato's philosophy in its entirety and detail in order to be a "Platonist"? Is it possible to distinguish the central and essential idea of a philosophy from the particular, relative, and even mistaken trappings in which it was originally expressed? What is the *perspective* that characterizes any Platonic philosophy?

For Further Reading

Julia Annas. *An Introduction to Plato's Republic.* Oxford: Clarendon Press, 1981. Chs. 8–10. An up-to-date discussion of Plato's theory of knowledge, theory of the Forms, and the Sun, Line, and the Cave.

Frederick Copleston. *A History of Philosophy.* Baltimore: Newman Press, 1946–1974. I, Parts 3 and 4. Readable and indispensable accounts of both Plato's and Aristotle's theories of reality and their relation to one another by an esteemed historian of philosophy.

G. M. A. Grube. *Plato's Thought.* London: Methuen, 1935. Ch. 1. A long and excellent chapter titled "The Theory of the Forms" in an old but useful work.

William J. Prior. *Unity and Development in Plato's Metaphysics.* LaSalle, IL: Open Court, 1985. A recent scholarly analysis of texts, showing the continuity and progress of Plato's metaphysical ideas throughout the most relevant of his dialogues.

David Ross. *Aristotle.* 5th ed. London: Methuen, 1949. Ch. 6. Discussion of Aristotle's doctrines of substance, matter, form, and other topics from an old but still standard work on Aristotle.

A. E. Taylor. *Plato: The Man and His Work.* London: Methuen, 1926. A standard work which provides an overview of Plato's philosophy and brief, running commentaries on his dialogues.

Gregory Vlastos (ed.). *Plato: A Collection of Critical Essays.* I. Garden City, NY: Anchor Books, 1971. Scholarly and sometimes technical discussions by Plato specialists, on a variety of metaphysical and epistemological issues in Plato's philosophy.

Nicholas White. *A Companion to Plato's Republic.* Indianapolis: Hackett Publishing Company, 1979.

*In addition, see the relevant articles ("Plato," "Aristotle," "Universals," etc.) in *The Encyclopedia of Philosophy*, ed. Paul Edwards. New York: Macmillan, 1967.

Mind
and
Matter

I F YOU were to meet someone on the street and ask what he or she thinks reality is, you might get a response something like this:

> Well, I know that I have a mind (or soul, or whatever you want to call it), and I know that in addition to my mind—and presumably other minds too—there is a world of material things like my own body, and tables and chairs, and all the other things "out there." And, well, I guess there is a real difference between mind and matter such that my mind might exist even *apart* from matter.

This view of reality, *mind-matter dualism*, is a very common one, held by many who have never heard its name or have never even heard of metaphysics. It is called a dualism because it reduces everything to two basic realities, in this case, mind and matter. As a genuine philosophical position, however, it is considerably more complex than the opinion expressed by our friend on the street. For its most forceful expression we turn to the French thinker René Descartes[1] (1596–1650).

DESCARTES: THE FATHER OF MODERN PHILOSOPHY

In addition to being a mathematician and scientist (he invented analytic geometry and made numerous contributions to physics), Descartes was also a philosopher and has been called, in fact, the father of modern philosophy. Everything changed with Descartes, and nearly all modern philosophies may be traced back, in one way or another, to his.

In a sense, modern philosophy originated in a dream, or a series of dreams, in which a new approach to knowledge was revealed to Descartes. It is not known exactly what "came" to Descartes in these dreams, but it appears that it had something to do with the unity of all branches of knowledge and perhaps the method of achieving this unity. In his *Discourse on Method*, Descartes tells of his disillusionment with traditional philosophy:

> . . . seeing that it has been cultivated for many centuries by the best minds that have ever lived, and that nevertheless no single thing is to be found in it which is not subject of dispute, and in consequence which is not dubious, I had not enough presumption to hope to fare better there than other men had done. And also, considering how many conflicting opinions there may be regarding the self-same matter, all supported by learned people, while there can never be more than one which is true, I esteemed as well-nigh false all that only went as far as being probable.[2]

On the other hand, he was much struck by the certainty of mathematical procedures:

> Most of all was I delighted with mathematics because of the certainty of its demonstration and the evidence of its reasoning.[3]

---

[1]Pronounced *Day-cart'*.

[2]René Descartes, *Discourse on Method*, in *The Philosophical Works of Descartes*, tr. Elizabeth S. Haldane and G. R. T. Ross (Cambridge: Cambridge University Press, 1911), I, pp. 85–86.

[3]Ibid., I, p. 85.

He determined that if philosophy too was to be successful it must annex to itself something like a "geometrical method" so that its starting-points and conclusions might be as certain as those of geometry.

It will be best to consider Descartes' conception of philosophical knowledge in Part II, "The Question of Knowledge." Here it should be enough to say only that Descartes turned his back on the doubtful truths delivered through the senses, and turned rather to what could be known with certainty through *reason alone*—an "inside-out" philosopher rather than an "outside-in" philosopher. In the intellect he found, as in geometry, two fundamental, foolproof operations: *intuition* and *deduction*. Through intuition he could know certain basic and undoubtable truths, and through deduction he could draw from these basic truths still further truths. Through both of them together he believed that he could construct a whole philosophy.

Armed with his geometrical method, Descartes set out to formulate a new and certain and definitive philosophy. The best expressions of this philosophy may be found in Descartes' *Discourse on Method* (especially Part IV) and his *Meditations on First Philosophy*. It may be helpful to anticipate a bit by saying that Descartes' philosophy unfolds in three major stages: First, the knowledge of the *mind*; second, the knowledge of *God*; and third, the knowledge of *matter.*

"WHAT CAN I KNOW FOR CERTAIN?"

We have already noted that Descartes was disillusioned with previous philosophies because of their contradictions and muddledness. This distress was genuine (one may even detect an element of personal crisis in it) and probably reflected certain recent upheavals in the medieval view of the world. We can imagine him peering out his window and exclaiming, "If I cannot be certain that the sun moves across the sky—something I can see with my own eyes—then of what *can* I be certain?" Descartes thus resolved, first, to doubt anything and everything that was doubtable, in hopes of discovering something, even one thing, that was not doubtable, something certain, something unshakable, some indubitable truth that might serve as a secure foundation of his philosophy. In this respect, Descartes likened himself to the ancient Archimedes who said in relation to his newly discovered principle of the fulcrum, "Give me a place to stand, and I will move the world!" Descartes said, in effect, "Give me just one certain truth, and I will build upon it an entire philosophy!"

Thus, Descartes embarked on his process of *systematic doubt*, that is, the process of doubting everything that can be doubted to see if there is anything that *cannot* be doubted. Since our senses sometimes deceive us, Descartes supposed that perhaps the world of sense experience was not at all as it seems to be. Since people make the simplest mistakes in reasoning, he rejected as false all the demonstrations he had previously accepted. And noticing the similarities between waking life and dreams, he even ventured that nothing was more real than dreams. And noticing that two plus three equals five even when dreaming, he went so far as to devise the hypothesis of an "evil genius" bent upon constantly deceiving Descartes even about mathematical truths. Descartes documents his progress in the *Meditations:*

> I shall proceed by setting aside all that in which the least doubt could be supposed to exist—just as if I had discovered that it was absolutely false; and I shall ever follow in this road until I have met with something which is certain, or at least, if I can do nothing else, until I have learned for certain that there is nothing in the world that is certain. Archimedes, in order that he might draw the terrestrial globe out of its place, and transport it elsewhere, demanded only that one point should be fixed and immoveable; in the same way I shall have the right to conceive high hopes if I am happy enough to discover one thing only which is certain and indubitable.

> I suppose, then, that all the things that I see are false; I persuade myself that nothing has ever existed of all that my fallacious memory represents to me. I consider that I possess no senses; I imagine that body, figure, extension, movement and place are but the fictions of my mind. What, then, can be esteemed as true? Perhaps nothing at all, unless that there is nothing in the world that is certain.[4]

THE INTUITION OF MIND

In this way Descartes sought to erase, as it were, everything from the chalkboard of human knowledge. Finally, he found himself exactly opposite to the naive realist who thinks that things are exactly as they appear. Descartes could doubt *everything*—except for one. In all of this doubting

---

[4]Descartes, *Meditations on First Philosophy*, in *Philosophical Works of Descartes*, I, p. 149.

and erasing, one thing finally presented itself as *undoubtable* and *unerasable*. As he expressed it in the famous line from the *Discourse, Cogito ergo sum,* "I think, therefore I am." After all, if I am mistaken about this, then there is no "I" to be mistaken!

> . . . whilst I thus wished to think all things false, it was absolutely essential that the "I" who thought this should be somewhat, and re-marking that this truth "I think, therefore I am" was so certain and so assured that all the most extravagant suppositions brought for-ward by the sceptics were incapable of shaking it, I came to the con-clusion that I could receive it without scruple as the first principle of the Philosophy for which I was seeking.[5]

Here, then, is rock-bottom certitude, unshakable even by the most radical doubt, a place for Descartes to stand as he sought to build a philosophy.

"I think, therefore I am." But *what* am I? What *is* mind? What *is* soul? What *is* my spirit? (Descartes uses all of these terms interchangeably.) Descartes' answer in the *Discourse:* It is "a substance the whole essence or nature of which is to think,"[6] or for short, a *thinking substance.* But here we must make our terms clear. We have a good idea what Descartes means by "thinking"; it means all the intellectual operations, such as affirming, deny-ing, imagining, doubting, reflecting, inferring, and the like. We may have more trouble with the word "substance." Some readers may find themselves almost hopelessly afflicted with the idea that substance means some con-crete, physical thing. But the word itself (from the Latin *substantia*) means, literally, "that which stands under," or "that which upholds" something. To use Descartes' own example, consider a ball of wax. It may be hard or soft and have a certain color, odor, and texture, and these may change from time to time, but then there is the wax *itself,* the substance of these qualities. Can you imagine texture or shape existing without something that *is* textured and shaped? Can you imagine thinking without something that *does* the thinking? Just as in grammar there could be no predicate without a subject, so in the world of sensible things there could be no qualities without a ma-terial substance, and in the intellectual world no thinking activities without a mental substance. But it is not just that there is no thinking apart from

---

[5]Descartes, *Discourse on Method,* I, p. 101.
[6]Ibid.

RENÉ DESCARTES

RENÉ DESCARTES was born in Touraine, France, in 1596. His mother died in giving him birth, and from her he appears to have inherited a frail constitution. At 8 years he was enrolled in the Jesuit school at La Flèche, where his poor health won for him certain privileges, including sleeping late, a habit that Descartes cherished throughout his life. At La Flèche, he displayed the inclination for mathematics and geometry which later exerted such an influence over his whole philosophy.

At 16, Descartes left La Flèche and journeyed to Paris, where, provided by his father with a valet and money, he especially enjoyed gambling. (His friends attributed his gambling successes to the fact that he bet according to his unusual knowledge of mathematics rather than to chance.) In Paris, he made the acquaintance of the celebrated mathematician Mydorge. A certain restlessness and eagerness to learn from "the book of the world," as

(continued on next page)

mind—mind *is* thinking, a thinking substance. It *may* affirm, deny, doubt, reflect, imagine, infer, etc., but it *must* think.

In the *Meditations*, Descartes provides a summary of this first stage of his reasoning: (1) It is certain that I exist, and (2) I am a mind or thinking substance.

> . . . I was persuaded that there is nothing in all the world, that there was no heaven, no earth, that there were no minds, nor any bodies: was I not then likewise persuaded that I did not exist? Not at all; of a surety I myself did exist since I persuaded myself of something [or

he put it, caused Descartes, in 1617, to go to Holland where he enlisted as a volunteer without pay in the army of Prince Maurice of Nassau. He was not much of a soldier, though it was during this stint that he discovered analytic geometry, thus ensuring his niche in the history of mathematics. In 1619, the Thirty Years War broke out, and Descartes joined the Catholic forces and found himself eventually in Prague. On November 10, 1619, Descartes had his famous three dreams in which a way of unifying all knowledge was revealed to him. Tired of soldiering, he returned to Paris (which he found too hectic), and then, in 1628, he went to the Netherlands where his serious philosophical and scientific activity and writing got under way, as well as other things: Here he had a mistress who bore him a daughter. It was during this period that Descartes published his major philosophical works, though, noting the fate of Galileo, he suspended the publication of a book on cosmology.

In time he was repeatedly entreated by Queen Christina of Sweden (a robust and masculine woman) to tutor her in his philosophy. Because of his physical condition he hesitated, but eventually accepted the invitation in 1649. Upon his arrival he learned to his horror that the queen insisted on receiving philosophy lessons at five o'clock in the morning! This first winter was especially severe, and Descartes quickly took pneumonia and died. To the end of his life he professed the Catholic faith. He is buried in Ste. Geneviève du Mont in Paris.

Some of Descartes' more important works are: *Rules for the Direction of the Mind, Discourse on Method, Meditations on First Philosophy, Optics, Geometry, Meteorology,* and *Principles of Philosophy.*

merely because I thought of something]. But there is some deceiver or other, very powerful and very cunning, who ever employs his ingenuity in deceiving me. Then without doubt I exist also if he deceives me, and let him deceive me as much as he will, he can never cause me to be nothing so long as I think that I am something. So that after having reflected well and carefully examined all things, we must come to the definite conclusion that this proposition: I am, I exist, is necessary true each time that I pronounce it, or that I mentally conceive it. . . .

But what am I, now that I suppose that there is a certain genius which is extremely powerful, and, if I may say so, malicious, who employs all his powers in deceiving me? Can I affirm that I possess the least of all those things which . . . pertain to the nature of body? I pause to consider, I revolve all these things in my mind, and I find none of which I can say that it pertains to me. It would be tedious to stop to enumerate them. Let us pass to the attributes of soul and see if there is any one which is in me? What of nutrition or walking . . . ? But if it is so that I have no body it is also true that I can neither walk nor take nourishment. Another attribute is sensation. But one cannot tell without body, and besides I have thought I perceived many things during sleep that I recognized in my waking moments as not having been experienced at all. What of thinking? I find here that thought is an attribute that belongs to me; it alone cannot be separated from me. I am, I exist, that is certain. But how often? Just when I think; for it might possibly be the case if I ceased entirely to think, that I should likewise cease altogether to exist. I do not now admit anything which is not necessarily true: to speak accurately I am not more than a thing which thinks, that is to say a mind or a soul, or an understanding, or a reason, which are terms whose significance was formerly unknown to me. I am, however, a real thing and really exist; but what thing? I have answered: a thing which thinks.[7]

Thus we are led to the first of Descartes' three major metaphysical conclusions: *There is mind.*

But that is not the only important thing that has been learned. Through reflection on the character of this primary certainty—I exist—Descartes has discovered what he can take as the hallmark or criterion of *any* indubitable and certain idea: *clarity* and *distinctness.*

After this I considered generally what in a proposition is requisite in order to be true and certain; for since I had just discovered one which I knew to be such, I thought that I ought also to know in what this certainty consisted. And having remarked that there was nothing at all in the statement, "*I think, therefore I am*" which assures me of having thereby made a true assertion, excepting that I see very clearly that to think it is necessary to be, I came to the conclusion

---

[7]Descartes, *Meditations on First Philosophy*, I, pp. 150, 151–52.

SUBSTANCE

"Substance" is popularly thought to be a *physical thing*. But the term was used by Descartes and subsequent thinkers in quite a different way, and with its original sense of "that which stands under" and thus "upholds" something (from the Latin *substantia*). In Descartes and others, mind is the substance which underlies mental activities, as matter is the substance underlying and upholding physical qualities.

that I might assume, as a general rule, that the things which we conceive very clearly and distinctly are all true—remembering, however, that there is some difficulty in ascertaining which are those that we distinctly conceive.[8]

THE DEDUCTION OF GOD

On the basis of mind as a thinking substance, along with the criterion of clear and distinct ideas, Descartes leads us to a further consideration: God. He provides two proofs for the existence of God, both of them rooted in the thinking self, both of them employing clear and distinct premises, and both of them involving the idea of perfection.

The first of these two proofs has no particular name, so we may propose for convenience the label Eidological Argument for God, from the Greek word for "idea." Descartes' reasoning is that God must exist in order to account for our *idea of perfection*. Descartes discovered in his mind the idea of a being more perfect than himself—after all, he doubted, and it is a greater perfection to know than to doubt—but where did this idea of something more perfect come from? Now it is absurd that this idea might have come from nothing, for I have a clear and distinct notion that nothing comes from nothing. Nor could it have come from myself, since it is no less absurd that the more perfect should come from the less perfect than that something should come from nothing. We are driven rationally

---

[8]Ibid., I, pp. 101–2.

to the only conclusion: The idea of perfection has been placed in our minds by a perfect being. This proof comes out best in the *Discourse:*

> Following upon this, and reflecting on the fact that I doubted, and that consequently my existence was not quite perfect (for I saw clearly that it was a greater perfection to know than to doubt), I resolved to inquire whence I had learnt to think of anything more perfect than I myself was; and I recognised very clearly that this conception must proceed from some nature which was really more perfect. As to the thoughts which I had of many other things outside of me, like the heavens, the earth, light, heat, and a thousand others, I had not so much difficulty in knowing whence they came, because, remarking nothing in them which seemed to render them superior to me, I could believe that, if they were true, they were dependencies upon my nature, in so far as it possessed some perfection; and if they were not true, that I held them from nought, that is to say, that they were in me because I had something lacking in my nature. But this could not apply to the idea of a Being more perfect than my own, for to hold it from nought would be manifestly impossible, and because it is no less contradictory to say of the more perfect that it is what results from and depends on the less perfect, than to say that there is something which proceeds from nothing, it was equally impossible that I should hold it from myself. In this way it could but follow that it had been placed in me by a Nature which was really more perfect than mine could be, and which even had within itself all the perfections of which I could form any idea—that is to say, to put it in a word, which was God.[9]

It should be noted that this is a *causal* argument for God; that is, it argues that God must exist as the only adequate cause of something, in this case, the cause of the idea of perfection. We are reminded, though, how seriously Descartes takes mind and ideas. Even an idea is some sort of reality or *thing* (though obviously not a physical thing), and a thing the existence of which needs explaining no less than tables or chairs or worlds or galaxies.

Descartes' second proof for God is a version of the Ontological Argument. As with the first, this one too is stated in the *Discourse*, though it is

---

[9]Descartes, *Discourse on Method*, I, p. 102.

developed further in the *Meditations*. And like the first, it begins with the idea of perfection or the idea of a most perfect being. Descartes observed that the very concept of God implies his real existence. For what does "God" mean? It means a being who is a supremely perfect being, and who therefore possesses the sum of all possible perfections. Thus, God must be—to name a few—omniscient (for that is a perfection), God must be omnibenevolent (for that is a perfection), and God must *exist* (for that *too* is a perfection). Is not real existence just as necessary to a supremely perfect being as any other of these perfections? Could God be the absolutely perfect being if he was not omnipotent? Could God be the absolutely perfect being if he did not even *exist?* Of course it does not follow from the fact that you cannot separate the idea of a mountain from the idea of a valley that there *are* any mountains or valleys. But that is because existence is not part of what it means to be a mountain or valley. But it *is* part of what it means to be God. On this reasoning, as soon as you get hold of the idea of God as a supremely perfect being, you get hold of a God who exists.

> . . . now, if just because I can draw the idea of something from my thought, it follows that all which I know clearly and distinctly as pertaining to this object does really belong to it, may I not derive from this an argument demonstrating the existence of God? It is certain that I no less find the idea of God, that is to say, the idea of a supremely perfect Being, in me, than that of any figure or number whatever it is; and I do not know any less clearly and distinctly that an [actual and] eternal existence pertains to this nature than I know that all that which I am able to demonstrate of some figure or number truly pertains to the nature of this figure or number, and therefore, although all that I concluded in the preceding Meditations were found to be false, the existence of God would pass with me as at least as certain as I have ever held the truths of mathematics (which concern only numbers and figures) to be.

This indeed is not at first manifest, since it would seem to present some appearance of being a sophism. For being accustomed in all other things to make a distinction between existence and essence, I easily persuade myself that the existence can be separated from the essence of God, and that we can thus conceive God as not actually existing. But, nevertheless, when I think of it with more attention, I clearly see that existence can no more be separated from the essence

of God than can its having its three angles equal to two right angles
to be separated from the essence of a [rectilinear] triangle, or the
idea of a mountain from the idea of a valley; and so there is not any
less repugnance to our conceiving a God (that is, a Being supremely
perfect) to whom existence is lacking (that is to say, to whom a certain perfection is lacking), than to conceive of a mountain which has
no valley.

But although I cannot really conceive of a God without existence any
more than a mountain without a valley, still from the fact that I conceive of a mountain with a valley, it does not follow that there is such
a mountain in the world; similarly although I conceive of God as
possessing existence, it would seem that it does not follow that there
is a God which exists; for my thought does not impose any necessity
upon things, and just as I may imagine a winged horse, although no
horse with wings exists, so I could perhaps attribute existence to
God, although no God existed.

But a sophism is concealed in this objection; for from the fact that I
cannot conceive a mountain without a valley, it does not follow that
there is any mountain or any valley in existence, but only that the
mountain and the valley, whether they exist or do not exist, cannot in
any way be separated one from the other. While from the fact that I
cannot conceive God without existence, it follows that existence is
inseparable from Him, and hence that He really exists; not that my
thought can bring this to pass, or impose any necessity on things,
but, on the contrary, because the necessity which lies in the thing itself, i.e. the necessity of the existence of God determines me to think
in this way. For it is not within my power to think of God without
existence (that is of a supremely perfect Being devoid of a supreme
perfection) though it is in my power to imagine a horse either with
wings or without wings.[10]

By means of his two arguments for God, Descartes brings us to his second main conclusion: *There is a God.*

---

[10]René Descartes, *Meditations on First Philosophy* I, pp. 180–82.

THE ONTOLOGICAL ARGUMENT

God is the greatest or most perfect being.
A being who exists is greater or more perfect than a
 being who does not exist.

Therefore, God must exist.

THE DEDUCTION OF MATTER

On the basis of God, and some other clear and distinct ideas, Descartes leads us to a further consideration: the world of material objects.

According to Descartes, it is only through the belief in God that we may be assured of the existence of the external world and the things in it: tables, chairs, dogs, cats, the earth, stars, our own bodies, and so on. How does Descartes arrive at this thesis? Surely, says Descartes, we can doubt the existence of such things. Aside from the inevitable distortions and mis-representations of our senses, is it not at least *possible* that we are now dreaming, and that the world "out there" is not at all as we perceive it, or even that it *is* not at all—period? Apart from God, it is possible. But *with* God, it is not possible. Why not? Because everything in us, including our clear and distinct ideas, has come from God, and God, a supremely per-fect being and the author of all good, is by his divine nature incapable of creating in us false or misleading ideas. And even if he could, he *wouldn't*, since deception is clearly a moral defect, whereas God is the supremely perfect being—can you imagine God being a deceiver?

To be sure, many of our ideas may be confused, obscure, or false, but that is because they have become contaminated with nothingness, "from below" as it were, whereas as created and implanted in us by God, "from above," they cannot fail to be true. And, to be sure, many of our judg-ments are mistaken. But that is because of a misuse of our will (also given by God) whereby because of passion, prejudice, or haste, we affirm as true or deny as false an idea that is not clear and distinct. If you look at the sun and judge it to be about two feet across, your decision has overstepped the boundaries of your clear and distinct ideas, and that is your problem, not God's. Descartes summarizes:

> . . . as often as I so restrain my will within the limits of my knowledge that it forms no judgment except on matters which are clearly and distinctly represented to it by the understanding, I can never be deceived; for every clear and distinct conception is without doubt something, and hence cannot derive its origin from what is nought, but must of necessity have God as its author—God, I say, who being supremely perfect, cannot be the cause of any error; and consequently we must conclude that such a conception [or such a judgment] is true.[11]

Thus God is the guarantor of our knowledge:

> . . . so I very clearly recognise that the certainty and truth of all knowledge depends alone on the knowledge of the true God, in so much that, before I knew Him, I could not have a perfect knowledge of any other thing. And now that I know Him I have the means of acquiring a perfect knowledge of an infinitude of things, not only of those which relate to God Himself and other intellectual matters, but also of those which pertain to corporeal nature. . . .[12]

And we are now in a position to reintroduce into our picture of reality what Descartes originally found it necessary to exclude: the external world of material objects.

Do we not have a clear and distinct idea of an external world? A world of tables, chairs, dogs, cats, the earth, stars, and our own bodies existing outside our minds and independently of us? Is not the "externality" of such a world and such things clearly and distinctly evident from the passivity of our sense perceptions? That is, we do not wish or imagine or dream up this world. It is just *there*, imposing itself on us, independently of our wills. Furthermore, is it not evident that just as it was required in the world of mind to believe in a *substance* which upholds and supports the various intellectual activities, so also in the external world there must be a

---

[11]Descartes, *Meditations on First Philosophy* I, p. 178.

[12]Ibid. I, p. 185.

substance which upholds and supports the various physical qualities which we experience—colors, tastes, shapes, and the like? We will call this substance *material* substance. And is it not evident that extension (to use Descartes' expression), or the ability to occupy space or possess dimensions (to use our own), is the very essence of material substance? We observed earlier that minds (or thinking substances) *may* deny, affirm, imagine, remember, and so on, but *think* they *must*. Likewise, we may say of material objects that they may be red, or blue, or rectangular, or hard, or sweet, and so on, but *extended* they *must* be. Of course, says Descartes, the things "out there" may not be entirely as they are represented to us by our senses, but they must at least possess the geometrical features which we clearly and distinctly perceive (such as length, breadth, and depth).

How many of the ideas in the above paragraph can you find substantiated in the following paragraph from the *Meditations?*

I further find in myself faculties employing modes of thinking peculiar to themselves, to wit, the faculties of imagination and feeling, without which I can easily conceive myself clearly and distinctly as a complete being; while, on the other hand, they cannot be so conceived apart from me, that is without an intelligent substance in which they reside, for [in the notion we have of these faculties, or, to use the language of the Schools] in their formal concept, some kind of intellection is comprised, from which I infer that they are distinct from me as its modes are from a thing. I observe also in me some other faculties such as that of change of position, the assumption of different figures and such like, which cannot be conceived, any more than can the preceding, apart from some substance to which they are attached, and consequently cannot exist without it; but it is very clear that these faculties, if it be true that they exist, must be attached to some corporeal or extended substance, and not to an intelligent substance, since in the clear and distinct conception of these there is some sort of extension found to be present, but no intellection at all. There is certainly further in me a certain passive faculty of perception, that is, of receiving and recognising the ideas of sensible things, but this would be useless to me [and I could in no way avail myself of it], if there were not either in me or in some other thing another active faculty capable of forming and producing these ideas. But this active faculty cannot exist in me [inasmuch as I am a thing that thinks] seeing that it does not presuppose thought, and also that those ideas are often produced in me without my contributing in any way to the same, and often even against my will; it is thus necessarily the case that the faculty resides in some substance different from me in which all the reality which is objectively in the ideas that are produced by this faculty is formally or eminently contained, as I remarked before. And this substance is either a body, that is, a corporeal nature in which there is contained formally [and really] all that which is objectively [and by representation] in those ideas, or it is God Himself, or some other creature more noble than body in which that same is contained eminently. But, since God is no deceiver, it is very manifest that He does not communicate to me these ideas immediately and by Himself, nor yet by the intervention of some creature in which their reality is not formally, but only eminently, contained. For since He has given me no faculty to recognise that this is the case, but, on the other hand, a very great inclination to believe [that they are sent to me or] that they are conveyed to me by corporeal objects, I do not see how He could be defended from the accusation of deceit if these ideas were produced by causes other than corporeal objects. Hence we must allow that corporeal things exist. However, they are perhaps not exactly what we perceive by the senses, since this comprehension by the senses is in many instances very obscure and confused; but we must at least admit that all things which I conceive in them clearly and distinctly, that is to say, all things which, speaking generally, are comprehended in the object of pure mathematics, are truly to be recognised as external objects.[13]

Thus we have arrived at Descartes' third conclusion: *There is matter.* And we have progressed from our knowledge of mind to a knowledge of God, and from knowledge of God to a knowledge of matter.

The essential movement in Descartes' philosophy and the three pivotal ideas may be represented by a simple diagram:

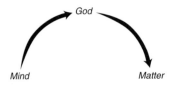

Mind   God   Matter

---

[13]Ibid., I, pp. 190–91.

SOME OBJECTIONS

For all its importance and influence, Descartes' theory of reality has hardly escaped criticism. We may mention a few of these, first some lesser ones and then one very big one.

First of all, there is the question of Descartes' method. Few philosophers would align themselves with such a rigorous exclusion of sense experience as a legitimate means of acquiring knowledge; indeed many, quite opposite to Descartes, have admitted *only* sense experience as the source of knowledge, and with the result that they have arrived at quite different conclusions about reality. We will speak of this again in Part II. Here it must suffice to say that there are more ways to begin a philosophy than with a *cogito*. And, speaking of the *cogito*, are we very sure that thinking requires a thinker? What would result if we simply denied the necessity of mental substance, or *any* substance. Why not let there be simply intellectual activities and physical qualities? We will see that some have in fact argued for just this view. Also, it has often been charged that Descartes has committed the informal fallacy of *Petitio Principii* or circular reasoning. Upon his reflection on the *Cogito ergo sum*, Descartes is willing to accept any clear and distinct idea as indubitable; he uses such ideas in his proofs for God, but then insists that it is God who ensures the reliability of these clear and distinct ideas.

And regarding Descartes' proofs for God: In his first proof, some have stumbled over the notion that ideas are *things*, that they possess some sort of objective reality, and thus that they must be caused in a way similar to tables and chairs. And are we sure that the idea of God could not be devised without God actually existing? Descartes' Ontological Argument clearly construes existence as if it were a predicate or defining property. But is it? Isn't the concept of a unicorn the same whether the unicorn exists or not? What is altered in the *concept* of a thing by adding that it *exists?* Nothing. Thus, existence is not a predicate.

THE MIND-BODY PROBLEM

But now we must address the really big problem posed by Descartes' philosophy. If we leave God aside and focus our attention just on the natural world (including ourselves as part of it), then Descartes' view of reality may appropriately be called *dualistic:* There are *two* essentially different substances, mind and matter, which constitute the "stuff" of this world.

This is, in fact, how Descartes' theory of reality is usually represented, and as such it poses one of the most vexing problems in the history of philosophy: *the mind-body problem.*

The mind-body problem simply stated is this: Once we define mind and matter as essentially different substances, which means that they can have nothing in common, no bridge between them, no causal connection, then *how do we get them back together again?* And we *must* get them back together again, for there clearly *is* some sort of connection between them. Obviously, our bodily states can affect our mental states. We are familiar with all sorts of ways in which physics and chemistry can affect the mind. Just think of the mental effects of caffeine, drugs, old age, the alteration of brain states, etc., and if someone beats you over the head long enough, you will become *depressed!* On the other hand, it is also obvious that mental states can give rise to bodily states. Psychosomatic medicine, with its mentally induced sicknesses, is evidence enough, and have you ever felt physically ill because of some idea—like the prospect of failing a course? That the mind and body stand in a causal relation to one another appears to be a fact. The question is *how*, if they are absolutely different in nature from one another:

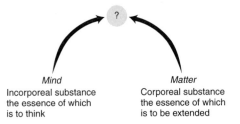

Mind
Incorporeal substance
the essence of which
is to think

Matter
Corporeal substance
the essence of which
is to be extended

So far we have represented the problem in terms of *causality.* But it may be represented in yet other ways. In the following, the contemporary philosopher John Searle suggests four aspects of our mental life which appear unconnectable (we might say) with the material world: (1) consciousness, (2) intentionality—but be careful, it does not mean what you may think, (3) subjectivity, and, of course, (4) causation.

There are four features of mental phenomena which have made them seem impossible to fit into our "scientific" conception of the world as made up of material things. . . .

The most important of these features is consciousness. I, at the moment of writing this, and you, at the moment of reading it, are both conscious. It is just a plain fact about the world that it contains such conscious mental states and events, but it is hard to see how mere physical systems could have consciousness. How could such a thing occur? How, for example, could this grey and white gook inside my skull be conscious? . . .

The second intractable feature of the mind is what philosophers and psychologists call "intentionality," the feature by which our mental states are directed at, or about, or refer to, or are of objects and states of affairs in the world other than themselves. . . . Now the question about intentionality is much like the question about consciousness. How can this stuff inside my head be *about* anything? How can it *refer* to anything? . . .

The third feature of the mind that seems difficult to accommodate within a scientific conception of reality is the subjectivity of mental states. This subjectivity is marked by such facts as that I can feel my pains, and you can't. I see the world from my point of view; you see it from your point of view. I am aware of myself and my internal mental states, as quite distinct from the selves and mental states of other people. . . .

Finally, there is a fourth problem, the problem of mental causation. We all suppose, as part of common sense, that our thoughts and feelings make a real difference to the way we behave, that they actually have some *causal* effect on the physical world. I decide, for example, to raise my arm and—lo and behold—my arm goes up. But if your thoughts and feelings are truly mental, how can they affect anything physical? . . . These four features, consciousness, intentionality, subjectivity, and mental causation are what make the mind-body problem seem so difficult. . . .[14]

But back to Descartes and the specifically *causal* issue involved in the mind-body problem. Descartes himself was not oblivious to the difficulty. The solution he proposed has been called *interactionism*. It is simply the view that there is, after all, some kind of interaction between the two essentially different substances.

---

[14]John Searle, *Minds, Brains and Science* (Cambridge, MA: Harvard University Press, 1984), pp. 15–17.

Nature also teaches me by these sensations of pain, hunger, thirst, etc., that I am not only lodged in my body as a pilot in a vessel, but that I am very closely united to it, and so to speak so intermingled with it that I seem to compose with it one whole. For if that were not the case, when my body is hurt, I, who am merely a thinking thing, should not feel pain, for I should perceive this wound by the understanding only, just as the sailor perceives by sight when something is damaged in his vessel; and when my body has need of drink or food, I should clearly understand the fact without being warned of it by confused feelings of hunger and thirst. For all these sensations of hunger, thirst, pain, etc. are in truth none other than certain confused modes of thought which are produced by the union and apparent intermingling of mind and body.[15]

Where does this "union" and "intermingling" of mind and body take place? Descartes' answer: the pineal gland, in the center of the brain. Apparently he thought that the pineal gland was a likely candidate for this honor because it is the most inward part of the brain, and perhaps, too, because it appeared to Descartes to be the only thing in the body without a double or counterpart. (It is reported that Descartes would secure discarded carcasses from the local butcher for the purpose of dissection and examination.)

It has seemed to many that Descartes' solution was, of course, no solution at all. It only moved the question one step further back, and the question now becomes, *How* do mind and matter interact in the pineal gland? Nonetheless, interactionism as a solution to the mind-body problem is here to stay. After all, what constitutes a causal connection even between *like* substances is no easy matter. And who is to say outright what substances can or cannot do? Further, talk of an unbridgeable "gap" between mind and matter is strange inasmuch as mind is not conceived as spatial at all. On the other hand, mind *is* in space and time in *some* sense: Does not your mind exist right *here* and right *now?* At least in some way, then, mind, and matter *do* occupy a common ground.

There have been other proposed solutions. Before mentioning two radical solutions, we shall mention three traditional ones. No sooner had Descartes presented the world with the mind-body problem than the French thinker Malebranche (1638–1715) proposed *occasionalism* as a solution: On the occasion of bodily stimuli or impressions, God creates the

---

[15]Descartes, *Meditations on First Philosophy* I, p. 192.

appropriate idea and response in the mind. The German philosopher Leibniz (1646–1716) proposed a *preestablished harmony,* according to which bodily and physical states have been preordained by God to correspond at every point with appropriate mental states, like two clocks synchronized and set to ticking at the same time. The Dutch philosopher Spinoza proposed what has been called the *double-aspect theory.* On this view there is only one reality, unknown to us except through its attributes of mind and matter, two of the infinite number of aspects of this one reality.

There is, however, a much more radical approach to the mind-body problem. Like some forms of radical surgery, which cut out the disease by cutting out the organ, this approach cuts out the problem by cutting out one or the other of the substances. But which has to go? How you answer that may determine whether you go the way of *idealism,* which denies the reality of material substance and reduces everything to mind and ideas, or *materialism,* which denies the reality of mind as a substance and reduces everything to matter. The materialistic option will be explored in the next chapter.

MIND: A SET OF DISPOSITIONS OR FUNCTIONS

In the meantime, however, we should consider looking at the issue in an entirely different way, involving some recent and analytic-style philosophizing. We mention here two important developments in philosophical psychology—critical thinking about mind and mental states—both of which nullify the mind-body problem. Notice we said "nullify" (not "solve"), for these approaches regard the mind-body problem itself, as traditionally posed in "substance"-talk, to be misguided, or a pseudo-problem, or a mistaken and misleading way of representing the situation.

This is the view of the recent British philosopher Gilbert Ryle and a long line of thinkers influenced by him. His 1949 book, *The Concept of Mind,* had the effect of an exploding bombshell in the sphere of philosophical psychology. Ryle said that the mind-body problem, like so many philosophical problems, is not a *real* problem, but results rather from *linguistic and conceptual confusion.* That is, it is a problem that results from our misunderstanding and misuse of *language* and *concepts.* (Ryle is a good example of an "analytic" philosopher, such as we mentioned in Chapter 1.) He begins by sketching the "official doctrine":

There is a doctrine about the nature and place of minds which is so prevalent among theorists and even among laymen that it deserves to be described as the official theory. Most philosophers, psychologists and religious teachers subscribe, with minor reservations, to its main articles and, although they admit certain theoretical difficulties in it, they tend to assume that these can be overcome without serious modifications being made to the architecture of the theory. It will be argued here that the central principles of the doctrine are unsound and conflict with the whole body of what we know about minds when we are not speculating about them.

The official doctrine, which hails chiefly from Descartes, is something like this. With the doubtful exceptions of idiots and infants in arms every human being has both a body and a mind. Some would prefer to say that every human being is both a body and a mind. His body and his mind are ordinarily harnessed together, but after the death of the body his mind may continue to exist and function.

Human bodies are in space and are subject to the mechanical laws which govern all other bodies in space. Bodily processes and states can be inspected by external observers. So a man's bodily life is as much a public affair as are the lives of animals and reptiles and even as the careers of trees, crystals and planets.

But minds are not in space, nor are their operations subject to mechanical laws. The workings of one mind are not witnessable by other observers; its career is private. Only I can take direct cognisance of the states and processes of my own mind. A person therefore lives through two collateral histories, one consisting of what happens in and to his body, the other consisting of what happens in and to his mind. The first is public, the second private. The events in the first history are events in the physical world; those in the second are events in the mental world.[16]

But what, exactly, is the confusion that Ryle sees in this "official doctrine"? Ryle said that Descartes, and most people after him, were guilty of a *category mistake*, as he called it. This is the mistake of treating a concept as if it belonged to one system or category of ideas when, in fact, it

---

[16]Gilbert Ryle, *The Concept of Mind* (London: Hutchinson, 1949), pp. 11–12.

belongs to another. An example will help. Imagine yourself showing a visitor around the campus. Your friend asks you to point out the library, and you point to a building and say, "Over there." He then asks to see the Student Union, and you take him to another building. He then asks to be shown the humanities building, and you show it to him. Then he asks to see the *college*. But you are puzzled by this request because your friend appears to think that the college is something you can *see*. You might say to him: "What do you mean, 'Show me the college'? The college is not a building or a *thing*; it is an organization of various departments and faculties. You have confused the idea of a college with *things*, such as buildings." Ryle makes the application:

> I shall often speak of [the "official doctrine"] with deliberate abusiveness, as "the dogma of the Ghost in the Machine." . . . It is not merely an assemblage of particular mistakes. It is one big mistake and a mistake of a special kind. It is, namely, a category-mistake. It represents the facts of mental life as if they belonged to one logical type or category (or range of types or categories), when they actually belong to another. The dogma is therefore a philosopher's myth.[17]

Surely we have minds and these minds display mental characteristics. This is not what Ryle objects to. He objects to the "official doctrine" of the Ghost in the Machine, the representation of mind as a kind of great, nonphysical *blob*. Where did Descartes (and all the other proponents of the "official doctrine") go wrong? Right at the start, when he began thinking about the mental world in terms that were only appropriate for the physical world: "thing," "stuff," "attribute," "state," "process," "change," "cause," and "effect." It was, says Ryle, a colossal category mistake to employ *thing*-language in the attempt to throw light on the world of mind.

We cannot give here a full account of Ryle's more positive theory of mind. But is not mind more like a college than a building? Is it not, rather, a way of representing the organization, interrelationships, and activities of faculties—in this case *mental* faculties? Furthermore, and more important, would it not be truer to our actual evidence and experience to represent mental states as *dispositions?* As an "ordinary language analyst," Ryle asks us to pay attention to and to take our cue from the way in which we usually speak about such matters, and the way we usually speak betrays nothing at

---

[17]Ibid., p. 16.

all of some private, concealed, sealed-off domain of mental processes, or any "ghost in the machine." What are we actually referring to when we speak of a person's thoughts, desires, convictions, moods, and inclinations? In our interpretation of such mental states do we not invariably include references to some relevant bodily and publicly accessible facts? What *is* a thought, desire, conviction, mood, or inclination apart from some accompanying physical states such as facial expressions, shrugs, weeping, speaking, gesturing, or other bodily and witnessable activity? Mental states would seem to have discernable meaning and real content only in relation to bodily states. And the task of the Rylean philosophers becomes, then, one of inquiring not into the spooky world of Cartesian minds, but into capacities, propensities, habits, and tendencies—in a word, dispositions—evident in what persons *do*.

One might be tempted to see here a form of materialism, but that would be a mistake. Ryle's point was not a metaphysical one involving the reduction of mind to matter, or mental states to bodily states, but rather an analytic-logical point: an attempt to clarify the logical status of the idea of mind, and to go from there—though certainly it can't be back to Descartes!

A second, related, and still more recent development is *functionalism*. It is, in fact, at present all the rage among those dealing with the philosophy of mind—which has become an ever-enlarging circle, including not only people from philosophy but also people from the fields of psychology, cybernetics, and linguistics, as well as many working in the areas of artificial intelligence and computational theory. All of this together is sometimes called cognitive science, which is the attempt to understand, from all relevant perspectives and on the basis of all possible data, the nature of knowing. We will encounter functionalism again, in the chapter on materialism, though it is appropriate here to provide a sketch, especially since it is in some ways the current philosophical heir to Ryle's work.

It is not called "functionalism" for nothing. Again, our attention is shifted from traditional Cartesian substance-talk to a radically different way of talking about the mind: The mind and its various states are to be understood in terms of *function*. You do not give a definition of a coffeepot when you tell what it is made of (plastic, metal, rubber, etc.) but when you describe how it is put together and what it does (contains water, percolates, filters the water through a batch of ground coffee beans, etc.). Likewise, say the functionalists, when addressing and assessing the significance of mental states, it is not a question of what they are made of—that is irrelevant—but what they *do*. More specifically, the definition of a mental state, such as a belief, should delineate what it does, what role it plays, how it relates to and what contribution it makes to input, output, and other mental states—such language naturally suggests that mental states, in the functionalist view, may be likened to the program of a computer. Still better is the concise statement (plus example) by Paul M. Churchland, a major figure in the field of cognitive science:

> According to *functionalism*, the essential or defining feature of any type of mental state is the set of causal relations it bears to (1) environmental effects of the body, (2) other types of mental states, and (3) bodily behavior. Pain, for example, characteristically results from some bodily damage or trauma; it causes distress, annoyance, and practical reasoning aimed at relief; and it causes wincing, blanching, and nursing of the traumatized area. Any state that plays exactly that functional role is a pain, according to functionalism. Similarly, other types of mental states (sensations, fears, beliefs, and so on) are also defined by their unique causal roles in a complex economy of internal states mediating sensory inputs and behavioral outputs.[18]

But *why* functionalism? What consideration compels us to adopt this view? What problem does it solve? Here is where the issue is best considered in terms of Chapter 5, except to say that the total evidence from a variety of perspectives (such as those mentioned above) urges upon the functionalist a *nonreductivist* view of the mind that accommodates features that cannot be reduced to bodily states, behavior, or environment. Still leaving aside the metaphysical question as to the nature of mind, it is nonetheless surely not *these* things pure and simple.

CHAPTER 4 IN REVIEW

Summary

Although the metaphysical theory known as mind-matter dualism has been widely held, it has nowhere received a more powerful expression than in Descartes, the father of modern philosophy.

---

[18]Paul M. Churchland, *Matter and Consciousness: A Contemporary Introduction to the Philosophy of Mind* (Cambridge, MA: M.I.T. Press, 1984), p. 36.

Descartes believed that it was possible to unfold a complete philosophy by reason alone (we will have more to say about his theory of knowledge in Part II) and to arrive, specifically, at a certain knowledge of the essentially different substances, mind ("a substance the essence of which is to think") and matter ("a substance the essence of which is to be extended"), with considerable help from his idea of God. He found that it was impossible to doubt the existence of the self—otherwise the very activity of doubting would be impossible. Thus, one of the best-known pronouncements in the history of philosophy: "I think, therefore I am." Armed with this fundamental certitude, Descartes then proceeded to demonstrate the existence of God from the presence in our minds of the idea of a perfect being (most notably, the Ontological Argument). On the basis of both our passivity to what must be external objects and the impossibility that God, the perfect being, should deceive us with respect to our faculty of clear and distinct ideas, we may also rest assured as to the existence and at least relative nature of the radically different world of material substances outside us. The main moves may be represented simply as: Mind $\rightarrow$ God $\rightarrow$ Matter.

However, any version of mind-matter dualism which portrays mind and matter as *essentially* different faces a tremendous problem: If they are so *different*, how can they relate to one another (as they obviously do) and therefore be in some necessary way the *same?* Traditionally, solutions were proposed in the form of interactionism, occasionalism, a preestablished harmony, and the double-aspect theory. More recently, however, it has been suggested that the whole problem stems from a mistaken concept of the mind. Ryle, for example, has argued that to view mind as if it were a substance underlying various activities is to import an inappropriate model: a category mistake.

Basic Ideas

- Dualism
- Descartes' method
- Two fundamental operations of the intellect
    Intuition
    Deduction
- Descartes' procedure of systematic doubt
- *Cogito ergo sum*

- Descartes' conception of mind
- Substance
- The nature and role of clear and distinct ideas
- Descartes' arguments for God
  Eidological Argument
  Ontological Argument
- God as the source of clear and distinct ideas
- How errors occur
- How we acquire knowledge of the external world
- Descartes' conception of matter
- Various objections to Descartes' philosophy
- The mind-body problem
- Some traditional solutions to the mind-body problem
  Interactionism
  Occasionalism
  Preestablished harmony
  Double-aspect theory
- Radical solutions to the mind-body problem: materialism and idealism
- The category mistake
- Mind as a set of dispositions
- Functionalism

Questions for Reflection

- At the beginning of the chapter it was asserted that mind-matter dualism is a very common metaphysical theory. Do you think so? Would you have answered the question of reality along these lines? What *would* have been your answer?
- It is sometimes observed that Descartes' way of viewing *mind* and its *activities* was too easily influenced by a prevailing way of talking about things in the external world in terms of *substance* and *qualities:* Would this in itself make Descartes' view of mind wrong? Might this be the origin of the category mistake that Ryle talks about?
- If you *do* maintain the mind-matter dualist position, what do *you* do about the mind-body problem?

For Further Reading

C. D. Broad. *The Mind and Its Place in Nature*. London: Routledge & Kegan Paul, 1925. Ch. 3. Treatment of "The Traditional Problem of Body and Mind" in an old but enduring work.

Frederick Copleston. *A History of Philosophy*. Baltimore: Newman Press, 1946–1974. IV, Chs. 3–5, 9, 11, 17. Chapters dealing with Descartes' dualistic theory of reality, his theory of interactionism, and the response of Leibniz and Spinoza, by a recognized historian of philosophy.

William Doney (ed.). *Descartes: A Collection of Critical Essays*. Garden City, NY: Anchor Books, 1967. Hefty essays by well-known philosophers on various aspects of Descartes' philosophy.

A. C. Ewing. *The Fundamental Questions of Philosophy*. New York: Collier, 1962. Ch. 6. Commonsensical discussion of "The Relation of Matter and Mind."

Owen J. Flanagan, Jr. *The Science of Mind*. Cambridge, MA: M.I.T. Press, 1984. A thorough and critical discussion of the central issues in contemporary cognitive science, including dualism, introspection, functionalism, etc.

Antony Flew (ed.). *Body, Mind, and Death*. New York: Macmillan, 1964. Selections from traditional and contemporary philosophers with a good introduction by a well-known philosopher of the analytic style.

Colin McGinn. *The Character of Mind*. New York: Oxford University Press, 1982. Provocative discussions of the nature of mind, including chapters on "Mind and Body" and "The Self."

Jerome A. Shaffer. *Philosophy of Mind*. Englewood Cliffs, NJ: Prentice Hall, 1968. Chs. 3–4. Student-oriented treatments of consciousness, its relation to the body, the mind-body problem, dualism, etc.

P. F. Strawson. *Individuals: An Essay in Descriptive Metaphysics*. Garden City, NY: Anchor Books, 1959. An influential work which, like Ryle, reflects the mind-body problem as a pseudoproblem, emphasizing the basic unity of the individual.

Richard Taylor. *Metaphysics*. Third ed. Englewood Cliffs, NJ: Prentice Hall, 1983. Chs. 1–2. Student-oriented discussions on "Persons and Bodies" and "Interactionism."

*In addition, see the relevant articles ("Mind-Body Problem," "Descartes," etc.) in *The Encyclopedia of Philosophy*, ed. Paul Edwards. New York: Macmillan, 1967.

CHAPTER 5

Materialism

M ATERIALISM IS actually a form of *naturalism*, and it might be best first to get an idea of this larger metaphysical perspective. All naturalisms share a repudiation of any supernatural or spiritual reality. The claim is: Only that exists which can, at least in principle, be investigated scientifically. And just as believers in the supernatural or the spiritual are often given to faith, dogma, intuition, authority, and the like, so naturalists are generally given to observation, experimentation, and healthy doses of skepticism. In a word, naturalists tend to be "tough-minded" philosophers.

But we must distinguish between a narrower and a wider naturalism, corresponding to a narrower and a wider view of nature itself. The narrower view defines nature as the physical world and may be called *materialism*. The wider naturalism, on the other hand, defines nature more broadly so as to include matter as but one of *many* dimensions or aspects of nature. In this chapter we will focus our attention on materialism.

WHAT IS MATERIALISM?

As with the word "idealism," the word "materialism" also has a popular and a more technical sense. In popular usage materialism means a preoccupation with earthly goods (such as money, ski chalets, and sailboats), and a materialist in this sense is one whose life revolves around the pursuit of such things. But here we intend "materialism" in its more technical and metaphysical sense: Matter with its motions and qualities is the ultimate reality of all things. More generally, what this means is that everything in the universe—from subatomic particles, to tables, chairs, dogs, and cats, to thoughts, feelings, perceptions, and ideals—*everything* is reducible to matter with its motions and qualities, to physical states, to a position in space and time, to what can be quantified.

There are few forks on the philosophical road that are more unmistakable than the one where idealism and materialism veer off from each other. We saw in our last chapter that one radical solution to the mind-body problem is simply to do away with matter. The result is *idealism*, the view that there is only one reality, and that is mind and its ideas. Materialism takes exactly the opposite course and denies the reality of mind, or at least reduces it (along with everything else) to matter. As a radical solution to the mind-body problem materialism is certainly as effective as idealism, for it too overcomes entirely the old problem of relating two essentially different substances, for there *is* no other substance, only matter. In the same way that Descartes, with his mind-matter dualism, unwittingly spawned modern idealism, so did he spawn modern materialism. This is not to say that the only reason for adopting materialism is that it is a way of avoiding the mind-body problem. As with idealism, materialism too has still other advantages. Advantages aside, certainly as a theory of reality it is in some respects the starkest and the most hard-headed.

Materialism is actually a very old philosophy. Already among the Pre-Socratics, Democritus and Leucippus taught that all things, including the

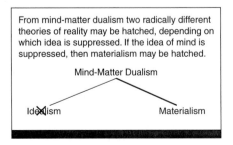

From mind-matter dualism two radically different theories of reality may be hatched, depending on which idea is suppressed. If the idea of mind is suppressed, then materialism may be hatched.

Mind-Matter Dualism

Idealism   Materialism

soul, are made of indivisible particles or atoms. This idea was adopted by
the Greek philosopher Epicurus (about 300 B.C.). He concluded from the
materialistic nature of the soul that upon death its parts disperse, and
therefore there can be no life after death—so eat, drink and be merry!
After Epicurus, the Roman poet Lucretius (about 60 B.C.) wrote as if he
himself were even then providing a materialist (and atomistic) response to
Descartes' mind-body problem:

> I now declare that mind and soul are joined
>> together, and form one single entity,
>> but the head so to speak, that rules in all the body,
>> is counsel, mind, and intellect, as we say,
>> and this is placed midway within the breast.
> For here leap terror and panic, this spot feels
>> sweet joy; here, then, are intellect and mind.
> The rest of the soul, dispersed through all the body,
>> obeys the mind and moves to its command.
> For mind thinks its own thoughts, knows it own pleasures,
>> when nothing has stimulated soul or body.
> And as when injury attacks our head
>> or eye, they hurt, but we're not agonized
>> all over, thus the mind sometimes feels pain
>> or joy and strength, and when other parts of soul
>> in limb and joint have felt no novel impulse.
> But when the mind is deeply stirred by terror,
>> all through the body we see the soul affected;
>> we pale, and over all the body sweat
>> pours out, the tongue stumbles, voice goes awry,
>> eyes are befogged, ears ring, the knees give way,
>> yes, from sheer terror of mind we often see
>> men fall in a faint; thus readily we perceive
>> the union of soul and mind, for soul, when struck
>> by mind, in turn strikes body and makes it move.
> This argument also proves that soul and mind
>> are physical things. Clearly, they move our limbs,
>> arouse the body from sleep, change our expression,
>> and guide and govern the man in all his being.
> Yet without touch, we see, such things can't happen,
>> nor touch without matter; must we not then admit
>> the soul and mind in act are physical things?

Besides, we see that in our bodies, soul
    and body act and react in sympathy.
If a bristling spear has driven deep, exposing
    sinew and bone, and yet not taking life,
    still faintness follows and sweet swooning down
    to earth, and there is a sense of rocking motion,
    sometimes with vaguely felt desire to rise.
And so the soul must be a physical thing,
    since physical weapon and wound can make it suffer.
I'll now proceed to argument and proof
    of what makes up the soul, and what its substance.
To begin, I say the soul is subtly built
    of infinitesimal atoms. You may see
    and learn that this is so from what's to come.
Nothing whatever, we see, can move as fast
    as the mind when it conceives and starts an action;
    thus nothing whose nature clearly lies within
    our range of vision moves faster than the mind.
But whatever is so mobile must be made
    of very round and very tiny atoms,
    so that the slightest impulse starts them moving.
Yes, just a touch makes water move and flow:
    it's made, you see, of small-sized shapes that roll.
But the nature of honey tends to be more stable;
    its fluid is thicker and less disposed to move.
For all the atoms of its substance cling
    more closely, being of particles less smooth,
    you see, and not so delicate or so round.
Take poppyseed: a gentle puff of air
    at the top will blow a tall heap helter-skelter,
    but not, on the other hand, a heap of stones
    or grain. According, then, as particles
    are smallest and smoothest, they will move with ease.
But on the other hand, as some are found
    rougher and heavier, so are they more stable.
Now since the soul has been revealed to be
    uncommonly mobile, we must grant it made
    of atoms very tiny, smooth, and round.
Take this to heart, good friend; in many ways
    you'll find it a useful, helpful thing to know.

This fact, too, tells the nature of the soul,
> how fine its fabric, and in how small a space
> it could be held, if it were all rolled up:
> when once the carefree peace of death has seized
> a man, and the substance of soul and mind has left him,
> from his whole body you'd see nothing lost
> in appearance or in weight; death leaves him all
> but the humid heat and sentience that mean life.
The entire soul, then, must consist of tiny
> atoms, strung out through sinews, vitals, veins,
> since, when it all has gone from all the body,
> the outer dimensions of body-parts remain
> unaltered, and not an ounce of weight is lost.
It's such as when bouquet of wine floats off,
> or breath of perfume is wafted to the winds,
> or when from a substance flavor dies away;
> to the eye, the physical thing appears no smaller
> for all of that, and suffers no loss of weight.
Why? Because many minuscule atoms make
> flavors and scents throughout the range of things.
Thus you may know the substance of the mind
> and soul, I insist, is formed of most minute
> atoms, for slipping away, it steals no weight.[1]

In the modern period, the eighteenth-century English philosopher Thomas Hobbes expressed the materialist thesis with a theistic twist: The notion of *spirit*, as opposed to *matter* or *body*, should be reserved for God alone.

From these Metaphysics, which are mingled with the Scripture to make School Divinity, we are told, there be in the world certain Essences separated from Bodies, which they call *Abstract Essences, and Substantial Forms:* For the Interpreting of which *Jargon*, there is need of somewhat more than ordinary attention in this place. Also I ask pardon of those that are not used to this kind of Discourse, for applying my self to those that are. The World, (I mean not the Earth only, that denominates the Lovers of it *Worldly men*, but the *Uni-*

---

[1]Lucretius, *The Nature of Things* III, pp. 136–230, tr. Frank O. Copley (New York: Norton, 1977).

verse, that is, the whole mass of all things that are) is Corporeal, that is to say, Body; and hath the dimensions of Magnitude, namely, Length, Breadth, and Depth: also every part of Body, is likewise Body, and hath the like dimensions; and consequently every part of the Universe, is Body; and that which is not Body, is no part of the Universe: And because the Universe is All, that which is no part of it, is *Nothing*; and consequently *no where*. Nor does it follow from hence, that Spirits are *nothing*: for they have dimensions, and are therefore really *Bodies*; though that name in common Speech be given to such Bodies only, as are visible, or palpable; that is, that have some degree of Opacity: But for Spirits, they call them Incorporeal; which is a name of more honour, and may therefore with more piety be attributed to God himself; in whom we consider not what Attribute expresseth best his Nature, which is Incomprehensible; but what best expresseth our desire to honour Him.[2]

Such a view of reality has taken several forms. No doubt the harshest is *mechanistic materialism*.

Thomas Hobbes, a modern materialist

---

[2]Thomas Hobbes, *Leviathan*, Ch 46, ed. A. D. Lindsay (New York: Dutton, 1950) (slightly edited).

MAN A MACHINE

The key to understanding mechanistic materialism lies in the word "mechanistic," which means "machinelike." According to this theory of reality, not only are all things reducible to matter and motion and locatable in space and time, but all things happen and have their particular features according to a finite number of fixed physical laws. That is to say, the world and everything in it is a *machine*.

Mechanistic materialism really took shape as a philosophical position (and in some ways even as a philosophical movement) soon after Descartes. The thinkers advocating this idea were very much influenced by the "new science," and were especially captivated by Sir Isaac Newton's Three Laws of Motion, the basis of Newtonian mechanics. They were also influenced by Descartes himself, who believed that—at least with respect to the *matter* part of his dualism—the world is ordered by fixed laws, and that animals, like everything else in the external world, are mechanisms.

It is important not to miss the full force of the claim that the universe is a machine. It is not just that all things (and everything *about* all things) are caused. We all believe that. It is, rather, that everything is caused in such a way that *it could not have been otherwise*. This pen, this desk, that paperclip in just that position, the smoke curling upward from this pipe, everything that *is* and is going on in this room, in all rooms, in all the world, in all worlds—everything in the universe down to the minutest detail is, on this view, *exhaustively predetermined* by infinitely long and converging chains of blind, irrational antecedent causes. One of the most concise expressions of

---

NEWTON'S THREE LAWS OF MOTION

1. A body remains at rest or in motion with a constant velocity unless acted on by an outside force.
2. The sum of the forces acting on a body is equal to the product of its mass and acceleration.
3. For every action there is an equal and opposite reaction.

How do these laws play into the hands of mechanistic materialism? Can you think of concrete examples?

this mechanistic point of view was provided by the French astronomer and mathematician Laplace:

> We ought then to regard the present state of the universe as the effect of its anterior state and as the cause of the one which is to follow. Given for one instant an intelligence which could comprehend all the forces by which nature is animated and the respective situation of the beings who compose it—an intelligence sufficiently vast to submit these data to analysis—it would embrace in the same formula the movements of the greatest bodies of the universe and those of the lightest atom; for it, nothing would be uncertain and the future, as the past, would be present to its eyes.[3]

That is, on the mechanistic view of things, if you could somehow know the exact status of every detail in the universe at one point, then you could know perfectly every detail in the universe at any point in the past or the future.

One cannot overestimate Sir Isaac Newton's influence on subsequent science and philosophy. It is not difficult to see how Newtonian mechanics, specifically, played into the hands of materialistic philosophy.

---

[3]Pierre Simon de Laplace, *A Philosophical Essay on Probabilities*, tr. Frederick Wilson Truscott and Frederick Lincoln Emory (New York: Dover, 1951), p. 4.

Even so, it is *still* possible that some may fail to note the full implications of the mechanistic claim. If *everything* in the universe is matter in motion and is governed by mechanistic laws, then so is man. And then so are his thinking, feeling, purposing, valuing, and willing. Man too, through and through, is a machine.

Man a Machine was in fact the title of a remarkable little volume published in 1748 by the French physician and agnostic La Mettrie. (He has been called "the scapegoat of eighteenth-century materialism.") Like many others before and after him, La Mettrie argued for a purely materialistic basis of human consciousness. Thoughts, sensations, and emotions are all a matter of organs, nerves, impulses, reflex movements, pumping blood, and the like. These in turn are physiological counterparts of springs, cogs, wheels, wire, and so on, so it all reduces to physics and chemistry. On such a view, as someone has said, the brain secretes thought in the same way that the liver secretes bile! A few passages from La Mettrie:

> Man is so complicated a machine that it is impossible to get a clear idea of the machine beforehand, and hence impossible to define it. . . .

> But since all the faculties of the soul depend to such a degree on the proper organization of the brain and of the whole body, that apparently they are but this organization itself, the soul is clearly an enlightened machine. . . .

> The soul is therefore but an empty word, of which no one has any idea, and which an enlightened man should use only to signify the part in us that thinks. Given the least principle of motion, animated

---

MAN, A COMPUTER?

Especially with the rise of computer technology the temptation to create man in the image of a computer has sometimes been irresistible.

"Each human being is a superbly constructed, astonishingly compact, self-ambulatory computer. . . ."

—Carl Sagan

bodies will have all that is necessary for moving, feeling, thinking, repenting, or in a word for conducting themselves in the physical realm, and in the moral realm which depends upon it. . . .

Grant only that organized matter is endowed with a principle of motion, which alone differentiates it from the inorganic (and can one deny this in the face of the most incontestable observation?) and that among animals, as I have sufficiently proved, everything depends upon the diversity of this organization: these admissions suffice for

L' H O M M E

M A C H I N E.

Eſt-ce là ce Raion de l'Eſſence ſuprème,
Que l'on nous peint ſi lumineux?
Eſt-ce là cet Eſprit ſurvivant à nous même?
Il naît avec nos ſens, croit, s'affoiblit
comme eux.
Helas! il périra de même.

VOLTAIRE.

_____

À LEYDE,

De l'Imp. d'ELIE LUZAC, Fils.

MDCCXLVIII.

Title page of La Mettrie's *Man a Machine,*
The verse by Voltaire: *Where is this reason,*
essence supreme, which so luminously is
painted? Where is this spirit outliving us? It is
born with our senses. And with the senses
waxes and wanes. Alas, it too will die.

guessing the riddle of substances and of man. It [thus] appears that
there is but one [type of organization] in the universe, and that man
is the most perfect [example]. . . .

Let us then conclude boldly that man is a machine, and that in the
whole universe there is but a single substance differently modified.
This is no hypothesis set forth by dint of a number of postulates and
assumptions; it is not the work of prejudice, nor even of my reason
alone; I should have disdained a guide which I think to be so untrust-
worthy, had not my senses, bearing a torch, so to speak, induced me
to follow reason by lighting the way themselves. Experience has thus
spoken to me in behalf of reason; and in this way I have combined
the two.

. . . Need I say that I refer to the empty and trivial notions, to the
pitiable and trite arguments that will be urged (as long as the shadow
of prejudice or of superstition remains on earth) for the supposed incompatibility of two substances which meet and move each other
unceasingly? Such is my system, or rather the truth, unless I am
much deceived. It is short and simple. Dispute it now who will.[4]

Amidst all the rest, do not fail to notice La Mettrie's concluding claim
for his materialistic-mechanistic theory: "It is short and simple." Here
again is the appeal to *simplicity* as a criterion of a better explanation. In fact,
it is often urged by materialists that the economy or simplicity of their theory decisively enhances its *explanatory power* over, say, dualistic theories.

THE NEW MATERIALISM

If you have the impression that the conception of man as a machine is
just an idle piece displayed in the historical museum of philosophical
ideas, your impression is quite wrong. It is true that the La Mettrie and
pre-La Mettrie type of mechanism was based on the "billiard-ball" model
of the universe (everything happens according to strict laws and direct or
indirect physical contacts), and that the billiard-ball model is now "out."
And even the classical Newtonian mechanics has now been succeeded by

---

[4]Julien Offray de La Mettrie, *Man a Machine*, tr. Gertrude C. Bussey et al. (La Salle,
IL: Open Court, 1912), pp. 18, 89, 140–41.

complicated things like *quantum mechanics* and Heisenberg's Uncertainty Principle, according to which there is no observable causal determinism at the level of atomic and subatomic particles. How this latter involves a "dematerialization" of matter is described by the scientist and philosopher N. R. Hanson:

> Matter has been dematerialized, not just as a concept of the philosophically real, but now as an idea of modern physics. Matter can be analyzed down to the level of fundamental particles. But at that depth the direction of the analysis changes, and this constitutes a major conceptual surprise in the history of science. The things which for Newton typified matter—e.g., an exactly determinable state, a point shape, absolute solidity—these are now the properties electrons do not, because theoretically they cannot, have. . . .

> The dematerialization of matter . . . has rocked mechanics at its foundations. . . . The 20th century's dematerialization of matter has made it conceptually impossible to accept a Newtonian picture of the properties of matter and still do a consistent physics.[5]

This rejection of mechanistic materialism by modern physics has strong implications for the relationship between humans and nature. Gary Zukav explains this in his book *The Dancing Wu Li Masters: An Overview of the New Physics:*

> . . . after three centuries, the Scientists have returned with their discoveries. They are as perplexed as we are (those of them who have given thought to what is happening).

> "We are not sure," they tell us, "but we have accumulated evidence which indicates that the key to understanding the universe is *you.*"

> This is not only different from the way that we have looked at the world for three hundred years, it is *opposite.* The distinction between the "in here" and the "out there" upon which science was founded, is blurred. This is a puzzling state of affairs. Scientists, using the "in

---

[5]N. R. Hanson, "The Dematerialization of Matter," in *The Concept of Matter*, ed. Ernan McMullen (Notre Dame, IN: University of Notre Dame Press, 1963), pp. 556–57.

here—out there" distinction, have discovered that the "in here—out there" distinction may not exist! What is "out there" apparently depends, in a rigorous mathematical sense as well as a philosophical one, upon what we decide "in here."

The new physics tells us that an observer cannot observe without altering what he sees. Observer and Observed are interrelated in a real and fundamental sense. The exact nature of this interrelation is not clear, but there is a growing body of evidence that the distinction between the "in here" and the "out there" is illusion.

The conceptual framework of quantum mechanics, supported by massive volumes of experimental data, forces contemporary physicists to express themselves in a manner that sounds, even to the uninitiated, like the language of the mystics.

Access to the physical world is through experience. The common denominator of all experiences is the "I" that does the experiencing. In short, what we experience is not external, but our *interaction* with it. . . .

The tables have been turned. "The exact sciences" no longer study an objective reality that runs its course regardless of our interest in it or not, leaving us to fare as best we can while it goes its predetermined way. Science, at the level of subatomic events, is no longer "exact," the distinction between objective and subjective has vanished, and the portals through which the universe manifests itself are, as we once knew a long time ago, those impotent, passive witnesses to its unfolding, the "I"s, of which we, insignificant we, are examples. The Cogs in the Machine have become the Creators of the Universe. . . .[6]

Nonetheless, the materialistic perspective thrives. Consider, for example, the materialism of the Australian J. J. C. Smart. Under the sway of contemporary physics he rejects complete causal determination, but asserts, nevertheless, a purely physicalistic theory of mind. More specifically, he asserts what is called the Identity Thesis.

---

[6]Gary Zukav, *The Dancing Wu Li Masters: An Overview of the New Physics* (New York: Morrow, 1979), pp. 92–93, 114.

First of all let me try to explain what I mean by "materialism." I shall then go on to try to defend the doctrine. By "materialism" I mean the theory that there is nothing in the world over and above those entities which are postulated by physics (or, of course, those entities which will be postulated by future and more adequate physical theories). Thus I do not hold materialism to be wedded to the billiard-ball physics of the nineteenth century. The less visualizable particles of modern physics count as matter. Note that energy counts as matter for my purposes: indeed in modern physics energy and matter are not sharply distinguishable. Nor do I hold that materialism implies determinism. If physics is indeterministic on the micro-level, so must be the materialist's theory. I regard materialism as compatible with a wide range of conceptions of the nature of matter and energy. For example, if matter and energy consist of regions of special curvature of an absolute space-time, with "worm holes" and what not, this is still compatible with materialism: we can still argue that in the last resort the world is made up entirely of the ultimate entities of physics, namely space-time points.

. . . [M]y definition will in some respects be narrower than those of some who have called themselves "materialists." I wish to lay down that it is incompatible with materialism that there should be any irreducibly "emergent" laws or properties, say in biology or psychology. According to the view I propose to defend, there are no irreducible laws or properties in biology, any more than there are in electronics. Given the "natural history" of a superheterodyne (its wiring diagram), a physicist is able to explain using only laws of physics, its mode of behavior and its properties (for example, the property of being able to receive such and such a radio station which broadcasts on 25 megacycles). Just as electronics gives the physical explanation of the workings of superheterodynes, etc., so biology gives (or approximates to giving) physical and chemical explanations of the workings of organisms or parts of organisms. The biologist needs natural history just as the engineer needs wiring diagrams, but neither needs nonphysical laws.

It will now become clear why I define materialism in the way I have done above. I am concerned to deny that in the world there are nonphysical entities and nonphysical laws. In particular I wish to deny the doctrine of psychophysical dualism. (I also want to deny any theory of "emergent properties," since irreducibly nonphysical properties are just about as repugnant to me as are irreducibly nonphysical entities.)

Popular theologians sometimes argue against materialism by saying that "you can't put love in a test tube." Well you can't put a gravitational field in a test tube (except in some rather strained sense of these words), but there is nothing incompatible with materialism, as I have defined it, in the notion of a gravitational field.

Similarly, even though love may elude test tubes, it does not elude materialistic metaphysics, since it can be analyzed as a pattern of bodily behavior or, perhaps better, as the internal state of the human organism that accounts for this behavior. (A dualist who analyzes love as an internal state will perhaps say that it is a soul state, whereas the materialist will say that it is a brain state. It seems to me that much of our ordinary language about the mental is neither dualistic nor materialist but is neutral between the two. Thus, to say that a locution is not materialistic is not to say that it is immaterialistic.)

But what about consciousness? Can we interpret the having of an after-image or of a painful sensation as something material, namely, a brain state or brain process? We seem to be immediately aware of pains and after-images, and we seem to be immediately aware of them as something different from a neurophysiological state or process. For example, the after-image may be green speckled with red, whereas the neurophysiologist looking into our brains would be unlikely to see something green speckled with red. However, if we object to materialism in this way we are victims of a confusion which U. T. Place has called "the phenomenological fallacy." To say that an image or sense datum is green is not to say that the conscious experience of having the image or sense datum is green. It is to say that it is the sort of experience we have when in normal conditions we look at a green apple, for example. Apples and unripe bananas can be green, but not the experiences of seeing them. An image or a sense datum can be green in a derivative sense, but this need not cause any worry, because, on the view I am defending, images and sense data are not constituents of the world, though the processes of having an image or a sense datum are actual processes in the world. The experience of having a green sense datum is not itself green; it is a process occurring in grey matter. The world contains plumbers, but does not contain the average plumber; it also contains the having of a sense datum, but does not contain the sense datum. . . .

It may be asked why I should demand of a tenable philosophy of mind that it should be compatible with materialism, in the sense in which I have defined it. One reason is as follows: How could a non-physical property or entity suddenly arise in the course of animal evolution? A change in a gene is a change in a complex molecule which causes a change in the biochemistry of the cell. This may lead to changes in the shape or organization of the developing embryo. But what sort of chemical process could lead to the springing into existence of something nonphysical? No enzyme can catalyze the production of a spook! Perhaps it will be said that the nonphysical comes into existence as a by-product: that whenever there is a certain complex physical structure, then, by an irreducible extraphysical law, there is also a nonphysical entity. Such laws would be quite outside normal scientific conceptions and quite inexplicable: they would be, in Herbert Feigl's phrase, "nomological danglers." To say the very least, we can vastly simplify our cosmological outlook if we can defend a materialistic philosophy of mind.[7]

ARE THE MIND AND BODY IDENTICAL?

Two major criticisms of materialism center around (1) the claimed identity of mind and body and (2) the claimed universality of strict determinism. A little later, in our discussion of B. F. Skinner, we will address the second of these. For the moment, consider the first.

All forms of materialism involve a physicalistic interpretation of mind. In the case of Smart, we have just seen that this takes the form of the Identity Thesis, so-called because it views the mind (including thoughts, perceptions, emotions, etc.) as identical with brain states (nerve cells, electrical impulses, etc.):

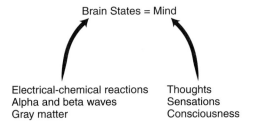

Brain States = Mind

Electrical-chemical reactions
Alpha and beta waves
Gray matter

Thoughts
Sensations
Consciousness

One of the most common objections to this view has already been anticipated by Smart. Are not the differences between mental states and brain
states so great that no amount of empirical or scientific analysis can bridge
them? For example, consider a surgeon who completes his last delicate and
precise penetration into an innermost recess of the brain. What does he see
there—*red* or *affection?* No. He sees more nerves, brain tissue, blood, cells,
and so on. It's a serious question: Do the sensations of red, the idea of a
table, the feeling of repulsion, and the desire for food sit right there in the
brain alongside veins and synapses, waiting to be exposed?

Some are not satisfied that Smart and others have successfully laid
this objection to rest. The American philosopher Richard Taylor presses
the difference between mind and body by raising *logical* problems with
identity-talk: I can be blamed, but can my *body* be blamed? I can be religious, but can my *body* be religious? My thoughts can be true or false,
but can my *brain* be true or false?

> By "identity" the materialist must mean a strict and total identity of
> himself and his body, nothing less. Now to say of anything, X, and
> anything, Y, that X and Y are identical, or that they are really one
> and the same thing, one must be willing to assert of X anything
> whatever that he asserts of Y, and vice versa. This is simply a conse-
> quence of their identity, for if there is anything whatever that can be
> truly asserted of any object X, but cannot be truly asserted of some
> object Y, then it logically follows that X and Y are two different
> things, and not the same thing. In saying, for instance, that the
> British wartime prime minister and Winston Churchill are one and
> the same person, one commits himself to saying of either whatever
> he is willing to say of the other—such as, that he lived to a great age,
> smoked cigars, was a resolute leader, was born in Blenheim, and so
> on. If there were any statement whatever that was true of, say, Mr.
> Churchill, but not true of the wartime prime minister, then it would
> follow that Mr. Churchill was not the wartime prime minister, that
> we are here referring to two different men, and not one.
>
> The question can now be asked, then, whether there is anything true
> of me that is not true of my body, and vice versa. There are, of
> course, ever so many things that can be asserted indifferently of both
> me and my body without absurdity. For instance, we can say that I
> was born at such and such place and time, and it is not the least odd
> to say this of my body as well. Or we can say that my body now

weighs exactly so many pounds, and it would be just as correct to give this as my weight; and so on.

But now consider more problematical assertions. It might, for instance, be true of me at a certain time that I am morally blameworthy or praiseworthy. Can we then say that my body or some part of it, such as my brain, is in exactly the same sense blameworthy or praiseworthy? Can moral predicates be applied without gross incongruity to any physical object at all? Or suppose I have some profound wish or desire, or some thought—the desire, say, to be in some foreign land at a given moment, or thoughts of the Homeric gods. It seems at least odd to assert that my body, or some part of it, wishes that it were elsewhere, or has thoughts of the gods. How, indeed, can any purely physical state of any purely physical object ever be a state that is *for* something, or *of* something, in the way that my desires and thoughts are such? And how, in particular, could a purely physical state be in this sense *for* or *of* something that is not real? Or again, suppose that I am religious, and can truly say that I love God and neighbor, for instance. Can I without absurdity say that my body or some part of it, such as my foot or brain, is religious, and loves God and neighbor? Or can one suppose that my being religious, or having such love, consists simply in my body's being in a certain state, or behaving in a certain way? If I claim the identity of myself with my body, I must say all these odd things; that is, I must be willing to assert of my body, or some part of it, everything I assert of myself. There is perhaps no logical absurdity or clear falsity in speaking thus of one's corporeal frame, but such assertions as these are at least strange, and it can be questioned whether, as applied to the body, they are even still meaningful.

The disparity between bodily and personal predicates becomes even more apparent, however, if we consider epistemological predicates, involved in statements about belief and knowledge. Thus, if I believe something—believe, for instance, that today is February 31—then I am in a certain state; the state, namely, of having a certain belief which is in this case necessarily a false one. Now how can a physical state of any physical object be identical with that? And how, in particular, can anything be a *false* physical state of an object? The physical states of things, it would seem, just *are*, and one cannot even think of anything that could ever distinguish one such state from another as being either true or false. A physiologist might give a complete physical description of a brain and nervous system at a particular time, but he could never distinguish some of those states as true and others as false, nor would he have any idea what to look for if he were asked to do this. At least, so it would certainly seem.[8]

An objection to the Identity Thesis has also been raised by the functionalists. We introduced functionalism at the end of Chapter 4, though we have put off until now an account of one of its major appeals. Functionalism is, quite simply, an alternative to the Identity Thesis, which it regards as utterly implausible. Why? The Identity Thesis insists on drawing straight lines, as it were, from specific mental states to specific brain states; it argues that all mental states of a given type, for example, being in pain, must be *identified* with a physical state of a certain type, for example, a C-fiber firing. But, the functionalist charges, could not many other physical systems be in pain without being in just the physical state we happen to be in when we are in pain? Through a well-known and imaginative device, Paul M. Churchland shows how this one-to-one correspondence of mental states to brain states need not hold.

Imagine a being from another planet, says the functionalist, a being with an alien physiological constitution, a constitution based on the chemical element silicon, for example, instead of on the element carbon, as ours is. The chemistry and even the physical structure of the alien's brain would have to be systematically different from ours. But even so, that alien brain could well sustain a functional economy of internal states whose mutual *relations* parallel perfectly the mutual relations that define our own mental states. The alien may have an internal state that meets all the conditions for being a pain state, as outlined earlier. That state, considered from a purely physical point of view, would have a very different makeup from a human pain state, but it could nevertheless be identical to a human pain state from a purely functional point of view. And so for all of his functional states.

If the alien's functional economy of internal states were indeed *functionally isomorphic* with our own internal economy—if those states

---

[8]Richard Taylor, *Metaphysics*, second ed. (Englewood Cliffs, NJ: Prentice Hall, 1974), pp. 13–15.

were causally connected to inputs, to one another, and to behavior in ways that parallel our own internal connections—then the alien would have pains, and desires, and hopes, and fears just as fully as we, despite the differences in the physical system that sustains or realizes those functional states. What is important for mentality is not the matter of which the creature is made, but the structure of the internal activities which that matter sustains.

If we can think of one alien constitution, we can think of many, and the point just made can also be made with an artificial system. Were we to create an electronic system—a computer of some kind—whose internal economy were functionally isomorphic with our own in all the relevant ways, then it too would be the subject of mental states.

What this illustrates is that there are almost certainly many more ways than one for nature, and perhaps even for man, to put together a thinking, feeling, perceiving creature. And this raises a problem for the identity theory, for it seems that there is no single type of physical state to which a given type of mental state must always correspond. Ironically, there are *too many* different kinds of physical systems that can realize the functional economy characteristic of conscious intelligence. . . . The prospects for universal identities, between types of mental states and types of brain states, are therefore slim.[9]

The same point is made by the contemporary philosopher Arthur C. Danto: Given a functionalist definition of mind, but also a non-brain support system for mental functions (think of a computer), it becomes impossible to identify the mind with the brain. On the other hand, as Danto states, the analogy (so precious to functionalists) between brain-states and computer-states is now itself being called into question.

Functionalism has . . . raised severe problems for certain materialist theories of the mind. Thus it is difficult to insist that the mind is nothing but the brain, hence nothing but that material system, if the mind itself can be functionally defined and then given something that supports all its functions but is otherwise different from the

[9]Paul M. Churchland, *Matter and Consciousness: A Contemporary Introduction to the Philosophy of Mind* (Cambridge, MA: M.I.T. Press, 1984), pp. 36f.

brain. How can the mind be identified with the brain when it can also be identified with the computer when the computer and the brain cannot be identified? Identity is transitive: if $a = b$ and $b = c$, then $a = c$. Of course, functionalism itself may be false. It may seem available only to a superficial knowledge of brains and computers. It may be that there really is only a distant analogy between mental functioning in human beings and input transformation in computers. Already today, for example, computer scientists are contending that computers circa 1987 really are inadequate to model mental functions like speech. There is already the sense that something far more complex takes place in brains than in even quite advanced machines.[10]

BEYOND FREEDOM AND DIGNITY: SKINNER

Probably the best recent example of one who asserts both a physicalistic view of mind and a pervasive causal determinism was not a philosopher but the behaviorist psychologist B. F. Skinner.

What is *behaviorism?* Generally, behaviorism is a school of psychology which emphasizes observable human behavior as the proper object of psychological study. Now here we have to draw a distinction. For there is a big difference between (1) the view that the description of observable behavior is the psychologist's task, which we may call descriptive or *soft* behaviorism, and (2) the view that observable behavior *is all there is*, which we may call *hard* behaviorism. Obviously, soft behaviorism is not our concern here inasmuch as it makes no claim at all about reality or human nature itself. Hard behaviorism, however, most certainly does involve a claim about reality—specifically a claim about the nature of human nature itself. This form of behaviorism is, therefore, at a certain level inseparable from a metaphysical perspective, and the perspective is a materialistic and mechanistic one. It is therefore appropriate to consider this form of behaviorism in a chapter on materialism, especially since, through Skinner's book *Beyond Freedom and Dignity*, it has enjoyed a renewed and far-reaching impact in recent years.

---

[10]Arthur C. Danto, *Connections to the World: The Basic Concepts of Philosophy* (New York: Harper & Row, 1989), p. 233.

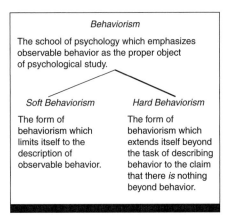

Behaviorism

The school of psychology which emphasizes observable behavior as the proper object of psychological study.

Soft Behaviorism

The form of behaviorism which limits itself to the description of observable behavior.

Hard Behaviorism

The form of behaviorism which extends itself beyond the task of describing behavior to the claim that there *is* nothing beyond behavior.

There can be no doubt about the physicalistic and mechanistic character of Skinner's appraisal of the human person. Though Skinner's physicalism, or reduction of the total person to physical states, underlies and pervades Skinner's work everywhere, it is nowhere really argued, at least not with any rigor. Rather, it is treated as an assumption that any enlightened twentieth-century person would surely embrace, in contrast to earlier and "prescientific" notions which uncritically employ ideas such as mind, transcendence, free will, and the like. Our interest in Skinner is not, therefore, so much with his defense of physicalism (because he gives none) but with what he does with it as the foundation of his proposed "technology of behavior," a program of psychological engineering, or manipulation of human nature in the interest of the improvement and progress of the species.

Almost all our major problems involve human behavior, and they cannot be solved by physical and biological technology alone. What is needed is a technology of behavior, but we have been slow to develop the science from which such a technology might be drawn. One difficulty is that almost all of what is called behavioral science continues to trace behavior to states of mind, feelings, traits of character, human nature, and so on. Physics and biology once followed similar practices and advanced only when they discarded them. The behavioral sciences have been slow to change partly because the explanatory entities often seem to be directly observed and partly because other kinds of explanations have been hard to find. The environment is obviously important, but its role has remained obscure. It does not push or pull, it *selects*, and this function is difficult to discover and analyze. The role of natural selection in evolution was formulated only a little more than a hundred years ago, and the selective role of the environment in shaping and maintaining the behavior of the individual is only beginning to be recognized and studied. As the interaction between organism and environment has come to be understood, however, effects once assigned to states of mind, feelings, and traits are beginning to be traced to accessible conditions, and a technology of behavior may therefore become available. It will not solve our problems, however, until it replaces traditional prescientific views, and these are strongly entrenched. Freedom and dignity illustrate the difficulty. They are the possessions of the autonomous man of traditional theory, and they are essential to practices in which a person is held responsible for his conduct and given credit for his achievements. A scientific analysis shifts both the responsibility and the achievement to the environment. It also raises questions concerning "values." Who will use a technology and to what ends? Until these issues are resolved, a technology of behavior will continue to be rejected, and with it possibly the only way to solve our problems. . . .

A child is born a member of the human species, with a genetic endowment showing many idiosyncratic features, and he begins at once to acquire a repertoire of behavior under the contingencies of reinforcement to which he is exposed as an individual. Most of these contingencies are arranged by other people. They are, in fact, what is called a culture, although the term is usually defined in other ways. Two eminent anthropologists have said, for example, that "the essential core of culture consists of traditional (i.e., historically derived and selected) ideas and especially their attached values." But those who observe cultures do not see ideas or values. They see how people live, how they raise their children, how they gather or cultivate food, what kinds of dwellings they live in, what they wear, what games they play, how they treat each other, how they govern themselves, and so on. These are the customs, the customary *behaviors*, of a people. To explain them we must turn to the contingencies which generate them.

Some contingencies are part of the physical environment, but they usually work in combination with social contingencies, and the latter are naturally emphasized by those who study cultures. The social contingencies, or the behaviors they generate, are the "ideas" of a culture; the reinforcers that appear in the contingencies are its "values."

A person is not only exposed to the contingencies that constitute a culture, he helps to maintain them, and to the extent that the contingencies induce him to do so the culture is self-perpetuating. The effective reinforcers are a matter of observation and cannot be disputed. What a given group of people calls good is a fact: it is what members of the group find reinforcing as the result of their genetic endowment and the natural and social contingencies to which they have been exposed. Each culture has its own set of goods, and what is good in one culture may not be good in another. To recognize this is to take the position of "cultural relativism." What is good for the Trobriand Islander is good for the Trobriand Islander, and that is that. Anthropologists have often emphasized relativism as a tolerant alternative to missionary zeal in converting all cultures to a single set of ethical, governmental, religious, or economic values. . . .

It is the nature of an experimental analysis of human behavior that it should strip away the functions previously assigned to autonomous man and transfer them one by one to the controlling environment. The analysis leaves less and less for autonomous man to do. But what about man himself? Is there not something about a person which is more than a living body? Unless something called a self survives, how can we speak of self-knowledge or self-control? To whom is the injunction "Know thyself" addressed?

It is an important part of the contingencies to which a young child is exposed that his own body is the only part of his environment which remains the same *(idem)* from moment to moment and day to day. We say that he discovers his *identity* as he learns to distinguish between his body and the rest of the world. He does this long before the community teaches him to call things by name and to distinguish "me" from "it" or "you."

A self is a repertoire of behavior appropriate to a given set of contingencies. A substantial part of the conditions to which a person is exposed may play a dominant role, and under other conditions a person may report, "I'm not myself today," or "I couldn't have done what you said I did, because that's not like me." The identity conferred upon a self arises from the contingencies responsible for the behavior. Two or more repertoires generated by different sets of contingencies compose two or more selves. A person possesses one repertoire appropriate to his life with his friends and another appropriate to his life with his family, and a friend may find him a very different person if he sees him with his family or his family if they see him with his friends. The problem of identity arises when situations are intermingled, as when a person finds himself with both his family and his friends at the same time.

Self-knowledge and self-control imply two selves in this sense. The self-knower is almost always a product of social contingencies, but the self that is known may come from other sources. The controlling self (the conscience or superego) is of social origin, but the controlled self is more likely to be the product of genetic susceptibilities to reinforcement (the id, or the Old Adam). The controlling self generally represents the interests of others, the controlled self the interests of the individual.

The late B. F. Skinner, the most
influential behaviorist, and advocate of a
"technology of behavior."

The picture which emerges from a scientific analysis is not of a body with a person inside, but of a body which is a person in the sense that it displays a complex repertoire of behavior. The picture is, of course, unfamiliar. The man thus portrayed is a stranger, and from the traditional point of view he may not seem to be a man at all. "For at least one hundred years," said Joseph Wood Krutch, "we have been prejudiced in every theory, including economic determinism, mechanistic behaviorism, and relativism, that reduces the stature of man until he ceases to be man at all in any sense that the humanists of an earlier generation would recognize." Matson has argued that "the empirical behavioral scientist . . . denies, if only by implication, that a unique being, called Man, exists." "What is now under attack," said Maslow, "is the 'being' of man." C. S. Lewis put it quite bluntly: Man is being abolished.

There is clearly some difficulty in identifying the man to whom these expressions refer. Lewis cannot have meant the human species, for not only is it not being abolished, it is filling the earth. (As a result it may eventually abolish itself through disease, famine, pollution, or a nuclear holocaust, but that is not what Lewis meant.) Nor are individual men growing less effective or productive. We are told that what is threatened is "man *qua* man," or "man in his humanity," or "man as Thou not It," or "man as a person not a thing." These are not very helpful expressions, but they supply a clue. What is being abolished is autonomous man—the inner man, the homunculus, the possessing demon, the man defended by the literatures of freedom and dignity.

His abolition has long been overdue. Autonomous man is a device used to explain what we cannot explain in any other way. He has been constructed from our ignorance, and as our understanding increases, the very stuff of which he is composed vanishes. Science does not dehumanize man, it de-homunculizes him, and it must do so if it is to prevent the abolition of the human species. To man *qua* man we readily say good riddance. Only by dispossessing him can we turn to the real causes of human behavior. Only then can we turn from the inferred to the observed, from the miraculous to the natural, from the inaccessible to the manipulable.[11]

---

[11]B. F. Skinner, *Beyond Freedom and Dignity* (New York: Bantam Books, 1972), pp. 22–23, 121–22, 189–91.

REVEALING EXPRESSIONS FROM SKINNER

- "technology of behavior"
- explanation by "antecedent physical events"
- person as "a repertoire of behavior"
- values as "social contingencies"
- good and bad as "positive" and "negative" reinforcement
- "responsibility and achievement" of "environment"
- "experimental analysis"
- "beyond freedom and dignity"

The above selections from Skinner emphasize several overlapping themes: the denial of free will and all human transcendence; a reinterpretation of values as being dependent on social contingencies or conditions; a purely physicalistic interpretation of all levels of human activity; the importance of the environment for the shaping of human nature. In sum, he argues for the abolition of man as traditionally conceived, and for a technology of human nature as conceived along "hard" behavioristic lines.

Is man a machine for Skinner? Although Skinner explicitly represents man as a "machine," in the following paragraph he appears to want to soften the blow.

Man is not made into a machine by analyzing his behavior in mechanical terms. Early theories of behavior, as we have seen, represented man as a push-pull automaton, close to the nineteenth-century notion of a machine, but progress has been made. Man is a machine in the sense that he is a complex system behaving in lawful ways, but the complexity is extraordinary. His capacity to adjust to contingencies of reinforcement will perhaps be eventually simulated by machines, but this has not yet been done, and the living system thus simulated will remain unique in other ways.[12]

---

[12]Ibid., pp. 192–93.

Nevertheless, many think that Skinner's conception of human nature is essentially indistinguishable from the old-fashioned mechanistic one. Surely if there is any recurring theme in Skinner's work it is the rejection of human autonomy and the invocation of a universal and strict causal determinism. And this brings us to the second major problem with materialism.

ARE ALL THINGS DETERMINED?

It should be apparent by now that while not every form of materialism embraces causal determinism (think of Smart), the two usually do go hand in hand (as in Skinner). All things are reducible to physical states; all things are causally determined. But for many philosophers causal determinism, especially as regards human activity, is extremely problematic.

It is important to recall an earlier point. The trouble is not over the principle of universal causality, pure and simple. Almost everyone believes that every event must have a cause; from nothing, nothing comes; or for everything that happens there must be a necessary (it couldn't happen without it) and sufficient (it can happen with it) condition. The problem arises with the further assertion that everything is causally *determined;* that is, for anything that happens, *it could not have happened otherwise.* To put it another way: There is a big difference (do you see it?) between saying (1) D could not occur without A, B, and C; and (2) given A, B, and C, D *must* occur. It is, of course, this second claim, the principle of universal determination, that is so vexing.

In the first place, it is vexing from the standpoint of the belief in genuine *morality.* If it is true that nothing can happen otherwise than it does, then this must apply also to our willing and choosing. And this means the denial of *free will.* On the other hand, is it not clear—so the argument goes—that morality presupposes free will? that *ought* implies *can?* What sense is there in praise and blame and talk of moral responsibility if one cannot choose to act *freely?* Is it not always relevant, when trying to establish blame or guilt or responsibility on the part of someone, to ascertain whether that person was forced, drugged, or suffering from some compulsion? Free will would seem to be a condition for responsible moral action.

More generally it may be asked whether the ideas of moral good and evil are even *meaningful* of the materialistic/determinist view of things. For on that view things just *are,* and they can't be otherwise. Whence, then, comes any *ought?* If you start with a morally neutral universe, how do

Causality and Determinism

- *Principle of universal causality:* Everything that comes into being is caused.
- *Principle of universal determinism:* Everything that comes into being is caused in such a way that it could not have been otherwise.

you account for objective values or ideals or universally binding rights and wrongs? Or maybe something can come from nothing. Or maybe values aren't universal and objective, but, as Skinner says, they're just by-products of environment and accidental social conditions. But is this what you mean by genuine morality? (These questions will have to be considered again in Chapter 12.)

In the second place, some think that determinism is downright incompatible with genuine *thinking*, using the word to cover a broad range of intellectual activities. Setting aside such intellectual experiences as intuition, flashes of insight, and creative imagination, which some think transcend the flux and flow of blind and mechanical causation, is not the determinist caught in a hopeless if not self-contradictory position? For we are told right and left that all things are causally determined, could not be otherwise, etc., and yet we are told also to think hard, to scrutinize, to evaluate, to analyze. But this puts the intellect in the position of *judging* things, which means that the intellect is different from, and higher than, those that it *judges*. That is, if your mind and intellectual processes themselves are but an example of physical and chemical processes, then how can your mind frame a theory *about* physics and chemistry? And what *is* truth?

But there may be worse. We are told by the determinist that all things are causally determined. But, then, that very statement too, as well as everything else the determinist maintains, *is itself causally determined.* But if it's causally determined and could not be otherwise, then why pay any attention to it? Do you usually take seriously the claims of someone whose claims you know to be blindly determined by antecedent causes? As in the case of determining moral responsibility, does not intellectual responsibility mean freedom from constraints such as drug-inducement, compulsions, force, and the like?

TWO MAJOR PROBLEMS FOR DETERMINISM

- Is moral experience compatible with universal causal determinism?
- Is cognitive experience compatible with universal causal determinism?

DETERMINIST: All things are causally determined.

INDETERMINIST: But is that statement itself therefore causally determined?

DETERMINIST: Why, of course. I just said that everything is!

INDETERMINIST: Well, then, why should I take it seriously?

DETERMINIST: Because I am a rational person, and I offer it as a rational position.

INDETERMINIST: But that's just the point. I don't call people or positions "rational" that are blind products of antecedent causes. I might as well argue with a turnip!

Inevitably, someone will counter with the analogy of computers: Are not human minds supercomplex and glorified computers? The proper answer is, of course, that computers—even the most supercomplex—do so well only because they are programmed by something essentially different, a *non*computer, namely, a *human mind*.

It is all a question of *transcendence:* Do you believe that the categories of materialism and/or determinism are adequate to your total experience as a human being, especially your moral and intellectual experience? Or must there be some reality or dimension of human nature, however dimly perceived and understood, that stands outside and above matter, motion, and causal determination:

CHAPTER 5 IN REVIEW

Summary

A radical solution to the mind/body problem is materialism, which entirely does away with mind (or mental substance) and affirms matter, with its motions and qualities, as the sole underlying reality of all things. This is a very old philosophical perspective with roots even before Socrates.

An extreme form of materialism is mechanistic materialism, which imports the further principle that the motions in the universe are determined by fixed and unalterable laws: The universe and everything in it is a *machine*. But, then, so are human beings, as La Mettrie announced in his book *Man a Machine*. Of course, the image of a person as consisting of wheels, springs, cogs, and bolts is out of date, as the idea of matter itself has become considerably refined. Nonetheless, the physicalistic conception of mind persists as in the Identity Thesis of J. J. C. Smart: Mental states are identical with brain states.

In recent times, something very much like mechanistic materialism has surfaced in conjunction with the behavioristic psychology of Skinner. We have called it "hard" behaviorism precisely because it assumes the truth of materialism as a theory of reality and a theory of human nature. Skinner's main purpose in *Beyond Freedom and Dignity* is to envision and advocate a "technology of human behavior," a manipulation of human behavior and transformation of values in accordance with the progress and ideals of the evolutionary process.

As materialism, and certainly *mechanistic* materialism, bears on human nature and life, it poses great problems. Specifically, if all things are exhaustively determined, and man is a machine, then what becomes of moral and cognitive experience? Many philosophers believe that moral responsibility and authentic thinking are immediately rendered impossible on the determinist view of things. This is to say nothing of the alleged self-refuting character of this thesis: If everything is causally determined, then so is this very claim, but then why pay attention to it? And Taylor has pointed out some problems with the Identity Thesis.

In the end, the question becomes: Is it possible to live with the intellectual and practical implications that follow from the denial of *human transcendence?*

Basic Ideas

- Naturalism
- Materialism
- Materialism as a solution to the mind-body problem
- Mechanism
- The "dematerialization" of matter

- The Identity Thesis
- Objections to the Identity Thesis
- Behaviorism
  Soft behaviorism
  Hard behaviorism
- Technology of behavior
- Causality vs. determinism
- Objections to causal determinism
- The question of transcendence

Questions for Reflection

- Are background, upbringing, education, etc., relevant to the adoption of the materialist perspective? Is this *philosophically* relevant?
- We will have occasion to look again at the problem of determinism (Chapter 12), but consider now: How serious a threat do you really think determinism is to morality and knowledge? How might materialists and/or determinists counter the charge that their position undermines morality and knowledge? And even if it does, so what? And just what does "transcendence" mean in this context, anyway? Is it a philosophically coherent and responsible concept?
- At the beginning of this chapter it was noted that some philosophers opt for a "wider naturalism," according to which both physical and mental reality should be subsumed under a higher nature, or regarded as dimensions of a single reality. Does this strike you as a plausible approach? Does it solve any problems? Does it create any new ones?

For Further Reading

John V. Canfield. *Purpose in Nature.* Englewood Cliffs, NJ: Prentice Hall, 1966. Essays by various thinkers, including "Behavior, Purpose, and Teleology," and "Comments on a Mechanistic Conception of Purposefulness."

Hubert L. Dreyfus. *What Computers Can't Do: The Limits of Artificial Intelligence.* Rev. ed. New York: Harper & Row, 1979. A critical account of work in artificial intelligence, arguing for the uniqueness of human cognition.

Gerald Dworkin (ed.). *Determinism, Free Will, and Moral Responsibility*. Englewood Cliffs, NJ: Prentice Hall, 1970. Essays by several thinkers on the topics indicated in the title.

Owen J. Flanagan, Jr. *The Science of Mind*. Cambridge, MA: M.I.T. Press, 1984. A thorough and critical discussion of the central issues in contemporary cognitive science, including behaviorism, Identity Theory, functionalism, etc.

Antony Flew (ed.). *Body, Mind, and Death*. New York: Macmillan, 1964. Traditional and contemporary statements on mind and body, including some discussion of behaviorism and consciousness as brain processes.

John McLeish. *The Development of Modern Behavioral Psychology*. Calgary: Detselig, 1981. A complete account of the historical roots and continuing development and interaction of the several branches of behaviorism.

John O'Conner (ed.). *Modern Materialism: Readings on Mind-Body Identity*. New York: Harcourt, Brace & World, 1969. Essays by well-known thinkers on mind and brain processes, materialism in relation to the mind-body problem, mechanism, identity theories, etc.

David Rosenthal. *Materialism and the Mind-Body Problem*. Englewood Cliffs, NJ: Prentice Hall, 1971. Good treatment of the mind-body problem and its contemporary solutions, including the materialistic.

Richard Taylor. *Metaphysics*. 3rd ed. Englewood Cliffs, NJ: Prentice Hall, 1983. Chs. 3–5. Brief, student-oriented discussions on "The Mind as a Function of the Body," "Freedom and Determinism," and "Fate."

John A. Weigel. *B. F. Skinner*. Boston: Twayne, 1977. A brief and very useful volume which argues that Skinner is a "good and true prophet" whose ideas have been misunderstood and maligned.

Gary Zukav. *The Dancing Wu Li Masters*. New York: Morrow, 1979.

*In addition, see the relevant articles ("Materialism," "Mechanism in Biology," "Naturalism," "Behaviorism," etc.) in *The Encyclopedia of Philosophy*, ed. Paul Edwards. New York: Macmillan, 1967.

PART TWO

THE
QUESTION
OF
KNOWLEDGE

I N OUR introductory note to Part 1 we said that the question of reality may be in some ways the most basic question. But a similar claim could be made for the question of knowledge.

It is true that our answers to the question of reality will largely determine our answers to many other questions. But we cannot really answer any questions at all, not even the question of reality, until we have become clear on the still prior question of knowledge. Think about this until you see it: Judgments about reality, morality, art, society, religion, politics, science, or anything else, presuppose judgments about knowledge itself— *whether* we can know, *how* we can know, and *what* we can know. Take, for example, your knowledge that "In fourteen hundred and ninety-two Columbus sailed the ocean blue." How did you arrive at this piece of knowledge? In your claim to "know" this there are surely contained already many implicit judgments about epistemological issues such as

- the limits of reason.
- the role of sense experience.
- the relevance of intuition.
- the assurances of historical investigation.
- the nature and criterion of truth.
- the nature and authority of "facts."
- the possibility of certainty.
- degrees of certainty.

If such a welter of considerations is necessarily involved in such a harm-less claim as "In fourteen hundred and ninety-two Columbus sailed the ocean blue," then how much more attention must we give the epistemo-logical underpinnings of claims about reality, value, moral responsibility, society, and God?

CHAPTER 6

The Way
of
Reason

W HERE DOES knowledge come from? What is the basis of knowledge? The question of the origin of knowledge is one of the most important questions of philosophy. In fact, it is a *crucial* question. As we have said already in the introduction to Part II, how you answer this question will have everything to do with the rest of your philosophy.

TWO MAIN THEORIES ABOUT THE BASIS OF KNOWLEDGE

Throughout the history of philosophy, thinkers have generally answered this question in two ways. On the one side, we have those philosophers who, in one way or another and in varying degrees, have emphasized *reason* as the source of knowledge ("inside-out" philosophers). On the other side, we have those philosophers who, in one way or another and in varying degrees, have emphasized *experience* as the source of knowledge ("outside-in" philosophers). The position stressing the role of the intellect or reason is called *rationalism,* and those holding to this position are called *rationalists*

141

(from the Latin word *ratio*, "reason"). The position stressing the role of experience is called *empiricism*, and those holding this view are called empiricists (from the Greek *empeiria*, "experience").

A special note is in order regarding the labels "rationalism" and "rationalist." This is because these terms, like so many other important terms, bear more than one meaning. Here again we must distinguish between a loose and a stricter sense of these terms. We have already encountered the loose sense of "rationalism" in the Introduction. There we said that rationalism is a dominating interest in reasoning, reflecting, criticizing, examining, and so on. This is what we meant when we defined philosophy as the attempt to provide, within limits, an essentially *rational* interpretation of reality as a whole, and when we characterized all philosophers as *rationalists*. Now, however, in the stricter or more technical sense of the word, rationalism is an *epistemological theory*, specifically a *theory about the basis of knowledge*. Note, then, that while a rationalist in the strict sense is necessarily a rationalist in the loose sense, it is not necessarily the case that a rationalist in the loose sense will be a rationalist in the strict sense—he or she may, rather, be an *empiricist*. As a term designating a theory about the basis of knowledge, rationalism is on a par with empiricism. Both empiricism and rationalism (in this technical sense) answer the question, "What is the basis of knowledge?" though in radically different ways.

REASON AS THE BASIS OF KNOWLEDGE

We will begin with rationalism. Above we said that rationalism emphasizes reason as the source of knowledge. This may now be refined somewhat: Rationalism is the belief that at least some knowledge about reality can be acquired through reason, independently of sense experience.

It is important here to stress, first, that the rationalist believes that *some* knowledge about reality can be acquired through reason alone. Few rationalists have ever insisted that sense experience plays absolutely no role whatsoever in the acquisition of knowledge. We will say more about this later, but for the moment just consider: Even if you are a strict rationalist, how do you know that swans are white? that in fourteen hundred and ninety-two Columbus sailed the ocean blue? Obviously there is much about the world that we could not possibly know apart from making observations, lighting Bunsen burners, taking field trips, and so on. The

HOW DO YOU KNOW, WHEN YOU KNOW?

Epistemology is concerned primarily with the kind of knowledge involved in truth-claims, that is, when the truth or falsity of something is asserted.

But truth-claims come in many colors, and, therefore, so does this kind of knowledge. Consider, for example, the following claims. In each of them something is claimed to be "known," but the "knowing" in each is quite different from all the others.

- I know that in fourteen hundred and ninety-two Columbus sailed the ocean blue.
- I know that I exist.
- I know that God exists.
- I know that all swans are white.
- I know that this table exists.
- I know that my Redeemer liveth.
- I know that every event must have a cause.
- I know that you are suffering.
- I know that all barking dogs bark.
- I know that it will rain tomorrow.

Obviously, the kind of knowledge involved in a straightforward historical claim like "I know that in fourteen hundred and ninety-two Columbus sailed the ocean blue" is quite different from the kind of knowledge delivered through an introspective intuition, as in "I know that I exist." And both of these are quite different from the knowledge involved in the religious assertion, "I know that my Redeemer liveth." And so on.

To see that these claims really involve quite different meanings of "know," just ask yourself in each case "how" that particular thing would be known—what sorts of considerations should be brought to bear, etc.

staunchest rationalists admit this. What they insist on is that at least *some* of the truths about reality (and usually the most important truths about reality) are known apart from sense experience.

Second, we must stress that for rationalists reason is the source of at least some of our knowledge about *reality*. We do have, after all, knowledge which is *not* about reality. For example, we know that all barking dogs bark, that a triangle has three sides, and in short, any statement of the form "A is A." Such statements, as we will emphasize later, are absolutely and universally and necessarily true. But that is because they are true by definition. As such they have no bearing on reality; they neither affirm nor deny the existence of anything; they must be true *no matter what*. Everyone agrees that such truths are known independently of sense experience; all you have to do is look at the proposition to see that it must be true. The rationalist, though, claims that at least some propositions which *are* about reality—which affirm or deny the existence of something—may be known independently of sense experience, through reason alone.

Do you yourself possess any universal and certain knowledge about reality? Think of some possible examples:

- Every event must have a cause.
- It is morally wrong to kill people for the fun of it.
- All individuals are endowed with basic rights.

Can you derive such universal and certain knowledge from the limited, fluctuating, and relative evidence of sense experience? Where, then, does such knowledge come from?

As two classic examples of rationalism we may mention Plato and Descartes. We have, of course, already dealt with the *metaphysical* doctrines of these thinkers in Part I, where we discussed Plato's theory of the Forms and Descartes' mind-matter dualism. But now we consider the *epistemological* side of their philosophies.

THE RATIONALISM OF PLATO

Along with many other Greek philosophers, Plato believed that the *reason*, which distinguishes humans from the lower animals, comprises the essential nature of the human being. (The classical definition of man as "a rational animal" comes from these Greek philosophers.) Human good and happiness, therefore, lie in the activity and fulfillment of the rational faculty. That is, they lie in contemplation and *knowledge*. On the other hand, it will be recalled from our earlier discussion that Plato believed that the only proper object of knowledge, or the only thing that can *really* be known, is *Being*. This means that we can have no real knowledge of the world about us, the relative and fluctuating world of *Becoming*. Of this world we have only opinion, not knowledge.

Now, Plato has Socrates announce in the *Phaedo* that not only do real philosophers have no fear of death, but they actually desire and look forward to it. In fact, real philosophers view their lives as lifelong preparations for death. Why? Because as long as we are in *this* world, we are held back from the attainment of real knowledge and therefore happiness. And why is this? For one thing, our bodies are a constant distraction from the higher pursuit of knowledge. The pursuit of knowledge does, after all, require some time and attention, but it seems that most of our time is taken up by the body: We must feed it, clothe it, cleanse it, and pay all sorts of attention to it. For another, and this is more important for the present point, as long as our souls are imprisoned in our bodies they have a natural tendency (if not necessity) to peer out, as it were, through the only windows of the prison, the five senses. As a result, our souls become contaminated by the distortions, illusions, and relativities of the sensible world.

Plato represents the twofold problem posed by the body as follows:

Now take the acquisition of knowledge. Is the body a hindrance or not, if one takes it into partnership to share an investigation? What I mean is this. Is there any certainty in human sight and hearing, or is it true, as the poets are always dinning into our ears, that we neither hear nor see anything accurately? Yet if these senses are not clear and accurate, the rest can hardly be so, because they are all inferior to the first two. Don't you agree?

Certainly.

Then when is it that the soul attains to truth? When it tries to investigate anything with the help of the body, it is obviously led astray.

Quite so.

Is it not in the course of reflection, if at all, that the soul gets a clear view of facts?

Yes.

Surely the soul can best reflect when it is free of all distractions such as hearing or sight or pain or pleasure of any kind—that is, when it ignores the body and becomes as far as possible independent, avoiding all physical contacts and associations as much as it can, in its search for reality.

That is so.

Then here too—in despising the body and avoiding it, and endeavoring to become independent—the philosopher's soul is ahead of all the rest.

It seems so.

Here are some more questions, Simmias. Do we recognize such a thing as absolute uprightness?

Indeed we do.

And absolute beauty and goodness too?

Of course.

Have you ever seen any of these things with your eyes?

Certainly not, said he.

Well, have you ever apprehended them with any other bodily sense? By "them" I mean not only absolute tallness or health or strength, but the real nature of any given thing—what it actually is. Is it through the body that we get the truest perception of them? Isn't it true that in any inquiry you are likely to attain more nearly to knowledge of your object in proportion to the care and accuracy with which you have prepared yourself to understand that object in itself?

Certainly.

Don't you think that the person who is likely to succeed in this attempt most perfectly is the one who approaches each object, as far as possible, with the unaided intellect, without taking account of any sense of sight in his thinking, or dragging any other sense into his reckoning—the man who pursues the truth by applying his pure and unadulterated thought to the pure and unadulterated object, cutting himself off as much as possible from his eyes and ears and virtually all the rest of his body, as an impediment which by its presence prevents the soul from attaining to truth and clear thinking? Is not this the person, Simmias, who will reach the goal of reality, if anybody can?

What you say is absolutely true, Socrates, said Simmias.

All these considerations, said Socrates, must surely prompt serious philosophers to review the position in some such way as this. It looks as though this were a bypath leading to the right track. So long as we keep to the body and our soul is contaminated with this imperfection, there is no chance of our ever attaining satisfactorily to our object, which we assert to be truth. In the first place, the body provides us with innumerable distractions in the pursuit of our necessary sustenance, and any diseases which attack us hinder our quest for reality. Besides, the body fills us with loves and desires and fears and all sorts of fancies and a great deal of nonsense, with the result that we literally never get an opportunity to think at all about anything. Wars and revolutions and battles are due simply and solely to the body and its desires. All wars are undertaken for the acquisition of wealth, and the reason why we have to acquire wealth is the body, because we are slaves in its service. That is why, on all these accounts, we have so little time for philosophy. Worst of all, if we do obtain any leisure from the body's claims and turn to some line of inquiry, the body intrudes once more into our investigations, interrupting, disturbing, distracting, and preventing us from getting a glimpse of the truth. We are in fact convinced that if we are ever to have pure knowledge of anything, we must get rid of the body and contemplate things by themselves with the soul by itself.[1]

O happy day, then, when the soul will finally be set free from the body by death! Only then will it come into the uninterrupted enjoyment of absolute knowledge of that other world, the world of truth and reality. In the meantime, we must minimize as much as possible the contamination of the senses.

It seems, to judge from the argument, that the wisdom which we desire and upon which we profess to have set our hearts will be attainable only when we are dead, and not in our lifetime. If no pure

---

[1]Plato, *Phaedo*, pp. 65A–66E, tr. Hugh Tredennick, in *Plato: The Collected Dialogues*, eds. Edith Hamilton and Huntington Cairns (New York: Pantheon Books, 1961).

knowledge is possible in the company of the body, then either it is totally impossible to acquire knowledge, or it is only possible after death, because it is only then that the soul will be separate and independent of the body. It seems that so long as we are alive, we shall continue closest to knowledge if we avoid as much as we can all contact and association with the body, except when they are absolutely necessary, and instead of allowing ourselves to become infected with its nature, purify ourselves from it until God himself gives us deliverance. In this way, by keeping ourselves uncontaminated by the follies of the body, we shall probably reach the company of others like ourselves and gain direct knowledge of all that is pure and uncontaminated—that is, presumably, of truth. For one who is not pure himself to attain to the realm of purity would no doubt be a breach of universal justice.[2]

Here then is a clearly rationalist view of knowledge. Sense experience is disdained as a hindrance to real knowledge. And true reality, by its very nature as transcendent and nonsensible, can be grasped adequately by the intellect alone.

But Plato's rationalism becomes clear in yet another way. Even in this world, knowledge—insofar as it is knowledge—is possible only because it is *innate*, that is, inborn. The theory of innate ideas is a popular one among rationalists. But it is important not to confuse innate ideas with *instinct*. Instinct is not a result of a cognitive activity; rather, it is the *subcognitive* and purely mechanistic behavior which enhances survival. Further, in none of its forms does the doctrine of innate ideas mean that the infant child is born into the world with its mind burgeoning with Einstein's theory of relativity. It usually means that fundamental ideas or principles are built right into the mind itself and require only to be developed and brought to maturity.

Plato himself sought to prove the immortality of the soul, or, more accurately, the *preexistence* of the soul, on the grounds that we have in our minds certain ideas that we could not possibly have derived from sense experience alone. Such an idea is that of equality. Where, Plato asks, did we acquire this and similar ideas? Certainly not from the sensible world around us, for there is no instance of absolute equality to be found anywhere in this world.

---

[2]Ibid., pp. 66E–67B.

In contrast to his friends, Socrates is glad at the prospect of his death, for death is
the liberation of the soul from the body, and this means the fulfillment of his
lifelong philosophical goal: knowledge.

Of course the sensible world is full of things which are *more or less* equal, but
you will search this world over, or any other world in space and time, and
never come across an instance of *absolute* equality. We are back in the world
of Heraclitus, where everything flows, and in Plato's world of Becoming,
which is populated by imperfect copies or mere approximations to the true
Realities, the eternal Forms.

Plato concludes that the only way to account for this knowledge is to
believe that prior to its embodiment in this world, the soul was in the
presence of the Forms, where it acquired knowledge of the realities, including knowledge of Equality. This knowledge was lost or forgotten
through the trauma of birth, though to some degree "recollected" subsequent to birth on the occasion of our experiences with more-or-less equality, that is, Equality as it is encountered imperfectly in the sensible world.
It is important to note that Plato's theory of knowledge as recollection, although it certainly emphasizes the innateness of our fundamental ideas,
also accords some role to sense experience after all. At least in this life, no
knowledge could be enjoyed at all were it not for the initial stimulation of
the senses.

As a possible theory of innate knowledge, you might find Plato's doctrine of recollection a bit silly. On the other hand, one should always be cautious in judging as silly the ideas of those who have exerted enormous influence on the way we ourselves think today. Plato's theory is both historically and philosophically interesting, and his own statement of it is worthy of close attention:

> We admit, I suppose, that there is such a thing as equality—not the equality of stick to stick and stone to stone, and so on, but something beyond all that and distinct from it—absolute equality. Are we to admit this or not?
>
> Yes indeed, said Simmias, most emphatically.
>
> And do we know what it is?
>
> Certainly.
>
> Where did we get our knowledge? Was it not from the particular examples that we mentioned just now? Was it not from seeing equal sticks or stones or other equal objects that we got the notion of equality, although it is something quite distinct from them? Look at it in this way. Is it not true that equal stones and sticks sometimes, without changing in themselves, appear equal to one person and unequal to another?
>
> Certainly.
>
> Well, now, have you ever thought that things which were absolutely equal were unequal, or that equality was inequality?
>
> No, never, Socrates.
>
> Then these equal things are not the same as absolute equality.
>
> Not in the least, as I see it, Socrates.
>
> And yet it is these equal things that have suggested and conveyed to you your knowledge of absolute equality, although they are distinct from it?
>
> Perfectly true.
>
> Whether it is similar to them or dissimilar?
>
> Certainly.

It makes no difference, said Socrates. So long as the sight of one thing suggests another to you, it must be a cause of recollection, whether the two things are alike or not.

Quite so.

Well, now, he said, what do we find in the case of the equal sticks and other things of which we were speaking just now? Do they seem to us to be equal in the sense of absolute equality, or do they fall short of it in so far as they only approximate to equality? Or don't they fall short at all?

They do, said Simmias, a long way.

Suppose that when you see something you say to yourself, This thing which I can see has a tendency to be like something else, but it falls short and cannot be really like it, only a poor imitation. Don't you agree with me that anyone who receives that impression must in fact have previous knowledge of that thing which he says that the other resembles, but inadequately?

Certainly he must.

Very well, then, is that our position with regard to equal things and absolute equality?

Exactly.

Then we must have had some previous knowledge of equality before the time when we first saw equal things and realized that they were striving after equality, but fell short of it.

That is so.

And at the same time we are agreed also upon this point, that we have not and could not have acquired this notion of equality except by sight or touch or one of the other senses. I am treating them as being all the same.

They are the same, Socrates, for the purpose of our argument.

So it must be through the senses that we obtained the notion that all sensible equals are striving after absolute equality but falling short of it. Is that correct?

Yes, it is.

So before we began to see and hear and use our other senses we must somewhere have acquired the knowledge that there is such a thing as absolute quality. Otherwise we could never have realized, by using it as a standard for comparison, that all equal objects of sense are desirous of being like it, but are only imperfect copies.

That is the logical conclusion, Socrates.

Did we not begin to see and hear and possess our other senses from the moment of birth?

Certainly.

But we admitted that we must have obtained our knowledge of equality before we obtained them.

Yes.

So we must have obtained it before birth.

So it seems.

Then if we obtained it before our birth, and possessed it when we were born, we had knowledge, both before and at the moment of birth, not only of equality and relative magnitudes, but of all absolute standards. Our present argument applies no more to equality than it does to absolute beauty, goodness, uprightness, holiness, and, as I maintain, all those characteristics which we designate in our discussions by the term "absolute." So we must have obtained knowledge of all these characteristics before our birth.

That is so.

And unless we invariably forget it after obtaining it we must always be born *knowing* and continue to *know* all through our lives, because "to know" means simply to retain the knowledge which one has acquired, and not to lose it. Is not what we call "forgetting" simply the loss of knowledge, Simmias?

Most certainly, Socrates.

And if it is true that we acquired our knowledge before our birth, and lost it at the moment of birth, but afterward, by the exercise of our senses upon sensible objects, recover the knowledge which we had once before, I suppose that what we call learning will be the

Innate Ideas

Rationalists, who believe that we can have existential knowledge (knowledge of the actual existence or nonexistence of things) apart from sense experience, are surely obligated to account for this knowledge. One way is through a doctrine of *innate ideas*. "Innate" means "inborn," thus theories of innate ideas are theories which teach that the mind in some way possesses at least fundamental ideas or intellectual structures from birth. The mind at birth is not a "blank tablet."

recovery of our knowledge, and surely we should be right in calling this recollection.[3]

THE RATIONALISM OF DESCARTES

Another classic example of a rationalist philosopher is Descartes. As with Plato, we have already considered Descartes' theory of reality and thus have already been introduced to at least something of his theory of knowledge.

It will be recalled that Descartes was repelled by the contradictions he discovered among philosophers, but was attracted by the certainties he discovered in mathematics:

> Most of all was I delighted with Mathematics because of the certainty of its demonstrations and the evidence of its reasoning; but I did not yet understand its true use, and, believing that it was of service only in the mechanical arts, I was astonished that seeing how firm and solid was its basis, no loftier edifice had been reared thereupon.[4]

---

[3]Ibid., pp. 74A–75D.

[4]René Descartes, *Discourse on Method*, in *Philosophical Works of Descartes*, tr. Elizabeth S. Haldane and G. R. T. Ross (Cambridge: Cambridge University Press, 1911), I, p. 85.

This preoccupation with mathematics immediately betrays Descartes' rationalist bent. For the reason why the truths of mathematics and the proofs of geometry are certain is that they are untainted by the tentativeness and fluctuations and relativities and illusions of sense experience. They are certain—*rationally* certain. Under the spell of mathematics, Descartes thus turned away from sense experience and toward *reason alone* as the source of philosophical certainty. And he conceived of a "geometrical method" for philosophy.

The essence of this new philosophical method may be found in Descartes' *Rules for the Direction of the Mind*. In Rule IV he stresses the absolute necessity of having a method and then explicitly defines it.

RULE IV. THERE IS NEED FOR A METHOD FOR FINDING OUT THE TRUTH

So blind is the curiosity by which mortals are possessed, that they often conduct their minds along unexplored routes, having no reason to hope for success, but merely being willing to risk the experiment of finding whether the truth they seek lies there. As well might a man burning with an unintelligent desire to find treasure, continuously roam the streets, seeking to find something that a passer-by might have chanced to drop. This is the way in which most Chemists, many Geometricians, and Philosophers not a few prosecute their studies. I do not deny that sometimes in these wanderings they are lucky enough to find something true. But I do not allow that this argues greater industry on their part, but only better luck. But however that may be, it were far better never to think of investigating truth at all, than to do so without a method. For it is very certain that unregulated inquiries and confused reflections of this kind only confound the natural light and blind our mental powers. . . . Moreover by a method I mean certain and simple rules, such that, if a man observe them accurately, he shall never assume what is false as true, and will never spend his mental efforts to no purpose, but will always gradually increase his knowledge and so arrive at a true understanding of all that does not surpass his powers.[5]

---

[5]Descartes, *Rules for the Direction of the Mind*, in *Philosophical Works of Descartes*, I, p. 9.

According to these last lines, anyone who follows Descartes' method would, in principle, be led to all possible knowledge. But what, more exactly, does this method consist in? Descartes reduces it, as we saw in Chapter 3, to two operations of the intellect: *intuition* and *deduction*. This, of course, is why Descartes' method has been called a "geometrical" method. As in geometry, it begins with fundamental and irreducible truths, and from these it deduces more truths. But now the notions of intuition and deduction require further comment.

The word "intuition" is used in many ways. In philosophy it means, usually, a direct and immediate knowledge of something. When we say that it is direct and immediate knowledge, we mean that it is not, like much of our other knowledge, *mediated*, or passed along through something else, say, through sense experience or through other ideas. An example of *mediated* knowledge is our knowledge that X is red, mediated or passed along through our sense experience of X and its color; or our knowledge that C is D, mediated or passed along through our prior understanding that if A is B then C is D, and A is B. In intuition, however, the truth or knowledge in question is grasped immediately by a direct awareness—it is *just there*. It is important to emphasize, though, that the intuitionist claims to know directly not only logical truths, as in "A is A," but truths about *reality*, as in our earlier examples: "Every event must have a cause"; "It is morally wrong to kill people for the fun of it"; and "All individuals are endowed with basic rights." As a theory about the basis of knowledge, intuitionism is the view that such truths may be known immediately and with certainty.

It is understandable why a doctrine of innate ideas has also been attributed to Descartes. Did he take, as it were, the Platonic Forms, place them in the mind, and then announce that we know them directly? Or does he believe that what is innate is a sort of *disposition* of the mind, or a *structure* by which universal and necessary truth about reality can be developed? Of course the latter would better explain why infants do not appreciate Einstein. In any event, what is really important is that for Descartes *something* is innate, and intuition is the faculty of direct awareness by which knowledge is derived from the mind alone. Although Descartes made a big thing of intuition, many other philosophers too have appealed to intuition as an important and even necessary epistemological tool.

But, Descartes continues, our knowledge is not limited to intuitions. For it is possible, says Descartes, to *deduce* further ideas and truths from

D E S C A R T E S '   R U L E S

In his *Rules for the Direction of the Mind*, Descartes presents a long list of rules which, if followed, ensure that the intellect will eventually grasp all that can be known. These rules are collapsed into four short paragraphs in the better-known *Discourse on Method:*

> The first of these was to accept nothing as true which I did not clearly recognize to be so: that is to say, carefully to avoid precipitation and prejudice in judgments, and to accept in them nothing more than what was presented to my mind so clearly and distinctly that I could have no occasion to doubt it.

> The second was to divide up each of the difficulties which I examined into as many parts as possible, and as seemed requisite in order that it might be resolved in the best manner possible.

> The third was to carry on my reflections in due order, commencing with objects that were the most simple and easy to understand, in order to rise little by little, or by degrees, to knowledge of the most

(continued on next page)

our intuited ones. You already have an idea of deduction from our chapter on logic. You will recall that it consists in the necessary inference of one proposition from others; in valid deductive reasoning, if the premises are true, the conclusion *must* be true. It is, thus, by the faculty of deduction that from the original intuitions we are enabled to expand our knowledge indefinitely—but without any loss of certainty. In the chapter on mind and matter we saw, in fact, how much Descartes deduced from his single intuition, "I think."

In the following, again from the *Rules for the Direction of the Mind*, Descartes emphasizes and clarifies intuition and deduction as the basic tools of knowledge.

complex, assuming an order, even if a fictitious one, among those which do not follow a natural sequence relatively to one another.

The last was in all cases to make enumerations so complete and reviews so general that I should be certain of having omitted nothing.

Descartes' optimism about the practice of these rules, as well as the mathematical character of his method, is evident from the continuing comment:

Those long chains of reasoning, simple and easy as they are, of which geometricians make use in order to arrive at the most difficult demonstrations, had caused me to imagine that all those things which fall under the cognizance of man might very likely be mutually related in the same fashion; and that, provided only that we abstain from receiving anything as true which is not so, and always retain the order which is necessary in order to deduce the one conclusion from the other, there can be nothing so remote that we cannot reach to it, nor so recondite that we cannot discover it.*

*Descartes, *Discourse on Method*, in *Philosophical Works of Descartes*, I, p. 92.

RULE III. IN THE SUBJECTS WE PROPOSE TO INVESTIGATE, OUR
INQUIRIES SHOULD BE DIRECTED, NOT TO WHAT OTHERS HAVE
THOUGHT, NOR TO WHAT WE OURSELVES CONJECTURE, BUT
TO WHAT WE CAN CLEARLY AND PERSPICUOUSLY BEHOLD
AND WITH CERTAINTY DEDUCE, FOR KNOWLEDGE IS
NOT WON IN ANY OTHER WAY

. . . we shall here take note of all those mental operations by which we are able, wholly without fear of illusion, to arrive at the knowledge of things. Now I admit only two, viz. intuition and deduction.

By *intuition* I understand, not the fluctuating testimony of the senses, nor the misleading judgment that proceeds from the blundering constructions of imagination, but the conception which an unclouded and attentive mind gives us so readily and distinctly that we are wholly freed from doubt about that which we understand. Or, what comes to the same thing, *intuition* is the undoubting conception of an unclouded and attentive mind, and springs from the light of reason alone; it is more certain than deduction itself, in that it is simpler, though deduction, as we have noted above, cannot by us be erroneously conducted. Thus each individual can mentally have intuition of the fact that he exists, and that he thinks; that the triangle is bounded by three lines only, the sphere by a single superficies, and so on. Facts of such a kind are far more numerous than many people think, disdaining as they do to direct their attention upon such simple matters.

This evidence and certitude, however, which belongs to intuition, is required not only in the enunciation of propositions, but also in discursive reasoning of whatever sort. For example consider this consequence: 2 and 2 amount to the same as 3 and 1. Now we need to see intuitively not only that 2 and 2 make 4, and that likewise 3 and 1 make 4, but further that the third of the above statements is a necessary conclusion from these two.

Hence now we are in a position to raise the question as to why we have, besides intuition, given this supplementary method of knowing, viz. knowing by *deduction*, by which we understand all necessary interference from other facts that are known with certainty. This, however, we could not avoid, because many things are known with certainty, though not by themselves evident, but only deduced from true and known principles by the continuous and uninterrupted action of a mind that has a clear vision of each step in the process. It is in a similar way that we know that the last link in a long chain is connected with the first, even though we do not take in by means of one and the same act of vision all the intermediate links on which that connection depends, but only remember that we have taken them successively under review and that each single one is united to its neighbor, from the first even to the last. Hence we distinguish this mental intuition from deduction by the fact that into the conception of the latter there enters a certain movement or succession, into that of the former there does not. Further deduction does not require an immediately presented evidence such as intuition possesses; its certitude is rather conferred upon it in some way by memory. The

DESCARTES' TWOFOLD BASIS OF KNOWLEDGE

- *Intuition:* The faculty by which truths are grasped immediately, without the intervention of sense-experience or other ideas.
- *Deduction:* The faculty by which subsequent truths are known with necessity from intuited truths, or from intuited truths taken together with other deduced truths.

upshot of the matter is that it is possible to say that those propositions indeed which are immediately deduced from first principles are known now by intuition, now by deduction, i.e. in a way that differs according to our point of view. But the first principles themselves are given by intuition alone, while, on the contrary, the remote conclusions are furnished only by deduction.

These two methods are the most certain routes to knowledge, and the mind should admit no others. All the rest should be rejected as suspect of error and dangerous. But this does not prevent us from believing matters that have been divinely revealed as being more certain than our surest knowledge, since belief in these things, as all faith in obscure matters, is an action not of our intelligence, but of our will. They should be heeded also since, if they have any basis in our understanding, they can and ought to be, more than all things else, discovered by one or other of the ways above-mentioned. . . .[6]

A CONTEMPORARY VERSION: CHOMSKY

It is true that modern and contemporary philosophy has been dominated not by rationalist but, rather, by empiricist epistemology—this probably has not a little to do with the ascendancy of the physical sciences and the scientific method beginning in the sixteenth century—and that theories of innate ideas and the like are looked upon as quaint leftovers from our

---

[6]Ibid., I, pp. 5–8.

philosophical past. Everything has been given a new twist, however, in the recent work of the linguist-philosopher Noam Chomsky of the Massachusetts Institute of Technology, and the philosophical world has had to take note. How has Chomsky's work suddenly derailed the empiricist approach which has for so long controlled the philosophical scene? How has it resulted in an unexpected new lease on life for the rationalist?

The answer has to do with Chomsky's contributions to philosophical linguistics—philosophical analyses, problems, and implications of language. More specifically, his original contribution was called *transformational grammar*, which attempts to relate the "surface" structure of sentences, or what is actually heard, and the "deep" structure of the sentences, what is meant. This, however, has already become out-of-date and unfashionable, and has been superseded by Chomsky's newer and more comprehensive idea of *generative grammar*, which supplements the earlier ideas with talk about "principles and parameters" of language.

The word "principle" here signals the belief that there are certain *universal principles* inherent in all languages, that is, features of language that we are born with. We may call these principles "language universals."

Noam Chomsky, whose linguistic studies
have proven relevant for the doctrine
of innate knowledge.

This claim may strike you as a sweeping generalization, but it appears to Chomskyites to be demonstrated conclusively by an in-depth analysis of, say, relative clauses and the referents of pronouns in English, as well as in a dozen or so of the other four thousand languages of the world. "Parameters" refers to what appears to be a *universal grammar* in the form of basic linguistic options which precede the learning of a language and are enacted or not in view of the demands of that particular language—you might think of them as hard-wire switches, built right into the mind, which are turned on and off at various points depending on the language being learned.

This is exceedingly difficult stuff, but what is important at the moment is this. The commonsensical model of language-acquisition has always been an empirical one: A child acquires language through stimulus-response, conditioning, trial and error, and so on. But in this major development of contemporary philosophy of language, with Chomsky leading the way, it is argued that the phenomenon of language is impossible except on the postulation of *innate intellectual structures*. The implications for epistemology, and specifically for rationalism, are too obvious to miss, as Chomsky himself points out in *Aspects of the Theory of Syntax:*

> On the basis of the best information now available, it seems reasonable to suppose that a child cannot help constructing a particular kind of transformational grammar to account for the data presented to him, any more than he can control his perception of solid objects or his attention to line and angle. Thus it may well be that the general features of language structure reflect, not so much the course of one's experience, but rather the general character of one's capacity to acquire knowledge—in the traditional sense, one's innate ideas and innate principles.[7]

The position is spelled out further in the following, from his essay "Language and the Mind." Note especially his rejection of empiricist explanations of language-acquisition, the recurring emphasis on innate structures as conditions for language, and, again, the relevance of this view of language for still other spheres of knowledge.

---

[7]Noam Chomsky, *Aspects of the Theory of Syntax* (Cambridge, MA: M.I.T. Press, 1965), p. 59.

As far as language learning is concerned, it seems to me that a rather convincing argument can be made for the view that certain principles intrinsic to the mind provide invariant structures that are a precondition for linguistic experience. . . .

The study of language, it seems to me, offers strong empirical evidence that empiricists' theories of learning are quite inadequate. Serious efforts have been made in recent years to develop principles of induction, generalization, and data analysis that would account for knowledge of a language. These efforts have been a total failure. The methods and principles fail not for any superficial reason such as lack of time or data. They fail because they are intrinsically incapable of giving rise to the system of rules that underlies the normal use of language. What evidence is now available supports the view that all human languages share deep-seated properties of organization and structure. These properties—these linguistic universals—can be plausibly assumed to be *an innate mental endowment* rather than the result of learning. If this is true, then the study of language sheds light on certain long-standing issues in the theory of knowledge. Once again, I see little reason to doubt that what is true of language is true of other forms of human knowledge as well.

There is one further question that might be raised at this point. How does the human mind come to have the innate properties that underlie acquisition of knowledge. Here linguistic evidence obviously provides no information at all. The process by which the human mind has achieved its present state of complexity and its particular form of innate organization is a complete mystery, as much of a mystery as the analogous questions that can be asked about any other complex organism. It is perfectly safe to attribute this to evolution, so long as we bear in mind that there is no substance to this assertion—it amounts to nothing more than the belief that there is surely some naturalistic explanation for these phenomena.

There are, however, important aspects of the problem of language and mind that can be studied sensibly within the limitations of present understanding and technique. I think that, for the moment, the most productive investigations are those dealing with the nature of particular grammars and with the universal conditions met by all human languages. I have tried to suggest how one can move, in successive steps of increasing abstractness, from the study of percepts to the study of grammar to the study of universal grammar and the mechanisms of learning.

In this area of convergence of linguistics, psychology, and philosophy, we can look forward to much exciting work in the coming years.[8]

But there are problems. In spite of the allegedly scientific character of Chomsky's procedure, it appears, at bottom, to be founded on *intuitions.* For example, it is not clear to everyone, as it is to Chomsky, just what does and does not count as a "sentence" in English—making for great cocktail party fights and lifelong feuds! More generally, it is certainly relevant to pose two questions. First, how does the mind come to possess this structure in the first place? Chomsky answers, as you just saw, that it is a "complete mystery," and he doesn't see at the moment that any purely naturalistic explanation (he cites evolutionary development) is any better than any other. Another question, and certainly more epistemologically relevant: However it got there, what is the relation of this innate intellectual structure to *truth?* Are we driven to a view of knowledge as *arbitrarily* determined by a purely accidental endowment within the brain? Or can we believe in some sort of *preestablished harmony* whereby this intellectual endowment is made to correspond to reality? Are we driven to something like Plato's doctrine of the *preexistence of the soul?* Or perhaps our experienced reality is itself *determined* by our innate intellectual structures? Or

---

REVEALING PHRASES IN CHOMSKY

- "Principles intrinsic to the mind"
- "Deep-rooted properties of organization and structure"
- "An innate mental endowment"

---

[8]Noam Chomsky, "Language and the Mind," in *Readings in Psychology Today* (Del Mar, CA: C.R.M. Books, 1969), pp. 282, 286.

maybe you can think of some other way out? Certainly the problem is an important one and worthy of serious discussion.

We have considered three rationalist conceptions of knowledge from three different periods. We do not raise here specific objections to these theories, because, in a way, the whole next chapter is itself a colossal challenge to them. Empiricism, with its doctrine that the mind is at birth a "blank tablet," rejects the very starting point of rationalism.

CHAPTER 6 IN REVIEW

Summary

One of the most basic questions of epistemology, and therefore a basic question of all philosophizing, is: What is the origin of knowledge? Philosophers have answered this question in two radically different ways. According to empiricism, all knowledge (at least "existential" knowledge, which informs us about existence) is derived from the five senses. Rationalism, on the other hand, teaches that at least some knowledge can be acquired apart from sense experience, through the intellect or reason alone.

In this chapter we have considered three ways in which rationalists have argued for their theories. We are already familiar with Plato's theory of reality (from Chapter 3), and we should recall that his image of the Divided Line represents as much a conception of knowledge as a conception of reality. The object of authentic knowledge is what *is*, as opposed to what is *becoming*. Such knowledge is hardly possible in this life, where the soul is imprisoned in the body, and where the body itself is a constant hindrance to the acquisition of knowledge. When the soul is liberated from the body at death, the soul comes into the possession of absolute knowledge. Until that time all we can do is cultivate as much as possible the innate truths that the mind is born with, but which, as they are "recollected," are invariably distorted by the world of Becoming, resulting in mere opinions, or *relative* knowledge.

Likewise, Descartes' theory of knowledge was anticipated in Chapter 4. Descartes, too, seeks to develop at least the foundation of his philosophy apart from the input of the senses. He saw in mathematics an especially good model for philosophical reasoning, and adopted intuition and deduction as the principles of his philosophical method. He believed that, in principle, it would be possible to unfold a complete system of knowledge by the rigorous practicing of this method. As with Plato, it is important to see that with Descartes every attempt is made to exclude or minimize the illusory and deceitful intrusions of the senses.

Rationalist theories of knowledge are regarded by many as a bit naive and quaint. However, the psycholinguistic research of Chomsky in particular has resurrected the theory of innate ideas. Specifically, his work has brought to light the presence of universal and innate intellectual structures which underlie all language, and which explain the process of language-acquisition better than the empirically oriented model of learning. Thus psycholinguistics (which is concerned with the connection between the mind and language) has emerged as an unexpected ally of the rationalist theory of knowledge.

Basic Ideas

- Empiricism
- Rationalism (strict sense)
- Plato: Why philosophers desire death
- Two bodily hindrances to knowledge
- Innate ideas
- Knowledge of recollection
- Descartes' "geometrical" method
- Intuitionism
- Descartes' two operations of the mind
  Intuition
  Deduction
- The empirical theory of language-acquisition
- Chomsky's generative grammar
  Principles
  Parameters

Questions for Reflection

- Does Plato's doctrine of recollection seem far-fetched or even bizarre? Even if it does, to what degree does it detract from his basic theory of knowledge? Is it itself basic? In evaluating philosophers' positions, is there a danger of throwing out the baby with the bath water?

- Both Plato and Descartes decry the illusions and distortions of sense experience. Can you provide your own evidence and examples of this? Can you think of *any* sense representation that is not, as it were, "contaminated"? Is it possible to overdo this point? Or, with the rationalists, are we at some point driven to some "purer" faculty than sense perception?

- Think about these propositions: "Every event must have a cause"; "It is morally wrong to kill people for the fun of it"; "All individuals are endowed with basic rights." Would you say that you *know* or are *certain* of these claims? Are any of them *universally* true? What, if anything, does sense experience contribute to this knowledge?

For Further Reading

Robert R. Ammerman and Marcus G. Singer (eds.). *Belief, Knowledge, and Truth: Readings in the Theory of Knowledge.* New York: Scribners, 1970. A collection of traditional, recent, and important statements on all aspects of knowledge, including some encountered in our chapter (e.g., the *a priori*, intuition, etc.).

Bruce Aune. *Rationalism, Empiricism, and Pragmatism: An Introduction.* New York: Random House, 1970. Ch. 1. A discussion on "Descartes and Rationalism."

Roderick M. Chisholm. *Theory of Knowledge.* Englewood Cliffs, NJ: Prentice Hall, 1966. Ch. 5. A beginner's chapter on "The Truths of Reason," dealing briefly with the most important issues and problems concerning the rationalist view of knowledge.

Frederick Copleston. *A History of Philosophy.* Baltimore: Newman Press, 1946–1974. I, Ch. 19, and IV, Ch. 3. Authoritative accounts of Plato's and Descartes' theories of knowledge by a respected historian of philosophy.

Willis Doney (ed.). *Descartes: A Collection of Critical Essays.* Garden City, NY: Anchor books, 1967. An anthology of advanced essays, including discussions of epistemological issues in Descartes.

A. C. Ewing. *The Fundamental Questions of Philosophy.* New York: Collier Books, 1962. Ch. 2. A lucid chapter on "The 'A Priori' and the Empirical," which considers the nature and necessity of knowledge acquired apart from sense experience.

Anthony Kenny. *Descartes: A Study of His Philosophy*. New York: Random House, 1968. Ch. 8. A brief and clearly presented chapter on Descartes' conception of "Reason and Intuition."

Paul K. Moser (ed.). *Empirical Knowledge: Readings in Contemporary Epistemology*. Sowage, MD: Rowman & Littlefield, 1986. A student-oriented anthology of 15 essays by prominent philosophers on issues and trends in contemporary epistemology.

A. Radford. *Transformational Syntax: A Student's Guide to Chomsky's Extended Standard Theory*. Cambridge: Cambridge University Press, 1988. A useful entrance into the obtuse and, for the beginner, seemingly inaccessible world of Chomsky's linguistic-epistemological theory.

Geoffrey Sampson. "Noam Chomsky and Generative Grammar," in *Schools of Linguistics*. Stanford, CA: Stanford University Press, 1980. A fairly simple overview with some criticisms of Chomsky's intuitions.

Gregory Vlastos (ed.). *Plato: A Collection of Critical Essays*. Garden City, NY: Anchor Books, 1971. An anthology of advanced essays on Plato's metaphysics and epistemology, including a discussion on "Learning as Recollection."

*In addition, see the relevant articles ("Rationalism," "A Priori and A Posteriori," "Innate Ideas," etc.) in *The Encyclopedia of Philosophy*, ed. Paul Edwards. New York: Macmillan, 1967.

CHAPTER 7

The Way
of
Experience

W E TURN next to the second general view of the basis of knowledge: *empiricism*. It was said earlier that empiricism is the view which emphasizes experience as the source of knowledge. We must now explain more carefully what we mean here by "experience."

WHAT IS EMPIRICISM?

There are many different sorts of experience, such as mystical experience, moral experience, aesthetic experience, lonely experience, and wild experience. But here we mean *sense* experience, that is, perceptions derived from the five senses: sight, sound, touch, taste, and smell. When empiricists say that experience is the basis of our knowledge, they mean sense experience, and therefore that the five senses are the foundation of all our knowledge.

As with rationalism, empiricism comes with varying emphases and in varying degrees. But as a general definition we may say that empiricism is the view that all knowledge of reality is derived from sense experience. This may be livened up somewhat by the empiricist metaphor of the *tabula rasa*, or "blank tablet." It is a shorthand way of expressing the empiricist denial that any ideas or even intellectual structure is inscribed on the mind from birth—the mind is at birth a *blank tablet*, devoid even of watermarks. The implication is, of course, that anything "written" on the tablet is written by the five senses.

CLASSICAL EMPIRICISM: ARISTOTLE AND ST. THOMAS

We will consider several forms of empiricism, beginning with the classical empiricism of Aristotle and St. Thomas. When we call the empiricism of Aristotle and St. Thomas *classical* empiricism, we not only reflect its Greek roots (Aristotle) but we also distinguish it from various forms of empiricism in the modern period.

It will be recalled from Chapter 3 that Aristotle rejected Plato's theory of the Forms. This was because Plato had created a great gulf between the Forms and the particular things they were the Forms *of.* We saw that Aristotle countered that the Form must be *in* the thing of which it is the Form: The Form, or essence, of the table or chair must be right *there*, along with the matter of the table or chair, constituting it. He insisted on this for many reasons, and one of them was *epistemological:* How can the Form—that which is knowable about the table or chair—make the table or chair knowable if it is not *in* the table or chair? It is therefore no surprise that Aristotle, quite unlike Plato, believed that knowledge comes through our sense experience of particular things in the world—like tables or chairs. And he was one of the first to employ the empiricist comparison of the mind to a *tabula rasa*, or blank tablet.

Let us close in on this a bit more. Like Plato, Aristotle believed that knowledge necessarily involves *general* or *universal ideas*—man, dog, table, chair, etc. Think about this. Where would thinking, speaking, and knowing be without such concepts? Is it possible to think or say or know *anything* apart from such ideas? "Socrates is a man." "In fourteen hundred and ninety-two Columbus sailed the ocean blue." "This table is rectangular." Are not general concepts like man, ocean, table, rectangularity, and

"[The Platonic Forms] help in no wise . . . towards the knowledge of the other things (for they are not even the substance of these, else they would have been in them), or towards their being, if they are not *in* the particulars which share in them; though if they were they might be thought to be causes, as white causes whiteness in a white object by entering into its composition."

—Aristotle

so on, necessary for thinking, speaking, and knowing? Now where do these ideas come from? *Unlike* Plato, Aristotle answered that they come from our *experience* of *particular* men, tables, chairs, dogs, oceans, etc.

The problem for such an approach is, of course, the same problem that bothered Plato: How do we arrive at *universal* ideas on the basis of our limited and fluctuating experience of *particular* things?

Aristotle's answer is that the universal and necessary elements of knowledge—the foundations of all subsequent reasoning—are built up in the mind through *induction*. This means, for Aristotle, that a wider and wider generalization is derived from repeated experiences of particular things until a *general* or *universal* concept is established in the mind: From the experience of the particular man Callias, the man Socrates, the man James, the man Tad, the man Bill . . . the intellect derives the general or universal idea of *man*, that is, *man as such*. From the experience of the particular dog Fido, the dog Lassie, the dog Rover, the dog Flip . . . the intellect derives the universal idea *dog*. And the universal ideas—man, dog, and innumerable other concepts derived from experience in the same manner—become the tools and building blocks of all reasoning. They then make it possible to say and know, "Socrates is a man," "In fourteen hundred and ninety-two Columbus sailed the ocean blue," etc.

Aristotle likens the process by which the universal concepts are established in the intellect to a company of soldiers retreating in disarray until a first soldier halts and makes a stand, then a second, then a third, and finally the whole company is put in order and established:

We conclude that these states of knowledge are neither innate in a determinate form, nor developed from other higher states of knowledge, but from sense-perception. It is like a rout in battle stopped by first one man making a stand and then another, until the original formation has been restored. The soul is so constituted as to be capable of this process.

. . . When one of a number of logically indiscriminable particulars has made a stand, the earliest universal is present in the soul: for though the act of sense-perception is of the particular, its content is universal—is man, for example, not the man Callias. A fresh stand is made among these rudimentary universals, and the process does not cease until the indivisible concepts, the true universals, are established: e.g. such and such a species of animals is a step towards the genus animal, which by the same process is a step towards a further generalization.

Thus it is clear that we must get to know the primary premises by induction; for the method by which even sense-perception implants the universal is inductive.[1]

This conception of the origin of knowledge was passed from Aristotle to St. Thomas, the dominant Christian philosopher of the thirteenth century. It may be helpful to see how St. Thomas expressed the matter.

We saw that Aristotle taught that the mind is a blank tablet waiting to be written upon by the senses. St. Thomas expresses the same empiricist idea with the words (everything sounds more profound in Latin) *Nihil in intellectu quod prius non fuerit in sensu*, "Nothing is in the intellect which was not first in the senses." For St. Thomas, as for Aristotle, the essences of things are locked inside the particular things of which they are the essences—individual human beings, animals, tables, chairs, dogs, and cats. The intellect, however, is able to liberate the essence in particular things and thus to "see" the universal idea of their common, essential nature: human, animal, table, chair, dog, and cat.

The intellectual faculty by which the essential or formal or universal element of particular things is unlocked and "seen" by the mind is called by St. Thomas *abstraction*. "To abstract" means to remove or separate something from something else. In this epistemological context, what is being abstracted is a common nature, and that from which it is being abstracted are the particular and varying instances of it. In abstracting the universal

---

[1]Aristotle, *Posterior Analytics*; 100a–100b, tr. G. R. G. Mure, in *Basic Works of Aristotle*, ed. Richard McKeon (New York: Random House, 1941).

human being from Callias, Socrates, James, Sue, Bill, and Sally, their individual and peculiar features are left behind (Socrates is bald and snub-nosed; James is tall, blue-eyed, and hairy; Bill has a nose shaped like an eagle's beak and is short; etc.) and their *common* and *essential* nature is grasped: *human being*.

It remains to stress that for both Aristotle and St. Thomas we can say, think, or know anything only because of universal ideas derived from experience. It is only by such ideas and truths as man, animal, equality, red, every event is caused, that the intellect can be guided amidst the particularities, relativities, deceptions, and fluctuations of the sensible world. We begin, then, with the particular things we encounter in the sensible world. From these we derive universal concepts and principles. With our universal concepts and principles we are enabled to return to the sensible world and speak of it, think about it, and know it: "Socrates is a human being." These three stages of knowledge according to Aristotle and St. Thomas may be represented more vividly:

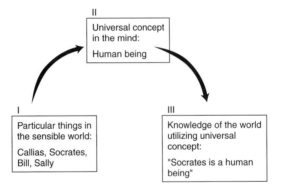

The following, from St. Thomas' *Summa Theologiae*, is brief but not easy. Try to see in it some of the above ideas at work, especially the movement: singular → universal → proposition. (In this quotation, "intelligible species" means the essence of a thing, and "phantasms" are the mental images of things.)

> Our intellect cannot know the singular in material things directly and primarily. The reason for this is that the principle of singularity in material things is individual matter; whereas our intellect understands by abstracting the intelligible species from such matter. Now what is abstracted from individual matter is universal. Hence our

"What the mind thinks must be in it just as characters may be said to be on a writing-tablet on which as yet nothing actually stands written."
—Aristotle

"Nothing is in the intellect which was not first in the senses."
—St. Thomas

intellect knows directly only universals. But indirectly, however, and as it were by a kind of reflexion, it can know the singular, because . . . even after abstracting the intelligible species, the intellect, in order to understand actually, needs to turn to the phantasms in which it understands the species. . . . Therefore it understands the universal directly through the intelligible species, and indirectly the singular represented by the phantasm. And thus it forms the proposition, "Socrates is a man."[2]

MODERN EMPIRICISM: LOCKE

It was the English philosopher John Locke (1632–1704) who laid the foundations of *modern* empiricism in his monumental *Essay Concerning Human Understanding*, published in 1690. Like Descartes, Locke was distressed over the muddles and uncertainties in metaphysics, theology, and moral philosophy. But unlike Descartes, who took the rationalistic method of geometry as his epistemological model, Locke took as his model the *experimental* methods of the new sciences, such as physics, astronomy, and medicine.

Locke begins on a negative note: a lengthy indictment of any theory of innate ideas. According to Locke, few philosophical theories are more firmly entrenched than the theory of innate ideas, which he characterizes as the belief that "there are in the understanding certain *innate principles;* some primary notions, *koinai ennoiai* [Greek: universal ideas], characters, as it were stamped upon the mind of man, which the soul receives in its very first

---

[2]St. Thomas, *Summa Theologiae*, Pt. I, Qu. 86, Art. I, in *Basic Writings of Saint Thomas Aquinas*, ed. Anton C. Pegis (New York: Random House, 1945), I.

being, and brings into the world with it."[3] He rejects the innateness of both "speculative" and "practical" principles, another way of saying "truths pertaining to reality and morality." In a word, Locke refutes the theory of innate ideas by charging that the arguments cited in support of it do not actually prove it, and that those who cite them do not pay sufficient attention to an altogether different and simpler explanation of the source of our ideas.

In the following excerpt he focuses on speculative principles, showing how innateness cannot be claimed even for the most certain of these, the Law of Identity ("What is, is") and the Law of Non-Contradiction ("It is impossible for the same thing to be, and not to be"): Such principles are neither universally agreed to, nor are they known by children, nor are they the products of reason. As with much of the quoted matter in this book, the following passages from Locke are classic statements and worthy of thoughtful scrutiny.

General Assent the Great Argument

There is nothing more commonly taken for granted, than that there are certain principles, both *speculative* and *practical* (for they speak of both), universally agreed upon by all mankind; which therefore, they argue, must needs be the constant impressions which the souls of men receive in their first beings, and which they bring into the world with them, as necessarily and really as they do any of their inherent faculties.

Universal Consent Proves Nothing Innate

This argument, drawn from universal consent, has this misfortune in it, that if it were true in matter of fact, that there were certain truths wherein all mankind agreed, it would not prove them innate, if there can be any other way shown, how men may come to that universal agreement in the things they do consent in; which I presume may be done.

"What Is, Is," and "It Is Impossible for the Same Thing to Be, and Not to Be," Not Universally Assented to

But, which is worse, this argument of universal consent, which is made use of to prove innate principles, seems to me a demonstration that there are none such; because there are none to which all mankind give an universal assent. I shall begin with the speculative,

---

[3]John Locke, *An Essay Concerning Human Understanding*, ed. A. S. Pringle-Pattison (London: Oxford University Press, 1924), I, 2, 1.

an instance in those magnified principles of demonstration: "Whatsoever is, is," and "It is impossible for the same thing to be, and not to be," which, of all others, I think, have the most allowed title to innate. These have so settled a reputation of maxims universally received, that it will, no doubt, be thought strange if any one should seem to question it. But yet I take liberty to say, that these propositions are so far from having an universal assent, that there are a great part of mankind to whom they are not so much as known.

NOT ON THE MIND, NATURALLY IMPRINTED, BECAUSE NOT KNOWN TO CHILDREN, IDIOTS, ETC.

For, first, it is evident, that all children and idiots have not the least apprehension or thought of them: and the want of that is enough to destroy that universal assent, which must needs be the necessary concomitant of all innate truths: it seeming to me near a contradiction to say, that there are truths imprinted on the soul which it perceives or understands not; imprinting, if it signify anything, being nothing else but the making certain truths to be perceived. No proposition can be said to be in the mind which it never yet knew, which it was never yet conscious of. . . . If truths can be imprinted on the understanding without being perceived, I can see no difference there can be between any truths the mind is capable of knowing in respect of their original: they must all be innate, or all adventitious; in vain shall a man go about to distinguish them. He therefore that talks of innate notions in the understanding, cannot (if he intend thereby any distinct sort of truths) mean such truths to be in the understanding as it never perceived, and is yet wholly ignorant of. For if these words "to be in the understanding" have any propriety, they signify to be understood. If therefore these two propositions: "Whatsoever is, is," and "It is impossible for the same thing to be, and not to be," are by nature imprinted, children cannot be ignorant of them; infants, and all that have souls, must necessarily have them in their understandings, know the truth of them, and assent to it.

THAT MEN KNOW THEM WHEN THEY COME TO THE USE OF REASON, ANSWERED

To avoid this, it is usually answered, that all men know and *assent* to them, *when they come to the use of reason*, and this is enough to prove them innate. To apply this answer with any tolerable sense to our present purpose, it must signify one of these two things; either, that as soon as men come to the use of reason, these supposed native in-scriptions come to be known and observed by them; or else, that the use and exercise of men's reasons assists them in the discovery of these principles, and certainly makes them known to them.

If Reason Discovered Them, That Would Not Prove Them Innate

If they mean that by the *use of reason* men may discover these princi-ples, and that this is sufficient to prove them innate, their way of ar-guing will stand thus: viz. That whatever truths reason can certainly discover to us, and make us firmly assent to, those are all naturally imprinted on the mind; and by this means there will be no difference between the maxims of the mathematicians and theorems they de-duce from them: all must be equally allowed innate, they being all discoveries made by the use of reason, and truths that a rational crea-ture may certainly come to know, if he apply his thoughts rightly that way.

It Is False That Reason Discovered Them

But how can these men think the use of reason necessary to discover principles that are supposed innate, when reason (if we may believe them) is nothing else but the faculty of deducing unknown truths from principles or propositions that are already known? That cer-tainly can never be thought innate which we have need of reason to discover, unless, as I have said, we will have all the certain truths that reason ever teaches us, to be innate. We may as well think the use of reason necessary to make our eyes discover visible objects, as that there should be need of reason, or the exercise thereof, to make the understanding see what is originally engraven in it. And I think those who give this answer will not be forward to affirm, that the knowledge of this maxim, "That it is impossible for the same thing to be, and not to be," is a deduction of our reason. For this would be to destroy that bounty of nature they seem so fond of, whilst they make the knowledge of those principles to depend on the labour of our thoughts. For all reasoning is search and casting about, and requires pains and application. And how can it with any tolerable sense be supposed, that what was imprinted by nature, as the foundation and guide of our reason, should need the use of reason to discover it?

Those who will take the pains to reflect with a little attention on the operations of the understanding, will find that this ready assent of the mind to some truths, depends not either on native inscription, or the use of reason, but on a faculty of the mind quite distinct from both of them, as we shall see hereafter.[4]

On the positive side, Locke is as explicit as one could hope for as to the actual origin of the ideas which undeniably exist in our minds: *experience*. But the next step is a little more subtle. For this experience takes two forms. First, there is what we might call the "external" experience by which objects in the external world, outside our minds, enter our minds through *sensation*, for example, hot, cold, red, yellow, hard, soft, sweet, and bitter. Second, there is the "internal" experience we have of the operations of our minds, or *reflection*, for example, thinking, willing, believing, doubting, affirming, denying, and comparing. Both of these are kinds of experience—reflection on what is going on inside no less than sensation of what is going on outside—and they are the two and only two means by which ideas become inscribed on the blank tablets of our minds. As just as the absence of ideas in infants is evidence against any doctrine of innate ideas, so the gradual development of ideas in children, corresponding to the development of their experience, is evidence for the empiricist doctrine that ideas originate in experience.

IDEA IS THE OBJECT OF THINKING

Every man being conscious to himself that he thinks, and that which his mind is applied about whilst thinking being the ideas that are there, it is past doubt that men have in their minds several ideas, such as are those expressed by the words, "whiteness, hardness, sweetness, thinking, motion, man, elephant, army, drunkenness," and others. It is in the first place then to be enquired. How he comes by them? I know it is a received doctrine, that men have native ideas and original characters stamped upon their minds in their very first being. This opinion I have at large examined already; and, I suppose, what I have said in the foregoing . . . will be much more easily admitted, when I have shown whence the understanding may get all the ideas it has, and by what ways and degrees they may come into the mind; for which I shall appeal to every one's own observation and experience.

---

[4]Ibid., I, pp. 2, 2–11.

ALL IDEAS COME FROM SENSATION OR REFLECTION

Let us then suppose the mind to be, as we say, white paper, void of all characters, without any ideas; how comes it to be furnished? Whence comes it by that vast store, which the busy and boundless fancy of man has painted on it with an almost endless variety? Whence has it all the materials of reason and knowledge? To this I answer, in one word, from EXPERIENCE; in that all our knowledge is founded, and from that it ultimately derives itself. Our observation, employed either about external sensible objects, or about the internal operations of our minds, perceived and reflected on by ourselves, is that which supplies our understandings with all the materials of thinking. These two are the fountains of knowledge, from whence all the ideas we have, or can naturally have, do spring.

THE OBJECTS OF SENSATION ONE SOURCE OF IDEAS

First, our senses, conversant about particular sensible objects, do convey into the mind several distinct perceptions of things, according to those various ways wherein those objects do affect them; and thus we come by those *ideas* we have of yellow, white, heat, cold, soft, hard, bitter, sweet, and all those which we call sensible qualities; which when I say the senses convey into the mind, I mean, they from external objects convey into the mind what produces there those perceptions. This great source of most of the ideas we have, depending wholly upon the senses, and derived by them to the understanding, I call, SENSATION.

THE OPERATIONS OF OUR MINDS THE OTHER SOURCE OF THEM

Secondly, the other fountain, from which experience furnisheth the understanding with ideas, is the perception of the operations of our minds within us, as it is employed about the ideas it has got; which operations when the soul comes to reflect on and consider, do furnish the understanding with another set of ideas which could not be had from things without: and such are perception, thinking, doubting, believing, reasoning, knowing, willing, and all the different actings of our minds; which we being conscious of, and observing in ourselves, do from these receive into our understanding as distinct ideas, as we do from bodies affecting our senses. This source of ideas every man has wholly in himself: and though it be not sense, as having nothing to do with external objects, yet it is very like it, and might properly enough be called internal sense. But as I call the other Sensation, so I call this REFLECTION, the ideas it affords being such only as the mind gets by reflecting on its own operations within itself. By Reflection, then, in the following part of this discourse, I would be understood to mean that notice which the mind takes of its own operations, and the manner of them, by reason whereof there comes to be ideas of these operations in the understanding. These two, I say, viz., external material things as the objects of Sensation, and the operations of our own minds within as the objects of Reflection, are, to me, the only originals from whence all our ideas take their beginnings. The term *operations* here, I use in a large sense, as comprehending not barely the actions of the mind about its ideas, but some sort of passions arising sometimes from them, such as the satisfaction or uneasiness arising from any thought.

ALL OUR IDEAS ARE OF THE ONE OR THE OTHER OF THESE

The understanding seems to me not to have the least glimmering of any ideas which it doth not receive from one of these two. *External objects* furnish the mind with the ideas of sensible qualities, which are all those different perceptions they produce in us; and *the mind* furnishes the understanding with ideas of its own operations. These, when we have taken a full survey of them, and their several modes, combinations, and relations, we shall find to contain all our whole stock of ideas; and that we have nothing in our minds which did not come in one of these two ways. Let any one examine his own thoughts, and thoroughly search into his understanding, and then let him tell me, whether all the original ideas he has there, are any other than of the objects of his senses, or of the operations of his mind considered as objects of his reflection; and how great a mass of knowledge soever he imagines to be lodged there, he will, upon taking a strict view, see that he has not any idea in his mind but what one of these two have imprinted, though perhaps with infinite variety compounded and enlarged by the understanding, as we shall see hereafter.

OBSERVABLE IN CHILDREN

He that attentively considers the state of a child at his first coming into the world, will have little reason to think him stored with plenty of ideas that are to be the matter of his future knowledge. It is by

degrees he comes to be furnished with them: and though the ideas of
obvious and familiar qualities imprint themselves before the memory
begins to keep a register of time and order, yet it is often so late before some unusual qualities come in the way, that there are few men
that cannot recollect the beginning of their acquaintance with them:
and if it were worth while, no doubt a child might be so ordered as
to have but a very few even of the ordinary ideas till he were grown
up to a man. But all that are born into the world being surrounded
with bodies that perpetually and diversely affect them, variety of
ideas, whether care be taken about it or no, are imprinted on the
minds of children. Light and colours are busy and at hand everywhere when the eye is but open; sounds and some tangible qualities
fail not to solicit their proper senses, and force an entrance to the
mind; but yet I think it will be granted easily, that if a child were
kept in a place where he never saw any other but black and white till
he were a man, he would have no more ideas of scarlet or green,
than he that from his childhood never tasted an oyster or a pineapple
has of those particular relishes.[5]

So far we have considered only the passive side of the mind, wherein it
receives what Locke will now call the *simple* ideas contributed by sensation and reflection. It also has an active side, whereby it constructs *complex* ideas out of the simple ones, by means of combining, comparing, and
abstracting.

UNCOMPOUNDED APPEARANCES

The better to understand the nature, manner, and extent of our
knowledge, one thing is carefully to be observed concerning the
ideas we have; and that is, that some of them are *simple*, and some
complex.

Though the qualities that affect our senses are, in the things themselves, so united and blended that there is no separation, no distance
between them; yet it is plain the ideas they produce in the mind enter
by the senses simple and unmixed. For though the sight and touch
often take in from the same object at the same time different ideas; as
a man sees at once motion and colour, the hand feels softness and

---

[5]Ibid., II, pp. 1–6.

warmth in the same piece of wax; yet the simple ideas thus united in the same subject are as perfectly distinct as those that come in by different senses. The coldness and hardness which a man feels in a piece of ice being as distinct ideas in the mind as the smell and whiteness of a lily, or as the taste of sugar and smell of a rose; and there is nothing can be plainer to a man than the clear and distinct perception he has of those simple ideas; which, being each in itself uncompounded, contains in it nothing but one uniform appearance or conception in the mind, and is not distinguishable into different ideas.

The Mind Can neither Make nor Destroy Them

These simple ideas, the materials of all our knowledge, are suggested and furnished to the mind only by those two ways above mentioned, viz., sensation and reflection. When the understanding is once stored with these simple ideas, it has the power to repeat, compare, and unite them, even to an almost infinite variety, and so can make at pleasure new complex ideas. But it is not in the power of the most exalted wit or enlarged understanding, by any quickness or variety of thought, to invent or frame one new simple idea in the mind, not taken in by the ways before mentioned; nor can any force of the understanding destroy those that are there. The dominion of man in this little world of his own understanding, being much-what the same as it is in the great world of visible things, wherein his power, however managed by art and skill, reaches no farther than to compound and divide the materials that are made to his hand, but can do nothing towards the making the least particle of new matter, or destroying one atom of what is already in being. The same inability will every one find in himself, who shall go about to fashion in his understanding any simple idea not received in by his senses from external objects, or by reflection from the operations of his own mind about them. I would have any one try to fancy any taste which had never affected his palate, or frame the idea of a scent he had never smelt: and when he can do this, I will also conclude, that a blind man hath ideas of colours, and a deaf man true distinct notions of sound. . . .

[Complex Ideas] Made by the Mind Out of Simple Ones

We have hitherto considered those ideas, in the reception whereof the mind is only passive, which are those simple ones received from sensation and reflection before mentioned, whereof the mind cannot make one to itself, nor have any idea which does not wholly consist of them. [But as the mind is wholly passive in the reception of all its simple ideas, so it exerts several acts of its own, whereby out of its simple ideas, as the materials and foundations of the rest, the others are framed. The acts of the mind wherein it exerts its power over its simple ideas are chiefly these three: (1) Combining several simple ideas into one compound one; and thus all complex ideas are made. (2) The second is bringing two ideas, whether simple or complex, together, and setting them by one another, so as to take a view of them at once, without uniting them into one; by which it gets all its ideas of relations. (3) The third is separating them from all other ideas that accompany them in their real existence; this is called abstraction: and thus all its general ideas are made. This shows man's power and its way of operation to be much-what the same in the material and intellectual world. For, the materials in both being such as he has no power over, either to make or destroy, all that man can do is either to unite them together, or to set them by one another, or wholly separate them. I shall here begin with the first of these in the consideration of complex ideas, and come to the other two in their due places.] As simple ideas are observed to exist in several combinations united together, so the mind has a power to consider several of them united together as one idea; and that not only as they are united in external objects, but as itself has joined them. Ideas thus made up of several simple ones put together I call *complex;* such as are beauty, gratitude, a man, an army, the universe; which, though complicated of various simple ideas or complex ideas made up of simple ones, yet are, when the mind pleases, considered each by itself as one entire thing, and signified by one name.

MADE VOLUNTARILY

In this faculty of repeating and joining together its ideas, the mind has great power in varying and multiplying the objects of its thoughts infinitely beyond what sensation or reflection furnished it with: but all this still confined to those simple ideas which it received from those two sources, and which are the ultimate materials of all its compositions. For simple ideas are all from things themselves; and of these the mind can have no more nor other than what are suggested to it. It can have no other ideas of sensible qualities than what come from without by the senses, nor any ideas of other kind of operations of thinking substance than what it finds in itself: but when it has once got these simple ideas, it is not confined barely to observation, and what offers itself from without; it can, by its own power, put together those ideas it has and make new complex ones which it never received so united.[6]

The essential points in all of this may be summarized visually:

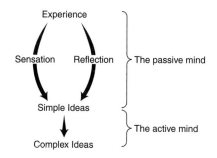

Locke's theory of knowledge gets much more complicated, but this will suffice to show its empirical character and how it all gets off the ground.

Yet, it is necessary to mention further features of Locke's theory. Perhaps more than anyone else, Locke emphasized what is sometimes called *epistemological dualism.* This is the view that there are two factors involved in knowing: the mind, which does the knowing, and its ideas, which are known. That this is Locke's view is clear from repeated statements such as, ". . . the mind, in all its thoughts and reasonings, hath no other immediate object but its own ideas. . . ."[7] But, of course, there is a third factor, namely, the object in the external world that is known by means of ideas. That Locke blithely believed that our ideas *represent* those objects, and therefore really inform us about the external world, is clear from statements such as:

. . . simple ideas are not fictions of our fancies, but the natural and regular productions of things without us, really operating upon us; and so carry with them all the conformity which is intended, or

---

[6]Ibid., II, pp. 2, 1–2, II, pp. 12, 1–2.
[7]Ibid., IV, 1, p. 1.

which our state requires; for they represent to us things under those appearances which they are fitted to produce in us: whereby we are enabled to distinguish the sorts of particular substances, to discern the states they are in, and so to take them for our necessities, and apply them to our uses. And this conformity between our simple ideas and the existence of things is sufficient for real knowledge.[8]

Thus we have also what is sometimes called *representative perception*, the theory that our ideas correspond to and faithfully represent objects in the external world.

So far so good. The trouble arises when we ask about this relation, or *correspondence*, of the perceived idea to anything "out there" in the external world. Any representative theory of knowledge, according to which the objects of the external world are represented to us by our ideas, immediately falls prey to the *egocentric predicament*, our hopeless inability to get outside our own minds and ideas. If all we can directly know is our own ideas (epistemological dualism), then how could we ever know whether our ideas correspond to anything, or even approximate anything, "out there" (representative theory of ideas)? Obviously, there is no standpoint from which we could look at an object in the external world and then look at our ideas in our minds, and announce: "Ah! They correspond. Our ideas really do represent things in the external world!" For in Locke's view, *all* we can perceive are *our own ideas*. That there *is* an external world we know from the passivity of our perceptions—our ideas simply *confront* us independently of our will. The question is: How do we know what it is *like?* Does this general theory end in a dismal skepticism about the things in the external world? How is the gap between the external world and our ideas of it to be overcome? This is a serious problem for anyone who holds both that all we can know is our own ideas and that our ideas represent the external world.

RADICAL EMPIRICISM: HUME

The forms of empiricism which we have looked at so far might be called "mild" forms. In spite of their emphasis on sense experience, both Aristotle and St. Thomas believed that from experience we can nonetheless derive

---

[8]Ibid., IV, 4, p. 4.

knowledge which is certain and universal, as with the principle of causality (every event must have a cause), and Locke believed this also and, similar to Descartes, that we can have a direct intuition of our own minds. Not so mild is the empiricism of the Scottish philosopher David Hume (1711–1776). It is, in fact, appropriately called *radical* empiricism.

It is important to follow the road from Locke to Berkeley to Hume: the three "British empiricists." Locke believed, as did Descartes, in two basic substances, mind and matter, though he confesses that while we have to believe in matter as something "out there" upholding the sensible qualities of things, we really cannot know what it is in itself; it is, Locke said, "something, I know not what." George Berkeley (1685–1753) followed Locke, but with his thoroughgoing idealist philosophy denied utterly the existence of matter, leaving only mind and its ideas. It remained for Hume to bring these ideas full circle to a kind of epistemological dead-end.

Hume's understanding of how knowledge arises is similar to Locke's, but the terminology is somewhat different. All we have are *perceptions*. These, however, are to be divided between *impressions*, which are vivid or lively sensations, or the immediate data of experience, and *ideas*, which are sort of pale copies of impressions, and which provide the material for thinking. Hume goes on to distinguish between simple and complex perceptions (both impressions and ideas), but insists in any case on the priority of impressions over ideas: First, we have sensations, and then, second, ideas which are based on these sensations. The crucial point is that we have no ideas unless they are derived from impressions, and this brings us to the crunch. For in the derivation of all our ideas from sense data, Hume was much more rigorous or consistent or *radical* than Locke. This radicalism shows up, first, in Hume's treatment of the idea of *substance*, both material substance in the external world and mental substance in the internal world.

THE EGOCENTRIC PREDICAMENT

Some philosophers claim that all we can know is our own ideas. But on this view we are trapped in the world of our own egos (or selves) and ideas. We could never get outside ourselves to verify whether ideas correspond to anything in the external world.

David Hume, who carried British
empiricism to its skeptical conclusion.

It is natural to *believe* that there is Something, some mental substance, which underlies our intellectual activities: How can there be thinking, etc., without something that *does* the thinking? Likewise, it is natural to *believe* that there is Something, some material substance, which underlies the sensible qualities in the external world: How can there be qualities without something that is *qualified?* But a "natural belief," as Hume calls it, for all its practical importance, is something very different from rational knowledge based on experience. Since we have no impressions whatsoever of substance, either external material substance or internal mental substance, we have no rational grounds at all for talk about matter or mind! As Hume says, the dissolution of the one paves the way for the dissolution of the other. From the *Treatise of Human Nature:*

> Philosophers begin to be reconcil'd to the principle, *that we have no idea of external substance, distinct from the ideas of particular qualities.* This must pave the way for a like principle with regard to the mind, *that we have no notion of it, distinct from the particular perceptions.* . . .

There are some philosophers, who imagine we are every moment intimately conscious of what we call our SELF; that we feel its existence and its continuance in existence; and are certain, beyond the evidence of a demonstration, both of its perfect identity and simplicity. The strongest sensation, the most violent passion, say they, instead of distracting us from this view, only fix it the more intensely, and make us consider their influence on *self* either by their pain or pleasure. To attempt a farther proof of this were to weaken its evidence; since no proof can be deriv'd from any fact, of which we are so intimately conscious; nor is there any thing, of which we can be certain, if we doubt of this.

Unluckily all these positive assertions are contrary to that very experience, which is pleaded for them, nor have we any idea of *self*, after the manner it is here explain'd. For from what impression cou'd this idea be deriv'd? This question 'tis impossible to answer without a manifest contradiction and absurdity; and yet 'tis a question, which must necessarily be answer'd, if we wou'd have the idea of self pass for clear and intelligible. It must be some one impression, that gives rise to every real idea. But self or person is not any one impression, but that to which our several impressions and ideas are suppos'd to have a reference. If any impression gives rise to the idea of self, that impression must continue invariably the same, thro' the whole course of our lives; since self is suppos'd to exist after that manner. But there is no impression constant and invariable. Pain and pleasure, grief and joy, passions and sensations succeed each other, and never all exist at the same time. It cannot, therefore, be from any of these impressions, or from any other, that the idea of self is deriv'd; and consequently there is no such idea.

Hume's "radical" empiricism is so-called because he applied the empiricist criterion of knowledge rigorously, consistently, and *exclusively*. Unlike previous empiricists, he allowed no rationalistic cracks or back doors: Our knowledge can extend absolutely no further than what is actually disclosed in sense experience.

But farther, what must become of all our particular perceptions upon this hypothesis? All these are different, and distinguishable, and separable from each other, and may be separately consider'd, and may exist separately, and have no need of any thing to support their existence. After what manner, therefore, do they belong to self; and how are they connected with it? For my part, when I enter most intimately into what I call *myself*, I always stumble on some particular perception or other, of heat or cold, light or shade, love or hatred, pain or pleasure. I never can catch *myself* at any time without a perception, and never can observe any thing but the perception. When my perceptions are remov'd for any time, as by sound sleep; so long am I insensible of *myself*, and may truly be said not to exist. And were all my perceptions remov'd by death, and cou'd I neither think, nor feel, nor see, nor love, nor hate after the dissolution of my body, I shou'd be entirely annihilated, nor do I conceive what is farther requisite to make me a perfect non-entity. If any one upon serious and unprejudic'd reflexion, thinks he has a different notion of *himself*, I must confess I can reason no longer with him. All I can allow him is, that he may be in the right as well as I, and that we are essentially different in this particular. He may, perhaps, perceive something simple and continu'd, which he calls *himself*; tho' I am certain there is no such principle in me.

But setting aside some metaphysicians of this kind, I may venture to affirm of the rest of mankind, that they are nothing but a bundle or collection of different perceptions, which succeed each other with an inconceivable rapidity, and are in a perpetual flux and movement. Our eyes cannot turn in their sockets without varying our perceptions. Our thought is still more variable than our sight; and all our other senses and faculties contribute to this change; nor is there any single power of the soul, which remains unalterably the same, perhaps for one moment. The mind is a kind of theatre, where several perceptions successively make their appearance; pass, re-pass, glide away, and mingle in an infinite variety of postures and situations. There is properly no *simplicity* in it at one time, nor *identity* in different; whatever natural propension we may have to imagine that simplicity and identity. The comparison of the theatre must not mislead us. They are the successive perceptions only, that constitute the mind; nor have we the most distant notion of the place, where these scenes are represented, or of the materials, of which it is compos'd.[9]

What am I? I look within, in search of some enduring, stable reality—a self, an ego, an "I." But all I can come up with is a passing parade of perceptions. We have come a long way from Descartes' introspective intuition of mind, the mental substance!

But Hume is not through. The implications of his relentless and radical empiricism touch every aspect of philosophy. A second important example is the context of *causality*. Again, do we not have a natural belief in a causal connection that binds things together in our experience? Is it not a universal and certain principle that every event must have a cause? Hume answers again: Natural belief, Yes; rational knowledge, No. Look at your experience once more. What do you actually *perceive?* What are your *impressions?* Is it true that in a supposed causal relation, such as A causing B, we have a perception of A coming before B, and we have a perception of A standing next to B (or next to something which stands next to B), but none of this is sufficient to explain a real causal connection between A and B: A could be before B, and be next to B, but still not be the cause of B. What is required, in addition to temporal succession and spatial proximity, is a *necessary connection*. And *that we don't* perceive. It is a metaphysical figment without any rational justification whatsoever.

The idea, then, of causation must be deriv'd from some *relation* among objects; and that relation we must now endeavor to discover. I find in the first place, that whatever objects are consider'd as causes or effects, are *contiguous;* and that nothing can operate in a time or place, which is ever so little remov'd from those of its existence. Tho' distant objects may sometimes seem productive of each other, they are commonly found upon examination to be link'd by a chain of causes, which are contiguous among themselves, and to the distant objects; and when in any particular instance we cannot discover this connexion, we still presume it to exist. We may therefore consider the relation of CONTIGUITY as essential to that of causation; at least may suppose it such, according to the general opinion, till we

---

[9]David Hume, *A Treatise of Human Nature*, ed. L. A. Selby-Bigge (London: Oxford University Press, 1888), pp. 251–53, 635.

can find a more proper occasion to clear up this matter, by examining what objects are or are not susceptible of juxtaposition and conjunction.

The second relation I shall observe as essential to causes and effects, is not so universally acknowledg'd, but is liable to some controversy. "Tis that of PRIORITY of time in the cause before the effect. Some pretend that 'tis not absolutely necessary a cause shou'd precede its effect; but that any object or action, in the very first moment of its existence, may exert its productive quality, and give rise to another object or action, perfectly co-temporary with itself. But beside that experience in most instances seems to contradict his opinion, we may establish the relation of priority by a kind of inference or reasoning. 'Tis an establish'd maxim both in natural and moral philosophy, that an object, which exists for any time in its full perfection without producing another, is not its sole cause; but is assisted by some other principle, which pushes it from its state of inactivity, and makes it exert that energy, of which it was secretly possessed. Now if any cause may be perfectly co-temporary with its effect, 'tis certain, according to this maxim, that they must all of them be so; since any one of them, which retards its operation for a single moment, exerts not itself at that very individual time, in which it might have operated; and therefore is no proper cause. The consequence of this wou'd be no less than the destruction of that succession of causes, which we observe in the world; and indeed, the utter annihilation of time. For if one cause were co-temporary with its effect, and this effect with its effect, and so on, 'tis plain there wou'd be no such thing as succession, and all objects must be coexistent.

If this argument appear satisfactory, 'tis well. If not, I beg the reader to allow me the same liberty, which I have us'd in the preceding case, of supposing it such. For he shall find, that the affair is of no great importance.

Having thus discover'd or suppos'd the two relations of *contiguity* and *succession* to be essential to causes and effects, I find I am stopt short, and can proceed no farther in considering any single instance of cause and effect. Motion in one body is regarded upon impulse as the cause of motion in another. When we consider these objects with the utmost attention, we find only that the one body approaches the other; and that the motion of it precedes that of the other, but without any sensible interval. 'Tis in vain to rack ourselves with *farther* thought and reflexion upon this subject. We can go no *farther* in considering this particular instance.

Shou'd any one leave this instance, and pretend to define a cause, by saying it is something productive of another, 'tis evident he wou'd say nothing. For what does he mean by *production?* Can he give any definition of it, that will not be the same with that of causation? If he can; I desire it may be produc'd. If he cannot; he here runs in a circle, and gives a synonimous term instead of a definition.

Shall we then rest contented with these two relations of contiguity and succession, as affording a complete idea of causation? By no means. An object may be contiguous and prior to another, without being consider'd as its cause. There is a NECESSARY CONNEXION to be taken into consideration; and that relation is of much greater importance, than any of the two above-mention'd.

Here again I turn the object on all sides, in order to discover the nature of this necessary connexion, and find the impression, or impressions, from which its idea may be deriv'd. When I cast my eye on the *known qualities* of objects, I immediately discover that the relation of cause and effect depends not in the least on *them*. When I consider their *relations*, I can find none but those of contiguity and succession; which I have already regarded as imperfect and unsatisfactory.[10]

Hume's position is appropriately called *phenomenalism*. This is the view that all we can actually know is the phenomena or appearances (*phenomenon* means, literally, "an appearance") that are presented to us in our perceptions. For the time-honored view that substance (both material and mental) is a metaphysical entity and that causality is a metaphysical connection, the phenomenalist substitutes the view that they are no more than bundles of perceptions: colors, sounds, pains, pleasures, location, succession, and the like. These two pillars of traditional philosophizing now lay in dust before the chisel of Hume's phenomenalism.

If you find yourself thinking of Hume as a *skeptic*, you are right. Specifically, his is the sort of skepticism which denies the knowledge of

---

[10] Ibid., pp. 75–77 (slightly edited).

metaphysical principles and relations is possible, "philosophical skepticism." Perhaps the best way of summarizing Hume's antimetaphysical skepticism is by means of his own derivation of all possible knowledge from two, and only two, sources: "relations of ideas" and "matters of fact." The following two paragraphs from Hume's *Enquiry Concerning Human Understanding* should be studied until the distinction is appreciated:

> All the objects of human reason or enquiry may naturally be divided into two kinds, to wit, *Relations of Ideas*, and *Matters of Fact*. Of the first kind are the sciences of Geometry, Algebra, and Arithmetic; and in short, every affirmation which is either intuitively or demonstratively certain. *That the square of the hypothenuse is equal to the square of the two sides*, is a proposition which expresses a relation between these figures. *That three times five is equal to the half of thirty*, expresses a relation between these numbers. Propositions of this kind are discoverable by the mere operation of thought, without dependence on what is anywhere existent in the universe. Though there never were a circle or triangle in nature, the truths demonstrated by Euclid would for ever retain their certainty and evidence.

> Matters of fact, which are the second objects of human reason, are not ascertained in the same manner; nor is our evidence of their truth, however great, of a like nature with the foregoing. The contrary of every matter of fact is still possible; because it can never imply a contradiction, and is conceived by the mind with the same facility and distinctness, as if ever so comfortable to reality. *That the sun will not rise to-morrow* is no less intelligible a proposition, and implies no more contradiction than the affirmation, *that it will rise*. We should in vain, therefore, attempt to demonstrate its falsehood. Were it demonstratively false, it would imply a contradiction, and could never be distinctly conceived by the mind.[11]

Our knowledge is either based on *relations of ideas*, in which case it is certain but has no connection with reality, as with "three times five is equal to half of thirty," which, though absolutely certain, is absolutely certain independently of anything in the world of reality; *or* our knowledge is

---

[11]David Hume, *An Enquiry Concerning Human Understanding*, in *Hume's Enquiries*, second ed., ed. L.A. Selby-Bigge, (Oxford: Clarendon Press, 1902), pp. 25–26.

HUME'S TWO BASES OF KNOWLEDGE

- *Relations of Ideas:* Ideas which, simply by virtue of their meanings and relations, are necessarily or *logically* true, but therefore irrelevant for the world of reality; for example, "The sun of the angles of a triangle equals 180 degrees."
- *Matters of Fact:* Ideas which bear upon and inform us about the world of reality, but which can never be certain because they are derived from specific experiences; for example, "Water freezes at 32 degrees Fahrenheit."

based on *matters of fact*, in which case it does inform us about the world of reality, as with "the sun will rise tomorrow," but can never be certain because it is derived from a limited and passing parade of perceptions. ("Relations of ideas" is a strange-sounding phrase. If it helps, draw the distinction between "matters of logic" and "matters of fact.")

This same skeptical and antimetaphysical distinction is restated in the celebrated outburst with which Hume concluded the *Enquiry:*

> When we run over libraries, persuaded of these principles, what havoc must we make? If we take in our hand any volume, of divinity or school metaphysics, for instance; let us ask, "Does it contain any abstract reasoning concerning quantity or number?" No. "Does it contain any experimental reasoning concerning matter of fact and existence?" No. Commit it then to the flames: for it can contain nothing but sophistry and illusion.[12]

Again, there is no halfway house: Our ideas are either certain but uninformative, or they are informative but never certain. And there we are stuck. But not for long.

---

[12]Ibid., p. 165.

CHAPTER 7 IN REVIEW

Summary

Empiricism is the epistemological claim that the mind at birth is a "blank tablet" and that all knowledge (exclusive of logical and mathematical knowledge) is derived ultimately from *sense experience*. In the previous chapter we considered three versions of rationalism, and in the present chapter we considered three versions of empiricism.

Classical empiricism has its origin in Greek philosophy and is most notably associated with Aristotle and, later, St. Thomas Aquinas. It will be recalled that Aristotle's is a Form-philosophy, wherein the object of knowledge is identified with the abiding essence of things. Unlike Plato, Aristotle believed that this essence is *in* particular things, and thus that it is with particular things that we must begin. From the particulars the mind is able to form a universal concept, which corresponds to the common essence in the particulars, and which guides knowledge and discourse amidst the flux and multiplicity of the sensible world. St. Thomas introduced the intellectual faculty of abstraction, whereby the mind is enabled to lift the universal features from particulars, leaving behind in the particulars all that is not *essential* to them.

In some ways, Locke is the giant of all empiricists, and certainly the one who set the empiricist agenda for the modern period. He began his famous *Essay Concerning Human Understanding* with a scathing rebuttal to the doctrine of innate ideas. In place of innate ideas Locke substitutes experience. This comes in two forms: sensation, our experience of external objects, and reflection, our experience of the internal workings of our minds. From sensation and reflection we form simple ideas, and from simple ideas the mind compounds complex ideas. In all of this the active and passive functions of the mind should be distinguished. Very important is Locke's epistemological or representative dualism, whereby our ideas are held to convey to us a likeness of the realities external to our minds: the perception of a tree, and the actual tree "out there." This, however, involves a great problem known as the egocentric predicament: If all we can know directly is our own idea, how can we ever know whether they correspond to anything that is not an idea?

Hume's *radical* empiricism pushes everything further. All we have are perceptions, divided into lively impressions and pale ideas; that's *all* we have. The time-honored concept of underlying but unperceived substance is, therefore, an unjustified figment, as is also the concept of causality, which, in its pre-Humean form, was thought to involve some unperceived metaphysical necessity. Hume's phenomenalism, which reduces knowledge to phenomena or appearances or "bundles of ideas," represents a serious skepticism: A proposition is either a mere relation of ideas ("A is A"), which says nothing about reality itself, or it is a matter of fact ("Swans are white"), which can never be known with certitude because of the limitations of our perceptions.

Basic Ideas

- Empiricism
- *Tabula rasa*
- Universal concepts
- Intellectual abstraction
- Aristotle and St. Thomas: Three stages of knowledge
- Locke's arguments against innate ideas
- Locke: Experience, sensation, and reflection
- Simple and complex ideas
- The mind as passive and active
- Epistemological dualism, or the representative theory of knowledge
- The egocentric predicament
- Hume: Perceptions, impressions, and ideas
- Hume's analysis of substance
- Hume's analysis of causality
- Phenomenalism
- Relations of ideas and matters of fact

Questions for Reflection

- When considering thinkers who belong to the same traditions, such as the empiricist tradition, be able to identify what they hold in common and where they differ. Can you compare in this way the thinkers in this chapter?
- What do you yourself make of the egocentric predicament? Is it a genuine problem? If not, why not? If so, how do you propose to escape the skepticism inherent in it?

- What do you think about Hume's rejection of mind (as a mental substance) or causality (as a metaphysical connection)? Does it make any difference to your philosophical perspective? To your practical life?

For Further Reading

Robert R. Ammerman and Marcus G. Singer (eds.). *Belief, Knowledge, and Truth: Readings in the Theory of Knowledge*. New York: Scribners, 1970. A collection of traditional, recent, and important statements on all aspects of knowledge, including some encountered in our chapter.

Bruce Aune. *Rationalism, Empiricism, and Pragmatism: An Introduction*. New York: Random House, 1970. Chs. 2–3. Discussions oriented to beginners on "Hume and Empiricism" and "Contemporary Empiricism."

V. C. Chappel (ed.). *Hume: A Collection of Critical Essays*. Garden City, NY: Anchor Books, 1966. An anthology of advanced essays on Hume's philosophy, including issues considered in our chapter.

Frederick Copleston. *A History of Philosophy*. Baltimore: Newman Press, 1946–1974. I, Ch. 29; II, Ch. 38; V, Chs. 4–6 and 14–15. Authoritative accounts on the empiricist epistemologies of Aristotle, St. Thomas, Locke, and Hume, by a recognized historian of philosophy.

A. C. Ewing. *The Fundamental Questions of Philosophy*. New York: Collier Books, 1962. Ch. 2. A beginner's discussion of the issue between rationalism and empiricism ("The 'A Priori' and the Empirical") by an intuitionist philosopher.

Antony Flew. *Hume's Philosophy of Belief: A Study of His First Inquiry*. London: Routledge & Kegan Paul, 1961. A standard treatment of the issues in Hume's *Enquiry*, including relations of ideas and matters of fact, the nature of empirical belief, the idea of necessary connection, etc.

Etienne Gilson. *The Christian Philosophy of St. Thomas Aquinas*, tr. L. K. Shook. New York: Random House, 1956. Part II, Chs. 5–7. Technical treatments of St. Thomas' theory of knowledge, by a foremost Thomas authority.

C. B. Martin and D. M. Armstrong (eds.) *Locke and Berkeley: A Collection of Critical Essays*. Garden City, NY: Anchor Books, 1968. An anthology which includes advanced discussions of some of Locke's positions encountered in our chapter.

Harold Morick (ed.). *Challenges to Empiricism*. Indianapolis: Hackett, 1980. Twelve contemporary thinkers criticize the fundamental empiricist thesis in relation to ontology, science, and linguistics.

Robert J. Swartz (ed.). *Perceiving, Sensing, and Knowing*. Garden City, NY: Anchor Books, 1965. A book of sometimes difficult readings from twentieth-century thinkers on perception and its role in the acquisition of knowledge.

*In addition, see the relevant articles ("Empiricism," "Phenomenalism," "Causation," "Aristotle," "Hume," etc.) in *The Encyclopedia of Philosophy*, ed. Paul Edwards. New York: Macmillan, 1967.

CHAPTER 8

The Problem of Certainty

I T MAY be fitting to conclude this part of the book with a chapter on *certainty*. To see that certainty really does pose a problem, just ask yourself whether you are certain of any of the following propositions, and whether you are certain about them in different ways:

- 2 + 2 = 4.
- In fourteen hundred and ninety-two Columbus sailed the ocean blue.
- I exist.
- You exist.
- The sun will rise tomorrow.
- Right now I am perceiving this page.
- Barking dogs bark.
- Humans have evolved from lower animals.
- Every event must have a cause.

As you can see, the idea of certainty is not a simple one. In this chapter we will consider the problem in only one of its aspects, but, philosophically, a very basic one. Still more specifically, we will discuss one philosopher's attempt to account for certainty, especially in light of the preceding chapter. A warning: This may not be easy going, and the quoted material will be a good challenge.

KANT AND HUME

"I openly confess my recollection of David Hume was the very thing which many years ago first interrupted my dogmatic slumber and gave my investigations in the field of speculative philosophy a quite new direction."[1] Thus spoke the German philosopher Immanuel Kant[2] (1724–1804), who marks a turning point in modern epistemology.

Kant observed that there must be something radically wrong with the whole way of thinking that led finally to the phenomenalism and skepticism of Hume. For, Kant says, I *am* certain of some of the truths which Hume called "matters of fact." He cites, as an example, all mathematical propositions, such as $7 + 5 = 12$ (though most philosophers now regard mathematical truths to be true by definition); from natural science he cites as an example Newton's Third Law of Motion, that in all motion action and reaction must always be equal; and from metaphysics he cites the principle of causality, that every event must have a cause. For Kant it was not a question of *whether* we possess such knowledge but *how*. In his explanation of how propositions can be at once genuinely informative about reality *and* absolutely certain, Kant signals an altogether different approach to the problem, provides us with a sort of halfway point between Rationalism and empiricism, and establishes himself as one of the greatest epistemologists of all time.

SOME IMPORTANT TERMINOLOGY

But, to begin at the beginning, it is necessary to study some terminology which Kant himself introduced into philosophical discussion.

---

[1] Immanuel Kant, *Prolegomena to Any Future Metaphysics*, tr. Lewis W. Beck (Indianapolis, IN: Bobbs-Merrill, 1950), p. 8.

[2] Rhymes with *font*.

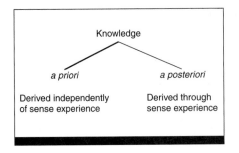

First, the distinction between *a priori* knowledge and *a posteriori* knowledge. You can pretty much guess the meaning of these Latin terms just by looking at them. *A priori* knowledge is knowledge which comes before (prior to) sense experience and is therefore *independent* of sense experience. This, of course, is the emphasis of the rationalist. *A posteriori* knowledge is knowledge which comes after (posterior to) sense experience and is therefore *dependent* on sense experience. This is the empiricist emphasis.

Second, we have the distinction between *analytic* and *synthetic* knowledge. Analytic knowledge is another way of expressing Hume's "relation of ideas." When this kind of knowledge is expressed in a proposition, the predicate is contained already in the subject. Examples are: "The sum of the angles of any triangle is 180 degrees"; "All barking dogs bark"; or any proposition of the form "A is A" (the predicate "A" is contained already in the subject "A"). Now all such knowledge or propositions "have to be true." For they are true by definition, or to say the same thing, they are *logically* true, and this means that you could deny them without self-contradiction. Do you recall the Law of Identity from the Three Laws of Thought? Who in their right minds would be interested in affirming that A is not A? (Such statements are sometimes called tautologies or redundancies.) Now no one questions the absolute truth of analytic propositions. Rationalists and empiricists alike agree that such propositions must be true no matter what. On the other hand, it is important to see that such truths do not really tell us anything about *reality*. They neither affirm nor deny the actual existence of anything. The proposition "All barking dogs bark" is necessarily true whether or not there are any dogs, or, for that matter, whether or not there is *anything*. A statement like "All barking dogs bark" only means "If there are any barking dogs, then they bark." The truth of these propositions is then *a priori* and utterly independent of sense experience and of the sensible world itself.

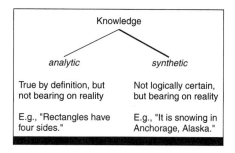

Synthetic knowledge, on the other hand, corresponds to Hume's "matters of fact." In synthetic propositions, the predicate *adds* something to the subject, and thus two ideas are "synthesized" in the proposition. Examples are: "Water freezes at 32 degrees Fahrenheit"; "Dogs bark"; and any proposition of the form "A is B" (the predicate "B" amplifies the subject "A"). In this way a synthetic proposition affirms or denies the existence of something (and is therefore sometimes called an "existential" proposition); it informs us about things; it really does tell us something about the actual universe.

IS THERE SYNTHETIC *A PRIORI* KNOWLEDGE?

Now we have just seen that everyone, rationalists and empiricists both, accepts the absolute truth of analytic propositions as *a priori* certain. It is also clear that few rationalists have ever insisted that sense experience plays absolutely no role *whatsoever* in the acquisition of synthetic knowledge. Just consider: Even if you are the staunchest rationalist, how do you know that swans are white? that in fourteen hundred and ninety-two Columbus sailed the ocean blue? Obviously there is much about the actual world that we could not possibly know except in an *a posteriori* way: making observations, lighting bunsen burners, taking field trips, and the like. Everyone admits this.

It turns out then that both rationalists and empiricists accept analytic propositions as *a priori* certain, and that they both accept at least *some* synthetic propositions as *a posteriori* probable. The real question and the real issue between rationalists and empiricists is this: Can we possess any knowledge that is both *a priori* certain and synthetically informative? *Is there such a thing as synthetic* a priori *knowledge?* This is a crucial question,

and how you answer it will make all the difference to your general philosophical perspective.

As we already have seen, Kant answered the question of synthetic *a priori* knowledge with a resounding Yes. But his explanation is hardly what traditional rationalists would have expected—or accepted. Kant turned the epistemological world upside-down. In fact, he likened his contribution to the Copernican revolution, which, by radically shifting our viewpoint (the sun does not go around the earth, but the earth goes around the sun), resulted immediately in a superior explanation of the phenomena to be explained. Kant's "Copernican revolution" consisted, similarly, in the startling announcement that ideas such as substance and causality do not make their way into our minds through experience, but are "*a priori* categories of the understanding" which mold and shape and, in fact, *constitute* our experience. That is, substance and causality (along with ten additional categories) are *part* of what we *mean* by experience. Indeed, even space and time, in which substances standing in causal relations are enabled to appear at all, are contributed by our intellects. Space and time too, therefore, are *a priori* conditions of experience.

In this way Kant redeems such principles as those of causality and substance from the skeptical clutches of Hume. As far as the world of appearance goes, "Every event must have a cause," for example, is a synthetic truth but also possesses *a priori* universality and necessity. We don't have any choice about it: We *have* to experience things as causally related because that is one of the ways our minds *create* experience; if we're all wearing rose-colored glasses, everything must appear to be rose-colored—to all of us.

SYNTHETIC *A PRIORI*, A CRUCIAL QUESTION

One of the questions that divides philosophers into two different camps is the question of synthetic *a priori* knowledge: Is it possible to know synthetic propositions with *a priori* certainty? Are there any nonanalytic truths that are, nonetheless, universally and necessarily true?

Kant's major work, the *Critique of Pure Reason*, was first published in 1781. In the following excerpts from the Introduction, Kant begins to explain in his own way the ideas we have already outlined. (1) He distinguishes between empirical and *a posteriori* knowledge derived from sense experience and pure or *a priori* knowledge which is completely independent of experience, and he raises the question whether such pure knowledge exists; (2) he establishes the two identifying marks by which pure or *a priori* knowledge may be recognized and distinguished from empirical or *a posteriori* knowledge:

- necessity
- universality

(3) he distinguishes between analytic and synthetic propositions, and explains the nature of synthetic *a priori* knowledge both as being existentially informative and also bearing the marks of necessity and universality, something unaccountable for on the basis of experience.

OF THE DIFFERENCE BETWEEN PURE AND EMPIRICAL KNOWLEDGE

That all our knowledge begins with experience there can be no doubt. For how should the faculty of knowledge be called into activity, if not by objects which affect our senses, and which either produce representations by themselves, or rouse the activity of our understanding to compare, to connect, or to separate them; and thus to convert the raw material of our sensuous impressions into a knowledge of objects, which we call experience? In respect of time, therefore, no knowledge within us is antecedent to experience, but all knowledge begins with it.

KANT'S COPERNICAN REVOLUTION IN PHILOSOPHY

". . . the pure concepts of the understanding . . . do not derive from experience, but experience derives from them."

But although all our knowledge begins with experience, it does not follow that it arises from experience. For it is quite possible that even our empirical experience is a compound of that which we receive through impressions, and of that which our own faculty of knowledge (incited only by sensuous impressions) supplies from itself, a supplement which we do not distinguish from that raw material, until long practice has roused our attention and rendered us capable of separating one from the other.

It is therefore a question which deserves at least closer investigation, and cannot be disposed of at first sight, whether there exists a knowledge independent of experience, and even of all impressions of the senses? Such *knowledge* is called *a priori*, and distinguished from *empirical* knowledge, which has its sources *a posteriori*, that is, in experience.

WE ARE IN POSSESSION OF CERTAIN COGNITIONS *A PRIORI*, AND EVEN THE ORDINARY UNDERSTANDING IS NEVER WITHOUT THEM

All depends here on a criterion, by which we may safely distinguish between pure and empirical knowledge. Now experience teaches us, no doubt, that something is so or so, but not that it cannot be different. *First*, then, if we have a proposition, which is thought, together with its necessity, we have a judgment *a priori;* and if, besides, it is not derived from any proposition, except such as is itself again considered as necessary, we have an absolutely *a priori* judgment. *Secondly*, experience never imparts to its judgments true or strict, but only assumed or relative universality (by means of induction), so that we ought always to say, so far as we have observed hitherto, there is no exception to this or that rule. If, therefore, a judgment is thought with strict universality, so that no exception is admitted as possible, it is not derived from experience, but valid absolutely *a priori*. . . . Necessity, therefore, and strict universality are safe criteria of knowledge *a priori*, and are inseparable one from the other. . . .

That there really exist in our knowledge such necessary, and in the strictest sense universal, and therefore pure judgments *a priori*, is easy to show. If we want a scientific example, we have only to look to any of the propositions of mathematics; if we want one from the sphere of the ordinary understanding, such a proposition as that each change must have a cause, will answer the purpose; nay, in the latter case, even the concept of cause contains so clearly the concept of the necessity of its connection with an effect, and of the strict universality of the rule, that it would be destroyed altogether if we attempted to derive it, as Hume does, from the frequent concomitancy of that which happens with that which precedes, and from a habit arising thence (therefore from a purely subjective necessity), or connecting representations. It is possible even, without having recourse to such examples in proof of the reality of pure propositions *a priori* within our knowledge, to prove their indispensability for the possibility of experience itself, thus proving it *a priori*. For whence should experience take its certainty, if all the rules which it follows were always again and again empirical, and therefore contingent and hardly fit to serve as first principles? For the present, however, we may be satisfied for having shown the pure employment of the faculty of our knowledge as a matter of fact, with the criteria of it.

Not only in judgments, however, but even in certain concepts, can we show their origin *a priori*. Take away, for example, from the concept of a body, as supplied by experience, everything that is empirical, one by one; such as colour, hardness or softness, weight, and even impenetrability, and there still remains the space which the body (now entirely vanished) occupied: that you cannot take away. And in the same manner, if you remove from your empirical concept of any object, corporeal or incorporeal, all properties which experience has taught you, you cannot take away from it that property by which you conceive it as a substance, or inherent in a substance (although such a concept contains more determinations than that of an object in general). Convinced, therefore, by the necessity with which that concept forces itself upon you, you will have to admit that it has its seat in your faculty of knowledge *a priori*. . . .

Of the Distinction between Analytical and Synthetical Judgments

In all judgments in which there is a relation between subject and predicate (I speak of affirmative judgments only, the application to negative ones being easy), that relation can be of two kinds. Either the predicate B belongs to the subject A as something contained (though covertly) in the concept A; or B lies outside the sphere of the concept A, though somehow connected with it. In the former case I call the judgment analytical, in the latter synthetical. Analytical judgments (affirmative) are therefore those in which the connection of the predicate with the subject is conceived through identity, while others in which that connection is conceived without identity, may be called synthetical. The former might be called illustrating, the latter expanding judgments, because in the former nothing is added by the predicate to the concept of the subject, but the concept is only divided into its constituent concepts which were always conceived as existing within it, though confusedly; while the latter add to the concept of the subject a predicate not conceived as existing within it, and not to be extracted from it by any process of mere analysis. If I say, for instance, All bodies are extended, this is an analytical judgment. I need not go beyond the concept connected with the name of body, in order to find that extension is connected with it. I have only to analyse that concept and become conscious of the manifold elements always contained in it, in order to find that predicate. This is therefore an analytical judgment. But if I say, All bodies are heavy, the predicate is something quite different from what I think as the mere concept of body. The addition of such a predicate gives us a synthetical judgment. . . .

Empirical judgments, as such, are all synthetical; for it would be absurd to found an analytical judgment on experience, because, in order to form such a judgment, I need not at all step out of my concept, or appeal to the testimony of experience. That a body is extended, is a proposition perfectly certain *a priori*, and not an empirical judgment. For, before I call in experience, I am already in possession of all the conditions of my judgment in the concept of body itself. I have only to draw out from it, according to the principle of contradiction, the required predicate, and I thus become conscious, at the same time, of the necessity of the judgment, which experience could never teach me. But, though I do not include the predicate of gravity in the general concept of body, that concept, nevertheless, indicates an object of experience through one of its parts: so that I may add other parts also of the same experience, besides those which belonged to the former concept. I may, first, by an analytical process, realize the concept of body, through the predicates of extension, impermeability, form, etc., all of which are contained in it. Afterwards I expand my knowledge, and looking back to the experience from which my concept of body was abstracted, I find gravity always connected with the before-mentioned predicates, and therefore I add it synthetically to that concept as a predicate. It is, therefore, experience on which the possibility of the synthesis of the predicate of gravity with the concept of body is founded: because both concepts, though neither of them is contained in the other, belong to each other, though accidentally only, as parts of a whole, namely, or experience, which is itself a synthetical connection of intuitions.

In synthetical judgments *a priori*, however, that help is entirely wanting. If I want to go beyond the concept A in order to find another concept B connected with it, where is there anything on which I may rest and through which a synthesis might become possible, considering that I cannot have the advantage of looking about in the field of experience? Take the proposition that all which happens has its cause. In the concept of something that happens I no doubt conceive of something existing preceded by time, and from this certain analytical judgments may be deduced. But the concept of cause is entirely outside that concept, and indicates something different from that which happens, and is by no means contained in that representation. How can I venture then to predicate of that which happens something totally different from it, and to represent the concept of cause, though not contained in it, as belonging to it, and belonging to it by necessity? What is here the unknown *x*, on which the understanding may rest in order to find beyond the concept A a foreign predicate B, which nevertheless is believed to be connected with it? It cannot be experience, because the proposition that all which happens has its cause represents this second predicate as added to the subject not only with greater generality than experience can ever supply, but also with a character of necessity, and therefore purely *a priori*, and based on concepts. . . .[3]

Later in the *Critique*, Kant proposes *how* synthetic *a priori* knowledge is possible. Pay close attention to his insistence on the role of *a priori* concepts as conditions of experience and the epistemological consequences of this, as in the statement, "If by them only it is possible to think any object of experience, it follows that they refer by necessity and *a priori* to all

---

[3]Immanuel Kant, *Critique of Pure Reason*, tr. F. Max Miller (Garden City, NY: Anchor Books, 1960), pp. 2–5, 7–9.

objects of experience." (By "intuition" Kant means the perception of objects as they are represented by the intellect.)

Two ways only are possible in which synthetical representations and their objects can agree, can refer to each other with necessity, and so to say meet each other. Either it is the object alone that makes the representation possible, or it is the representation alone that makes the object possible. In the former case their relation is empirical only, and the representation therefore never possible *a priori*. This applies to phenomena with reference to whatever in them belongs to sensation. In the latter case, though representation by itself (for we do not speak here of its causality by means of the will) cannot produce its object so far as its existence is concerned, nevertheless the representation determines the object *a priori*, if through it alone it is possible to know anything as an object. To know a thing as an object is possible only under two conditions. First, there must be intuition by which the object is given us, though as a phenomenon only, secondly, there must be a concept by which an object is thought as corresponding to that intuition. From what we have said before it is clear that the first condition, namely, that under which alone objects can be seen, exists, so far as the form of intuition is concerned, in the soul *a priori*. All phenomena therefore must conform to that formal condition of sensibility, because it is through it alone that they appear, that is, that they are given and empirically seen.

Now the question arises whether there are not also antecedent concepts *a priori*, forming conditions under which alone something can be, if not seen, yet thought as an object in general; for in that case all empirical knowledge of objects would necessarily conform to such concepts, it being impossible that anything should become an object of experience without them. All experience contains, besides the intuition of the senses by which something is given, a concept also of the object, which is given in intuition as a phenomenon. Such concepts of objects in general therefore must form conditions *a priori* of all knowledge produced by experience, and the objective validity of the categories, as being such concepts *a priori*, rests on this very fact that by them alone, so far as the form of thought is concerned, experience becomes possible. If by them only it is possible to think any object of experience, it follows that they refer by necessity and *a priori* to all objects of experience.

There is therefore a principle for the transcendental deduction of all concepts *a priori* which must guide the whole of our investigation, namely, that all must be recognised as conditions *a priori* of the possibility of experience, whether of intuition, which is found in it, or of thought. . . .[4]

Kant goes on immediately to contrast his own theory of knowledge with that of his empiricist predecessors, Locke and Hume, and to show where they went wrong: *Locke* correctly recognized the existence of pure (necessary and universal) concepts but mistakenly sought them from sense experience and, at the same time, applied them *beyond* sense experience (for example, every event must have a cause, and God, a transcendent being, is the cause of the world); *Hume* on the other hand, correctly saw that such concepts (necessary and universal) could not be derived from sense experience, and so mistakenly denied that they are, after all, necessary and universal. Now, says Kant, neither Locke's "extravagance" nor Hume's "skepticism" squares with the epistemological facts (the givenness of synthetic *a priori* knowledge), whereas his own theory does account for the facts by steering a middle course between the false alternatives of his misguided predecessors.

Locke, for want of this reflection, and because he met with pure concepts of the understanding in experience, derived them also from experience, and yet acted so *inconsistently* that he attempted to use them for knowledge which far exceeds all limits of experience. David Hume saw that, in order to be able to do this, these concepts ought to have their origin *a priori*; but as he could not explain how it was possible that the understanding should be constrained to think concepts, which by themselves are not united in the understanding, as necessarily united in the object, and never thought that possibly the understanding might itself, through these concepts, be the author of that experience in which its objects are found, he was driven by necessity to derive them from experience (namely, from a subjective necessity, produced by frequent association in experience, which at last is wrongly supposed to be *objective*, that is, from habit). He acted, however, very consistently, by declaring it to be impossible to go with these concepts, and with the principles arising from them, beyond the

---

[4]Ibid., pp. 72–73.

limits of experience. This empirical deduction, which was adopted by both philosophers, cannot be reconciled with the reality of our scientific knowledge *a priori*, namely, pure *mathematics* and *general natural science*, and is therefore refuted by facts. The former of these two celebrated men opened a wide door to *fantastic extravagance*, because reason, if it has once established such pretensions, can no longer be checked by vague praises of moderation; the other, thinking that he had once discovered so general an illusion of our faculty of knowledge, which had formerly been accepted as reason, gave himself over entirely to *scepticism*.[5]

THE LIMITS OF REASON

It is important to note, however, what price must be paid for synthetic *a priori* knowledge. It is a very high price. One of the implications of Kant's analysis is that we can know nothing of reality as it is in itself (what Kant calls the *noumenal* world) but only as it appears to us through experience (he calls this the *phenomenal* world). The reason is clear: The *a priori* categories or concepts of the understanding are, as we have said, constitutive of our experience, and therefore they have no legitimate application *beyond* experience. Causality, for example, applies only to objects of possible experience. And when we try to apply such concepts beyond experience, what results is nonsense and absurdities.

This necessary limitation of the concepts of the understanding to the phenomenal world comes out well in the following from Kant's *Prolegomena to Any Future Metaphysics*, published in 1783 as a simplified version of the *Critique of Pure Reason*. (In these paragraphs, "intuition" again refers to what we normally might call perceptions, and the "Aesthetic" refers to a section of the *Critique*.)

> Since the oldest days of philosophy, inquirers into pure reason have conceived, besides the things of sense, or appearances (*phenomena*), which make up the sensible world, certain beings of the understanding (*noumena*), which should constitute an intelligible world. And as appearance and illusion were by those men identified (a thing which we may well excuse in an undeveloped epoch), actuality was only conceded to the beings of the understanding.

---

[5]Ibid., pp. 74–75.

- *What we gain through Kant's theoretical reason: a priori* certainty and universality of fundamental concepts, such as causality and substance.
- *What we lose through Kant's theoretical reason:* the possibility of any theoretical knowledge of reality beyond objects of possible experience.

And we indeed, rightly considering objects of sense as mere appearances, confess thereby that they are based upon a thing in itself, though we know not this thing as it is in itself but only know its appearances, namely, the way in which our senses are affected by this unknown something. The understanding, therefore, by assuming appearances, grants the existence of things in themselves also; and to this extent we may say that the representation of such things as are the basis of appearances, consequently of mere beings of the understanding, is not only admissible but unavoidable.

Our critical deduction by no means excludes things of that sort (*noumena*), but rather limits the principles of the Aesthetic to this, that they shall not extend to all things—as everything would then be turned into mere appearance—but that they shall hold good only of objects of possible experience. Hereby, then, beings of the understanding are granted, but with the inculcation of this rule which admits of no exception: that we neither know nor can know anything at all definite of these pure beings of the understanding, because our pure concepts of the understanding as well as our pure intuitions extend to nothing but objects of possible experience, consequently to mere things of sense; and as soon as we leave this sphere, these concepts retain no meaning whatever.[6]

Thus, if we have gained *a priori* certainty and universality for synthetic knowledge, it has been at the cost of giving up any knowledge of reality beyond space and time. We will see in Chapter 9 that for Kant this included, naturally, God. But Kant believed that in addition to the "theoretical" reason, which is guided and limited by the *a priori* concepts of the understanding, there is open to us the "practical" reason, which builds on the entirely different foundation of *moral* experience, and which *does* give us, in a way, knowledge of God, freedom, and immortality.

---

[6]Kant, *Prolegomena to Any Future Metaphysics*, pp. 61–62.

Postmodernism: "Star Trek: The Next Generation"

Modernity has been under attack since Friedrich Nietzsche (1844–1900) lobbed the first volley in the late nineteenth century. But the full-scale frontal assault did not begin until the 1970s. The immediate impulse for the dismantling of the Enlightenment project came from the rise of deconstruction as a literary theory, which influenced a new movement in philosophy.

Deconstruction arose in response to a theory in literature called "structuralism." Structuralists theorized that cultures develop literary documents—texts—in an attempt to provide structures of meaning by which people can make sense out of the meaninglessness of their experience. Literature, therefore, provides categories with which we can organize and understand our experience of reality. Further, all societies and cultures possess a common, invariant structure.

The deconstructionists (or poststructuralists) rejected the tenets of structuralism. Meaning is not inherent in a text itself, they argued, but emerges only as the interpreter enters into dialogue with the text. Consequently, the meaning of a text depends on the perspective of the one who enters into dialogue with it, so there are as many interpretations of a text as readers (or readings).

Postmodern philosophers applied the theories of the literary deconstructionists to the world as a whole. Just as the meaning of a text depends on the reader, so also reality can be "read" differently depending on the perspectives of the knowing selves that encounter it. This means that there is no one meaning of the world, no transcendent center to reality as a whole.

On the basis of ideas such as these, the French philosopher Jacques Derrida called for the destruction of "onto-theory" (the attempt to set forth ontological descriptions of reality) as well as the "metaphysics of presence" (the idea that a transcendent something is present in reality). Because nothing transcendent inheres in reality, all that emerges in the knowing process is the perspective of the self who interprets reality.

Michel Foucault added a moral twist to Derrida's call. Every interpretation is put forward by those in power, he theorized. Because "knowledge"

(continued on next page)

is always the result of the use of power, to name something is to exercise power and hence to do violence to what is named. Social institutions do violence by imposing their own understanding on the centerless flux of experience. Thus, in contrast to Bacon, who sought knowledge in order to gain power over nature, Foucault claimed that every assertion of knowledge is an act of power.

Richard Rorty, in turn, jettisoned the classic conception of truth as either the mind or language mirroring nature. Truth is established neither by the correspondence of an assertion with objective reality nor by the internal coherence of the assertions themselves. Rorty argued that we should simply disband the search for truth and be content with interpretation. Hence, he proposed to replace classic "systematic philosophy" with "edifying philosophy," which "aims at continuing a conversation rather than at discovering truth."

The work of Derrida, Foucault, and Rorty reflects what seems to have become the central dictum of postmodern philosophy: "All is difference." This view sweeps away the "uni" of the "universe" sought by the Enlightenment project, the quest for a unified grasp of objective reality. The world has no center, only differing viewpoints and perspectives. In fact, even the concept of "world" presupposes an objective unity or a coherent whole that does not exist "out there." In the end, the postmodern world is merely an arena of dueling texts.

Although philosophers such as Derrida, Foucault, and Rorty have been influential on university campuses, they are only a part of a larger shift in thinking reflected in Western culture. What unifies the otherwise diverse strands of postmodernism is the questioning of the central assumptions of Enlightenment epistemology.

In the postmodern world, people are no longer convinced that knowledge is inherently good. In eschewing the Enlightenment myth of inevitable progress, postmodernism replaces the optimism of the last century with a gnawing pessimism. It is simply not the case that "each and every day in each and every way we are getting better and better." For the first time in many years, members of the emerging generation do not share the conviction of their parents that we will solve the enormous problems of the planet or that their economic situation will surpass that of

(continued on next page)

their parents. They know that life on the earth is fragile, and the continued existence of humankind is dependent on a new attitude which replaces
the image of conquest with cooperation.

The new emphasis on wholism is related to the postmodern rejection
of the second Enlightenment assumption, namely, that truth is certain and
hence purely rational. The postmodern mind refuses to limit truth to its
rational dimension and thus dethrones the human intellect as the arbiter
of truth. Because truth is nonrational, there are other ways of knowing,
including through the emotions and the intuition.

Finally, the postmodern mind no longer accepts the Enlightenment
belief that knowledge is objective. Knowledge cannot be merely objective, because the postmodern model of the world does not see the universe as mechanistic and dualistic, but historical, relational, and personal. The world is not simply an objective given that is "out there,"
waiting to be discovered and known. Instead it is relative, indeterminate,
and participatory.

In rejecting the modern assumption of the objectivity of knowledge,
the postmodern mind likewise dismisses the Enlightenment ideal of the
dispassionate, autonomous knower. Knowledge is not eternal and culturally neutral. Nor is it waiting to be discovered by scientists who bring
their rational talents to the givenness of the world. Rather, knowledge is
historically and culturally implicated, and consequently, our knowledge is
always incomplete.

The postmodern world view operates with a community-based understanding of truth. Not only the specific truths we accept, but even our understanding of truth, are a function of the community in which we participate. This basis in community, in turn, leads to a new conception of the
relativity of truth. Not only is there no absolute truth; more significantly,
truth is relative to the community in which we participate. With this in
view, the postmodern thinker has given up the Enlightenment quest for
the one, universal, supracultural, timeless truth. In its place, truth is what
fits within a specific community; truth consists in the ground rules that facilitate the well-being of the community in which one participates.

The postmodern perspective is reflected in the second "Star Trek"
series, "The Next Generation." The humans who make up the original
Enterprise are now joined by humanoid life forms from other parts of the

(continued on next page)

universe. This change represents the broader universality of postmodernity: humans are no longer the only advanced beings operative throughout the cosmos. More importantly, the understanding of the quest for knowledge has changed. Humankind is not capable of completing the mandate alone; nor does the burden of the quest fall to humans alone. Hence, the crew of the Enterprise symbolizes the "new ecology" of humankind in partnership with the universe. Their mission is no longer "to boldly go where no man has gone before," but "where no *one* has gone before."

In "The Next Generation," Data replaces Spock. In a sense, Data is Spock, the fully rational thinker capable of superhuman intellectual feats. Despite his seemingly perfect intellect, rather than being the transcendent human ideal Spock embodies, he is an android—-a subhuman machine. His desire is not only to understand what it means to be human, but also to become human. However, he lacks certain necessary aspects of humanness, including a sense of humor, emotion, and the ability to dream (at least until he learns that his maker programmed dreaming into his circuitry).

Although Data often provides valuable assistance in dealing with problems, he is only one of several who contribute to finding solutions. In addition to the master of rationality, the Enterprise crew includes persons skilled in the affective and intuitive dimensions of human life. Especially prominent is Counselor Troi, a woman gifted with the ability to perceive the hidden feelings of others.

The new voyages of the Enterprise lead its varied crew into a postmodern universe. In this new world, time is no longer simply linear, appearance is not necessarily reality, and the rational is not always to be trusted. In contrast to the older series, which in typical modern fashion generally ignores questions of God and religious belief, the postmodern world of "The Next Generation" also includes the supernatural, embodied in the strange character "Q." Yet its picture of the divine is not simply that of traditional Christian theology. Although possessing the classical attributes of divine power (such as omniscience), the godlike being "Q" is morally ambiguous, displaying both benevolence and a bent toward cynicism and self-gratification.

Stanley J. Grenz, "Star Trek and the Next Generation: Postmodernism and the Future of Evangelical Theology," *CRUX* 30 (March 1994), pp. 24–32.

CHAPTER 8 IN REVIEW

Summary

In the previous chapter we saw how the skeptical Hume brought traditional thinking about knowledge to a sort of dead-end. This is precisely where Kant began.

Unlike Hume, Kant was certain of many truths of the sort Hume rejected, for example, that every event must have a cause. According to Kant, the universality and necessity that characterize such truths cannot be accounted for on empiricist, or *a posteriori*, grounds and require, rather, an *a priori* origin. On the other hand, such truths are not analytic, or empty redundancies, but synthetic, or existential. But how is synthetic *a priori* knowledge possible? Kant himself rightly regarded his answer as a revolution in epistemology, and even now one frequently encounters the expressions "pre-Kantian" and "post-Kantian" as demarcations of a watershed in the history of philosophy.

Kant distinguished between things as they are in themselves (the noumenal world) and things as they appear to us (the phenomenal world). Things-in-themselves are wholly unknown to us. Things-as-they-appear (that is, experience) are made possible first of all by the *a priori* conditions of space and time, and then by the *a priori* categories of the understanding, which further structure our experience into the world that we apprehend. It is crucial to see how Kant, with this reinterpretation of the origin and nature of knowledge, accounts for synthetic *a priori* knowledge. For example, *every* event *must* have a cause, because that is the only way in which our intellects work. On the other hand, this means that our "theoretical" reason, operating with substance, causality, and the like, has proper application only to objects of possible experience. And *this* means that we can have no theoretical knowledge of anything *beyond* experience. For such knowledge we must have recourse to an entirely different kind of reason, the "practical" reason, which begins not with experiential categories but with moral categories.

Basic Ideas

- Kant's rejection of Humean skepticism
- *A priori* and *a posteriori* knowledge
- Analytic and synthetic knowledge

- Synthetic *a priori* knowledge
- Kant's "Copernican revolution" in philosophy
- Space and time as *a priori* conditions of experience
- The categories of the understanding as conditions of experience
- The noumenal and phenomenal worlds
- The theoretical reason and the practical reason
- The limitations of theoretical reason

Questions for Reflection

- It would be a mistake to call Kant either a rationalist or an empiricist. Do you see why? On the other hand, he effected a sort of synthesis of the two. What is the rationalist element? What is the empiricist element?
- With this doctrine of the *a priori* conditions of experience, Kant sought to explain how we enjoy certitude of certain important claims. What are some of these claims? Are *you* certain of them? If not, are you a skeptic? If so, how do *you* account for the certainty?

For Further Reading

Frederick Copleston. *A History of Philosophy*. Baltimore: Newman Press, 1946–1974. VI, Chs. 11–12. An authoritative account of Kant's theory of knowledge, by a recognized historian of philosophy.

A. C. Ewing. *Idealism: A Critical Survey*. London: Methuen, 1934. Ch. 3. A good summary account of Kant's metaphysics and epistemology, including his solution to the problem of synthetic *a priori* knowledge.

A. C. Ewing. *A Short Commentary on Kant's Critique of Pure Reason*. 2nd ed. London: Methuen, 1950. A comprehensible commentary on an incomprehensible book, along with a highly instructive introduction.

Justus Hartnack. *Kant's Theory of Knowledge*. Tr. M. Holmes Hartshorne. New York: Harcourt, Brace & World, 1967. A highly useful and lucid summary of the *Critique of Pure Reason*.

H. A. Prichard. *Kant's Theory of Knowledge*. Oxford: Clarendon Press, 1909. An old but useful exposition of Kant's epistemology, with special reference to the *Critique of Pure Reason*, by an important twentieth-century philosopher.

W. H. Werkmeister. *Kant: The Architectonic and Development of His Philosophy.* La Salle, IL: Open Court, 1980. Ch. 5. A recent, learned, concentrated, and understandable treatment of Kant's theory of knowledge, by an esteemed Kant scholar.

Robert Paul Wolff. *Kant: A Collection of Critical Essays.* Garden City, NY: Anchor Books, 1967. An anthology of advanced discussions of various aspects of Kant's philosophy, including epistemological issues.

*In addition, see the relevant articles ("Certainty," "Synthetic and Analytic Statements," "Kant," etc.) in *The Encyclopedia of Philosophy*, ed. Paul Edwards. New York: Macmillan, 1967.

PART THREE

THE QUESTION OF GOD

W | HEN MARK TWAIN was once traveling abroad he received news of a mistaken obituary back in the United States giving notice of his death. He sent back the message: "Reports of my death are greatly exaggerated." In the last century the German philosopher Friedrich Nietzsche boldly proclaimed, "God is dead." Again in the 1960s the proclamation was issued by the Death of God theologians. They were not the only ones (nor will they be the last) to give, in one way or another, notice of the demise of the deity, but many would insist that in every case the report has been greatly exaggerated. As the well-known piece of graffiti expresses it:

GOD IS DEAD!
—Nietzsche

NIETZSCHE IS DEAD!
—God

Certainly it is true that God is alive and well if the continuing interest in and discussion of God are any indication.

Still, some may sense a difference with the question of God. It has something to do with the fact that our society is such a melting pot of religious and antireligious views. Even under "Churches" the yellow pages list, side by side, everything from Methodists, Baptists, Lutherans, and Catholics, to the Congregation of the Kindred Spirits, the Church of Good Science, and the Homosexual Church of the Universe. The difference also has to do with the sometimes passionate nature of belief or disbelief. How many times have we all heard it said that friends should never talk religion or politics lest they suddenly find themselves friends no longer. It is true that arguments over religion can become the most heated and can bring out the worst of all participants—atheists no less than believers. This is just to say that here, perhaps more than anywhere else, a special plea must be issued for identifying and laying aside (as best we can) prejudices, mental blind spots, and wishful thinking.

What we have called here "the question of God" actually includes much more than just God. The following are only some of the issues that are usually encompassed in what is known as "philosophy of religion," or perhaps better, "philosophical theology":

- What does "God" mean?
- Can the existence of God be proven?
- What is the relation between God and morality?

- How does philosophical knowledge of God relate to divine revelation?
- What is the nature and relevance of religious faith?
- Does God care about the world?
- Are religious experiences relevant data for the existence of God?
- Can an all-powerful and all-loving God be reconciled with the evil in the world?
- Do we have immortal souls?
- What are the special features of religious language?

Obviously such issues overlap with metaphysical and epistemological issues. Nonetheless, there is here an identifiable core of connected issues. At the center lies the specific question of God, and radiating from that, all sorts of related questions. And a whole history of philosophy could be written around the question of God and related matters, which only shows that it must be one of the questions that matter.

CHAPTER 9

God
and
the
World

I T MAKES sense, of course, that the question of God's existence should come first in discussions concerning God and related matters. For, as St. Thomas Aquinas says near the beginning of his multi-volumed *Summa Contra Gentiles*, if we don't first establish that he at least exists, then there is no point in going on:

> Now, among the inquiries that we must undertake concerning God in Himself, we must set down in the beginning that whereby His Existence is demonstrated, as the necessary foundation of the whole work. For, if we do not demonstrate that God exists, all consideration of divine things is necessarily suppressed.[1]

---

[1] St. Thomas Aquinas, *Summa Contra Gentiles* I, 9, 5, tr. and ed. Anton C. Pegis (South Bend, IN: Notre Dame University Press, 1955), I.

In this chapter and the next, we too will raise the question of God's existence, and we will consider some of the best-known arguments, pro and con.

NATURAL THEOLOGY

Before really getting into the arguments for God, the idea of *natural theology* must be introduced. First, what is *theology?* "Theology" comes from the Greek word *theos*, which means "God." Theology is therefore the study or science or knowledge of God. What then is *natural* theology? Caution: It does *not* mean the study or science or knowledge of God through *nature*. It is true that some of the arguments for God are based on the physical world, but we will see too that many are not. Natural theology is the study or science or knowledge of God through the *natural intellect.* This means the intellect in its natural state, unaided by any special or supernatural input. It may be helpful to know that natural theology is sometimes known also by the less ambiguous labels *philosophical theology* and *rational theology.*

Natural theology is therefore to be distinguished from *revealed theology,* which means the knowledge of God through special revelation, such as the Bible, the Church, Moses, Christ, the Holy Spirit, and the like. If it is not overly simplistic, we may say that in natural theology people attempt through their own natural faculties to approach God, whereas in revealed theology God has in his own special way approached humanity:

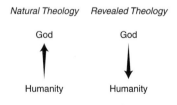

It is important to note, though, that those who accept both natural and revealed theology do not confuse what people do in natural theology with what God does in revealed theology. Natural theology, if successful, delivers some basic knowledge of God which may bear on people's philosophical life, such as knowledge of God's existence and perhaps something of his nature. But revealed theology, if true, delivers a knowledge which bears on human *salvation*. This was the point of the quip by Søren

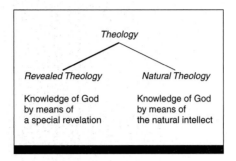

Kierkegaard (Danish philosopher of about 1850) that "to stand on one leg and prove God's existence is a very different thing from going on one's knees and thanking him," or from the exclamation of Tertullian (Church Father of about 200), "What has Athens to do with Jerusalem? What has the Academy to do with the Church?" or the distinction made by Blaise Pascal (French philosopher of about 1650) between "the God of the philosophers, and the God of Abraham, Isaac, and Jacob." Indeed, a whole string of thinkers has repudiated as irrelevant if not misguided the philosophical or rational approach to God in favor of the approach through *faith*. (By the way, what *is* faith anyway?)

As usual, however, such a distinction as that between natural and revealed theology is not as neat and tidy as one might wish, and in the actual history of philosophy and theology they have tended to blur into one another. This is not surprising in view of the fact that most philosophers who have propounded arguments for God's existence have already believed in divine revelation while at the same time believing that it is useful to demonstrate and understand through reason what they had already accepted through faith. Still, the distinction is an important and helpful one, and natural theology must be distinguished and understood. For, as we have seen, natural theology is itself a philosophical problem. Further, while some have rejected such (natural) knowledge of God, it has obviously not been rejected by those who have presented philosophical arguments for God's existence. Which brings us to . . .

THE COSMOLOGICAL ARGUMENT

Many arguments for the existence of God have been formulated over the centuries. Here we will consider two of them, surely the most important: the Cosmological and Teleological Arguments. These are *a posteriori* argu-

Is Belief in God "Properly Basic"?

Some recent philosophers (including Alvin Plantinga, William Alston, Nicholas Woltersdorff, and others) have introduced what they call "reformed epistemology" and have argued that belief in God is a "properly basic" belief, that is, a belief that may be accepted immediately, without evidence, as with "2 + 2 = 4," "The world has existed for longer than five minutes," "I had breakfast this morning," and "It is wrong to kill people for the fun of it." This of course does not mean that belief in God can be arbitrary or unjustified any more than any other properly basic beliefs, and this is where reformed epistemology comes in. These thinkers find in the sixteenth-century Protestant reformer John Calvin an account of a possible and appropriate ground for the properly basic belief in God:

> There is within the human mind, and indeed by natural instinct, an awareness of divinity. . . . God himself has implanted in all men a certain understanding of his divine majesty. . . . men one and all perceive that there is a God and that he is their maker.*

Belief in God may be embraced apart from rational evidence, and at the same time be justified as a natural disposition implanted in the soul by God himself.

---

*John Calvin, *Institutes of the Christian Religion,* tr. Ford Lewis Battles (Philadelphia: Westminster Press, 1960), I, pp. 43–44.

---

ments which, as we know from an earlier discussion, means that they attempt to demonstrate the existence of God *by means of sense experience.*

The most familiar attempts to prove the existence of God are variations of the *Cosmological Argument.* How many times have you heard something like this: "There has to be a God, because, well, the universe couldn't just *happen.* Do you think things just popped into being from *nowhere?* There must be a first cause of everything." This may not be the most sophisticated reasoning in the world, but it *is* a thumbnail expression of the Cosmological Argument. Why is this argument called "cosmological"? Because it is based

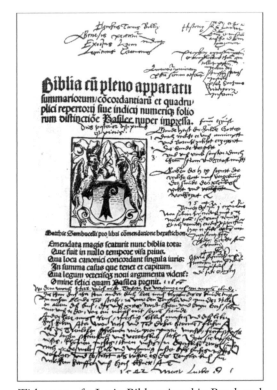

Title page of a Latin Bible printed in Basel, and
bearing the handwritten notations of Martin
Luther, the great sixteenth-century reformer,
who took a very dim view of natural theology,
knowledge of God through reason. Many who
believe in *revealed* theology find the revelation
in sacred scriptures, such as the Bible.

on the *kosmos*, the Greek word for *world*. Of course, "world" means here not
just the earth but the whole physical universe, or the sum total of space and
time. It is also called, for short, the First-Cause Argument, since it attempts
to show that there must be a first cause of the world.

The Cosmological Argument has been propounded by numerous
thinkers and in various forms down through the ages, but most formulations of it involve the following reasoning:

1. Here is the world, or space and time.
2. It could not be the cause of itself.
3. It could not come from nothing.

4. It could not be an effect in an infinite series of causes and effects.

5. Therefore, it must be caused by something outside space and time, something uncaused and ultimate.

Stated in this way, it begins with the fact of the physical world and then by a process of elimination arrives at the only possible explanation for it: God, or the First Cause. But why cannot something be the cause of itself? Why cannot something come from nothing? Why cannot something be the final effect in an infinite series of causes and effects?

These are, indeed, difficult questions. They are addressed, or at least involved, in the most famous proofs for God ever formulated, the "Five Ways" of St. Thomas Aquinas. He presents them in his *Summa Theologiae*:

The existence of God can be proved in five ways.

The first and more manifest way is the argument from motion. It is certain, and evident to our senses, that in the world some things are in motion. Now whatever is moved is moved by another, for nothing can be moved except it is in potentiality to that towards which it is moved; whereas a thing moves inasmuch as it is in act. For motion is nothing else than the reduction of something from potentiality to

THE COSMOLOGICAL ARGUMENT

Compressed into the form of a categorical syllogism, all Cosmological Arguments for God may be expressed as follows:

All contingent (or caused) being depends for its existence
  on some uncaused being.
The cosmos is a contingent being.

Therefore, the cosmos depends for its existence on some uncaused being.

As always, no conclusion in a deductive argument can be stronger than the premises. What questions, doubts, or challenges might be raised against the premises here? And does the "being" of the conclusion have to mean *God?*

actuality. But nothing can be reduced from potentiality to actuality, except by something in a state of actuality. Thus that which is hot, as fire, makes wood, which is potentially hot, to be actually hot, and thereby moves and changes it. Now it is not possible that the same thing should be at once in actuality and potentiality in the same respect, but only in different respects. For what is actually hot cannot simultaneously be potentially hot; but it is simultaneously potentially cold. It is therefore impossible that in the same respect and in the same way a thing should be both mover and moved, i.e., that it should move itself. Therefore, whatever is moved must be moved by another. If that by which it is moved be itself moved, then this also must needs be moved by another, and that by another again. But this cannot go on to infinity, because then there would be no first mover, and, consequently, no other mover, seeing that subsequent movers move only inasmuch as they are moved by the first mover; as the staff moves only because it is moved by the hand. Therefore it is necessary to arrive at a first mover, moved by no other; and this everyone understands to be God.

The second way is from the nature of efficient cause. In the world of sensible things we find there is an order of efficient causes. There is no case known (neither is it, indeed, possible) in which a thing is found to be the efficient cause of itself; for so it would be prior to itself, which is impossible. Now in efficient causes it is not possible to go on to infinity, because in all efficient causes following in order, the first is the cause of the intermediate cause, and the intermediate is the cause of the ultimate cause, whether the intermediate cause be several, or one only. Now to take away the cause is to take away the effect. Therefore, if there be no first cause among efficient causes, there will be no ultimate, nor any intermediate, cause. But if in efficient causes it is possible to go on to infinity, there will be no first efficient cause, neither will there be an ultimate effect, nor any intermediate efficient causes; all of which is plainly false. Therefore it is necessary to admit a first efficient cause, to which everyone gives the name of God.

The third way is taken from possibility and necessity, and runs thus. We find in nature things that are possible to be and not to be, since they are found to be generated, and to be corrupted, and consequently, it is possible for them to be and not to be. But it is impossible for all things which are, to be of this sort,[2] for that which can not-be at some time is not. Therefore, if everything can not-be, then at one time there was nothing in existence. Now if this is true, even now there would be nothing in existence, because that which does not exist begins to exist only through something already existing. Therefore, if at one time nothing was in existence, it would have been impossible for anything to have begun to exist; and thus even now nothing would be in existence—which is absurd. Therefore, not all beings are merely possible, but there must exist something the existence of which is necessary. But every necessary thing either has its necessity caused by another, or not. Now it is impossible to go on to infinity in necessary things which have their necessity caused by another, as has been already proved in regard to efficient causes. Therefore we cannot but admit the existence of some being having of itself its own necessity, and not receiving it from another, but rather causing in others their necessity. This all men speak of as God.

The fourth way is taken from the gradation to be found in things. Among beings there are some more and some less good, true, noble, and the like. But "more" or "less" are predicted of different things according as they resemble in their different ways something which is the maximum, as a thing is said to be hotter according as it more nearly resembles that which is hottest; so that there is something which is truest, something best, something noblest, and, consequently, something which is most being, for those things that are greatest in truth are greatest in being, as it is written in *Metaph*. ii. Now the maximum in any genus is the cause of all in that genus, as fire, which is the maximum of heat, is the cause of all hot things, as is said in the same book. Therefore there must also be something which is to all beings the cause of their being, goodness, and every other perfection; and this we call God.

The fifth way is taken from the governance of the world. We see that things which lack knowledge, such as natural bodies, act for an end, and this is evident from their acting always, or nearly always, in the same way, so as to obtain the best result. Hence it is plain that they achieve their end, not fortuitously, but designedly. Now whatever

---

[2]I have emended the translation in accordance with the best textual reading of this line: *Impossibile est autem omnia quae sunt, talia esse.*

lacks knowledge cannot move towards an end, unless it is directed by some being endowed with knowledge and intelligence; as the arrow is directed by the archer. Therefore some intelligent being exists by whom all natural things are directed to their end; and this being we call God.[3]

It should be noted what all of the Five Ways have in common. Each of them begins in an *a posteriori* way with the created world, and each of them presupposes the metaphysical principle *ex nihilo, nihil fit,* "from nothing, nothing comes." More specifically, St. Thomas shows in the Second Way why something cannot be the cause of itself (it would have to exist before it exists), and the impossibility of an infinite series of causes and effects is explicitly argued in the first three Ways. But here is a surprise. When St. Thomas argues against an infinite series of causes and effects he is not thinking of a *temporal* series, or one that *stretches infinitely backwards in time,* but rather a *hierarchical* series, or one that *extends infinitely upwards in being.* This is a crucial point for understanding St. Thomas' argument, and a picture may be worth a thousand words:

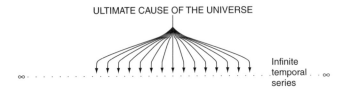

ULTIMATE CAUSE OF THE UNIVERSE

Infinite temporal series

That is, every moment in the universe, even if the universe has always been here, is dependent for its existence, *at that moment,* upon an ultimate cause. Although he believed, on the basis of Genesis 1:1, that the world, and therefore time, had a beginning, for the sake of his proofs for God he grants the world has always existed. After all, he reasons, if we can show that God must exist to account for a world that has always been here, how much more must he exist to account for a world that hasn't?

---

[3]St. Thomas Aquinas, *Summa Theologiae,* Pt. 1, Qu. 2, Art. 3, in *Basic Writings of Saint Thomas Aquinas,* ed. Anton C. Pegis (New York: Random House, 1945), I.

The most efficacious way to prove that God exists is on the supposition that the world is eternal. Granted this supposition, that God exists is less manifest. For, if the world and motion have a first beginning, some cause must clearly be posited to account for this origin of the world and of motion.[4]

Although each of the Five Ways assumes the eternity of the world, this is most evident in the Third Way. There it is argued that not all things are merely possible, or can not-be, for that would mean that even now nothing would exist; for, given *enough time* all possible states, including the possible nonbeing of things, would come about, and such a state at some point in the *infinite* past must have by now come about; but from such a state of nothingness, nothing could possibly come (*ex nihilo, nihil fit*); but right now there *is* a world, and therefore it was wrong at the start to think that all things are merely possible; so there must be something necessary, and ultimately something necessary of itself. Stay with this until you see how this argument cannot possibly work except on the assumption that the world has always existed.

St. Thomas really thought of his Five Ways as variations on a single idea, which is the substance of all of them: We know from experience that the world is *contingent*, that is, it depends on something outside itself for its existence. And this would be true even if the world has always been here, for an infinite collection of contingent things is no less contingent than a finite one. But there must be some *unconditional, ultimate* being upon which the world depends; otherwise it would have no *final* basis for existence.

There is, of course, a more obvious and more popular version of the argument. In philosophical circles this is sometimes called the *Kalam* Cosmological Argument (*kalam* is arabic for "rational") because of its prominence in medieval arabic philosophy, though it certainly has had its advocates in the Judeo-Christian tradition as well. Here, the infinite series of causes and effects *is* conceived as a temporal one stretching backwards in time; it is denied that this series could be infinite, and it is concluded that God must exist as the "First" Cause, that is, the originator of this temporal series. We saw that even though St. Thomas accepted this as an article of faith (Gen. 1:1), from a purely philosophical standpoint he left the question open, and actually *argued* as if the world had no beginning.

---

[4]St. Thomas Aquinas, *Summa Contra Gentiles*, I, 13, 30.

ST. THOMAS AQUINAS

St. Thomas Aquinas was born at the end of 1224 or the beginning of 1225 in a castle near Naples. His aristocratic father was the count of Aquino. He received his earliest education in the Benedictine monastery of Monte Cassino, where he was placed by his parents when he was 5, and at 14 he went to the University of Naples. In Naples he was attracted to the Dominican brothers and entered the Dominican Order. His family disapproved of this move, and Thomas' brothers kidnapped him during a journey to Bologna. His father, who was a military man and no doubt advocated the ideals of "breeding, leading, and bleeding," had Thomas imprisoned in a tower. He tried to draw Thomas back to sanity, even tempting him with a woman. But, faithful to his commitment, Thomas escaped after a year and traveled to Paris.

In Paris and then in Cologne, Thomas was the pupil of St. Albert the Great, whose interest in adapting the philosophy of Aristotle to Christianity

(continued on next page)

Others believe that it is philosophically *necessary* to believe in a beginning of the world. The reasoning goes like this. If the world *has* always existed, then an infinite number of years (or months, minutes, or whatever) has *already gone by*. But surely this is a self-contradictory claim. For an *infinite* series of years (or whatever) can never (by its very nature as being *infinite*) go by or be completed. How can one claim that prior to this moment (what lies in the future is irrelevant) the world has *passed through* an infinite number of years? Of course, you can *think* of an infinite number of was decisive for the direction of Thomas' own work. During this time Thomas was taunted as "the Dumb Ox" by his fellow students. (Thomas was exceedingly quiet, and was immensely fat, with a frame not unlike a wine cask.) But Albert the Great announced: "You call our brother Thomas a dumb ox, do you? I tell you that someday the whole world will listen to his bellows." In 1252, Thomas returned to Paris where he resumed his formal education at the university there, receiving his licentiate and his master's degree and lecturing as well.

In 1259, he returned to Italy where he taught theology at the papal court in Rome and was commissioned by Pope Urban IV to compose the litrugy of the feast of Corpus Christi. During the years 1268–1272 he was once again lecturing in Paris. He was then sent to Naples to establish a Dominican *Studium Generale*, where he remained until 1274, when he was called by Pope Gregory X to participate in the Council of Lyons. It was on the journey to Lyons that Thomas died, on March 7, 1274.

There is a tradition that toward the end of his life Thomas enjoyed mystic experiences which made all that he had previously written "seem as straw worthy to be burned." He became known as the Angelic Doctor, and was canonized in 1323. In 1879 Pope Leo XIII proclaimed Thomism as the official philosophy of the Roman Catholic Church. St. Thomas bellowed loudly indeed.

St Thomas was a prolific writer. In addition to many commentaries on the works of Aristotle, commentaries on Biblical books, and works on specific philosophical and theological topics, he produced two of the most influential and majestic works of the entire history of philosophy: *Summa Theologiae* and *Summa Contra Gentiles*.

---

years, but you can't *count* them; you can entertain the *idea* of an infinite series, but you can't actually *pass through* one and come out the other end. Or try this: If the universe has always existed, then it has taken *forever* to reach this point. But then it could never reach this point. But here we are! So it *didn't* take forever.

It will be noted that this argument for the beginning of the world is purely rational or logical. Some have enlisted further and very different evidence from cosmology, the study of the origin and nature of the physical

THE COSMOLOGICAL ARGUMENT: THOMISTIC FORM

Any form of the Cosmological Argument for God reasons, in one way or another, from the *contingency* of the world's being to the necessity of God's being. According to St. Thomas' version, no matter how long the world has existed—or even if it has always existed—it is *contingent*, or dependent, upon something else for its existence, and, finally, on Something which is *not* dependent. By its nature, this Something must be a transcendent (outside space and time) and ultimate being.

---

universe. You may be familiar with the theory of the "Big Bang." According to this theory, the present "expanding universe," or the recession of galaxies at unimaginable velocities, points to a moment, about 15 or 20 billion years ago, when all the matter in the universe was condensed into something like a superdense atom and exploded. Understandably, it is a temptation for some to identify this Big Bang with the origin of the universe. Others point to the Second Law of Thermodynamics: It is universally accepted that the energy in the universe is, at least on the large scale, irreversibly and evenly being distributed throughout—the universe is cooling down. But if the universe is running down, like a clock, must it not have once been wound up?

Thus Robert Jastrow, a well-known astronomer, on the implications of the Big Bang:

> When an astronomer writes about God, his colleagues assume he is either over the hill or going bonkers. In my case it should be understood from the start that I am an agnostic in religious matters. However, I am fascinated by some strange developments going on in astronomy—partly because of their religious implications and partly because of the peculiar reactions of my colleagues.

> The essence of the strange developments is that the Universe had, in some sense, a beginning—that it began at a certain moment in time, and under circumstances that seem to make it impossible—not just now, but ever—to find out what force or forces brought the world

THE COSMOLOGICAL ARGUMENT: POPULAR FORM

Whereas the Thomistic version of the Cosmological Argument is interested only in the *nature* of the world (as contingent), the more popular version is more interested in its *age*. According to this reasoning, it is impossible that the world has always existed, for that would mean that an infinite number of years (or whatever) has already gone by, but that is impossible because it is self-contradictory. Time must therefore have a beginning. And the cause of time must itself be Something transcendent (outside space and time) and ultimate.

According to the medieval picture of the universe, the earth is at the center, partly covered by water, surrounded by air and fire; then come the heavenly spheres, which carry round the moon, sun, and planets, followed by the *primum mobile,* the "first moved"; beyond this is "the Dwelling of God and all the Saints." Is St. Thomas' argument for God as the Unmoved Mover dependent on this picture of the universe?

into being at that moment. Was it, as the Bible says, that "Thou, Lord, in the beginning hast laid the foundations of the earth, and the heavens are the work of thine hands?" No scientist can answer that question; we can never tell whether the Prime Mover willed the world into being, or the creative agent was one of the familiar forces of physics; for the astronomical evidence proves that the Universe was created twenty billion years ago in a fiery explosion, and in the searing heat of that first moment, all the evidence needed for a scientific study of the cause of the great explosion was melted down and destroyed.

This is the crux of the new story of Genesis. It has been familiar for years as the "Big Bang" theory, and has shared the limelight with other theories, especially the Steady State cosmology; but adverse evidence has led to the abandonment of the Steady State theory by nearly everyone, leaving the Big Bang theory exposed as the only adequate explanation of the facts.

The general scientific picture that leads to the Big Bang theory is well known. We have been aware for fifty years that we live in an expanding Universe, in which all the galaxies around us are moving apart from us and one another at enormous speeds. The Universe is blowing up before our eyes, as if we are witnessing the aftermath of a gigantic explosion. If we retrace the motions of the outward-moving galaxies backward in time, we find that they all come together, so to speak, fifteen or twenty billion years ago.

At that time all the matter in the Universe was packed into a dense mass, at temperatures of many trillions of degrees. The dazzling brilliance of the radiation in this dense, hot Universe must have been beyond description. The picture suggests the explosion of a cosmic hydrogen bomb. The instant in which the cosmic bomb exploded marked the birth of the Universe.

Now we see how the astronomical evidence leads to a biblical view of the origin of the world. The details differ, but the essential elements in the astronomical and biblical accounts of Genesis are the same: the chain of events leading to man commenced suddenly and sharply at a definite moment in time, in a flash of light and energy. . . .

For the scientist who has lived by his faith in the power of reason, the story ends like a bad dream. He has scaled the mountains of ignorance; he is about to conquer the highest peak; as he pulls himself over the final rock, he is greeted by a band of theologians who have been sitting there for centuries.[5]

THE TELEOLOGICAL ARGUMENT

Closely related to the Cosmological Argument is the *Teleological Argument*. Obviously, this argument will have to do with *teleology* (from the Greek word *telos:* "purpose, design") and is called, for short, the Design Argument.

This argument is closely associated with the Cosmological Argument, and it will be recalled that St. Thomas listed it as the Fifth Way, alongside the other four. As with the Cosmological Argument, the Teleological Argument is an *a posteriori* reasoning that employs the idea of causality. In this case God is posited as the only adequate explanation for the apparent order, purpose, unity, harmony, and beauty of the cosmos. It may go beyond the Cosmological Argument, however, in further identifying the ultimate cause as a *rational* cause: The rationality displayed in the cosmos must be the product of *mind.*

One of the best-known, though now out-of-date, statements of this argument is provided by the Anglican divine William Paley (1743–1805). In his famous *watch analogy*, Paley argued that the human eyeball demands an intelligent creator no less than a watch, and the reasoning should recall our discussion of inductive arguments by analogy in Chapter 2. From Paley's *Natural Theology:*

> In crossing a heath, suppose I pitched my foot against a *stone* and were asked how the stone came to be there, I might possibly answer that for anything I knew to the contrary it had lain there forever, nor would it, perhaps, be very easy to show the absurdity of this answer. But suppose I had found a *watch* upon the ground, and it should be inquired how the watch happened to be in that place, I should hardly

---

[5]Robert Jastrow, *God and the Astronomers* (New York: Warner Books, 1978), pp. 1–4, 115–16.

"God does not play dice with the universe."
—Einstein

think of the answer which I had before given, that for anything I knew the watch might have always been there. Yet why should not this answer serve for the watch as well as for the stone; why is it not as admissible in the second case as in the first? For this reason, and for no other, namely, that when we come to inspect the watch, we perceive—what we could not discover in the stone—that its several parts are framed and put together for a purpose, e.g., that they are so formed and adjusted as to produce motion, and that motion so regulated as to point out the hour of the day; that if the different parts had been differently shaped from what they are, or placed after any other manner or in any other order than that in which they are placed, either no motion at all would have been carried on in the machine, or none which would have answered the use that is now served by it. To reckon up a few of the plainest of these parts and of their offices, all tending to one result: we see a cylindrical box containing a coiled elastic spring, which, by its endeavor to relax itself, turns round the box. We next observe a flexible chain—artificially wrought for the sake of flexure—communicating the action of the spring from the box to the fusee. We then find a series of wheels, the teeth of which catch in and apply to each other, conducting the motion from the fusee to the balance and from the balance to the pointer, and at the same time, by the size and shape of those wheels, so regulating that motion as to terminate in causing an index, by an equable and measured progression, to pass over a given space in a given time. We take notice that the wheels are made of brass, in order to keep them from rust; the springs of steel, no other metal being so elastic; that over the face of the watch there is placed a glass, a material employed in no other part of the work, but in the room of which, if there had been any other than a transparent substance, the hour could not be seen without opening the case. This mechanism being observed—it requires indeed an examination of the instrument, and perhaps some previous knowledge of the subject, to perceive and understand it; but being once, as we have said, observed and understood—the inference we think is inevitable, that the watch must have had a maker—that there must have existed, at some time and at some place or other, an artificer or artificers who formed it for the purpose which we find it actually to answer, who completely comprehended its construction and designed its use. . . .

Were there no example in the world of contrivance except that of the eye, it would be alone sufficient to support the conclusion which we draw from it, as to the necessity of an intelligent Creator. It could never be got rid of, because it could not be accounted for by any other supposition which did not contradict all the principles we possess of knowledge—the principles according to which things do, as often as they can be brought to the test of experience, turn out to be true or false. Its coats and humors, constructed as the lenses of a telescope are constructed, for the refraction of rays of light to a point, which forms the proper action of the organ; the provision in

In 1802 William Paley, an English clergyman, published his *Natural Theology*, in which he argued for God's existence on the basis of design in the cosmos. From this work comes the famous watch analogy: The world is to God as a watch is to a watchmaker.

its muscular tendons for turning its pupil to the object, similar to that which is given to the telescope by screws, and upon which power of direction in the eye the exercise of its office as an optical instrument depends; the further provision for its defense, for its constant lubricity and moisture, which we see in its socket and its lids, in its glands for the secretion of the matter of tears, its outlet or communication with the nose for carrying off the liquid after the eye is washed with it; these provisions compose altogether an apparatus, a system of parts, a preparation of means, so manifest in their design, so exquisite in their contrivance, so successful in their issue, so precious, and so infinitely beneficial in their use, as, in my opinion, to bear down all doubt that can be raised upon the subject. And what I wish, under the title of the present chapter, to observe is that, if other parts of nature were inaccessible to our inquiries, or even if other parts of nature presented nothing to our examination but disorder and confusion, the validity of this example would remain the same. If there were but one watch in the world, it would not be less certain that it had a maker. If we had never in our lives seen any but one single kind of hydraulic machine, yet if of that one kind we understood the mechanism and use, we should be as perfectly assured that it proceeded from the hand and thought and skill of a workman, as if we visited a museum of the arts and saw collected there twenty different kinds of machines for drawing water, or a thousand different kinds for other purposes. Of this point each machine is a proof independently of all the rest. So it is with the evidences of a divine agency. The proof is not a conclusion which lies at the end of a chain of reasoning, of which chain each instance of contrivance is only a link, and of which, if one link fail, the whole fails; but it is an argument separately supplied by every separate example. An error in stating an example affects only that example. The argument is cumulative in the fullest sense of that term. The eye proves it without the ear; the ear without the eye. The proof in each example is complete; for when the design of the part and the conduciveness of its structure to that design is shown, the mind may set itself at rest; no future consideration can detract anything from the force of the example.[6]

---

[6]William Paley, *Natural Theology: Selections*, ed. Frederick Ferré (New York: Bobbs-Merrill, 1963), pp. 3–4, 32–33.

Paley's watch analogy is striking but irrelevant, at least after 1859, the year in which Darwin published the *Origin of Species*. Paley, as well as almost everyone of his time, believed in a *special* creation of the universe and humans all at once, once upon a time, as a watchmaker makes a watch. Darwin, with his doctrine of the gradual and evolutionary development of man over an untold number of years, slowly but surely dealt the deathblow to any Paleyan type of teleology. In the place of a God directly and immediately fashioning, say, the human eye, evolution substituted long and progressive sequences of natural causes and effects. It became possible to explain the human species, and everything about it, as well as much of the rest of the biological and physical universe, in purely naturalistic terms. To be sure, the name of Darwin is often associated with atheism, but this is a mistake. Darwin (whose sole earned academic degree was in theology) did not himself turn his theory of evolution against the existence of God but only against a certain view of *how* God created things, the Paleyan view.

Indeed, though Darwin's theory of evolution dealt the deathblow to Paleyan teleology, it hardly dealt the deathblow to God. Enter *theistic evolution*. Is it not possible to reconcile evolution with a theistic interpretation of the world? Might not evolution itself be viewed as an instrument by which God has brought about, and is bringing about, his purpose in the cosmos? Many have answered Yes, including F. R. Tennant (1866–1957), one of the most persuasive of theistic evolutionists.

Tennant, who was himself a scientist before he was a philosopher and theologian, laid aside previous and, as he regarded them, dubious

THE TELEOLOGICAL ARGUMENT

Most versions of the Teleological Argument are arguments from analogy and take some such form as:

Watches, houses, ships, machines, etc., all exhibit design,
   and they are planned and produced by intelligent beings.
The universe exhibits design.

Therefore, the universe was planned and produced by an intelligent being.

approaches to God, and set out in an "empirically-minded" and scientific way. He asks us whether it is not possible in this way to establish a "reasonable belief" in God that is as respectable as what any scientific theory can deliver. He asks us further whether the evidence does not cause us to set aside once and for all the *narrow* teleology of Paley and to adopt a *wider*, or *cosmic* teleology. He asks us to shift our attention from specific instances of design to the *design of the whole*, and to appreciate natural processes and laws, including evolution, as "conspiring," as it were, upon the production of an intelligible universe, and upon humanity—the bearer of moral and aesthetic values—as its crowning glory.

> The empirically-minded theologian adopts a different procedure. He asks how the world, inclusive of man, is to be explained. He would let the Actual world tell its own story and offer its own suggestions: not silence it while abstractive speculation, setting out with presuppositions possibly irrelevant to Actuality, weaves a system of thought which may prove to conflict with facts. . . .
>
> . . . [he] sets out from facts and inductions; its premises are as firmly established and as universally acknowledged as any of the stable generalisations of science. Here there is at least common ground, as distinct from private certitude, from which argumentation may proceed. Coercive demonstration being confessedly unattainable, it is to be inquired what kind of justification for reasonable belief natural theology can afford. And the first step is to set forth the facts and generalisations which collectively constitute our data or premises.
>
> The forcibleness of Nature's suggestion that she is the outcome of intelligent design lies not in particular cases of adaptedness in the world, nor even in the multiplicity of them. It is conceivable that every such instance may individually admit of explanation in terms of proximate causes or, in the first instance, of explanation other than in terms of cosmic or "external" teleology. And if it also admits of teleological interpretation, that fact will not of itself constitute a rigorous certification of external design. The forcibleness of the world's appeal consists rather in the conspiration of innumerable causes to produce, by their united and reciprocal action, and to maintain, a general order of Nature. Narrower kinds of teleological argument, based on surveys of restricted spheres of fact, are much more precarious than that for which the name of "the wider teleology" may be appropriated in that

the comprehensive design-argument is the outcome of synopsis or conspection of the knowable world.

. . . So long as organisms were believed to have originated, in their present forms and with all their specialised organs, "ready made," the argument that adaptation of part to whole, of whole to environment, and of organ to function, implied design, was forcible. But its premiss became untenable when Darwin shewed that every organic structure had come to be what it now is through a long series of successive and gradual modifications. Gradualness of construction is in itself no proof of the absence of external design: it is not at this point that Darwinism delivered its alleged death-blow to teleology. The sting of Darwinism rather lay in the suggestion that proximate and "mechanical" causes were sufficient to produce the adaptations from which the teleology of the eighteenth century had argued to God. Assignable proximate causes, whether mechanical or not, are sufficient to dispose of the particular kind of teleological proof supplied by Paley. But the fact of organic evolution, even when the maximum of instrumentality is accredited to what is figuratively called natural selection, is not incompatible with teleology on a grander scale: as exponents of Darwinism were perhaps the first to recognise and to proclaim. Subversive of Paley's argument, it does not invalidate his theistic conclusion, nor even his view that every organism and organ is an end as well as a means. Indeed the science of evolution was the primary source of the wider teleology current for the last half century, as well as the main incentive to the recovery of the closely connected doctrine of divine immanence. This kind of teleology does not set out from the particular adaptations in individual organisms or species so much as from considerations as to the progressiveness of the evolutionary process and as to the organic realm as a whole. . . .

In an exposition of the significance of the moral order for theistic philosophy, the first step is to point out that man belongs to Nature, and is an essential part of it, in such a sense that the world cannot be described or explained as a whole without taking him and his moral values into account. Prof. Pringle-Pattison, especially, has elaborated the doctrine that, as he expresses it, "man is organic to the world." What precisely this, or the similar phrase "man is the child of Nature," should mean, if either is to be more than a half-truth, needs to be made clear. In so far as man's soul, *i.e.* man as *noümenon*, or (in the language of spiritualistic pluralism) the dominant monad in the

Charles Darwin published his *Origin of
Species* in 1859 and his *Descent of Man* in
1871. His theory of evolution held
revolutionary implications for many
fields of thought—not the least of
which was theology.

empirical self, is concerned, we are not authorised by known facts to
regard man as organic to Nature, or as the child of Nature, in the
sense that he is an emergent product of cosmic evolution. We are
rather forbidden by psychology to entertain any such notion. But, this
proviso being observed—it must qualify all that is further said in the
present connexion—we can affirm that man's body, with all its conditioning of his mentality, his sociality, knowledge and morality, is "of a
piece" with Nature; and that, in so far as he is a phenomenal being,
man is organic to Nature, or a product of the world. And this fact is
as significant for our estimation of Nature as for our anthropology. If
man is Nature's child, Nature is the wonderful mother of such a child.
Any account of her which ignores the fact of her maturity is scientifically partial and philosophically insignificant. Her capacity to produce
man must be reckoned among her potencies, explain it how we may.
And man is no monstrous birth out of due time, no freak or sport. In
respect of his body and the bodily conditioning of his mentality, man
is like, and has genetic continuity with, Nature's humbler and earlier-
born children. In the fulness of time Nature found self-utterance in a

NARROW VS. WIDER TELEOLOGY

- *Paley.* The world is full of particular instances of design, for example, the human eye. Each of these is an evidence for the direct creating and designing activity of God.
- *Tennant.* Particular instances of design, such as the human eye, can be adequately explained by natural causes, such as evolution. These natural causes, however, have produced a world which *as a whole* is an overwhelming evidence for the creating and designing activity of God.

son possessed of the intelligent and moral status. Maybe she was pregnant with him from the beginning, and the world-ages are the period of her gestation. As to this anthropocentric view of the world-process, and its co-extensiveness with teleological interpretation, more will presently be said. But in the light of man's continuity with the rest of the world we can at once dismiss the view that Nature suddenly "stumbled" or "darkly blundered" on man, while "churning the universe with mindless motion." The world-process is a *praeparatio anthropologica*, whether designedly or not, and man is the culmination, up to the present stage of the knowable history of Nature, of a gradual ascent. We cannot explain man in terms of physical Nature; conceivably Nature may be found explicable—in another sense of the word—in terms of man, and can be called "the threshold of spirit." Judging the genealogical tree by its roots, naturalism once preached that Darwin had put an end to the assumption that man occupies an exceptional position on our planet; apparently implying that there is no difference of status between man and the primordial slime because stages between the two are traceable. But if we judge the tree by its fruits, Darwin may rather be said to have restored man to the position from which Copernicus seemed to have ousted him, in making it possible to read the humanising of Nature in the naturalising of man, and to regard man as not only the last term and the crown of Nature's long upward effort, but also as its end or goal.[7]

---

[7]F. R. Tennant, *Philosophical Theology* (Cambridge: Cambridge University Press, 1930), II, pp. 78–79, 84, 100–102.

BLACK ELK ON THE ONENESS OF NATURE

One of the salient features of the Western religious tradition is its emphasis on the distinction between nature and the supernatural, and the human being's essential connection with the latter. This emphasis stands in stark contrast with other traditions. For example, Native American traditions stress humanity's unity with nature, as is evident in the following excerpt from *Black Elk Speaks:*

My friend, I am going to tell you the story of my life, as you wish; and if it were only the story of my life I think I would not tell it. . . .

It is the story of all life that is holy and is good to tell, and of us two-leggeds sharing in it with the four-leggeds and the wings of the air and all green things; for these are children of one mother and their father is one Spirit. . . .

So I know that it is a good thing I am going to do; and because no good thing can be done by any man alone, I will first make an offering and send a voice to the Spirit of the World, that it may help me to be true. See, I fill this sacred pipe with the bark of the red willow; but before we smoke it, you must see how it is made and what it means. These four ribbons hanging here on the stem are the four quarters of the universe. The black one is for the west where the thunder beings live to send us rain; the white one for the north, whence comes the great white-cleansing wind; the red one for the east, whence springs the light and where the morning star lives to give men wisdom; the yellow for the south, whence come the summer and the power to grow.

But these four spirits are only one Spirit after all, and this eagle feather here is for that One, which is like a father, and also it is for thoughts of men that should rise high as eagles do. Is not the sky a father and the earth a mother, and are not all living things with feet or wings or roots their children? And this hide upon the mouthpiece here, which should be bison hide, is for the earth, from whence we came and at whose breast we suck as babies all our lives, along with

(continued on next page)

all the animals and birds and trees and grasses. And because it means all this, and more than any man can understand, the pipe is holy. . . .

Now I light the pipe, and after I have offered it to the powers that are one Power, and sent forth a voice to them, we shall smoke together. Offering the mouthpiece first of all to the One above—so—I send a voice:

Hey hey! hey hey! hey hey! hey hey !

Grandfather, Great Spirit, you have been always, and before you no one has been. There is no other one to pray to but you. You yourself, everything that you see, everything has been made by you. The star nations all over the universe you have finished. The four quarters of the earth you have finished. The day, and in that day, everything you have finished. Grandfather, Great Spirit, lean close to the earth that you may hear the voice I send. You towards where the sun goes down, behold me; Thunder Beings, behold me! You where the White Giant lives in power, behold me! You where the sun shines continually, whence come the day-break star and the day, behold me! You where the summer lives, behold me! You in the depths of the heavens, an eagle of power, behold! And you, Mother Earth, the only Mother, you who have shown mercy to your children!

Hear me, four quarters of the world—a relative I am! Give me the strength to walk the soft earth, a relative to all that is! Give me the eyes to see and the strength to understand, that I may be like you. With your power only can I face the winds.

Great Spirit, Great Spirit, my Grandfather, all over the earth the faces of living things are all alike. With the tenderness have these come up out of the ground. Look upon these faces of children without number and with children in their arms, that they may face the winds and walk the good road to the day of quiet.

This is my prayer; hear me! The voice I have sent is weak, yet with earnestness I have sent it. Hear me!*

---

*Black Elk Speaks: Being the Life Story of a Holy Man of the Oglala Sioux, as told through John G. Neihardt (Lincoln: University of Nebraska Press, 1932), pp. 1–6.

THE PROBLEM OF CAUSALITY

Both the Cosmological and the Teleological Arguments for God have been criticized in many ways. Here we can mention only one minor criticism and then the major one.

Inevitably someone will ask: "If everything has to have a cause, then what caused God?" But this is to miss the point. It is not that every *thing* must have a cause, but that every *event*, or everything that *comes into being*, must have a cause. Now is God an event or something that comes into being? Of course not. How could he be, if he is the *cause* of events or things that come into being? It is hopeless confusion to try to think of God, who is by his nature transcendent and ultimate, as a being that comes into being or passes away. Similarly, some smart aleck might ask: "What was God doing before he created the world?" To this, one is tempted, with some ancients, to answer: "What was God doing before he created the world? Why, he was preparing hell for people who pry into divine mysteries!" More seriously, it is to be answered again that the questioner must not be paying attention to what he or she is saying. How can there by a "before" without creation? Apart from creation there *is* no time and therefore no "before." We must, in a word, take absolutely seriously the idea of God as a *transcendent* and *absolute* being.

Other problems for these arguments may be posed:

- Must the cause or designer of the universe be *God?*
- Just because everything in the universe is contingent, must the universe itself be contingent?
- How does the Cosmological Argument square with the scientific principle of the conservation of energy?
- Would we not *perceive* the universe as ordered whether it actually is or not?
- Even if the universe does display order, would not this particular configuration of matter necessarily arise sooner or later by sheer chance?

We cannot consider such questions here, but they might be discussed and considered with profit.

For our part, we must raise what is surely the most troublesome feature of the Cosmological and Teleological Arguments for the existence of God.

We have seen repeatedly that central to both of the arguments is the *principle of causality:* "From nothing, nothing comes," or "every event must have a cause." But the concept of causality is far and away one of the most difficult in all philosophy. And this is especially true when it is applied to God's relation to the world.

We have already seen how both Hume and Kant in different ways destroyed the traditional concept of causality. Now we are in a better position to emphasize the implications for metaphysics, and specifically for discussions of God. In a way, Hume and Kant make the same criticism: *The concept of causality cannot be legitimately extended beyond the objects of possible sense experience, and therefore cannot be extended to God.* On the other hand, it is crucial to appreciate that Hume and Kant would interpret and justify this claim in radically different ways.

Hume. Aside from Hume's skepticism about causality as such (after all, we have no basis in experience for the claimed universality and necessity of the cause-effect relation) he raises a further question: Are we not limited by our experience to a small part of reality? What possible basis do we have for thinking that the causal relation holds for anything *beyond* our experience? Our idea of causality—insofar as we possess one—is based on our experience of causes (for example, carpenters) and effects (for example, houses) joined together over and over again right before our eyes. But surely God's creation of the world is hardly an object of possible experience, and is totally without analogy in the universe we know.

This is Hume's main and recurring point in the following passage from his *Dialogues Concerning Natural Religion*, in which, more or less, his own position is represented by Philo, who speaks the following:

> That all inferences, Cleanthes, concerning fact are founded on experience, and that all experimental reasonings are founded on the supposition that similar causes prove similar effects, and similar effects similar causes, I shall not at present much dispute with you. But observe, I entreat you, with what extreme caution all just reasoners proceed in the transferring of experiments to similar cases. Unless the cases be exactly similar, they repose no perfect confidence in applying their past observation to any particular phenomenon. Every alteration of circumstances occasions a doubt concerning the event; and it requires new experiments to prove certainly that the new circumstances are of no moment or importance. A change in bulk, situation, arrangement, age, disposition of the air, or surrounding

bodies—any of these particulars may be attended with the most unexpected consequences. And unless the objects be quite familiar to us, it is the highest temerity to expect with assurance, after any of these changes, an event similar to that which before fell under our observation. The slow and deliberate steps of philosophers here, if anywhere, are distinguished from the precipitate march of the vulgar, who, hurried on by the smallest similitude, are incapable of all discernment or consideration.

But can you think, Cleanthes, that your usual phlegm and philosophy have been preserved in so wide a step as you have taken when you compared to the universe houses, ships, furniture, machines, and, from their similarity in some circumstances, inferred a similarity in their causes? Thought, design, intelligence, such as we discover in men and other animals, is no more than one of the springs and principles of the universe, as well as heat or cold, attraction or repulsion, and a hundred others which fall under daily observation. It is an active cause by which some particular parts of nature, we find, produce alterations on other parts. But can a conclusion, with any propriety, be transferred from parts to the whole? Does not the great disproportion bar all comparison and inference? From observing the growth of a hair, can we learn anything concerning the generation of a man? Would the manner of a leaf's blowing, even though perfectly known, afford us any instruction concerning the vegetation of a tree?

But allowing that we were to take the *operations* of one part of nature upon another for the foundation of our judgment concerning the *origin* of the whole (which never can be admitted), yet why select so minute, so weak, so bounded a principle as the reason and design of animals is found to be upon this planet? What peculiar privilege has this little agitation of the brain which we call *thought*, that we must thus make it the model of the whole universe? Our partiality in our own favour does indeed present it on all occasions, but sound philosophy ought carefully to guard against so natural an illusion.

So far from admitting, continued Philo, that the operations of a part can afford us any just conclusion concerning the origin of the whole, I will not allow any one part to form a rule for another part if the latter be very remote from the former. Is there any reasonable ground to conclude that the inhabitants of other planets possess thought, intelligence, reason, or anything similar to these faculties in men? When nature has so extremely diversified her manner of operation in this small globe, can we imagine that she incessantly copies herself throughout so immense a universe? And if thought, as we may well suppose, be confined merely to this narrow corner and has even there so limited a sphere of action, with what propriety can we assign it for the original cause of all things? The narrow views of a peasant who makes his domestic economy the rule for the government of kingdoms is in comparison a pardonable sophism. . . .

A very small part of this great system, during a very short time, is very imperfectly discovered to us; and do we thence pronounce decisively concerning the origin of the whole?

Admirable conclusion! Stone, wood, brick, iron, brass, have not, at this time, in this minute globe of earth, an order or arrangement without human art and contrivance; therefore, the universe could not originally attain its order and arrangement without something similar to human art. But is a part of nature a rule for another part very wide of the former? Is it a rule for the whole? Is a very small part a rule for the universe? Is nature in one situation a certain rule for nature in another situation vastly different from the former?

And can you blame me, Cleanthes, if I here imitate the prudent reserve of Simonides, who, according to the noted story, being asked by Hiero, *What God was?* desired a day to think of it, and then two days more; and after that manner continually prolonged the term, without ever bringing his definition or description? Could you even blame me if I had answered, at first, *that I did not know,* and was sensible that this subject lay vastly beyond the reach of my faculties? You might cry out sceptic and rallier, as much as you pleased; but, having found in so many other subjects much more familiar the imperfections and even contradictions of human reason, I never should expect any success from its feeble conjectures in a subject so sublime and so remote from the sphere of our observation. When two *species* of objects have always been observed to be conjoined together, I can *infer,* by custom, the existence of one wherever I *see* the existence of the other; and this I call an argument from experience. But how this argument can have place where the objects, as in the present case, are single, individual, without parallel or specific resemblance, may be difficult to explain. And will any man tell me with a serious countenance that an orderly universe must arise from some thought and art like the human because we have experience of it? To ascertain this reasoning it were requisite that we had experience of the origin of worlds; and it is not sufficient, surely, that we have seen ships and cities arise from human art and contrivance.[8]

Do you see, then, just what Hume, the radical empiricist, would mean by the charge that the Cosmological and Teleological Arguments involve an unjustified application of the concept of causality to God?

Kant. But Kant would mean something very different. We saw earlier how Kant, contrary to Hume, *did* believe in "Every event must have a cause" as a certain and universal principle, but only because it is a way in which our minds necessarily grasp and *represent* reality. Do you recall the role-colored glasses from our earlier discussion of Kant? We cannot help but experience things as standing in cause-effect relations, because causality is one of the ways in which our mind organizes or makes possible experience itself. But then, of course, causality can have no possible bearing on anything *outside* our sense experience, such as God.

In the following from the *Critique of Pure Reason*, Kant calls the Cosmological Argument a "transcendental illusion," and lists four lines of objection. The first of these concerns explicitly the proper, and limited, application of the principle of causality, though the limitation of the theoretical reason to objects of possible experience is a theme which otherwise recurs throughout.

There are so many sophistical propositions in this cosmological argument, that it really seems as if speculative reason had spent all her dialectical skill in order to produce the greatest possible transcendental illusion. . . .

I said before that a whole nest of dialectical assumptions was hidden in that cosmological proof, and that transcendental criticism might easily detect and destroy it. I shall here enumerate them only, leaving it to the experience of the reader to follow up the fallacies and remove them.

---

[8]David Hume, *Dialogues Concerning Natural Religion*, ed. Henry D. Aiken (New York: Hafner, 1948), pp. 20–23.

We find, first, the transcendental principle of inferring a cause for the accidental. This principle, that everything contingent must have a cause, is valid in the world of sense only, and has not even a meaning outside it. For the purely intellectual concept of the contingent cannot produce a synthetical proposition like that of causality, and the principle of causality has no meaning and no criterion of its use, except in the world of sense, while here it is meant to help us beyond the world of sense.

Secondly. The inference of a first cause, based on the impossibility of an infinite ascending series of given causes in this world of sense,— an inference which the principles of the use of reason do not allow us to draw even in experience, while here we extend that principle beyond experience, whither that series can never be prolonged.

Thirdly. The false self-satisfaction of reason with regard to the completion of that series, brought about by removing in the end every kind of condition, without which, nevertheless, no concept of necessity is possible, and by then, when any definite concepts have become impossible, accepting this as a completion of our concept.

Fourthly. The mistaking the logical possibility of a concept of all united reality (without any internal contradiction) for the transcendental, which requires a principle for the practicability of such a synthesis, such principle however being applicable to the field of possible experience only, etc.[9]

DOES CAUSALITY APPLY TO GOD?

- *Hume:* No. Causality is limited to the sensible world because we know it only through sense experience. We have no grounds for applying it to a transcendent God.
- *Kant.* No. Causality is limited to the sensible world because it is *constitutive* of sense experience, it is part of what experience *means*. It therefore has no possible application to a transcendent God.

---

[9]Immanuel Kant, *Critique of Pure Reason*, tr. F. Max Müller (Garden City, NY: Anchor Books, 1966), pp. 405–8.

As with Hume, Kant charges that the Cosmological and Teleological Arguments involve an illegitimate extension of the idea of causality to a sphere where it has no proper application. But he means something very different: It is not just that we have no basis for such an application of causality (Hume), but that causality could not *possibly* apply to God.

It must be seen that Hume's and Kant's criticisms of these theistic arguments follow from their respective views of knowledge. In both cases, it is important to appreciate this connection, and to appreciate, therefore, the importance of the starting point. And that takes us back to Chapters 7 and 8.

CHAPTER 9 IN REVIEW

Summary

One of the most interesting and instructive phenomena in the history of philosophy is found in the arguments for God's existence. Natural theology means knowledge of God acquired through our natural faculties of reason and/or experience. The best examples of this are the traditional arguments for the existence of God. We have considered two of these in this chapter:

- The Cosmological Argument
- The Teleological Argument

These are *a posteriori* arguments in that they attempt to demonstrate the existence of God on the basis of sense experience.

More specifically, the Cosmological Argument (First-Cause Argument) concludes that a transcendent and absolute being must exist as the only possible cause of the contingent universe. Actually there are two forms of this argument. If one grants that the world must have had a temporal beginning (as in the more common, or popular version), then God is posited as the first cause of the cosmos in the sense of its originator at a definite point in the past. If, on the other hand, one grants that the cosmos has always existed (as in the Thomistic version), then God is posited as the first cause of the cosmos in the sense of the ultimate being upon whom it depends at every moment in its (even infinite) existence. It is important to see that in either case, the world is regarded as *contingent* and therefore dependent upon something beyond itself, and finally upon something ultimate, for its existence.

The Teleological Argument (Design Argument) concludes that there must exist a transcendent and intelligent being as the only possible cause of the order and design in the universe. This argument also assumes two forms. In the older version of Paley, God is regarded as the direct cause of *specific* designs, say the human eye. In the more recent version of Tennant, who was much influenced by the theory of evolution, God is responsible for the design of the *whole*, which he has achieved by long sequences of innumerable natural processes. This latter view involves theistic evolution, the idea that evolution itself is one of the natural processes instituted by God and employed as an instrument for his production of humanity and human values.

Numerous complaints have been filed against these arguments, but the most critical have to do with the concept of causality. Aside from the intrinsic problems with this concept (is it really a metaphysical certainty that "from nothing, nothing comes" or that "every event must have a cause"?), some important philosophers (for example, Hume and Kant) have charged that whatever its application may be to the sensible world, it is certainly less clear how the concept of causality may relate to anything beyond the sensible world. According to Hume, we have no rational right to ascribe to some transcendent being the attributes and activities, such as *causal* activity, which we know only from our limited experience of the sensible world around us. According to Kant, it is not even *possible* that a concept of causality could be ascribed to God, since by its nature it is a principle of sense experience and therefore has no application beyond sense experience.

Basic Ideas

- Natural theology
- Revealed theology
- *A posteriori* arguments for God
- The Cosmological Argument
     Thomistic version
     Popular version
- St. Thomas' Five Ways
- Two meanings of "First" Cause
- Big Bang theory of the universe
- Second Law of Thermodynamics

- The Teleological Argument
- Teleology
- Paley's watch analogy
- Special creation vs. evolution
- Theistic evolution
- Narrow vs. wider teleology
- Miscellaneous objections to the *a posteriori* proofs
- Causality as the central problem
- Hume's criticism of divine causality
- Kant's criticism of divine causality

Questions for Reflection

- It is often observed that there is an essential difference between metaphysical and scientific reasoning. Do you agree with this? Can scientific theories, such as the Big Bang theory, hold any real relevance for metaphysical questions, such as the question of God? Can a scientific claim also be a metaphysical claim?

- It is sometimes said that St. Thomas' Five Ways are really different expressions of the same argument. Do you see any truth in this? How might you defend it?

- For some people, the idea of "theistic evolution" is a contradiction in terms. But is evolution in itself necessarily atheistic? What does "evolution" mean? Does God work through nature in other respects? What, suddenly, becomes so important about the interpretation of religious language, the use of symbols, etc. (think of the first chapters of the Bible)?

- If you were St. Thomas, would you feel devastated by either Hume's or Kant's attacks on your arguments for God? If not, why not?

For Further Reading

Donald R. Burrill (ed.). *The Cosmological Arguments.* Garden City, NY. Anchor Books, 1967. A useful collection of the standard statements both classical and contemporary, both positive and critical, on the Cosmological and Teleological Arguments.

William Lane Craig. *The Kalam Cosmological Argument*. New York: Barnes and Noble, 1977. A modern proposal of a medieval, Arabic form of the Cosmological Argument (the "popular" version), and involving discussions of contemporary physics, mathematics, philosophy, and theology.

Lecomte du Noüys. *Human Destiny*. New York: Longmans, Green & Co., 1947. One of the best known of modern versions of the Teleological Argument, arguing from the infinitesimal odds against the chance occurrences required for the production of life.

Anthony Kenny. *Five Ways: St. Thomas Aquinas' Proofs of God's Existence*. London: Routledge & Kegan Paul, 1969. Commentary on the Five Ways of St. Thomas in an analytic style.

J. L. Mackie. *The Miracle of Theism: Arguments for and against the Existence of God*. Oxford: Clarendon Press, 1982. Chs. 5, 8. Heavy-duty treatments of the Cosmological and Teleological Arguments by an eminent contemporary philosopher, tying together traditional and recent moves.

Jacques Maritain. *Approaches to God*. San Francisco: Harper & Row, 1954. Readable chapters reflecting the Thomistic approach to God (especially Ch. 2) by a recent and esteemed Catholic thinker.

Hugo A. Meynell. *The Intelligible Universe: A Cosmological Argument*. New York: Barnes & Noble, 1982. A redevelopment of an earlier version of the Cosmological Argument, taking into account critical discussions of recent years.

Ed. L. Miller. *God and Reason: An Invitation to Philosophical Theology*, 2nd ed. Englewood Cliffs, NJ: Prentice Hall, 1995. Chs. 1, 3–4. Introductory discussions of natural theology and the Cosmological and Teleological Arguments, reflecting standard historical and recent positions, pro and con.

Alvin Plantinga. *God, Freedom, and Evil*. Grand Rapids, MI: Eerdmans, 1974. Part 2, a–b. Brief and logically tight discussions and rejection of the Cosmological and Teleological Arguments by an influential contemporary philosopher of religion.

William L. Rowe. *The Cosmological Argument*. Princeton, NJ: Princeton University Press, 1975. A somewhat advanced discussion on all aspects of the subject, especially the principle of causality.

Jagjit Singh. *Great Ideas and Theories of Modern Cosmology.knowledge* New York: Dover, 1961. Ch. 16. Brief and mildly critical consideration of the cosmological-astronomical evidence for God.

Richard Swineburne. *The Existence of God.* Oxford: Clarendon Press, 1979. Chs. 7–8. Discussions in an analytic style, concluding that the Cosmological and Teleological Arguments hold no deductive validity though they do contribute inductive support.

Richard Taylor. *Metaphysics.* 3rd ed. Englewood Cliffs, NJ: Prentice Hall, 1983. Ch. 10. Recent and readable treatments of the issues involved in the Cosmological and Teleological Arguments, reflecting a sympathetic approach.

Religious
Experience

NATURALLY, THERE will be many who will balk at arguments for the
existence of God right from the start. Nor will they necessarily
be atheists. Some of the critics will be themselves believers, objecting that
somehow such proofs are irrelevant or inappropriate to the overpowering
majesty of God. "No," they will say, "God is not known in this way. Just as
he transcends the world and our reason, so is he known in a way that transcends our ordinary knowledge." It is just as silly to think that God can be
captured by an argument as it is to think that he can be confined to
Solomon's Temple: "Even heaven and the highest heaven cannot contain
you, much less this house that I have built!" (New Revised Standard Version). On the more human side, do not religious experiences come *first*,
and the arguments and rationalizations *second?* The French contemplative
philosopher Simone Weil[1] thought so:

259

When we are eating bread, and even when we have eaten it, we know that it is real. We can nevertheless raise doubts about the reality of the bread. Philosophers raise doubts about the reality of the world of the senses. Such doubts are however purely verbal; they leave the certainty intact and actually serve only to make it more obvious to a well-balanced mind. In the same way he to whom God has revealed his reality can raise doubts about this reality without any harm. They are purely verbal doubts, a form of exercise to keep his intelligence in good health.[2]

Enter the *non*rational approach to God, the approach of *religious experience* in its various and sundry forms.

THE EXPERIENCE OF THE NUMINOUS

It is important to review an earlier point: the distinction between *nonrational* and *irrational*. That which is irrational is that which is in some way contrary to or incompatible with reason. Certainly this is not intended by those who press for a nonrational approach to God. On the contrary, they intend a knowledge of God which is *other* than rational, and, indeed, they usually mean a knowledge that is higher than, or *superior* to, what is knowable through ordinary reason or experience.

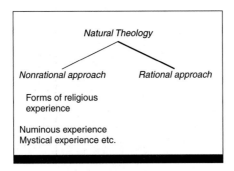

---

[1]Pronounced *vay*.

[2]Simone Weil, *Waiting for God*, tr. Emma Crauford (New York: Harper & Row, 1973), p. 212.

This was exactly the view of the German religious thinker Rudolf Otto (1869–1937). Otto was much annoyed by the distortions and trivialities that result from an intellectualist approach to religion. At the beginning of his influential work, *The Idea of the Holy*, Otto explains how the rational perspective on religion has come to dominate, and warns against the "one-sidedly intellectualistic and rationalistic interpretation":

. . . we have to be on our guard against an error which would lead to a wrong and one-sided interpretation of religion. This is the view that the essence of deity can be given completely and exhaustively in . . . "rational" attributions. . . . It is not an unnatural misconception. We are prompted to it by the traditional language of edification, with its characteristic phraseology and ideas; by the learned treatment of religious themes in sermon and theological instruction; and further even by our Holy Scriptures themselves. In all these cases the "rational" element occupies the foreground, and often nothing else seems to be present at all. But this is after all to be expected. All language, in so far as it consists of words, purports to convey ideas or concepts;—that is what language means—and the more clearly and unequivocally it does so, the better the language. And hence expositions of religious truth in language inevitably tend to stress the "rational" attributes of God.

But though the above mistake is thus a natural one enough, it is none the less seriously misleading. For so far are these "rational" attributes from exhausting the idea of deity, that they in fact imply a nonrational or suprarational Subject of which they are predicates. They are "essential" (and not merely "accidental") attributes of that subject, but they are also, it is important to notice, *synthetic* essential attributes. That is to say, we have to predicate them of a subject which they qualify, but which in its deeper essence is not, nor indeed can be, comprehended in them; which rather requires comprehension of a quite different kind. Yet, though it eludes the conceptual way of understanding, it must be in some way or other within our grasp, else absolutely nothing could be asserted of it. And even mysticism, in speaking of it as *to arrēton*, the ineffable, does not really mean to imply that absolutely nothing can be asserted of the object of the religious consciousness; otherwise, mysticism could exist only in unbroken silence, whereas what has generally been a characteristic of the mystics in their copious eloquence.

Here for the first time we come up against the contrast between rationalism and profounder religion. . . . All depends upon this: in our idea of God is the nonrational overborne, even perhaps wholly excluded, by the rational? Or conversely, does the nonrational itself preponderate over the rational? Looking at the matter thus, we see that the common dictum, that orthodoxy itself has been the mother of rationalism, is in some measure well founded. It is not simply that orthodoxy was preoccupied with doctrine and the framing of dogma, for these have been no less a concern of the wildest mystics. It is rather that orthodoxy found in the construction of dogma and doctrine no way to do justice to the nonrational aspect of its subject. So far from keeping the nonrational element in religion alive in the heart of the religious experience, orthodox Christianity manifestly failed to recognize its value, and by this failure gave to the idea of God a one-sidedly intellectualistic and rationalistic interpretation.[3]

Mind you, for Otto it is not just that there is a nonrational side or aspect of religion in addition to others. The nonrational lies at the *center* of religion; he calls it the heart of any religion worthy of the name. And as soon as you let some philosopher or theologian—some *rationalist*—get hold of religion, he or she will immediately cut out its heart! Otto insisted that we must recover and preserve the *non*rational core of authentic religion.

To this point, Otto's appraisal of religion is largely negative and not all that unusual: We must reject any rationalistic perspective which preempts or excludes what is in fact the nonrational core of religion. But what exactly is this nonrational core? Here is where Otto made his special contribution. He believed that he had isolated an experience which, though varying in its manifestations, may be recognized the world over, in all periods, and which is the foundation of true religious consciousness. It is the sense or awareness—sometimes quiet, sometimes frenzied, but always a bit uncanny—of *Something*. Here we are trying to talk about an encounter which, really, defies talking about. But it may help to describe this as a feeling or even a sense—even a kind of sensation—of a presence that is holy, wholly other, absolute, overpowering, and divine and before which

[3]Rudolf Otto, *The Idea of the Holy*, second ed., tr. John W. Harvey (New York: Oxford University Press, 1950), pp. 1–3.

we only want to cower in our creatureliness. For this experience Otto coined the expression "numinous feeling" and, better, "feeling of the numinous," from the Latin *numen*, which at one time signified the divine power or presence.

Otto invites you to reflect on such an experience as possibly your own:

> Let us consider the deepest and most fundamental element in all strong and sincerely felt religious emotion. Faith unto salvation, trust, love—all these are there. But over and above these is an element which may also on occasion, quite apart from them, profoundly affect us and occupy the mind with a wellnigh bewildering strength. Let us follow up with every effort of sympathy and imaginative intuition wherever it is to be found, in the lives of those around us, in sudden, strong ebullitions of personal piety and the frames of mind such ebullitions evince, in the fixed and ordered solemnities of rites and liturgies, and again in the atmosphere that clings to old religious monuments and buildings, to temples and to churches. If we do so we shall find we are dealing with something for which there is only one appropriate expression, *"mysterium tremendum."* The feeling of it may at times come sweeping like a gentle tide, pervading the mind with a tranquil mood of deepest worship. It may pass over into a more set and lasting attitude of the soul, continuing, as it were, thrillingly vibrant and resonant, until at last it dies away and the soul resumes its "profane," non-religious mood of everyday experience. It may burst in sudden eruption up from the depths of the soul with spasms and convulsions, or lead to the strangest excitements, to intoxicated frenzy, to transport, and to ecstasy. It has its wild and demonic forms and can sink to an almost grisly horror and shuddering. It has its crude, barbaric antecedents and early manifestations, and again it may be developed into something beautiful and pure and glorious. It may become the hushed, trembling, and speechless humility of the creature in the presence of—whom or what? In the presence of that which is a *mystery* inexpressible and above all creatures.[4]

---

[4]Ibid., pp. 12–13.

Does this suggest anything from your own experience? If not, Otto would recommend, perhaps, visiting an old and great cathedral, or maybe listening to Bach's B Minor Mass, or reading sacred scriptures. For in such things may be found, as it were, a less fleeting experience of the numinous inasmuch it has been to some degree captured and embodied for the contemplation of all.

THE MYSTICAL ASCENT

The word "mysticism" is surely one of the foggiest and most abused in our intellectual vocabulary. It is important, though, to clarify it, since mystical experience is perhaps the most dramatic and fascinating of the nonrational or experiential ways of knowing God.

Ouija boards, astrology, crystal balls, Tarot cards—all these and similar things have, at times, been associated with mysticism. The problem is, of course, that they are beset from the start with a certain occult or spooky nature. This not only renders them immediately suspect from a rational or scientific standpoint, but it also removes them from the arena of serious investigation and validation/invalidation. Mysticism in this sense should be set aside as a sort of slur on the real thing.

More recently, the use (and abuse) of drugs, such as LSD and the like, has intruded onto the religious and philosophical scene, promising a sort of "instant mysticism." One of the popularizers of this experience was the writer Aldous Huxley, who in his much-read little book *The Doors of Perception*, described the mescaline experience:

> . . . what happens to the majority of the few who have taken mescalin under supervision can be summarized as follows.
>
> (1) The ability to remember and to "think straight" is little if at all reduced. (Listening to the recordings of my conversation under the influence of the drug, I cannot discover that I was then any stupider than I am at ordinary times.)
>
> (2) Visual impressions are greatly intensified and the eye recovers some of the perceptual innocence of childhood, when the sensum was not immediately and automatically subordinated to the concept. Interest in space is diminished and interest in time falls almost to zero.

(3) Though the intellect remains unimpaired and though perception is enormously improved, the will suffers a profound change for the worse. The mescalin taker sees no reason for doing anything in particular and finds most of the causes for which, at ordinary times, he was prepared to act and suffer, profoundly uninteresting. He can't be bothered with them, for the good reason that he has better things to think about.

(4) These betters things may be experienced (as I experienced them) "out there," or "in here," or in both worlds, the inner and the outer, simultaneously or successively. That they are better seems to be self-evident to all mescalin takers who come to the drug with a sound liver and an untroubled mind.

These effects of mescalin are the sort of effects you could expect to follow the administration of a drug having the power to impair the efficiency of the cerebral reducing valve. When the brain runs out of sugar, the undernourished ego grows weak, can't be bothered to undertake the necessary chores, and loses all interest in those spatial and temporal relationships which mean so much to an organism bent on getting on in the world. As Mind at Large seeps past the no longer watertight valve, all kinds of biologically useless things start to happen. In some cases there may be extrasensory perceptions. Other persons discover a world of visionary beauty. To others again is revealed the glory, the infinite value and meaningfulness of naked existence, of the given, unconceptualized event. In the final stage of egolessness there is an "obscure-knowledge" that All is in all—that All is actually each. This is as near, I take it, as a finite mind can ever come to "perceiving everything that is happening everywhere in the universe."

In this context, how significant is the enormous heightening, under mescalin, of the perception of color! For certain animals it is biologically very important to be able to distinguish certain hues. But beyond the limits of their utilitarian spectrum, most creatures are completely color blind. Bees, for example, spend most of their time "deflowering the fresh virgins of the spring"; but, as Von Frisch has shown, they can recognize only a very few colors. Man's highly developed color sense is a biological luxury—inestimably precious to him as an intellectual and spiritual being, but unnecessary to his survival as an animal. To judge by the adjectives which Homer puts into their mouths, the heroes of the Trojan War hardly excelled the bees in their capacity to distinguish colors. In this respect, at least, mankind's advance has been prodigious.

Mescalin raises all colors to a higher power and makes the percipient aware of innumerable fine shades of difference, to which, at ordinary times, he is completely blind. It would seem that, for Mind at Large, the so-called secondary characters of things are primary. Unlike Locke, it evidently feels that colors are more important, better worth attending to, than masses, positions and dimension. Like mescalin takers, many mystics perceive supernaturally brilliant colors, not only with the inward eye, but even in the objective world around them. Similar reports are made by psychics and sensitives. There are certain mediums to whom the mescalin taker's brief revelation is a matter, during long periods, of daily and hourly experience.[5]

Huxley speaks here of the loss of interest in space and time, of focused attention, of "Mind at Large," "a world of visionary beauty," "the infinite value and meaningfulness of naked existence," and the "All." It is no wonder that some have seen in such experiences a shortcut to religious, or at least heightened, consciousness. Maybe so. But *mysticism?* Again, it depends on what you mean. Notice that Huxley speaks also of "visual impressions greatly intensified," "extrasensory perceptions," "perceiving everything that is happening," and "heightening of the perception of color." Such talk precisely distinguishes this kind of experience (whatever kind it is) from what we might call a more traditional and *classical* form of mysticism.

It is difficult to give a precise definition of classical mysticism, and the problem isn't helped any by the fact that the mystics describe their experience as something which can't be described! But we may venture the following: Mysticism is the pursuit of a transcendent, unitive experience with the absolute reality. It may also be helpful to list more completely some characteristic features of this experience. It is:

- *Transcendent*. Not localizable in space or time.
- *Ineffable*. Not expressible in language.

---

[5]Aldous Huxley, *The Doors of Perception* (New York: Harper & Row, 1970), pp. 25–27.

- *Noetic.* Conveying illumination, truth.
- *Ecstatic.* Filling the soul with bliss, peace.
- *Unitive.* Uniting the soul with reality.

Here we have in mind the experiences of, say St. Augustine, St. Francis, St. Teresa, St. John of the Cross, and Meister Eckhart. What distinguishes classical mysticism from the other forms of mysticism is its interest not in intensifying the consciousness but rather in *emptying* the consciousness of all sense impressions and ideas, so that, abandoning and transcending these, the soul may attain a reality of an altogether different and *higher* nature. One is tempted to make a distinction between these "higher" mystics and the merely "high" mystics.

It is important here to recall Plato. These mystics certainly were not Platonists, but they did hold to a Platonic view of reality as a ladder or scale of being. The point is to escape, even in this life as much as possible, all multiplicity and change and to become united with true being. And this in turn means a sometimes difficult ascent, as in struggling up a steep mountain, from the sensible world, to our ideas of the world, to pure intellectual ideas, to our own selves, and beyond to the One. This "ascent of the soul" may otherwise and variously be represented as an ascent from nonbeing to being, from ignorance to knowledge, from multiplicity and change to unity and immutability, and from evil to goodness. Recalling also Plato's Allegory of the Cave, the mystical ascent may further be characterized, allegorically, as an ascent from darkness to light.

Different mystics may represent differently the number and nature of the several steps involved in this ascent, and the following diagram is only suggestive of the basic ones. It is important to see that as one passes from the sensible world to internal-world images, to the pure intellectual operations of the mind, to pure self-consciousness, to *beyond* the self, one leaves further and further behind the crudities of space-time experience, multiplicity and change, ignorance, evil, and attachment to things, ideas, and one's own self. Thus is the soul prepared for the ecstatic ("ecstasy" means, literally, "to stand outside one's own self") infilling of the divine illumination, love, and will.

One of the greatest of the mystics was a Spaniard, St. John of the Cross (1542–1591). It is no accident that he called his greatest work *The Ascent of Mount Carmel.* The significance of the word "ascent" should certainly by now be clear, and Mount Carmel is where Elijah called down the true God to overthrow the claims of the idolaters (I Kings 18:20–40). This

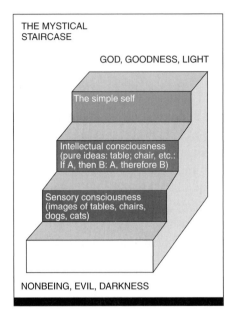

THE MYSTICAL
STAIRCASE

GOD, GOODNESS, LIGHT

The simple self

Intellectual consciousness
(pure ideas: table; chair, etc.:
If A, then B: A, therefore B)

Sensory consciousness
(images of tables, chairs,
dogs, cats)

NONBEING, EVIL, DARKNESS

work begins with a mystical poem and continues with a long and detailed commentary on it. That St. John sought to express the mystical experience by means of a *poem* is suggestive of the ineffability (or unspeakability) of the experience, and the poem otherwise reflects important aspects of the experience, such as the ascent, the withdrawal from the world and ideas, transcendence, ecstatic union, and the like. It would be a good exercise to see how many of these features you can recognize in the lines of St. John's poem:

1
In a dark night,
My longing heart, aglow with love,
—Oh, blessed lot!—
I went forth unseen
From my house that was at last in deepest rest.

2
Secure and protected by darkness,
I climbed the secret ladder, in disguise,
—Oh, blessed lot!—
In darkness, veiled and concealed I went
Leaving behind my house in deepest rest.

3
Oh, blissful night!
Oh, secret night, when I remained unseeing and unseen,
When the flame burning in my heart
Was my only light and guide.

4
This inward light,
A safer guide than noonday's brightness,
Showed me the place where He awaited me
—My soul's Beloved—
A place of solitude.

5
Oh, night that guided me!
Oh, night more lovely than the rosy dawn!
Oh, night whose darkness guided me
To that sweet union,
In which the lover and Beloved are made one.

6
Upon the flower of my breast,
Kept undefiled for Him alone,
He fell asleep,
While I was waking
Caressing Him with gentle cedars' breeze.

7
And when Aurora's breath
Began to spread His curled hair,
His gentle hand
He placed upon my neck.
And all my senses were in bliss suspended.

8
Forgetful of myself,
My head reclined on my Beloved,
The world was gone
And all my cares at rest,
Forgotten all my grief among the lilies.[6]

---

[6]St. John of the Cross, *The Dark Night of the Soul*, tr. and ed. Kurt F. Reinhardt (New York: Ungar, 1957), pp. 1–3.

We have spoken here and there of "mystical union," of the "unitive" aspect of the mystical experience, etc. But it is now important to realize that *Western* mystics (Christians, Jews, Muslims) don't and can't mean a *literal* union with God, at least not generally. For it is a fundamental idea of Western theology that there is an essential difference between God and what he has created. And the soul can never overcome—not even in the heights of mystical experience—the distinction between uncreated and created being. No, it is rather a matter of the soul becoming *conformed* to the divine will and love, or becoming *transparent* to the divine will and love. It is precisely to make this clear that St. John himself introduces his window-pane analogy, and otherwise comments on the mystical experience:

Let me clarify [the nature of this union] by a simile. Picture a ray of sunlight that is striking a window. Now if the window is coated with stains or vapors, the ray will be unable to illumine it and transform it into its own light; this it could do only if the window were stainless and pure. And the greater or lesser degree of illumination will be strictly in proportion to the window's greater or lesser purity; and this will be so, not because of the ray of sunlight but because of the condition of the window. Thus, if the window were entirely clean and pure, the ray would transform and illumine it in such a way that it would become almost undistinguishable from the brightness of the ray and would diffuse the same light as the ray. And yet, however much the window may resemble the ray of sunlight, it actually retains its own distinct nature. But this does not prevent us from saying that this window is luminous as a ray of the sun or is sunlight by participation. Now the soul is like this window: the Divine light of the Being of God is unceasingly beating upon it, or to use a better expression, the Divine light is ever dwelling in it.

When the soul thus allows God to work in it, it will soon be transformed and transfigured in God, and God will communicate to it His supernatural Being in such a way that the soul appears to be God Himself, and it will indeed be God by participation. Yet it remains true nevertheless that the soul's natural being—notwithstanding the soul's supernatural transformation—remains as distinct from the Being of God as it was before, even as the window has and retains a nature of its own, distinct from the nature of the ray, although it owes its luminosity to the light of the sun.

This consideration should make it clearer why a soul cannot dispose itself for this union by either understanding, or sensory apperception, or inner feelings and imaginings, or by any other experiences relating either to God or to anything else, but only by purity and love, that is, by perfect resignation and total detachment from all things for the sake of God alone. And as there can be no transformation unless there be perfect purity, the soul will not be perfect unless it be totally cleansed and wholly pure.

Those souls [who attain to Divine union] do so according to their greater or smaller capacity and thus not in the same degree; and the degree of union depends also on what the Lord wishes to grant to each soul. And it is similar in the beatific vision: though some souls will have a more perfect vision of God in Heaven than others, they all see God, and all are content, since their capacity is satisfied. And in this life, too, all souls [who have attained to the state of perfection] will be equally satisfied, each one according to its knowledge of God and thus according to its capacity. A soul, on the other hand, that does not attain to a degree of purity corresponding to its capacity, will never find true peace and contentment. . . .

This blissful night darkens the spirit, but only in order to illuminate it afterwards with respect to all things; it humbles the spirit and makes it miserable, but only in order to raise it up and exalt it; it impoverishes the spirit and deprives it of every natural possession and affection, but only to enable it to rise, divinely, in unfettered spiritual freedom, to a perfect fruition of all things in Heaven and on earth. And, owing to its purity, the spirit tastes the sweetness of all things in a preeminently sublime manner.

We know that the children of Israel could not relish, in the desert, the sweetness of the manna—the bread of angels—solely because they had retained a single affectionate remembrance of the fleshpots and meals which they had tasted in Egypt. Similarly, the spirit cannot attain to the delights of the supernatural as long as it remains attached to any actual or habitual desire or to any particular object or apprehension of the understanding.

The light which is here imparted to the soul is truly a most sublime Divine light, which transcends every natural light, and which cannot be grasped by the understanding in a natural manner. If, then, the understanding is to be united with this light and is to become Divine in the state of perfection, it must first be purged and annihilated with respect to its natural light and led into darkness by means of this dark contemplation. When this has been done, the Divine light and illumination will take the place of the natural mode and manner of the soul's understanding.

Moreover, in order to attain to the union to which this dark night is leading it, the soul must be filled with a certain glorious splendor, to become disposed for its communication with God. Included herein are innumerable blessings and delights which far exceed all the abundance which the soul can naturally possess. For, as Isaiah says: "No eye has seen, and no ear has heard, nor has it ever entered into a human heart, what God has prepared for those who love Him" [Isa. 64:4]. And this is the reason why the soul must first become empty and poor in spirit and purged from all natural support, so that, in total poverty of spirit and liberated from the old man, it may be able to live that new and blessed life which is attained by means of this night, and which is the state of union with God.[7]

Passing reference has already been made to St. Teresa of Avila (1515–1582), a nun of the Carmelite (there's that word again) Order. She became distressed at the laxity of her Order and inaugurated an energetic and successful reform, beginning with the founding of a convent at Avila, Spain, and involving a more disciplined practice of the life of prayer. She also authored several works on Christian spirituality (addressed primarily to her Sisters) and was, in fact, the one who so greatly influenced St. John of the Cross. She has always been cited as evidence for the way in which the contemplative life is not incompatible with the active life.

One of St. Teresa's books is called *The Interior Castle*. Think about this title. It would surely be desirable to live in a castle—say that splendid one sitting up there on the hill. St. Teresa tells us, however, that the *most* splendid castle is not outside us but *inside* us, namely the *soul*. Moreover, it has many wonderful rooms or dwellings (an allusion to John 14:2)—seven, to be exact (in the Biblical tradition seven is the number of perfection). At the center of all these dwellings is the most glorious and brilliantly lit dwelling place of the King, the light from which radiates outwards, illuminating in

---

[7]Ibid., pp. 35–37, 196–97.

St. Teresa of Avila, Christian mystical
writer and one of only two women on
whom the Roman Catholic Church has
conferred the title of "Doctor."

various degrees the other dwellings, depending on their proximity to the King's dwelling. It is necessary to occupy the several rooms, beginning with the room of self-knowledge, for the sake of their cleansing and purging powers. But the goal, of course, is to occupy the central room and to experience "spiritual marriage" with the divine. St. Teresa represents this as occurring "in the interior, in some place very deep within [the soul]".[8]

As with St. John's image of Mt. Carmel, so St. Teresa's image of The Interior Castle is about the progressive struggle of the individual to attain heightened levels of spiritual existence, culminating in the indescribable mystical union. And, as with St. John of the Cross, she attempts to dispel from her readers any illusions about the difficulty of this spiritual journey.

---

[8]St. Teresa of Avila, *The Interior Castle*, in *The Collected Works*, tr. Kiernan Kavanaugh and Otilio Rodrequez (Washington, D.C.: ICS Publications, 1980), II, p. 430.

In *The Way of Perfection*, she gives us a short but striking account of just how difficult it is—it is as difficult as it is important.

> Do not be frightened, daughters, by the many things you need to consider in order to begin this divine journey which is the royal road to heaven. A great treasure is gained by traveling this road; no wonder we have to pay what seems to us a high price. The time will come when you will understand how trifling everything is next to so precious a reward.

> Now returning to those who want to journey on this road and continue until they reach the end, which is to drink from this water of life, I say that how they are to begin is very important—in fact, all important. They must have a great and very resolute determination to persevere until reaching the end, come what may, happen what may, whatever work is involved, whatever criticism arises, whether they arrive or whether they die on the road, or even if they don't have courage for the trials that are met, or if the whole world collapses.[9]

MYSTICISMS EAST

It is sometimes said that the Western perspective tends to be academic, logical, and argumentative, whereas the Eastern way is essentially meditative, mystical, and inscrutable. Such characterizations are surely a distortion of the facts. We have just seen that various mystical traditions are strongly embedded in the West, and there are strong intellectualist traditions just as embedded in the Eastern perspectives of China, India, and Japan. Nonetheless, there is at least a grain of truth in the notion that the West tends to be intellectualist in its approach to reality whereas the East is spiritualist. It is certainly the spirituality of the East that has been borne across the ocean and has made the biggest impact on Western culture.

Religious experience is as varied in the East as in the West. But here too we encounter a solid core of the "higher" mysticism, with its emphasis on the renunciation of all distractions—both on the outside and on the inside—in the attempt to attain self-transcendence and unity with the ultimate principle of all things.

---

[9]St. Teresa of Avila, *The Way of Perfection*, in *The Collected Works*, II, pp. 117–18.

Probably the best-known of Eastern religious writings is the *Bhagavad-Gita*, a secret text of Hinduism, composed between 600 B.C. and 300 B.C. You will want to read the following passage from the *Gita* in the light of what you have already read from St. John of the Cross. (*Atman* denotes the self, which after enlightenment is understood to be identical with *Brahman*, the supreme reality and principle of all things.)

> He knows bliss in the Atman
> And wants nothing else.
> Cravings torment the heart:
> He renounces cravings.
> I call him illumined.
>
> Not shaken by adversity,
> Not hankering after happiness:
> Free from fear, free from anger,
> Free from the things of desire.
> I call him a seer, and illumined.
> The bonds of his flesh are broken.
> He is lucky, and does not rejoice:
> He is unlucky, and does not weep.
> I call him illumined.
>
> The tortoise can draw in his legs:
> The seer can draw in his senses.
> I call him illumined.
>
> The abstinent run away from what they desire
> But carry their desires with them:
> When a man enters Reality,
> He leaves his desires behind him.
>
> Even a mind that knows the path
> Can be dragged from the path:
> The senses are so unruly.
> But he controls the senses
> And recollects the mind
> And fixes it on me.
> I call him illumined.

Thinking about sense-objects
Will attach you to sense-objects;
Grow attached, and you become addicted;
Thwart your addiction, it turns to anger;

Be angry, and you confuse your mind;
Confuse your mind, you forget the lesson of experience;
Forget experience, you lose discrimination;
Lose discrimination, and you miss life's only purpose.

When he has no lust, no hatred,
A man walks safely among the things of lust and hatred.
To obey the Atman
Is his peaceful joy:
Sorrow melts
Into that clear peace:
His quiet mind
Is soon established in peace.

The uncontrolled mind
Does not guess that the Atman is present:
How can it meditate?
Without meditation, where is peace?
Without peace, where is happiness?

The wind turns a ship
From its course upon the waters:
The wandering winds of the senses
Cast man's mind adrift
And turns his better judgment from its course.

When a man can still the senses
I call him illumined.
The recollected mind is awake
In the knowledge of the Atman
Which is dark night to the ignorant:
The ignorant are awake in their sense-life
Which they think is daylight:
To the seer it is darkness.

Water flows continually into the ocean
But the ocean is never disturbed:
Desire flows into the mind of the seer
But he is never disturbed.
The seer know peace:
The man who stirs up his own lusts

Can never know peace.
He knows peace who has forgotten desire.
He lives without craving:
Free from ego, free from pride.

This is the state of enlightenment in Brahman:
A man does not fall back from it
Into delusion.
Even at the moment of death
He is alive in that enlightenment:
Brahman and he are one.[10]

You may, rightfully, be struck by the similarity of this passage to what has been discussed above and quoted from St. John of the Cross. In fact, it may seem to you that we have here only a different expression of the exact same idea and experience. Many do, indeed, take just this view of the matter. This sort of mysticism, they will say, is really a *universal* experience, though understandably and necessarily grasped and expressed in accordance with the language, images, and world-view of a particular mystic's time, place, and culture. Others are not so sure. And still others *are* sure that this is *not* the case.

It is true that underlying the *experiential* similarities there are important *conceptual* differences. That is, while mystics East and West describe and represent what they *experience* in similar ways, they understand *what* they experience in very different ways. We will mention only one of these conceptual differences, but a very basic one. We emphasized above that in Western mysticism—for example, Christian mysticism—the interpretation of the mystical experience is controlled by the philosophical and theological doctrine of the essential difference between God and his creation, and

---

[10]*The Song of God: Bhagavad-Gita,* tr. Swami Prabhavananda and Christopher Isherwood (New York: New American Library, 1951), pp. 41–44.

MYSTICISM EAST AND WEST

Western and Eastern mystics share many ideas and images in the description of their experience: the renunciation of the sensible world, transcendence of ideas, abandonment of all interests, blissful union with the ultimate reality, the "darkness" which leads to "light," etc.

On a more theoretical level, however, an important difference divides them. Western mystics (Christians, Jews, Muslims) all hold to an essential difference between God and his creatures; and, thus, mystical union can only mean a unity of will, love, etc. Eastern mystics, on the other hand, characteristically hold to the unity of all being; and, thus, mystical union means for them a quite literal unity of the individual with ultimate reality—indeed a unity that has always existed but is discovered in mystical illumination.

mystical "union," therefore, cannot be understood strictly or metaphysically. However, in Hindu thought (at least that which underlies the *Gita*) the matter is conceived quite otherwise. Here we have a strictly *monistic* view: Reality is One; all things are part of the One; there is no essential difference between creator and created. And mystical enlightenment consists of the *realization* of one's actual unity with the One. There are, then, important differences here which bear very much on the actual nature of the experience, and we must not be blinded to these by the similarities.

THE WAY OF ZEN

We have seen that in the case of both Western and Eastern mysticism an emphasis is placed on the ineffability of the mystical experience, the inability to express adequately in language the truth or reality that is encountered therein. But with Buddhism it gets even worse—or better, depending on your point of view.

Most of us have at least a bare knowledge of the origins and teaching of Buddhism. The story (a mixture of fact and legend) is: About 560 B.C., below the Himalayan foothills inside present-day Nepal, Siddhartha ("he

THE BASIC PRINCIPLES OF THE BUDDHA

Under the sacred Bodhi Tree, in a place called Budd Gaya (hence, "Buddha"), Siddhartha Gautama received Enlightenment concerning the following principles.

The Four Noble Truths
1. Life is permeated by suffering.
2. The origin of suffering lies with desire.
3. The cessation of suffering is possible through the cessation of desire.
4. The way to the latter is the Eightfold Noble Path.

The Eightfold Noble Path
1. Right views.
2. Right aspiration.
3. Right speech.
4. Right conduct.
5. Right effort.
6. Right mindfulness.
7. Right contemplation.
8. Right livelihood.

who has achieved his goal") Gautama was miraculously conceived, and upon his birth was pronounced a Bodhisattva ("future Buddha"); he was raised in an overprotective and wealthy family, and at age 29 ventured out only to be shocked by the suffering he encountered; deeply moved by this suffering, he renounced his opulent surroundings and left his wife and infant son in order to become an ascetic in search of Enlightenment; disappointed by several teachers, he sat himself under a sacred Bodhi Tree, vowing not to rise unenlightened; finally, he attained Enlightenment; he then removed himself to Banaras, where he preached a sermon disclosing the Four Noble Truths and the Eightfold Noble Path (see Box, above).

From this has grown centuries of Buddhist traditions, innumerable Buddhist sects, and a mountain of Buddhist literature. If we tried to reduce it all to the least common denominator, it might well be the experience of *emptiness*. All forms of Buddhism emphasize the transitoriness or impermanence of things. Of course, classical mysticism emphasizes this too, but whereas it attempts to scale the heights, transcend this fluctuating level of reality, and penetrate the Absolute, Unchanging reality, Buddhism seeks to penetrate the indescribable *Emptiness* beneath, behind, or beyond things. It is important not to confuse this Emptiness with Nothingness: What is denied (at least according to Mahayana Buddhism) is any absolute, abiding, reality either "out there" (God or Brahman) or "in here" (the self), and to cultivate an appreciation or awareness of things simply as they are—effervescent, transitory, fluctuating, superficial. This means, on the *theoretical* side, that all "substantial" or "dualistic" talk about subject and object, absolute and relative, and good and bad is misguided. On the *practical* side—and this is, after all, what Buddhism is most concerned with—this Enlightenment of the true nature of things as Emptiness constitutes a kind of healing or (perhaps better) balancing or harmonizing of our otherwise distorted minds and emotions.

How to achieve this enlightened state? The best-known way is the way of *Zen* Buddhism. Zen Buddhism, as a distinct brand of Buddhism, took shape in the seventh century and involved a mixture of Indian, Chinese, and earlier Buddhist ideas, especially of the Mahayana tradition. It became predominantly a Japanese movement and recently has taken root in the Western world. This is especially true in the United States, where Robert Pirsig's *Zen and the Art of Motorcycle Maintenance* has been for many years a paperback best-seller, where Haiku poems have been in some circles all the rage, as with the famous

> Old pond—
> and a frog-jump-in
> water-sound[11]

and where college students are titillated by the Zen riddle,

---

[11]Basho (17th century Zen monk), tr. in Harold G. Henderson, *An Introduction to Haiku: An Anthology of Poems and Poets from Basho to Shiki* (Garden City, NY: Doubleday, 1958), p. 20.

We know what is the sound of two hands clapping. But what is the sound of one hand clapping?

But amidst all this, an ancient wisdom and path of spirituality draws many honest truth-seekers to itself.

"Zen" is the Japanese word for "meditation" (*ch'an* in Chinese), and this immediately suggests something of the nature of the spiritual exercise required of the initiate. More specifically, and according to the Rinzai school, there are two aspects of the exercise. The first is, strictly, meditation in the *yoga* position, and involves breathing exercises in which the disciple contemplates a *koan*, a Zen riddle or paradox (such as the one mentioned above). This is given by the master, for the purpose of liberating the disciple from logical and conceptual modes of thought and cultivating an open and accepting mode. Second, there are more external exercises, such as the tea ceremony and archery, geared to the breaking down of the distinction between sacred and secular. Generally, all of this is intended to cultivate a perspective in which everything is seen to be utterly natural and one, and even the most mundane is seen as sacred and revelatory. But there is something yet more specific and, yes, wonderful, that is aimed at: the Zen experience of *satori*, a sudden and illuminating experience (*satori* is Japanese for "enlightenment") that overtakes the successful disciple. What is the specific content of the illuminating experience? Well, that is what cannot be expressed, except perhaps to say that everything is seen in a new light and experienced in perfect rapport.

D. T. Suzuki has done more than anyone to make Zen accessible to Westerners—he has been called the man who made "Zen" an English word. In the following, Suzuki represents the general nature of Zen and clarifies several points with respect to the central experience of *satori*. Special attention might be given to the way in which he distinguishes *satori* from what we have called classical mystical experience, and his expression of the nontheistic character of Zen.

The essence of Zen Buddhism consists in acquiring a new viewpoint of looking at life and things generally. By this I mean that if we want to get into the inmost life of Zen, we must forgo all our ordinary habits of thinking which control our everyday life, we must try to see if there is any other way of judging things, or rather if our ordinary way is always sufficient to give us the ultimate satisfaction of our spiritual needs. If we feel dissatisfied somehow with this life, if there is something in our ordinary way of living that deprives us of freedom in its most sanctified sense, we must endeavour to find a way somewhere which gives us a sense of finality and contentment. Zen proposes to do this for us and assures us of the acquirement of a new point of view in which life assumes a fresher, deeper, and more satisfying aspect. This acquirement, however, is really and naturally the greatest mental cataclysm one can go through with in life. It is no easy task, it is a kind of fiery baptism, and one has to go through the storm, the earthquake, the overthrowing of the mountains, and the breaking in pieces of the rocks.

This acquiring of a new point of view in our dealings with life and the world is popularly called by Japanese Zen students "satori" (*wu* in Chinese). It is really another name for enlightenment (*annuttara-samyak-sambodhi*), which is the word used by the Buddha and his Indian followers ever since his realization under the Bodhi-tree by the River Nairañjanā. There are several other phrases in Chinese designating this spiritual experience, each of which has a special connotation, showing tentatively how this phenomenon is interpreted. At all events there is no Zen without satori, which is indeed the Alpha and Omega of Zen Buddhism. Zen devoid of satori is like a sun without its light and heat. Zen may lose all its literature, all its monasteries, and all its paraphernalia; but as long as there is satori in it it will survive to eternity. I want to emphasize this most fundamental fact concerning the very life of Zen; for there are some even among the students of Zen themselves who are blind to this central fact and are apt to think when Zen has been explained away logically or psychologically, or as one of the Buddhist philosophies which can be summed up by using highly technical and conceptual Buddhist phrases, Zen is exhausted, and there remains nothing in it that makes it what it is. But my contention is, the life of Zen begins with the opening of satori (*kai wu* in Chinese).

Satori may be defined as an intuitive looking into the nature of things in contradistinction to the analytical or logical understanding of it. Practically, it means the unfolding of a new world hitherto unperceived in the confusion of a dualistically-trained mind. Or we may say that with satori our entire surroundings are viewed from quite an unexpected angle of perception. Whatever this is, the world for those who have gained a satori is no more the old world as it used to be; even with all its flowing streams and burning fires, it is never the same one again. Logically stated, all its opposites and contradictions are united and harmonized into a consistent organic whole. This is a mystery and a miracle, but according to the Zen masters such is being performed every day. Satori can thus be had only through our once personally experiencing it. . . .

I wish to close this Essay by making a few general remarks in the way of recapitulation on the Buddhist experience known as satori. . . .

2. Without the attainment of satori no one can enter into the mystery of Zen. It is the sudden flashing of a new truth hitherto altogether undreamed of. It is a sort of mental catastrophe taking place all at once after so much piling of matters intellectual and demonstrative. The piling has reached its limit and the whole edifice has now come to the ground, when behold a new heaven is opened to your full survey. Water freezes suddenly when it reaches a certain point, the liquid has turned into a solidity, and it no more flows. Satori comes upon you unawares when you feel you have exhausted your whole being. Religiously this is a new birth, and, morally, the revaluation of one's relationship to the world. The latter now appears to be dressed in a different garment which covers up all the ugliness of dualism, which is called in Buddhist phraseology delusion (*māyā*) born of reasoning (*tarka*) and error (*vikalpa*). . . .

4. This emphasizing in Zen of satori above everything else makes the fact quite significant that Zen is not a system of dhyāna as practised in India and by other schools of Buddhism than the Zen. By dhyāna is understood popularly a kind of meditation or contemplation; that is the fixing of thought, especially in Mahāyāna Buddhism, on the doctrine of emptiness (*śūnyatā*). When the mind is so trained as to be able to realize the state of perfect void in which there is not a trace of consciousness left, even the sense of being unconscious having departed—in other words, when all forms of mental activity are swept clean from the field of consciousness, which is now like a sky devoid of every speck of cloud, a mere broad expanse of blue—dhyāna is said to have reached its perfection. This may be called ecstasy or trance, but it is not Zen. In Zen there must be a satori; there must be a general mental upheaval which destroys the old accumulations of intellectuality and lays down a foundation for a new faith; there must

Landscape, by the painter-monk Sesshu (1420–1506),
done in the Zen "flung ink" style. The poem
celebrates nature as a ready-made poem.

be the awakening of a new sense which will review the old things from an angle of perception entirely and most refreshingly new. In dhyāna there are none of these things, for it is merely a quieting exercise of the mind. As such it has doubtless its own merits, but Zen ought not to be identified with such dhyānas. The Buddha therefore got dissatisfied with his two Sankhya teachers, in whose teaching the meditations were so many stages of self-abstraction or thought-annihilation.

5. Satori is not seeing God as he is, as may be contended by some Christian mystics. Zen has from the very beginning made clear its principal thesis, which is to see into the work of creation and not interview the creator himself. The latter may be found then busy moulding his universe, but Zen can go along with its own work even when he is not found there. It is not depending on his support. When it grasps the reason of living a life, it is satisfied. Hōyen, of Gosozan, used to produce his own hand and asked his disciples why it is called a hand. When one knows the reason, there is satori and one has Zen. Whereas with the God of mysticism there is the grasping of a definite object, and when you have God, what is not God is excluded. This is self-limiting. Zen wants absolute freedom, even from God. "No abiding place" means that; "Cleanse your mouth even when you utter the word 'Buddha'" amounts to the same thing. It is not that Zen wants to be morbidly unholy and godless, but that it knows the incompleteness of a name. Therefore when Yakusan (Yüehshan) was asked to give a lecture, he did not say a word, but instead came down from the pulpit and went off to his own room. Hyakujo (Pai-chang) merely walked forward a few steps, stood still, and opened his arms—which was his exposition of a great principle of Buddhism.

6. Satori is the most intimate individual experience and therefore cannot be expressed in words or described in any manner. All that one can do in the way of communicating the experience to others is to suggest or indicate, and this only tentatively. The one who has had it understands readily when such indications are given, but when we try to have a glimpse of it through the indices given we utterly fail. We are then like the man who says that he loves the most beautiful woman in the world and yet who knows nothing of her pedigree or social position, of her personal name or family name,

The *Tao*

The "Wisdom of China" is derived primarily from two ancient sages, Confucius (fifth century B.C.) and Lao Tzu (sixth century B.C.). Confucius' teachings were practical in intention, concerned largely with conduct and the ordering of society, i.e., with the "outer person"; Lao Tzu's teachings, on the other hand, were abstract, concerned with the principle of the *Tao* ("The Way," or the Law according to which everything happens) and our participation in it, i.e., with the "inner person."

Lao Tzu's teachings are recorded in the eighty-one lessons of the *Tao te Ching*. The following is the sixteenth of these, and its connection with the later Zen should be apparent.

> Empty yourself of everything.
> Let the mind rest at peace.
> The ten thousand things rise and fall while the Self watches their
>   return.
> They grow and flourish and then return to the source.
> Returning to the source is stillness, which is the way of nature.
> The way of nature is unchanging.
> Knowing constancy is insight.
> Not knowing constancy leads to disaster.
> Knowing constancy, the mind is open.
> With an open mind, you will be openhearted.
> Being openhearted, you will act royally.
> Being royal, you will attain the divine.
> Being divine, you will be at one with the Tao.
> Being at one with the Tao is eternal.
> And though the body dies, the Tao will never pass away.*

---

*Lao Tzu, *Tao Te Ching*, tr. Gia-Fu Feng and Hane English (New York: Vintage Books, 1972).

knows nothing of her individuality, physical as well as moral. We are again like the man who puts up a staircase in a place where four crossroads meet, to mount up thereby into the upper story of a mansion, and yet who knows not just where that mansion is, in the East or West, in the North or South. The Buddha was quite to the point when he thus derided all those philosophers and vain talkers of his day, who merely dealt in abstractions, empty hearsays, and fruitless indications. Zen therefore wants us to build the staircase right at the front of the very palace into whose upper story we are to mount up. When we can say "This is the very personality, this is the very house," we have the satori interviewed face to face and realized by oneself. (*Diṭṭhe va dhamme sayaṁ abhiññā acchikatvā.*) . . .

9. Satori is Enlightenment (*sambodhi*). So long as Buddhism is the doctrine of Enlightenment, as we know it to be, from its earliest as well as from its later literature, and so long as Zen asserts satori to be its culmination, satori must be said to represent the very spirit of the Buddhist teaching.[12]

IS RELIGIOUS EXPERIENCE EVIDENCE FOR GOD?

The question now is this: Is religious experience evidence for the existence of God? The answer, clearly, is both Yes and No. Obviously, it is evidence for the one who has enjoyed such an experience. And, to return to the point we began this chapter with, for such an individual it is an evidence for the existence of God which, far and away, surpasses any other evidence. "Seeing is believing." And such individuals have "seen" more directly and personally than they possibly could by means of any abstract argumentation. In fact, even if all the rational evidence were *against* the existence of God, the person who has had a religious experience would hardly be swayed. The immediacy and personalness of his or her religious experience would no doubt be decisive.

But, of course, this is exactly the problem. The individual or *private* nature of such experiences is, some skeptics would say, just what makes them philosophically irrelevant. All the outsider has is the *claim* of those who

---

[12]Daisetz Teitaro Suzuki, *Essays in Zen Buddhism* (First Series) (London: Rider, 1926), pp. 227–28, 259, 260–62, 264.

have had such experiences. From what standpoint can one possibly compare the claim with reality? Are not such claims, by their nature, insulated against any objective investigation or verification? In some sense this is surely true, but maybe not entirely so. C. D. Broad, a contemporary philosopher who is as hard-nosed as they come, has argued that there may be, in fact, some considerations that could tip the scales in favor of the integrity of, say, mystical experience:

> When there is a nucleus of agreement between the experiences of men in different places, times, and traditions, and when they all tend to put much the same kind of interpretation on the cognitive content of these experiences, it is reasonable to ascribe this agreement to their all being in contact with a certain objective aspect of reality *unless* there be some positive reason to think otherwise. The practical postulate which we go upon everywhere else is to treat cognitive claims as veridical unless there be some positive reason to think them delusive. This, after all, is our only guarantee for believing that ordinary sense-perception is veridical. We cannot *prove* that what people agree in perceiving really exists independently of them; but we do always assume that ordinary waking sense-perception is veridical unless we can produce some positive ground for thinking that it is delusive in any give case. I think it would be inconsistent to treat the experiences of religious mystics on different principles. So far as they agree they should be provisionally accepted as veridical unless there be some positive ground for thinking that they are not. So the next question is whether there is any positive ground for holding that they are delusive.[13]

But notice Broad's important proviso: ". . . unless there be some positive ground for thinking that they are not." Certainly many have argued that such grounds may, indeed, be cited. It is sometimes charged, for example, that such experiences may be explained (away) as manifestations of physiological problems, sexual hang-ups, psychological abnormalities, and the like. In a very lively passage in his *The Varieties of Religious Experience* (first published in 1902), William James takes on precisely this accusation and, in turn, accuses it of simple-mindedly confusing the "facts of mental

---

[13]C. D. Broad, *Religion, Philosophy, and Psychical Research* (New York: Harcourt, Brace & Co., 1953), p. 197.

RELIGIOUS EXPERIENCE:
PERSONAL AND PRIVATE

The personalness of religious experience renders it decisive for the participant. But the privacy of religious experience renders it sterile as an objective and investigable evidence for God. Or does it?

history" with "their spiritual significance." That is, what is important is not how person X got that way, but whether what he or she says is worthy, true, etc. He asks, furthermore, why any other state of mind—for example, that of the skeptic or the atheist—should be exempt from the same trivializing explanation: What is good for the goose is good for the gander. Pay close attention to his indictment of "medical materialism":

> Perhaps the commonest expression of this assumption that spiritual value is undone if lowly origin be asserted is seen in those comments which unsentimental people so often pass on their more sentimental acquaintances. Alfred believes in immortality so strongly because his temperament is so emotional. Fanny's extraordinary conscientiousness is merely a matter of overinstigated nerves. William's melancholy about the universe is due to bad digestion—probably his liver is torpid. Eliza's delight in her church is a symptom of her hysterical constitution. Peter would be less troubled about his soul if he would take more exercise in the open air, etc. A more fully developed example of the same kind of reasoning is the fashion, quite common nowadays among certain writers, of criticizing the religious emotions of showing a connection between them and the sexual life. Conversion is a crisis of puberty and adolescence. The macerations of saints, and the devotion of missionaries, are only instances of the parental instinct of self-sacrifice gone astray. For the hysterical nun, starving for natural life, Christ is but an imaginary substitute for a more earthly object of affection. And the like.

We are surely all familiar in a general way with this method of discrediting states of mind for which we have an antipathy. We all use it to some degree in criticizing persons whose states of mind we regard as overstrained. But when other people criticize our own more exalted soul-flights by calling them "nothing but" expressions of our organic disposition, we feel outraged and hurt, for we know that, whatever be our organism's peculiarities, our mental states have their substantive value as revelations of the living truth; and we wish that all this medical materialism could be made to hold its tongue.

Medical materialism seems indeed a good appellation for the two simpleminded systems of thought which we are considering. Medical materialism finishes up Saint Paul by calling his vision on the road to Damascus a discharging lesion of the occipital cortex, he being an epileptic. It snuffs out Saint Teresa as an hysteric, Saint Francis of Assisi as an hereditary degenerate, George Fox's discontent with the shams of his age, and his pining for spiritual veracity, it treats as a symptom of a disordered colon. Carlyle's organ-tones of misery it accounts for by a gastroduodenal catarrh. All such mental overtensions, it says, are, when you come to the bottom of the matter, mere affairs of diathesis (auto-intoxications most probably), due to the perverted action of various glands which physiology will yet discover.

And medical materialism then thinks that the spiritual authority of all such personages is successfully undermined.

Let us ourselves look at the matter in the largest possible way. Modern psychology, finding definite psycho-physical connections to hold good, assumes as a convenient hypothesis that the dependence of mental states upon bodily conditions must be thorough-going and complete. If we adopt the assumption, then of course what medical materialism insists on must be true in a general way, if not in every detail: Saint Paul certainly had once an epileptoid, if not an epileptic seizure; George Fox was an hereditary degenerate; Carlyle was undoubtedly auto-intoxicated by some organ or other, no matter which—and the rest. But now, I ask you, how can such an existential account of facts of mental history decide in one way or another upon their spiritual significance? According to the general postulate of psychology just referred to, there is not a single one of our states of mind, high or low, healthy or morbid, that has not some organic process as its condition. Scientific theories are organically conditioned just as much as religious emotions are; and if we only knew the facts intimately enough, we should doubtless see "the liver" determining the dicta of the sturdy atheist as decisively as it does those of the Methodist under conviction anxious about his soul. When it alters in one way the blood that percolates it, we get the Methodist, when in another way, we get the atheist form of mind. So of all our raptures and our drynesses, our longings and paintings, our questions and beliefs. They are equally organically founded, be they religious or of nonreligious content.

To plead the organic causation of a religious state of mind, then, in refutation of its claim to possess superior spiritual value, is quite illogical and arbitrary, unless one has already worked out in advance some psycho-physical theory connecting spiritual values in general with determinate sorts of physiological change. Otherwise none of our thoughts and feelings, not even our scientific doctrines, not even our *dis*-beliefs, could retain any value as revelations of the truth, for every one of them without exception flows from the state of its possessor's body at the time. . . .

William James' *Varieties of Religious Experience* is a classic of religious philosophy, and the chapters dealing with mysticism are perhaps the most frequently consulted discussions of the subject.

In the natural sciences and industrial arts it never occurs to anyone to try to refute opinions by showing up their author's neurotic constitution. Opinions here are invariably tested by logic and by experiment, no matter what may be their author's neurological type. It should be no otherwise with religious opinions. Their value can only be ascertained by spiritual judgments directly passed upon them, judgments based on our own immediate feeling primarily; and secondarily on what we can ascertain of their experiential relations to our moral needs and to the rest of what we hold as true.

Immediate luminousness, in short, *philosophical reasonableness*, and *moral helpfulness* are the only available criteria. Saint Teresa might have had the nervous system of the placidest cow, and it would not now save her theology, if the trial of the theology by these other tests should show it to be contemptible. And conversely if her theology can stand these other tests, it will make no difference how hysterical or nervously off her balance Saint Teresa may have been when she was with us here below.[14]

Surely James is right about the epistemological irrelevance of medical materialism's criticism of religious claims. On the other hand, that does not make those claims true. As he himself insists in the last two paragraphs above, those claims, like others, must satisfy some tests before they are accepted: They must be philosophically reasonable, and they must cohere with and advance the rest of our moral and intellectual life. And here is James' more positive contribution to the discussion. James was a major contributor to Pragmatism, a philosophy that stressed practicality, workability, usefulness, and consequences or results as the criteria of true beliefs. And he did, in fact, believe that the claims advanced by the world's great religious or theological personalities satisfy the test—at least when reduced to their common, universal essence. Following his indictment of medical materialism, the main part of *The Varieties of Religious Experience* is an extended consideration of the relevance and worthiness of various religious claims and perspectives, and at the end, he states clearly his positive assessment. In the following brief extract from his Postscript, James sets himself squarely against the prevailing "current" and votes in

---

[14]William James, *The Varieties of Religious Experience* (New York: Longmans, Green, and Co., 1902), pp. 10–18.

"MEDICAL MATERIALISM"

A term which William James contemptuously applies to the attempts to undermine the religious and spiritual significance of religious experiences by attributing them to disorders of a psychological or even physiological nature.

favor of a religious reality (by "piecemeal supernaturalism" James means a conception of the supernatural which envisions it as actually intruding into and affecting our world).

> . . . the current of thought in academic circles runs against me, and I feel like a man who must set his back against an open door quickly if he does not wish to see it closed and locked. In spite of its being so shocking to the reigning intellectual tastes, I believe that a candid consideration of piecemeal supernaturalism and a complete discussion of all its metaphysical bearings will show it to be the hypothesis by which the largest number of legitimate requirements are met. That of course would be a program for other books than this; what I now say sufficiently indicates to the philosophic reader the place where I belong.

> If asked just where the differences in fact which are due to God's existence come in, I should have to say that in general I have no hypothesis to offer beyond what the phenomenon of "prayerful communion," especially when certain kinds of incursion from the subconscious region take part in it, immediately suggests. The appearance is that in this phenomenon something ideal, which in one sense is part of ourselves and in another sense is not ourselves, actually exerts an influence, raises our centre of personal energy, and produces regenerative effects unattainable in other ways. If, then, there be a wider world of being than that of our every-day consciousness, if in it there be forces whose effects on us are intermittent, if one facilitating condition of the effects be the openness of the "subliminal" door, we have the elements of a theory to which the phenomena of religious life lend plausibility. I am so impressed by the importance of these phenomena that I adopt the hypothesis

Is Religion an Illusion?

One of the most famous attacks on religion was that of Sigmund Freud, who explained it away as the result of various psychological needs and complexes. But it is often observed that his attack involved a gigantic informal fallacy. What was it?

> . . . we turn our attention to the psychical origin of religious ideas. These, which are given out as teachings, are not precipitates of experience or end-results of thinking: they are illusions, fulfilments of the oldest, strongest and most urgent wishes of mankind. The secret of their strength lies in the strength of those wishes. As we already know, the terrifying impression of helplessness in childhood aroused the need for protection—for protection through love—which was provided by the father; and the recognition that this helplessness lasts throughout life made it necessary to cling to the existence of a father, but this time a more powerful one. Thus the benevolent rule of a divine Providence allays our fear of the dangers of life; the establishment of a moral world-order ensures the fulfilment of the demands of justice, which have so often remained unfulfilled in human civilization; and the prolongation of earthly existence in a future life provides the local and temporal framework in which these wish-fulfilments shall take place. Answers to the riddles that tempt the curiosity of man, such as how the universe began or what the relation is between body and mind, are developed in conformity with the underlying assumptions of this system.*

---

*Sigmund Freud, *The Future of an Illusion*, tr. W. D. Robson-Scott, rev. and ed. James Strachey (Garden City, N.Y.: Anchor Books, 1964), pp. 47–48.

---

which they so naturally suggest. At these places at least, I say, it would seem as though transmundane energies, God, if you will, produced immediate effects within the natural world to which the rest of our experience belongs.[15]

---

[15]Ibid., pp. 523–24.

James aside, many are drawn at least to a more general conclusion: It is true that the world is full of kooks, liars, and deluded persons, and surely this should put us on guard against accepting, willy-nilly, every claim to direct experience with God. On the other hand, is it a bit nervy to scoff at such claims when they are made by some of the finest, most articulate, and most positively influential people the world has ever known?

CHAPTER 10 IN REVIEW

Summary

Knowledge of God by way of religious experience is, in contrast to the rational and argumentative approach, *non*rational or *supra*rational. And this means, for the proponent of religious experience, a directness and personalness about this knowledge which immediately make it superior to all other approaches, except, of course, for supernatural revelation, which one might claim to have, say, in the Bible or through Christ.

There are many varieties of religious experience, just a few of which we have considered in this chapter. One of the most interesting, and perhaps the most universal, is the experience described by Rudolf Otto as the experience of the numinous. Even this experience takes many and diverse forms, but Otto claims that almost everyone has had a brush with the divine, a feeling or sense of the divine presence, such as he describes.

A more important, and certainly persistent, experience is that of the mystic. A great deal of ambiguity and sloppiness is associated with the word "mysticism" which has been used to cover everything from saintliness to drug experiences. But a fairly clearly defined experience has been expressed (though it cannot really be expressed) by a long train of what we have called the "higher" mystics. An excellent representative of these is St. John of the Cross, who taught that a (metaphorical) union with God could be attained in an ecstatic state in which all multiplicity and movement (whether in the sensible world, the intellectual sphere, or the soul itself) have been transcended. Such an experience has also been regarded by many as a universal phenomenon, though both similarities and differences may be perceived in Western and Eastern accounts of the mystical consciousness.

Although the participant in religious experience will have no interest in skeptical attacks on its validity ("He who sees, sees, and he who does not see, does not see"), the directness and personalness (or subjectivity) of the experience are exactly what make for great difficulties in treating it as an evidence for God. On the other hand, the attempt to explain away such experiences as originating in psychological or physiological states is a simple case of the Genetic Fallacy.

Basic Ideas

- The nonrational approach to God
- The numinous experience
- "Instant" mysticism
- Classical mysticism (definition)
- Features of classical mysticism
- The mystical ascent
- Sensory and intellectual consciousness
- Mystical union: Western
- Mystical union: Eastern
- Brahman
- The Four Noble Truths/The Eightfold Path
- Emptiness
- Zen
- *Satori*
- Religious experience as evidence for God: Pro and con
- "Medical materialism"
- The pragmatic value of religion

Questions for Reflection

- In this chapter different levels or kinds of religious experience have been noted. Can you yourself identify with any of them? Might one feel, without believing in *God*, that such experiences are significant? How so, or why not?
- Can you explain in your own way how classical mysticism is inseparably bound up with a certain view of reality? Which comes first: this view of reality or the mystic experience?
- What is your own honest evaluation of the claims of religious experience? Do the subjectivity and privacy of such experiences render them irrelevant as evidence for an unseen reality? Can you think of any consideration pro or con not mentioned in the text?

• Could one believe that mysticism is a universal and legitimate religious experience and accept at the same time the exclusive authority of a particular religion, say, Christianity or Judaism? Might there be a difference between general spiritual illumination and personal salvation?

For Further Reading

Brian Davies. *An Introduction to the Philosophy of Religion.* New York: Oxford University Press, 1982. Ch. 7. A brief, readable, and skeptical treatment of "experience of God."

Philip Kaplaav. *The Three Pillars of Zen.* Garden City, NY: Doubleday, 1980. An oft-cited, excellent introduction of Zen.

H. D. Lewis. *Our Experience of God.* New York: Macmillan, 1959. An exposition of religious experience from a specifically Christian standpoint.

J. L. Mackie. *The Miracle of Theism: Arguments for and against the Existence of God.* Oxford: Clarendon Press, 1982. Ch. 10 (a). A highly critical analysis of religious-experience claims, by a recognized philosopher of religion.

Ed. L. Miller. *God and Reason: An Invitation to Philosophical Theology.* Englewood Cliffs, NJ: Prentice Hall, 1995. Ch. 6. A student-oriented summary of many of the ideas discussed in this chapter, from a somewhat sympathetic perspective.

Rudolf Otto. *Mysticism East and West: A Comparative Analysis of the Nature of Mysticism.* Tr. Bertha L. Bracey and Richenda C. Payne. New York: Macmillan, 1932. A standard work which delineates the common and different features of Eastern and Western mysticism.

E. Allison Peers. *Studies in the Spanish Mystics.* London: Sheldon Press, 1928–30. I, Ch. 5. A standard exposition of St. John of the Cross.

S. Radhakrishnan. *The Bhagavadgītā.* London: George Allen and Unwin, 1948. A series of essays on the *Gita* and a commentary on the translation.

W. T. Stace (ed.). *The Teachings of the Mystics.* New York: New American Library, 1960. A very useful compendium of the original mystic statements, with an excellent introduction by the editor.

Richard Swinburne. *The Existence of God.* Oxford: Clarendon Press, 1979. Ch. 13. An excellent discussion of religious experience (five types) in terms of contemporary issues, concluding that it possesses "considerable evidential force."

R. C. Zaehner. *Mysticism: Sacred and Profane.* Oxford: Clarendon Press, 1957. A somewhat standard work which includes a treatment of the relation of mysticism to hallucinogenic experiences. (Ch. I and Appendices A and B.)

*In addition, see the relevant articles ("Mysticism, History of," "Religious Experience, Argument for the Existence of God," "Zen," etc.) in *The Encyclopedia of Philosophy*, ed. Paul Edwards. New York: Macmillan, 1967.

CHAPTER 11

God
and
Evil

O NE MIGHT easily imagine that just as the theists are able to line up their evidence *for* the existence of God, say the traditional arguments, the atheists likewise are able to marshal a long list of arguments *against* the existence of God. But this is not quite the case. If you stop and reflect, you will probably agree that you have seldom heard anyone really propound an argument against the existence of God. What you probably *have* heard are many arguments *against* the arguments *for* the existence of God. That is, the atheist, unable to present any positive *dis*proof of God's existence, is usually content, or forced, to find flaws in the theist's position. There is, of course, one notable exception to this: *the argument against the existence of God on the basis of the evil in the world.* But this alone has wrought plenty of havoc for the theist.

WHAT IS THE PROBLEM?

What is meant by "evil"? Two things. *First*, we have *natural* evil, or the evil that results from natural causes. This is otherwise known as the *evil of suffering*. Starvation, cancerous pain, physical deformity, disease—these and innumerable other sources of undeserved anguish are, rightfully, called *evils* in our world. *Second*, we have *moral* evil, the evil that results from personal depravity. Torture, murder, war, cheating, exploitation—these too, though very different from natural evils, are certainly evils. Either one or both of these types of evil figure in the "problem of evil."

But what is the problem? The problem is how to reconcile the evil in the world with a God who is at once omnipotent (all-powerful) and omnibenevolent (all-loving). The problem is also called *theodicy*, which means, literally, "the justification of God." The idea here is: How can God, in the traditional sense of the word, be justified or vindicated in the face of all, or even any, of the evil in the world?

Hardly a more powerful statement of the problem may be found than in the outburst of the English philosopher John Stuart Mill, for whom the impossibility of reconciling God and evil played an important role in his rejection of Christianity:

> Not even on the most distorted and contracted theory of good which ever was framed by religious or philosophical fanaticism, can the government of Nature be made to resemble the work of a being at once good and omnipotent.[1]

A more extended statement may be cited from Hume's *Dialogues Concerning Natural Religion*, from which we have already noted the attack on God's causal ordering of the world. Note how both natural and moral evil figure in his "catalogue of woes."

> The whole earth, believe me, Philo, is cursed and polluted. A perpetual war is kindled amongst all living creatures. Necessity, hunger, want stimulate the strong and courageous; fear, anxiety, terror agitate the weak and infirm. The first entrance into life gives anguish to the new-born infant and to its wretched parent; weakness, impotence, distress attend each stage of that life, and it is, at last finished in agony and horror.

---

[1]John Stuart Mill, *Three Essays on Religion* (New York: Henry Holt & Co., 1874), p. 38.

Observe, too, says Philo, the curious artifices of nature in order to embitter the life of every living being. The stronger prey upon the weaker and keep them in perpetual terror and anxiety. The weaker, too, in their turn, often prey upon the stronger, and vex and molest them without relaxation. Consider that innumerable race of insects, which either are bred on the body of each animal or, flying about, infix their stings in him. These insects have others still less than themselves which torment them. And thus on each hand, before and behind, above and below, every animal is surrounded with enemies which incessantly seek his misery and destruction.

Man alone, said Demea, seems to be, in part, an exception to this rule. For by combination in society he can easily master lions, tigers, and bears, whose greater strength and agility naturally enable them to prey upon him.

On the contrary, it is here chiefly, cried Philo, that the uniform and equal maxims of nature are most apparent. Man, it is true, can, by combination, surmount all his real enemies, and become master of the whole animal creation; but does he not immediately raise up to himself imaginary enemies, the demons of his fancy, who haunt him with superstitious terrors and blast every enjoyment of life? His pleasure, as he imagines, becomes in their eyes a crime; his food and repose give them umbrage and offence; and even death, his refuge from every other ill, presents only the dread of endless and unnumerable woes. Nor does the wolf molest more the timid flock than superstition does the anxious breast of wretched mortals.

Besides, consider, Demea: This very society by which we surmount those wild beasts, our natural enemies, what new enemies does it not raise to us? What woe and misery does it not occasion? Man is the greatest enemy of man. Oppression, injustice, contempt, contumely, violence, sedition, war, calumny, treachery, fraud—by these they mutually torment each other, and they would soon dissolve that society which they had formed were it not for the dread of still greater ills which must attend their separation.

But though these external insults, said Demea, from animals, from men, from all the elements, which assault us form a frightful catalogue of woes, they are nothing in comparison of those which arise within ourselves, from the distempered condition of our mind and body. How many lie under the lingering torment of diseases? Hear the pathetic enumeration of the great poet.

> Intestine stone and ulcer, colic-pangs,
> Demoniac frenzy, moping melancholy,
> And moon-struck madness, pining atrophy,
> Marasmus, and wide-wasting pestilence.
> Dire was the tossing, deep the groans: *Despair*
> Tended the sick, busiest from couch to couch.
> And over them triumphant *Death* his dart
> Shook: but delay'd to strike, though oft invok'd
> With vows, as their chief good and final hope.

The disorders of the mind, continued Demea, though more secret, are not perhaps less dismal and vexatious. Remorse, shame, anguish, rage, disappointment, anxiety, fear, dejection, despair—who has ever passed through life without cruel inroads from these tormentors? How many have scarcely ever felt any better sensations? Labour and poverty, so abhorred by everyone, are the certain lot of the far greater number; and those few privileged persons who enjoy ease and opulence never reach contentment or true felicity. All the goods of life united would not make a very happy man, but all the ills united would make a wretch indeed; and any one of them almost (and who can be free from every one?), nay, often the absence of one good (and who can possess all?) is sufficient to render life ineligible.

Were a stranger to drop on a sudden into this world, I would show him, as a specimen of its ills, an hospital full of diseases, a prison crowded with malefactors and debtors, a field of battle strewed with carcases, a fleet floundering in the ocean, a nation languishing under tyranny, famine, or pestilence. To turn the gay side of life to him and give him a notion of its pleasures—whither should I conduct him? To a ball, to an opera, to court? He might justly think that I was only showing him a diversity of distress and sorrow.

There is no evading such striking instances, said Philo, but by apologies which still further aggravate the charge. Why have all men, I ask, in all ages, complained incessantly of the miseries of life? . . .

And is it possible, Cleanthes, said Philo, that after all these reflections, and infinitely more which might be suggested, you can still persevere in your anthropomorphism, and assert the moral attributes of the Deity, his justice, benevolence, mercy, and rectitude, to be of the same nature with these virtues in human creatures? His power, we allow, is infinite; whatever he wills is executed; but neither man nor any other animal is happy; therefore, he does not will their happiness. His wisdom is infinite; he is never mistaken in choosing the means to any end; but the course of nature tends not to human or animal felicity; therefore, it is not established for that purpose. Through the whole compass of human knowledge there are no inferences more certain and infallible than these. In what respect, then, do his benevolence and mercy resemble the benevolence and mercy of men?

Epicurus' old questions are yet unanswered.

Is he willing to prevent evil, but not able? then is he impotent. Is he able, but not willing? then is he malevolent. Is he both able and willing? whence then is evil?[2]

Pay special attention to the concluding lines of the above quotation. These questions embody the best-known and simplest expression of the problem of evil.

SOME SOLUTIONS

The believer who seriously confronts this dilemma might appreciate the saying, "There are many ways to skin a cat, but whatever way you choose, don't expect the cat to cooperate." That is, the problem is indeed a difficult one, and the believer should be cautioned against any glibness or overconfidence. There are no easy answers. Still, the bottom line is this: It is clear to most theists that neither God's omnipotence nor his omnibenevolence can be given up.

Or can they? Mill himself resorted to just this "radical surgery": Let us simply deny, flat-out, that God is omnipotent. He states this rather startling thesis in his *Three Essays on Religion* (1874):

It is not too much to say that every indication of Design in the Kosmos is so much evidence against the Omnipotence of the Designer.

---

[2]David Hume, *Dialogues Concerning Natural Religion*, ed. Henry D. Aiken (New York: Hafner, 1948), pp. 62–64.

For what is meant by Design? Contrivance: the adaptation of means to an end. But the necessity for contrivance—the need of employing means—is a consequence of the limitation of power. Who would have recourse to means if to attain his end his mere word was sufficient? The very idea of means implies that the means have an efficacy which the direct action of the being who employs them has not. Otherwise they are not means, but an incumbrance. A man does not use machinery to move his arms. If he did, it could only be when paralysis had deprived him of the power of moving them by volition. But if the employment of contrivance is in itself a sign of limited power, how much more so is the careful and skilful choice of contrivances? Can any wisdom be shown in the selection of means, when the means have no efficacy but what is given them by the will of him who employs them, and when his will could have bestowed the same efficacy on any other means? Wisdom and contrivance are shown in overcoming difficulties, and there is no room for them in a Being for whom no difficulties exist. The evidences, therefore, of Natural Theology distinctly imply that the author of the Kosmos worked under limitations; that he was obliged to adapt himself to conditions independent of his will, and to attain his ends by such arrangements as those conditions admitted of.

And this hypothesis agrees with what we have seen to be the tendency of the evidences in another respect. We found that the appearances in Nature point indeed to an origin of the Kosmos, or order in Nature, and indicate that origin to be Design but do not point to any commencement, still less creation, of the two great active elements of the Universe, the passive element and the active element, Matter and Force. There is in Nature no reason whatever to suppose that either Matter or Force, or any of their properties, were made by the Being who was the author of the collocations by which the world is adapted to what we consider as its purposes; or that he has power to alter any of those properties. It is only when we consent to entertain this negative supposition that there arises a need for wisdom and contrivance in the order of the universe. The Deity had on this hypothesis to work out his ends by combining materials of a given nature and properties. Out of these materials he had to construct a world in which his designs should be carried into effect through given properties of Matter and Force, working together and fitting into one another. This did require skill and contrivance, and the means by which it is effected are often such as justly excite our wonder and admiration: but exactly because it requires wisdom, it implies limitation of power, or rather the two phrases express different sides of the same fact.[3]

The believer will find this thesis considerably more than "startling." Mill's statement involves an interesting piece of reasoning and is well worth digesting. But, some would say, the idea of a limited or *finite* God is as absurd as that of a malevolent or *evil* God. There must be another way.

We are stuck, then, with these two claims:

1. There is an omnipotent, omnibenevolent God.
2. There is evil.

That these two propositions seem to be incompatible with one another is clear. But the first question to be asked is whether the incompatibility here is a *logical* incompatibility, that is to say, a logical contradiction. If the two propositions are *logically* incompatible, well, that is the end of the matter—one of them must be false. And since we can hardly deny the existence of evil, we must deny the existence of an omnipotent and omnibenevolent God. But *are* they logically incompatible? It would seem not. However difficult it may be to reconcile the two propositions, there is nothing in the concept of an omnipotent and omnibenevolent God that *logically* excludes there being evil in the world. If so, it is at least *possible* for both propositions to be true, and the traditional believer's job is to show how.

One of the most popular proposals is to invoke the transcendence and inscrutability of God: God lies so far above us that it is impossible to understand his ways and purposes, and presumptuous even to try. Was this not God's own answer to the suffering Job?

> Then the LORD answered Job out
> of the whirlwind:
> "Who is this that darkens counsel
> by words without
> knowledge?

---

[3]John Stuart Mill, *Three Essays on Religion*, pp. 176–78.

Gird up your loins like a man,
    I will question you, and you
    shall declare to me.

"Where were you when I laid the
    foundation of the earth?
Tell me, if you have
    understanding.
Who determined its
    measurements—surely you
    know!
Or who stretched the line upon
    it?
On what were its bases sunk,
    or who laid its cornerstone
    when the morning stars sang
    together
    and all the heavenly beings
    shouted for joy?

"Or who shut the sea with
    doors
    when it burst out from the
    womb?—
    when I made the clouds its
    garment,
    and thick darkness its swaddling
    band,
    and prescribed bounds for it,
    and set bars and doors,
    and said, 'Thus far shall you
    come, and no farther,
    and here shall your proud waves
    be stopped'?
Job 38:1–11 (New Revised Standard Version)

And what does he say in *Isaiah?*

For my thoughts are not your
    thoughts.
    nor are your ways my ways,
    says the LORD.

> For as the heavens are higher than
>   the earth,
>   so are my ways higher than
>   your ways
>   and my thoughts than your
>   thoughts.
>   Isaiah 55:8–9 (NRSV)

But though this may be an appropriate and satisfying approach from a *religious* standpoint, from a *philosophical* standpoint it is a retreat, and issues a *carte blanche* for ignorance and uncritical reflection on the most urgent of issues.

Some other attempted resolutions may be mentioned. Closely related to the last is the emphasis on the goodness of the whole: If everything could be viewed from the divine standpoint, then it would immediately be appreciated how everything, even evil, actually contributes to the unity, harmony, beauty, and, in a word, goodness of things considered as a *totality*. A quite different angle was proposed by Leibniz, who taught that it would in fact be *logically impossible* to have a world without evil: Anything created by God would have to be *less* than God just by virtue of being *dependent* on him, and this means immediately that it must be less than perfect, and *this* means immediately the presence of various sorts of imperfections. How could God create something that was perfect, and therefore independent, and therefore uncreated? It is *logically* impossible. Similar is the view of Tennant. In an earlier chapter we saw that he emphasized the

---

SOME SOLUTIONS TO THE PROBLEM OF EVIL

- God is not omnipotent after all.
- God's plan for the world is inscrutable.
- All things, including evil, actually contribute to the goodness of the whole.
- A perfect world is a logical impossibility.
- Evil is a necessary by-product of nature.

presence of order in the world. But even Tennant saw that unfortunate and unhappy things are inevitable by-products of nature. It is impossible (*logically* impossible?) to have a physical cosmos, with its multiplicity, change, and natural processes, and not also have mishaps, accidents, disease, famines, and the like.

Some of these solutions to the problem of evil may strike you as more relevant than others, but each of them deserves, at least, to be understood and weighed. Two further views, however, must be considered somewhat more carefully: the privation theory of evil and the therapy theory of evil.

EVIL AS A PRIVATION OF GOODNESS

The first of these has a long tradition, but is most notably associated with the medieval Christian philosopher and theologian St. Augustine (354–430).

It is our natural tendency to think of evil as some kind of thing, a "stuff," a substance, or a *blob*. However, Augustine and many others have argued, exactly counter to this grain, that evil is no *thing* at all. It is, rather, the absence or privation of something, namely, of being and goodness. And this is true both of natural evil and of moral evil. It is true that when God created the world and the human race he said, "It is good." But he did not mean—*could* not mean—that they were *absolutely* good or good in the same way that God is. How could they be? For then they would not be created things, but God himself.

St. Augustine was a Christian Platonist, though as a Christian he certainly disagreed with much of Plato's philosophy. But he did hold broadly to the Platonic idea that the world is necessarily a mixture, as it were, of being and nonbeing: It is becoming. And one of the hallmarks of the relative nonbeing in the world is its multiplicity and change—the *absence* of full being along with its unity and unchangeableness. But this multiplicity and change give rise to natural processes, and these in turn give rise to famines, disease, plagues, etc., and these in turn give rise to suffering, which St. Augustine believed is visited on human beings as a just punishment for their sins. But, then, what about sin? Moral evil, or sin, likewise may be traced to an absence of goodness. It results when something goes wrong with the will; when it breaks down; when it falls short; when it fails to will the good; when it is derailed and turns aside from the good; when it is corrupted. As disease is the absence of health in the body, so sin is the absence of health in the will.

The basic idea here may not be easy to get hold of, but if you think about it enough, it might come to you in a sort of intuitive flash. Perhaps Augustine's own statements will help. The general principle of evil as a privation of goodness is explained in the following from *The Enchiridion on Faith, Hope, and Love:*

WHAT IS CALLED EVIL IN THE UNIVERSE IS BUT THE ABSENCE OF GOOD

. . . in the universe, even that which is called evil, when it is regulated and put in its own place, only enhances our admiration of the good; for we enjoy and value the good more when we compare it with the evil. For the Almighty God, who, as even the heathen acknowledge, has supreme power over all things, being Himself supremely good, would never permit the existence of anything evil among His works, if He were not so omnipotent and good that He can bring good even out of evil. For what is that which we call evil but the absence of good? In the bodies of animals, disease and wounds mean nothing but the absence of health; for when a cure is effected, that does not mean that the evils which were present—namely, the diseases and wounds—go away from the body and dwell elsewhere: they altogether cease to exist; for the wound or disease is not a substance, but a defect in the fleshly substance—the flesh itself being a substance, and therefore something good, of which those evils—that is, privations of the good which we call health—are accidents. Just in the same way, what are called vices in the soul are nothing but privations of natural good. And when they are cured, they are not transferred elsewhere: when they cease to exist in the healthy soul, they cannot exist anywhere else.

ALL BEINGS WERE MADE GOOD, BUT NOT BEING MADE PERFECTLY GOOD, ARE LIABLE TO CORRUPTION

All things that exist, therefore, seeing that the Creator of them all is supremely good, are themselves good. But because they are not, like their Creator, supremely and unchangeably good, their good may be diminished and increased. But for good to be diminished is an evil, although, however much it may be diminished, it is necessary, if the being is to continue, that some good should remain to constitute the being. For however small or of whatever kind the being may be, the good which makes it a being cannot be destroyed without destroying the being itself. An uncorrupted nature is justly held in esteem. But if, still further, it be incorruptible, it is undoubtedly considered of still higher value. When it is corrupted, however, its corruption is an evil, because it is deprived of some sort of good. For if it be deprived of no good, it receives no injury; but it does receive injury, therefore it is deprived of good. Therefore, so long as a being is in process of corruption, there is in it some good of which it is being deprived; and if a part of the being should remain which cannot be corrupted, this will certainly be an incorruptible being, and accordingly the process of corruption will result in the manifestation of this great good. But if it does not cease to be corrupted, neither can it cease to possess good of which corruption may deprive it. But if it should be thoroughly and completely consumed by corruption, there will then be no good left, because there will be no being. Wherefore corruption can consume the good only by consuming the being. Every being, therefore, is a good; a great good, if it cannot be corrupted; a little good, if it can; but in any case, only the foolish or ignorant will deny that it is a good. And if it be wholly consumed by corruption, then the corruption itself must cease to exist, as there is no being left in which it can dwell.[4]

The principle is further explained and applied specifically to sin in the following from *On Free Choice of the Will*:

Because the will is moved when it turns from an immutable good to a changeable one, you may perhaps ask how this movement arises. For the movement itself is certainly evil, although the free will must be numbered among the goods, because without it no one can live rightly. Even if this movement, that is, the turning of the will from the Lord God, is without doubt a sin, we cannot say, can we, that God is the cause of sin? This movement will not be from God, but what then is its origin? If I should answer your question by saying that I do not know, you would perhaps be disappointed; yet that would be the truth, for that which is nothing cannot be known. Only hold to your firm faith, since no good thing comes to your perception, understanding, or thought which is not from God. Nothing of

---

[4]St. Augustine, *The Enchiridion on Faith, Hope, and Love*, tr. J. F. Shaw, ed. Henry Paolucci (Chicago: Henry Regnery, 1961), pp. 12–13.

any kind can be discovered which is not from God. Wherever you see measure, number, and order, you cannot hesitate to attribute all these to God, their Maker. When you remove measure, number, and order, nothing at all remains. Even if the beginning of some form were to remain, where you do not find order or measure or number (since wherever these exist, form is complete), you must remove even that very beginning of form which seems to be the artisan's raw material. If the completion of form is a good, there is some good even in the rudimentary beginning of form. Thus, if all good is completely removed, no vestige of reality persists; indeed, nothing remains. Every good is from God. There is nothing of any kind that is not from God. Therefore, since the movement of turning away from good, which we admit to be sin, is a defective movement and since, moreover, every defect comes from nothing, see where this movement belongs: you may be sure that it does not belong to God.

Yet since this defect is voluntary, it lies within our power. You must not be willing to fear this defect, for if you do not desire it, it will not exist. What greater security can there be than to live a life where what you do not will cannot happen to you? Since a man cannot rise of his own will as he fell by his own will, let us hold with firm faith the right hand of God, Jesus Christ our Lord, which is stretched out to us. Let us wait for Him with steadfast hope; let us love Him with burning love.[5]

Is it clear? While God, who is the highest being, is the cause of all lesser being, he is not, nor can he be, the cause of the relative nonbeing in the world, for nonbeing is nothing at all. The advocate of the evil-is-a-privation-of-goodness position might therefore exclaim: "Rather than blame God for the relative nonbeing present in the world, and least of all for the wickedness that people themselves freely introduce, praise him for the relative beauty, harmony, goodness, and being in the world which *he* has introduced!"

One very big caution is in order. In view of this talk about evil as a privation or absence of goodness, you may be tempted to think that the reality of evil is simply being denied. But that would be to miss an important

---

[5]St. Augustine, *On Free Choice of the Will*, tr. Anna S. Benjamin and L. H. Hackstaff (Indianapolis: Library of Liberal Arts, 1964), pp. 83–84.

EVIL AS A PRIVATION OF GOODNESS

One of the most enduring solutions to the problem of evil is to interpret evil, both natural and moral, not as a positive substance but as the absence of being and goodness. The world and human souls are seen as created by the highest being (who is goodness) "from above," but at the same time as corruptible by nonbeing (or evil) "from below." God is, thus, responsible for the *isness* and *goodness* in the world, not the *nonbeing* and *evil*.

point. Who in his or her right mind would care to deny the reality of evil? What is involved here is a question not about the *reality* of evil, but, rather, about the *nature* of evil. And though St. Augustine denied that evil is a substance and called it the absence of goodness, few have been more sensitive to its awful reality.

THE FREE-WILL DEFENSE

You may have a kind of nagging feeling that at least the moral evil in the world is not God's fault but rather is due to the free choices and acts of human beings. And you might suspect that moral evil is just the price that has to be paid if there is to be any genuine moral responsibility and human goodness in the world. All of this suggests, in fact, an important angle to the problem of God and evil, and raises at the same time a host of difficult questions:

- Why did God endow humans with free will, knowing that they would abuse it?
- Is free will a condition for real humanhood?
- Does God's foreknowledge of what we will do mean that what we do is actually predetermined?
- Could God have made us free *and* unable to sin?

Some of these issues you will have to ponder or discuss on your own. Others, however, will have to be considered, along with that "important angle" mentioned above.

Note Augustine's reference, in the last passage quoted on page 311, to the "voluntary" defection of human beings from the good. He is very emphatic on the necessity of free will as a condition of morality and as the source of moral evil in the world. In another place in the same work he says explicitly that

> no righteous act could be performed except by free choice of the will, and I asserted that God gave it for this reason.[6]

Actually, Augustine means that God gave *Adam* and *Eve* free will. Adam and Eve misused (note again the negative tone) their free will, and sin thus made its entry into the world. Everyone after Adam and Eve has inherited the effects of the Fall, and this includes a loss of free will and a consequent "bondage of the will." Nonetheless, at least in the case of the first human beings, Adam and Eve, free will was a condition of authentic humanhood, though it also meant the possibility of sin. Leaving aside the difficult question of Adam and Eve's fall and its consequences for their descendents, this view is essentially what is nowadays called the *Free-will Defense*.

The contemporary American philosopher Alvin Plantinga summarizes the idea:

> . . . among good states of affairs there are some that not even God can bring about without bringing about evil: those goods, namely, that *entail* or *include* evil states of affairs. The Free Will Defense can be looked upon as an effort to show that there may be a very different kind of good that God can't bring about without permitting evil. These are good states of affairs that don't include evil; they do not entail the existence of any evil whatever; nonetheless God Himself can't bring them about without permitting evil.

> So how does the Free Will Defense work? And what does the Free Will Defender mean when he says that people are or may be free? What is relevant to the Free Will Defense is the idea of *being free with respect to an action*. If a person is free with respect to a given action, then he is free to perform that action and free to refrain from performing it; no antecedent conditions and/or causal laws determine that he will perform the action, or that he won't. It is within his

---

[6]Ibid., p. 78.

St. Augustine

The main writers of the early centuries of the Christian church are called the Church Fathers. The last and greatest of these was St. Augustine.

He was born in a Roman province on the north coast of Africa in 354. His father was a pagan, and his mother, who wielded a great deal of influence over him, was a Christian: St. Monica. He did not particularly excel at his early studies, though eventually he became expert in rhetoric when he moved as a student in 370 to Carthage. The loose morals of the city, however, undermined the Christian morals of this impressionable young man, and he gradually fell away from Christianity. He took a mistress by whom he had a son during his second year in Carthage.

During this time, Augustine rejected not only Christian morals but also Christian doctrines. He was especially troubled by the failure of Christianity to explain how a good God could be responsible for a world with so much evil in it. He turned to the materialistic ideas of Manichaeism, the doctrine that the world is dominated by two external and opposed principles,

(continued on next page)

power, at the time in question, to take or perform the action and within his power to refrain from it. Freedom so conceived is not to be confused with unpredictability. You might be able to predict what you will do in a given situation even if you are free, in that situation, to do something else. If I know you well, I may be able to predict good and evil, light and darkness. In 383 Augustine traveled to Rome, where he opened his own school of rhetoric, but he had so much trouble getting his students to pay their tuition that he moved to Milan. This was decisive for Augustine. His commitment to Manichaeism was by this time wavering anyway, and his discovery of certain "Platonic writings" (probably the writings of the Neoplatonist Plotinus, who lived about A.D. 200) introduced him to an altogether different and superior idea of things: a spiritual and transcendent conception of God, and the view that evil is a privation of goodness. This discovery, along with the influence of the sermons of St. Ambrose, bishop of Milan, and Augustine's own study of the New Testament, set the stage for his conversion to Christianity in the summer of 386. On Holy Saturday, 387, he was baptized by St. Ambrose, and in the autumn of 388 he departed for Africa.

Back in Africa, Augustine was ordained as a priest by the bishop of Hippo, a seaport city about 150 miles west of Carthage, and he himself became bishop of that city in 396. During this period his literary output continued and included three of the most important theological and philosophical works ever written: the *Confessions* (the world's first autobiography), the *City of God* (the first philosophy of history), and *On the Trinity*. At the same time, he was combating the heresies of Manichaeism, Donatism (which claimed to be the only true church), and Pelagianism (which overemphasized the role of free will in man's salvation), and developing further his own philosophy of Christian Platonism. Augustine died on August 28, 430, as the Vandals laid seige to Hippo, and as he was reciting the Penitential Psalms.

In addition to being one of the world's greatest philosophers and theologians, Augustine was also one of the world's great authors. In addition to the *Confessions*, the *City of God*, and *On the Trinity*, he wrote innumerable commentaries on Biblical books and a prodigious number of works on various topics and against various heresies.

what action you will take in response to a certain set of conditions; it does not follow that you are not free with respect to that action. Secondly, I shall say that an action is *morally significant*, for a given person, if it would be wrong for him to perform the action but right to refrain or *vice versa*. Keeping a promise, for example, would ordinarily be morally significant for a person, as would refusing induction into the army. On the other hand, having Cheerios for breakfast (instead of Wheaties) would not normally be morally significant. Further, suppose we say that a person is *significantly free*, on a given occasion, if he is then free with respect to a morally significant action. And finally we must distinguish between *moral evil* and *natural evil*. The former is evil that results from free human activity; natural evil is any other kind of evil.

Given these definitions and distinctions, we can make a preliminary statement of the Free Will Defense as follows. A world containing creatures who are significantly free (and freely perform more good than evil actions) is more valuable, all else being equal, than a world containing no free creatures at all. Now God can create free creatures, but He can't *cause* or *determine* them to do only what is right. For if He does so, then they aren't significantly free after all; they do not do what is right *freely*. To create creatures capable of *moral good*, therefore, He must create creatures capable of moral evil; and He can't give these creatures the freedom to perform evil and at the same time prevent them from doing so. As it turned out, sadly enough, some of the free creatures God created went wrong in the exercise of their freedom; this is the source of moral evil. The fact that free creatures sometimes go wrong, however, counts neither against God's omnipotence nor against His goodness; for He could have forestalled the occurrence of moral evil only by removing the possibility of moral good.[7]

To this, however, an objection is frequently heard: But is there a real contradiction in the idea that God might have so constituted his creatures that they *always* choose the right? This is the point made by the late British philosopher, J. L. Mackie:

> If God has made men such that in their free choices they sometimes prefer what is good and sometimes what is evil, why could he not have made men such that they always freely choose the good? If there is no logical impossibility in a man's freely choosing the

---

[7]Alvin Plantinga, *God, Freedom, and Evil* (New York: Harper & Row, 1974).

THE FREE-WILL DEFENSE

By means of the Free-will Defense, many thinkers, ancient and modern, have undertaken to defend God from the charge that he is responsible for moral evil: In order for human beings to be truly capable of moral goodness, they must also be capable of moral evil; but this means that with respect to good and evil they must have genuine free choice; but this means the real possibility (or inevitability?) of the introduction of moral evil into the scheme of things.

good on one, or on several occasions, there cannot be a logical impossibility in his freely choosing the good on every occasion. God was not, then, faced with a choice between making innocent automata and making beings who, in acting freely, would sometimes go wrong: there was open to him the obviously better possibility of making beings who would act freely but always go right. Clearly, his failure to avail himself of this possibility is inconsistent with his being both omnipotent and wholly good.[8]

Now, many who are "incompatibilists" (people who believe that genuine free will is logically incompatible with determinism) have an immediate intuition that there is something wrong with the idea that God can so *constitute* us that we always *freely* choose to do good. It is true that there is no logical contradiction in the proposition,

#1. All people always freely choose to do good.

But there is a contradiction in the proposition,

#2. God so constitutes all people that they always freely choose to do good.

---

[8]J. L. Mackie, "Evil and Omnipotence," in *The Philosophy of Religion*, ed. Basil Mitchell (London: Oxford University Press, 1971), p. 92.

because that entails #1, plus the proposition,

#3. No one can do otherwise than choose to do good.

which is incompatible with #1.

Similarly, Plantinga himself asks us to consider the Mackie-type claim that God can bring about a world in which everyone freely chooses to do good. Is this really a coherent idea? Virtually everyone has accepted that even an omnipotent Being must be bound by the laws of reason—it is a mark of God's *perfect* nature and *un*limited power that he is prevented from creating irrational things like four-sided triangles and dogs that don't bark while they're barking—in fact, these latter "things" can't be *things* at all, right? Now, Plantinga asks, how can *God* bring about a world in which all people freely choose to do good, a world that must, at least in part, be brought about by *someone else*, namely those people he creates to freely bring it about? It is, even for God, an impossible state of affairs. Thus the debate can become very sticky, though at least for incompatibilists the Free-will Defense stands. In the next section we will encounter yet another example.

EVIL AS THERAPY

Alongside the theory of evil as a privation of goodness we may mention another very important theory: evil as *therapy*. To call evil "therapeutic" may strike you not only as being a bit odd but also as silly or trivializing. But you must bear in mind that "therapy" involves more than aches, pains, exercise, and massages. It means, literally, *healing*: a healing power applied to physical and psychological disabilities and disorders. Thus, to press the therapeutic character of evil as a way of solving the problem of evil is to argue that evil is the instrument by which God has determined to correct,

What Even God Cannot Do

"Nothing which implies contradiction falls under the omnipotence of God."
—St. Thomas

purify, and instruct his creatures—in a word, *to bring them to spiritual health and maturity.*

This view, too, is both a very old and a very modern one. One of its most ardent advocates is the contemporary philosopher of religion John Hick. In his important book *Evil and the God of Love,* Hick enlists an early example of this approach in the ancient Christian writer Irenaeus[9] (130?–202?), bishop of Lyons. Irenaeus emphasized the *development* that goes on in human beings, as well as the whole human race, and the methods God has chosen to bring this development about. The experience of evil is a necessary part of this "soul-making" activity of God. From Irenaeus' *Against Heresies:*

> Man has received the knowledge of good and evil. It is good to obey God, and to believe in Him, and to keep His commandment, and this is the life of man; as not to obey God is evil, and this is his death. Since God, therefore, gave [no man] such mental power man knew both the good of obedience and the evil of disobedience, that the eye of the mind, receiving experience of both, may with judgment make choice of the better things; and that he may never become indolent or neglectful of God's command; and learning by experience that it is an evil thing which deprives him of life, that is, disobedience to God, may never attempt it at all, but that, knowing that what preserves his life, namely, obedience to God, is good, he may diligently keep it with all earnestness. Wherefore he has also had a twofold experience, possessing knowledge of both kinds, that with discipline he may make choice of the better things. But how, if he had no knowledge of the contrary, could he have had instruction in that which is good? For there is thus a surer and an undoubted comprehension of matters submitted to us than the mere surmise arising from an opinion regarding them. For just as the tongue receives experience of sweet and bitter by means of tasting, and the eye discriminates between black and white by means of vision, and the ear recognises the distinctions of sound by hearing; so also does the mind, receiving through the experience of both the knowledge of what is good, become more tenacious of its preservation, by acting in obedience to God; in the first place, casting away, by means of repentance, disobedience, as being something disagreeable and nauseous; and afterwards coming to understand what it really is,

---

[9]Pronounced *eye-ray-neé-us.*

John Hick, an advocate of a contemporary
Irenaean theodicy.

that it is contrary to goodness and sweetness, so that the mind may
never even attempt to taste disobedience to God. But if any one do
shun the knowledge of both these kinds of things, and the twofold
perception of knowledge, he unawares divests himself of the character of a human being.

. . . If, then, thou are God's workmanship, await the hand of thy
Maker which creates everything in due time; in due time as far as
thou art concerned, whose creation is being carried out. Offer to
Him thy heart in a soft and tractable state, and preserve the form in
which the Creator has fashioned thee, having moisture in thyself,
lest, by becoming hardened, thou lose the impressions of His fingers.
But by preserving the framework thou shalt ascend to that which is
perfect, for the moist clay which is in thee is hidden [there] by the
workmanship of God. . . . If, then, thou shalt deliver up to Him
what is thine, that is, faith towards Him and subjection, thou shalt
receive his handiwork, and shalt be a perfect work of God.[10]

---

[10]Irenaeus, *Against Heresies*, IV, 39, 1–2, tr. Alexander Roberts and James Donaldson,
in *The Ante-Nicene Fathers*, I (Grand Rapids, MI: Eerdmans, 1979).

Hick provides a useful summary of the differences between the Irenaean and Augustinian theodicies, and stresses (he calls it a "significant fact") the antiquity of the Irenaean.

> There is thus to be found in Irenaeus the outline of an approach to the problem of evil which stands in important respects in contrast to the Augustinian type of theodicy. Instead of the doctrine that man was created finitely perfect and then incomprehensibly destroyed his own perfection and plunged into sin and misery, Irenaeus suggests that man was created as an imperfect, immature creature who was to undergo moral development and growth and finally be brought to the perfection intended for him by his Maker. Instead of the fall of Adam being presented, as in the Augustinian tradition, as an utterly malignant and catastrophic event, completely disrupting God's plan, Irenaeus pictures it as something that occurred in the childhood of the race, an understandable lapse due to weakness and immaturity rather than an adult crime full of malice and pregnant with perpetual guilt. And instead of the Augustinian view of life's trials as a divine punishment for Adam's sin, Irenaeus sees our world of mingled good and evil as a divinely appointed environment for man's development towards the perfection that represents the fulfilment of God's good purpose for him.

> Irenaeus was the first great Christian theologian to think at all systematically along these lines, and although he was far from working out a comprehensive theodicy his hints are sufficiently explicit to justify his name being associated with the approach that we are studying in this part. It is true that Irenaeus' name does not belong to this type of theodicy as clearly and indisputably as Augustine's name belongs to the predominant theodicy of Western Christendom; it is also true that within Irenaeus' own writings there are cross-currents and alternative suggestions that I have left aside here. Nevertheless, to speak of the Irenaean type of theodicy is both to name a tradition by its first great representative and at the same time to indicate the significant fact that this mode of responding to the problem of evil originated in the earliest and most ecumenical phase of Christian thought.[11]

---

[11]John Hick, *Evil and the God of Love*, rev. ed. (San Francisco: Harper & Row, 1978), pp. 214–15.

It is not hard to see how *natural* evil, with its sufferings and hardships, may contribute to the development of a mature and virtuous soul, but what about *moral* evil? And how do the innocent victims of murder and torture fit into the picture? We are back to the Free-will Defense. At this point Hick adopts the same sort of reasoning as Augustine: Free will is a condition of humanhood, and sin enters the world through human free will. And he provides his own response to the Mackie-type view that God could have so made humans that they would freely but always choose the right. Hick's position is that while there may be no contradiction in God so making his creatures that they always act freely but rightly, there *is* a contradiction in God so constituting his creatures that they freely respond to him in a loving, trusting, and faithful relationship. Why? Because such a relationship is *two-sided,* and if the freely proffered love, trust, or faith of the one party is, as it were, programmed by the other party, then for that party it could not possibly *be* a relationship of love, trust, or faith, at least not *authentic* love, trust, or faith, to use Hick's word. Free will and *independence* from the Creator are, in this way, marks of genuine humanity. But, of course, this makes for the possiblity of disobedience, and that means *sin.*

Hick's argument for this version of the Free-will Defense is especially effective because of his analogy involving posthypnotic suggestion.

> Is it logically possible for God so to make men that they will freely respond to Himself in love and trust and faith?
>
> I believe that the answer is no. The grounds for this answer may be presented by means of an analogy with posthypnotic suggestion, which Flew uses in this connection. A patient can, under hypnosis, be given a series of instructions, which he is to carry out after waking— say, to go at a certain time to a certain library and borrow a certain book—and he may at the same time be told that he will forget having received these instructions. On coming out of the hypnotic trance he will then be obediently unaware of what transpired in it, but will nevertheless at the prescribed time feel an imperious desire to go to the library and borrow the book, a desire that the ordinary resources of the educated intellect will find no difficulty in rationalizing. The patient will thus carry out the hypnotist's commands whilst seeming both to himself and to others to be doing so of his own free will and for his own sufficient reasons. In terms of the definition of a free act as one that is not externally compelled but flows from the character

of the agent, the actions of one carrying out post-hypnotic suggestions are free actions and the patient is a free agent in his performance of them. Nevertheless, taking account of the wider situation, including the previous hypnotic trance, we must say the patient is not free as far as these particular actions are concerned *in relation to the hypnotist*. In relation to the hypnotist he is a kind of puppet or tool. And if the hypnotist's suggestion had been that the patient would agree with him about some controversial matter or, coming closer to an analogy with our relationship with God, trust the hypnotist, or love him, or devotedly serve him, there would be something inauthentic about the resulting trust, love, or service. They would be inauthentic in the sense that to the hypnotist, who knows that he has himself directly planted these personal attitudes by his professional techniques, there would be an all-important difference between the good opinion and trust and friendship of the patient and that of someone else whose mind has not been conditioned by hypnotic suggestion. He would regard and value the two attitudes in quite different ways. His patient's post-hypnotic friendship and trust would represent a purely technical achievement, whereas the friendship and trust of the other would represent a response to his own personal qualities and merits. The difference would be that between genuine and spurious personal attitudes—genuine and spurious, not in respect of their present observed and felt characters but in respect of the ways in which they have come about. For it is of the essential nature of "fiduciary" personal attitudes such as trust, respect, and affection to arise in a free being as an uncompelled response to the personal qualities of others. If trust, love, admiration, respect, affection, are produced by some kind of psychological manipulation which by-passes the conscious responsible centre of the personality, then they are not real trust and love, etc., but something else of an entirely different nature and quality which does not have at all the same value in the contexts of personal life and personal relationship. The authentic fiduciary attitudes are thus such that it is impossible—logically impossible—for them to be produced by miraculous manipulation: "it is logically impossible for God to obtain your love-unforced-by-anything-outside-you and yet himself force it." . . .

. . . It would not be logically possible for God so to make men that they could be guaranteed freely to respond to Himself in genuine trust and love. The nature of these personal attitudes precludes their being caused in such a way. Just as the patient's trust in, and devotion to, the hypnotist would lack for the latter the value of a freely given trust and devotion, so our human worship and obedience to God would lack for Him the value of a freely offered worship and obedience. We should, in relation to God, be mere puppets, precluded from entering into any truly personal relationshp with Him.[12]

Thus Hick, renewing the therapy thinking of Irenaeus and pressing a new version of the Free-will Defense, argues that this mortal existence, with its authentic freedoms and its disciplining and healing and maturing environment, is "a vale of soul-making." Some readers will of course respond with an incredulous outburst: "How naive can you be? This is obviously not a vale of soul-making but a vale of soul-*breaking!* Are we supposed to believe, to take just one example, that the Nazi death camps were divinely appointed means of spritual progress?" And if it is answered that somehow the position holds true at least for the race as a whole, the second response will immediately be: "Large consolation for those *individuals* whose innocent lives were snuffed out in the gas chambers." Naturally, Hick's actual view is much richer than what we have been able to recount here, and naive it certainly is not. Nonetheless, the point is well taken. And it leads to the next section.

EVIL IS IRRATIONAL

We have now mentioned several attempts to reconcile evil with God. In spite of their differences, they all have in common at least a faith in the ability of reason to unravel to some degree the mystery of evil. They all say, in one way or another: "If only we think hard about the matter—draw the right distinctions, introduce the relevant concepts, etc.—we are able to see that the problem of good and evil is not as desperate as we thought." Not all are so optimistic. In fact, some abandon all hope of explaining evil and see it, rather, as the supreme evidence of the ultimate *irrationality* of human existence.

We are, of course, now in the presence of a radically different philosophical perspective. It is not only an atheistic one but also, in some sense, a *nihilistic* one. "Nihilism" means, literally, "nothingism" (from the Latin *nihil,* "nothing"). As a label, nihilism usually refers specifically to values

---

[12]Ibid., pp. 308–10.

and ideals, and is the denial that they have any objective reality. It is understandable how, for such a perspective, evil is the most vivid expression of our finally hopeless situation.

If we take nihilism to mean the *utter* and *absolute* rejection of all value and meaning, then there have not been very many nihilists. And, if there ever was one, he or she should have just sat down and died. For even the barest pursuit of one's life is an affirmation of *some* value and meaning, isn't it? But with some philosophers the irrationalist or absurdist position takes a truly interesting turn. First, these philosophers are atheists or *humanists*. Humanism, as one could guess from the word, is the exaltation of humanity itself as the ultimate reality. Second, for these thinkers the problem of evil becomes one of reconciling evil not with God (there is no God) but, rather, with *man*—not theodicy, but, if you will, *anthropodicy*.

One way in which this may be done is suggested in certain strains of atheistic or humanistic existentialism. We spoke of existentialism in Chapter 1 and will have more to say about it in Chapter 12. For now, we just remind ourselves that existentialism, which was renewed by the horrors of the world wars, generally rejects most philosophizing as abstract and irrelevant, and emphasizes the concrete business of living authentically. The late French writer Albert Camus is a good example:

> Judging whether life is or is not worth living amounts to answering the fundamental question of philosophy. All the rest—whether or not the world has three dimensions, whether the mind has nine or twelve categories—come afterwards. These are games. . . . I have never seen anyone die for the ontological argument. . . . the meaning of life is the most urgent of questions.[13]

But what about evil, specifically? Camus, the atheist, says that we must *recognize* it in all its horror and irrationality, but we must not *accept* it. Human dignity lies precisely in our struggle against evil, in living in constant revolt against its reign. This comes out well in Camus' novel *The Plague*. In this novel the plague itself may be understood on several levels. But on the most basic level it represents evil, and at least one of the characters in the novel expresses vividly the absence of God and the necessity of defiance as the only meaningful response to evil.

---

[13]Albert Camus, *The Myth of Sisyphus and Other Essays*, tr. Justin O'Brien (New York: Vintage Books, 1955), pp. 3–4.

". . . since the order of the world is shaped by death, mightn't it be better for God if we refuse to believe in Him and struggle with all our might against death, without raising our eyes toward the heaven where He sits in silence."

Tarrou nodded.

"Yes. But your victories will never be lasting; that's all."

Rieux's face darkened.

"Yes, I know that. But it's no reason for giving up the struggle."

"No reason, I agree. Only, I now can picture what this plague must mean for you."

"Yes. A never ending defeat." . . .

"Who taught you all this, doctor?"

The reply came promptly:

"Suffering."[14]

And in his *The Myth of Sisyphus and Other Essays*, Camus juxtaposes the two most extreme possible responses to the human condition: suicide, which is "giving in," and conscious revolt. It is already clear which path Camus urges us to follow.

Now I can broach the notion of suicide. It has already been felt what solution might be given. At this point the problem is reversed. It was previously a question of finding out whether or not life had to have a meaning to be lived. It now becomes clear, on the contrary, that it will be lived all the better if it has no meaning. Living an experience, a particular fate, is accepting it fully. Now, no one will live this fate, knowing it to be absurd, unless he does everything to keep before him that absurd brought to light by consciousness. Negating one of the terms of the opposition on which he lives amounts to escaping it.

---

[14]Albert Camus, *The Plague*, tr. Stuart Gilbert (New York: Modern Library, 1948), pp. 117–18.

Through novels, plays, and essays, Albert
Camus addressed the futility of the
human situation.

To abolish conscious revolt is to elude the problem. The theme of
permanent revolution is thus carried into individual experience. Living is keeping the absurd alive. Keeping it alive is, above all, contemplating it. Unlike Eurydice, the absurd dies only when we turn away
from it. One of the only coherent philosophical positions is thus revolt. It is a constant confrontation between man and his own obscurity. It is an insistence upon an impossible transparency. It challenges
the world anew every second. Just as danger provided man the
unique opportunity of seizing awareness, so metaphysical revolt extends awareness to the whole of experience. It is that constant presence of man in his own eyes. It is not aspiration, for it is devoid of
hope. That revolt is the certainty of a crushing fate, without the resignation that ought to accompany it.

This is where it is seen to what a degree absurd experience is remote
from suicide. It may be thought that suicide follows revolt—but

wrongly. For it does not represent the logical outcome of revolt. It is just the contrary by the consent it presupposes. Suicide, like the leap, is acceptance at its extreme. Everything is over and man returns to his essential history. His future, his unique and dreadful future—he sees and rushes toward it. In its way, suicide settles the absurd. It engulfs the absurd in the same death. But I know that in order to keep alive, the absurd cannot be settled. It escapes suicide to the extent that it is simultaneously awareness and rejection of death. It is, at the extreme limit of the condemned man's last thought, that shoelace that despite everything he sees a few yards away, on the very brink of his dizzying fall. The contrary of suicide, in fact, is the man condemned to death.

That revolt gives life its value. Spread out over the whole length of a life, it restores its majesty to that life. To a man devoid of blinders, there is no finer sight than that of the intelligence at grips with a reality that transcends it. The sight of human pride is unequaled. No disparagement is of any use. That discipline that the mind imposes on itself, that will conjured up out of nothing, that face-to-face struggle have something exceptional about them. To impoverish that reality whose inhumanity constitutes man's majesty is tantamount to impoverishing him himself. I understand then why the doctrines that explain everything to me also debilitate me at the same time. They relieve me of the weight of my own life, and yet I must carry it alone. At this juncture, I cannot conceive that a skeptical metaphysics can be joined to an ethics of renunciation.

Consciousness and revolt, these rejections are the contrary of renunciation. Everything that is indomitable and passionate in a human heart quickens them, on the contrary, with its own life. It is essential to die unreconciled and not of one's own free will. Suicide is a repudiation. The absurd man can only drain everything to the bitter end, and deplete himself. The absurd is his extreme tension, which he maintains constantly by solitary effort, for he knows that in that consciousness and in that day-to-day revolt he gives proof of his only truth, which is defiance. This is a first consequence.[15]

---

[15]Camus, *The Myth of Sisyphus*, pp. 39–41.

Such a stance is not without problems, as we will see in Chapter 12. For the moment: any philosophy which rejects the objective reality of values will surely have a hard time when it turns right around and argues passionately for certain values. In the case of Camus, it might be asked: In a universe devoid of real values, what is it that justifies and gives value to the life of revolt? Why is the revolt itself a value? Of course Camus might just as easily respond, "There you go again with your academic questions! Don't you understand that in a world such as this it is not reasoning but *acting* that is called for?"

Be that as it may. With the emphasis on evil as the supreme evidence for the ultimate irrationality of the world, we appear to have come full circle: God may be dead, but the Devil is very much alive! And now the *theist* might attack:

THEIST: You atheists are always attacking us theists on the ground that we cannot show how evil in the world can be reconciled with an all-powerful and all-loving God. You call it "the problem of evil."

ATHEIST: Right!

THEIST: But don't you have a similar problem? Why is it any more difficult to have evil *with* God than to have goodness *without* him? On your atheistic view, how can you account for all the goodwill, generosity, and self-sacrifice in the world? Call it "the problem of goodness."

ATHEIST: But all those good things come from *human beings!*

THEIST: Well, I doubt it. But even so, I will insist just as emphatically that sin *also* comes from humans.

ATHEIST: But if your God is all-powerful he could have prevented men from sinning.

THEIST: I invoke the Free-will Defense.

ATHEIST: Oh. But what about natural evil? Your Free-will Defense will not explain *that.*

THEIST: You're right. But I have all sorts of other ideas about it—I'll tell you about them sometime. In the meantime, what's *your* explanation for natural evil? Isn't it as big a problem for you as for me? Give a little and take a little!

CHAPTER 11 IN REVIEW

Summary

The presence in the world of evil, both natural and moral, is surely the biggest stumbling-block to belief in an all-powerful and all-loving God.

Many attempts have been made on the theistic side to overcome this difficulty. We have considered several of them, but especially two. One of the most enduring is the view of evil as a privation, or absence, of good. Associated most notably with St. Augustine, this view emphasizes that God is responsible for the creation of *things*, not *no-things*. But evil is a no-thing; it is the absence of being and goodness. It cannot therefore be attributed to God. Natural evil has its origin in the (necessary) relative non-being of the natural world, and moral evil has its root in the relative nonbeing of the will. The denial that evil is a substance should not be confused with the denial that evil is real. Very different, but also enduring, is the therapeutic view of evil. Here the emphasis is primarily on natural evil, which is seen to be conducive to the development and strengthening of individuals and the race. Thus John Hick calls this mortal existence "a vale of soul-making."

Both of these positions make use, in their own ways, of the Free-will Defense, which has figured prominently in recent philosophical discussions: If individuals are to be genuinely capable of doing what is right, they must also be capable of doing what is wrong. That is, human free will is a logically necessary limitation on God's power if moral creatures are to exist.

In contrast to those theists who attempt to reconcile evil with God, there are those atheists who simply, as it were, abandon the world to evil. God is dead, and the world is ultimately irrational. Camus provides one possible stance: We can at least recover something of human dignity by defying the irrational forces that will, finally, "do us in." But theists want to know why this belief in the world as ultimately irrational is, philosophically, any less distasteful and problematic than their own belief in God.

Basic Ideas

- Natural evil and moral evil
- The problem of evil

- Theodicy
- Hume's statement of the problem
- Some standard solutions
  A limited God
  An inscrutable God
  The goodness of the whole
  The logical impossibility of a perfect world
  Evil as the necessary by-product of nature
- Evil as a privation of goodness
- The Free-will Defense: For and against
- Evil as therapy
- Soul-making vs. soul-breaking
- Evil as irrational
- Nihilism
- Anthropodicy
- The dignity of defiance

Questions for Reflection

- Do you think that the standard solutions to the problem of evil tend to trivialize the problem, or do any of them have real merit?
- In the last chapter we saw how classical mysticism has its roots in a certain metaphysical view. Can you explain how St. Augustine's position on evil has its roots in the same view? By contrast, how would you characterize the metaphysical perspective that underlies Camus' position?
- Is it possible that what one feels about the problem of evil depends largely on what side of the fence he or she starts out on? Is it likely that a theist will find the problem insuperable? Is it not likely that an atheist will see it as devastating to the theist position? What side of the fence are you on, and what difference does it make in your own view of the problem?
- The Free-will Defense always figures strongly in discussions about the problem of evil. Can you argue the Free-will Defense back and forth? What do *you* make of this maneuver?

For Further Reading

John Cruickshank. *Albert Camus and the Literature of Revolt.* Oxford: Oxford University Press, 1959. A lucid treatment of Camus' idea of revolt in relation to his life, politics, and literature, and prefaced by a summarized and highly instructive "tribute" to Camus.

Brian Davies. *An Introduction to the Philosophy of Religion.* New York: Oxford University Press, 1982. Ch. 3. A brief, student-oriented chapter, raising relevant issues and concluding that evil is not a decisive evidence against God.

Austin Farrer. *Love Almighty and Ills Unlimited.* New York: Doubleday, 1961. A treatment of evil along specifically Augustinian lines, by a well-known philosopher.

Antony Flew. *Hume's Philosophy of Belief: A Study of His First Inquiry.* London: Routledge & Kegan Paul, 1961. Ch. 9. A thorough discussion of Hume's critical position on "the religious hypothesis."

Etienne Gilson. *The Christian Philosophy of St. Augustine.* Tr. L. E. M. Lynch. New York: Random House, 1960. Part II, sec. 3, and *passim.* A brief but helpful elucidation of Augustine's privation theory of evil, by a renowned medieval scholar.

Walter Kaufmann. *The Faith of a Heretic.* New York: McGraw-Hill, 1959. A lively rejection of the attempt to resolve the problem of evil from a Biblical standpoint.

C. S. Lewis. *The Problem of Pain.* New York: Macmillan, 1962. A lucid and popular treatment of the problem of suffering (including animal suffering) by a foremost Christian apologist.

J. L. Mackie. *The Miracle of Theism: Arguments For and Against the Existence of God.* Oxford: Clarendon Press, 1982. Ch. 9. Hefty discussions of standard and continuing issues pertaining to the problem of evil (survey of solutions, Free-will Defense, divine omnipotence, etc.), with generally negative conclusions.

Ed. L. Miller. *God and Reason: An Invitation to Philosophical Theology.* Englewood Cliffs, NJ: Prentice Hall, 1995. Ch. 8. A discussion, for beginners, of the problem of evil, with special reference to the Augustinian position.

Michael Peterson. *Evil and the Christian God.* Grand Rapids, MI: Baker, 1982. An Evangelical's attempt to reconcile evil with the God of the Bible and of classical theism, with special reference to the argument from gratuitous evil.

Michael Peterson et al. *Reason and Religious Belief: An Introduction to the Philosophy of Religion.* New York: Oxford University Press, 1991. Ch. 6. An introductory but sophisticated treatment of the problem of evil, reflecting current and influential options.

Nelson Pike (ed.). *God and Evil: Readings on the Theological Problem of Evil.* Englewood Cliffs, NJ: Prentice Hall, 1964. A much-used collection of seven enduring statements, traditional and contemporary.

Alvin Plantinga. *God and Other Minds: A Study of the Rational Justification of Belief in God.* Ithaca, NY: Cornell University Press, 1967. Chs. 5–6 and 7, Part II. A sometimes technical discussion of God and evil, emphasizing recent debates concerning, for example, the Free-will Defense and problems of divine omnipotence.

James F. Ross. *Philosophical Theology.* Indianapolis: Bobbs-Merrill, 1969. Chs. 5–6. An approach to the problem of evil along Thomistic-analytic lines.

Richard Swinburne. *The Existence of God.* Oxford: Clarendon Press, 1979. Ch. 11. A clear account of relevant issues (traditional approaches, Free-will Defense, quantity of evil, etc.) rejecting evil as evidence against God.

R. A. Tsanoff. *The Nature of Evil.* New York: Macmillan, 1931. A complete history of the philosophical problem of evil and proposed solutions.

*In addition, see the relevant articles (e.g., "Evil, the Problems of") in *The Encyclopedia of Philosophy*, ed. Paul Edwards. New York: Macmillan, 1967.

PART FOUR

THE
QUESTION
OF
MORALITY

 s WAS explained in Chapter 1, value theory raises the question of
value in general. The value of filets mignons, human deeds,
works of art, political ideologies—all values are the concern of value theory. It is not possible to consider all spheres of value, but it would seem
necessary to consider at least two of them. In this part of our book we will
examine *ethical* or *moral values,* those values which define personal decisions and actions as good or evil, moral or immoral. In the final part we
will look at *social* and *political values,* the values which determine the principles and institutions of our life together in society and the state.

Talk of moral and political values probably brings immediately to mind
all sorts of exciting and dramatic issues, such as abortion, capital punishment, the draft, war, sex, nuclear armament, ERA, politics, minority
rights, imperialism, genetic engineering, and euthanasia. And rightfully
so. All such issues presuppose, involve, and imply many kinds of values.
But while it is expected, also rightfully, that value theory must in the end

illuminate such problems, it is usually not with these problems that value theory directly concerns itself. More specifically, as a theoretical endeavor, moral philosophy or ethics is concerned with the clarification of fundamental ethical concepts, the elucidation of principles, and the critical discussion of positions and perspectives. It should be apparent that these tasks are, after all, much more important than the excited arguments about specific issues (such as those mentioned above) which all too often proceed without due regard for more fundamental questions. In the case of ethics, such questions are:

- What is moral goodness?
- Is morality relative or absolute?
- Do moral claims have cognitive (truth/falsity) status?
- Are all moral values derived from an ultimate value?
- What are the epistemological bases of the ethical theories?
- Is there a distinction between what *is* and what *ought* to be?
- Does moral responsibility require free will?
- What is the relation between the private and the public good?

The truth is, of course, that even with its theoretical concerns the philosophical question of morality stands more obviously related to concrete situations and practical questions than do the other fields of philosophy. And it is, therefore, here, with the question of morality (and again in Part V, with the question of society), that philosophical activity will seem to many to be most related to the question of *living*.

CHAPTER 12

Challenges
to
Morality

B FORE WE consider some of the more important ways philosophers have answered the question of morality, we must consider
the prior question: Is morality, or at least traditional morality, even possible? Some have, indeed, maintained for various reasons that morality, as
it is usually conceived, is *not* possible. *First*, there are those who judge
right from the start that ethical propositions are meaningless. *Second*, we
have the relativists or subjectivists, who argue that morality is a matter of
individual judgment and that there are no common or universal moral
obligations. *Third*, we have to reckon with those who locate the basis of
morality in evolving human nature itself. *Fourth*, we must confront the
determinist, who denies free will and asks: If all things, including our
choices, are completely predetermined, then how can there be any basis
for moral responsibility?

THE CHALLENGE
OF LOGICAL POSITIVISM

Logical positivism challenges traditional morality by maintaining that *its language is meaningless.*

When we raise the question whether morality is *meaningless*, it is important to introduce a distinction. There is a big difference between *existential* meaning (as in "I saw a meaningful movie") and *cognitive* meaning (as in "'Creech creech' is meaningless"). In the first case it is a question of relevance or *importance*, whereas in the second case it is a question of *truth status*. To say of a claim that it is irrelevant (it has no existential meaning) is very different from saying that it is neither true nor false and therefore doesn't say anything literal at all (it has no cognitive meaning). In the logical positivists' challenge to morality, it is asserted that traditional moral claims, such as "X is good" or "You ought not to do Y," are cognitively meaningless; they are neither true nor false; they make no claim about anything whatsoever; they are no more significant than "Creech creech"; they are gibberish.

Logical positivism is a superempiricist philosophy after the manner of Hume. Do you recall Hume's pronouncement about casting into the flames those volumes containing claims that are neither relations of ideas (analytic) nor matters of fact (synthetic *a posteriori*)? At the heart of logical positivism lies the Humean-sounding *verification principle:* A proposition is cognitively meaningful if and only if it is either analytic or in principle empirically verifiable. Say it another way: If you cannot conceive of the actual empirical conditions under which your claim could be shown to be true or false, then you are talking nonsense. The implications of this principle are, of course, devastating. All metaphysical claims (about God, souls, free will, necessary causal relations, underlying substances, etc.) are

---

Two Meanings of "Meaning"

- *Existential meaning:* The importance or relevance that something holds.
- *Cognitive meaning:* The truth/falsity status of a claim.

immediately excluded as *cognitively meaningless*. And the verificationists deliver an identical judgment on *moral claims*. They are purportedly not empty analytic propositions, or tautologies, and they cannot even in principle be verified by means of sense experience, so they are *cognitively meaningless*.

How, then, do the logical positivists handle ethical claims and propositions? The most popular of their views is known as *emotivism*. Look at the word. You can tell immediately that this interpretation of moral propositions has something to do with *emotions*. Actually, emotivism is the view that moral propositions are really emotional expressions, expressions or pronouncements of one's own likes and dislikes: anger, elation, disgust, approval, disapproval. At the same time, they are attempts to arouse a similar feeling in others and to provoke action. Obviously, such expressions as "X is right" only reveal something about the one uttering them. They do not refer to any objective or factual or common state of affairs. They make no claim about anything "out there." They possess no truth value. In this way, the ethical statement "Stealing is wrong" is equivalent both to the exclamation "Stealing!" and to the command "Do not steal." But none of these expressions have any cognitive meaning, for they express not truth but emotions. They are not value claims but psychological claims.

The way in which the emotivist theory of morality follows naturally from a preconceived theory of knowledge has been represented as follows:

> As positivists, these writers held that every judgment belongs to one or other of two types. On the one hand, it may be *a priori* or necessary. But then it is always analytic, i.e., it unpacks in its predicate part or all of its subject. Can we safely say that 7 + 5 makes 12? Yes, because 12 is what we mean by "7 + 5." On the other hand, the judgment may be empirical, and then, if we are to verify it, we can no longer look to our meanings only; it refers to sense experience and there we must look for its warrant. Having arrived at this division of judgments, the positivists raised the question where value judgments fall. The judgment that knowledge is good, for example, did not seem to be analytic; the value that knowledge might have did not seem to be part of our concept of knowledge. But neither was the statement empirical, for goodness was not a quality like red or squeaky that could be seen or heard. What were they to do, then, with these awkward judgments of value? To find a place for them in their theory of knowledge would require them to revise the theory

radically, and yet that theory was what they regarded as their most important discovery. It appeared that the theory could be saved in one way only. If it could be shown that judgments of good and bad were not judgments at all, that they asserted nothing true or false, but merely expressed emotions like "Hurrah" or "Fiddlesticks," then these wayward judgments would cease from troubling and weary heads could be at rest. This is the course the positivists took. They explained value judgments by explaining them away.[1]

True to the above characterization, A. J. Ayer, the arch-representative of logical positivism, presents his own case thus:

> . . . it is our business to give an account of "judgements of value" which is both satisfactory in itself and consistent with our general empiricist principles. We shall set ourselves to show that in so far as statements of value are significant, they are ordinary "scientific" statements; and that in so far as they are not scientific, they are not in the literal sense significant, but are simply expressions of emotion which can be neither true nor false. . . .
>
> We begin by admitting that the fundamental ethical concepts are un-analysable, inasmuch as there is no criterion by which one can test the validity of the judgements in which they occur. So far we are in agreement with the absolutists. But, unlike the absolutists, we are able to give an explanation of this fact about ethical concepts. We say that the reason why they are unanalysable is that they are mere pseudo-concepts. The presence of an ethical symbol in a proposition adds nothing to its factual content. Thus if I say to someone, "You acted wrongly in stealing that money," I am not stating anything more than if I had simply said, "You stole that money." In adding that this action is wrong I am not making any further statement about it. I am simply evincing my moral disapproval of it. It is as if I had said, "You stole that money," in a peculiar tone of horror, or written it with the addition of some special exclamation marks. The tone, or the exclamation marks, adds nothing to the literal meaning of the sentence. It merely serves to show that the expression of it is attended by certain feelings in the speaker.

---

[1]Brand Blanshard, "The New Subjectivism in Ethics," *Philosophy and Phenomenological Research* 9 (1949), pp. 504–5.

If now I generalise my previous statement and say, "Stealing money is wrong," I produce a sentence which has no factual meaning—that is, expresses no proposition which can be either true or false. It is as if I had written "Stealing money!!"—where the shape and thickness of the exclamation marks show, by a suitable convention, that a special sort of moral disapproval is the feeling which is being expressed. It is clear that there is nothing said here which can be true or false. Another man may disagree with me about the wrongness of stealing, in the sense that he may not have the same feelings about stealing as I have, and he may quarrel with me on account of my moral sentiments. But he cannot, strictly speaking, contradict me. For in saying that a certain type of action is right or wrong, I am not making any factual statement, not even a statement about my own state of mind. I am merely expressing certain moral sentiments. And the man who is ostensibly contradicting me is merely expressing his moral sentiments. So that there is plainly no sense in asking which of us is in the right. For neither of us is asserting a genuine proposition.

What we have just been saying about the symbol "wrong" applies to all normative ethical symbols. Sometimes they occur in sentences which record ordinary empirical facts besides expressing ethical feeling about those facts: sometimes they occur in sentences which simply express ethical feeling about a certain type of action, or situation, without making any statement of fact. But in every case in which one would commonly be said to be making an ethical judgement, the function of the relevant ethical word is purely "emotive." It is used to express feeling about certain objects, but not to make any assertion about them.

It is worth mentioning that ethical terms do not serve only to express feeling. They are calculated also to arouse feeling, and so to stimulate action. Indeed some of them are used in such a way as to give the sentences in which they occur the effect of commands. Thus the sentence "It is your duty to tell the truth" may be regarded both as the expression of a certain sort of ethical feeling about truthfulness and as the expression of the command "Tell the truth." The sentence "You ought to tell the truth" also involves the command "Tell the truth," but here the tone of the command is less emphatic. In the sentence "It is good to tell the truth" the command has become little more than a suggestion. And thus the "meaning" of the word "good," in its ethical usage, is differentiated from that of the word "duty" or the word "ought." In fact we may define the meaning of the various ethical words in terms both of the different feelings they are ordinarily taken to express, and also the different responses which they are calculated to provoke.

We can now see why it is impossible to find a criterion for determining the validity of ethical judgements. It is not because they have an "absolute" validity which is mysteriously independent of ordinary sense-experience, but because they have no objective validity whatsoever. If a sentence makes no statement at all, there is obviously no sense in asking whether what it says is true or false. And we have seen that sentences which simply express moral judgements do not say anything. They are pure expressions of feeling and as such do not come under the category of truth and falsehood. They are unverifiable for the same reason as a cry of pain or a word of command is unverifiable—because they do not express genuine propositions.

. . . the main objection to the ordinary subjectivist theory is that the validity of ethical judgements is not determined by the nature of their author's feelings. And this is an objection which our theory escapes. For it does not imply that the existence of any feelings is a necessary and sufficient condition of the validity of an ethical judgement. It implies, on the contrary, that ethical judgements have no validity.[2]

What do you make of this view of morality? First, some rather theoretical considerations. Obviously, as with the logical positivist rejection of metaphysical claims, its rejection of moral claims depends on the verification principle, but the verification principle must reckon with several lines of objection: Does it rather arbitrarily exalt the language of sense experience as *the* language? Is it insensitive to other and equally important spheres of discourse with their own different criteria of meaningfulness? Is it not meaningless on its own showing, since it claims to be nonanalytic but cannot be verified empirically? And are you satisfied with this bifurcation of meaningful knowledge into either analytic *a priori* or synthetic *a posteriori*? And do you accept its repudiation of synthetic *a priori* knowledge, and can you live with the epistemological consequences of this?

---

[2]A. J. Ayer, *Language, Truth and Logic*, 2nd ed. (London: Gollancz, 1946), pp. 102–3, 107–10.

On the more practical side, even if emotivism could work as a *theory* about moral propositions, can it work in *practice?* What becomes of the practical necessity of legislation, praise and blame, and moral disputes? More specifically, consider these odd implications of emotivism. If emotivism were true, then no one could be mistaken in matters of morality, for, in the first place, moral judgments would not be about *truth*, and, in the second place, a person's feelings and attitudes would be just whatever they *are*, and that is that. Closely related to this is the awkward consequence that something approved by an insane person might for that reason alone be good: Imagine a murder wherein the victim was dispatched so immediately as to have no time to formulate his own disapproval, and the crime so perfectly executed that no others beside the murderer should ever know it. The only attitude of feeling about the murder would be the murderer's own. And his feeling about it would be: "I like it!" The murder was therefore "good." Finally, what becomes of occurrences which happened before anyone registered approval or disapproval? Were they not good or bad already, then, when they occurred? In a word: At the practical level, is anything really important resolved with the view that "X is bad" means simply "X—ugh!"?

SELF-REFUTING PROPOSITIONS

Propositions make claims, of course, about many things. When, however, a proposition is itself one of the things it makes a claim about, it sometimes turns out to be *self-refuting*. This means that if the proposition is taken seriously, then it backfires on itself—if it's true, it must be false!

A well-known example of a self-refuting proposition is: "All generalizations are false." If all generalizations are false, then the claim itself, which is a generalization, must be false. Especially puzzling is the proposition

> The sentence in this box is false.

If it's false, then it must be true; if it's true, it must be false! Does the verification principle backfire in a similar way? If it's true, then it itself must be meaningless!

THE CHALLENGE OF RELATIVISM

We have already encountered the idea of *ethical relativism* in the person of Protagoras. In fact, he provided this view with a motto for all time when he said that "a man is the measure of all things." Though Protagoras himself did not limit his statement to moral claims, it was natural that it was in the realm of morality that it was most obviously applied.

Ethical relativism holds, unlike emotivism, that moral claims *are* cognitively meaningful (that is, true or false) and that the criterion of their truth or falsity is the *individual*—the individual's perceptions, opinions, experiences, inclinations, and desires. This sort of relativism can take different forms, depending on what is meant by "individual." It might make ethical truth relative to the individual person, or the individual society, or community, or nation, or culture, or even the whole human race. But *any* form of ethical relativism denies that there are common or universal or *objective* moral values. It insists, rather, that moral values are private, individual, or *subjective*. Hence, ethical relativism vs. ethical absolutism may be expressed also as ethical subjectivism vs. ethical objectivism. However it is expressed, the issue is the same: What is the source or foundation of moral values and ideals? Are ethical values relative and subjective, or absolute and objective? Are they dependent upon the individual, or do moral values and ideals exist irrespective and independent of the individual? Is morality a matter of "different strokes for different folks"?

For those who embrace ethical relativism, more often than not it is the particular or individual *culture* that is said to define morality. We have encountered an instance of this already in B. F. Skinner's *Beyond Freedom and Dignity:*

> What a given group of people calls good is a fact; it is what members of the group find reinforcing as the result of their genetic endowment and the natural and social contingencies to which they have been exposed. Each culture has its own set of goods, and what is good in one culture may not be good in another. To recognize this is to take the position of "cultural relativism." What is good for the Trobriand Islander is good for the Trobriand Islander, and that is that. Anthropologists have often emphasized relativism as a tolerant alternative to missionary zeal in converting all cultures to a single set of ethical, governmental, religious, or economic values.[3]

---

[3]B. F. Skinner, *Beyond Freedom and Dignity* (New York: Bantam Books, 1972), p. 122.

One such anthropologist was Ruth Benedict, author of the much-read *Patterns of Culture*. In her essay, "Anthropology and the Abnormal," she, like Skinner, equates cultural relativism and ethical relativism:

> Every society, beginning with some slight inclination in one direction or another, carries its preference farther and farther, integrating itself more and more completely upon its chosen basis, and discarding those types of behavior that are uncongenial. Most of those organizations of personality that seem to us most incontrovertibly abnormal have been used by different civilizations in the very foundations of their institutional life. Conversely the most valued traits of our normal individuals have been looked on in differently organized cultures as aberrant. Normality, in short, within a very wide range, is culturally defined. It is primarily a term for the socially elaborated segment of human behavior in any culture; and abnormality, a term for the segment that that particular civilization does not use. The very eyes with which we see the problem are conditioned by the long traditional habits of our own society.
>
> It is a point that has been made more often in relation to ethics than in relation to psychiatry. We do not any longer make the mistake of deriving the morality of our own locality and decade directly from the inevitable constitution of human nature. We do not elevate it to the dignity of a first principle. We recognize that morality differs in every society, and is a convenient term for socially approved habits. Mankind has always preferred to say, "It is morally good," rather than "It is habitual," and the fact of this preference is matter enough for a critical science of ethics. But historically the two phrases are synonymous.
>
> The concept of the normal is properly a variant of the concept of the good. It is that which society has approved. A normal action is one which falls well within the limits of expected behavior for a particular society. Its variability among different peoples is essentially a function of the variability of the behavior patterns that different societies have created for themselves, and can never be wholly divorced from a consideration of culturally institutionalized types of behavior.
>
> Each culture is a more or less elaborate working-out of the potentialities of the segment it has chosen. In so far as a civilization is well integrated and consistent within itself, it will tend to carry farther and

farther, according to its nature, its initial impulse toward a particular type of action, and from the point of view of any other culture those elaborations will induce more and more extreme and aberrant traits.

Each of these traits, in proportion as it reinforces the chosen behavior patterns of that culture, is for that culture normal. Those individuals to whom it is congenial either congenitally, or as the result of childhood sets, are accorded prestige in that culture, and are not visited with the social contempt or disapproval which their traits would call down upon them in a society that was differently organized. On the other hand, those individuals whose characteristics are not congenial to the selected type of human behavior in that community are the deviants, no matter how valued their personality traits may be in a contrasted civilization.[4]

Why would one be an ethical relativist? Why would one ever assert with Protagoras that in matters of morality, "a man is the measure of all things"? Well, there is one gigantic but two-sided argument that relativists give over and over again. And, in fact, it is the argument that Protagoras himself gave. The argument is, first, that ethical views, opinions, and exhortations are largely or even completely conditioned by our circumstances. Obviously, whether you think that X is right and Y is wrong is very much dependent upon—relative to—when and where you were born, your upbringing, your education, your religious instruction, and maybe even your skin color and your height. Do you really think that you would hold the same moral opinions if your fundamental circumstances had been radically different? Second, and aside from our circumstances, relativists usually take very seriously the differences, disputes, and downright confusion that reign everywhere in the area of morality.

When both of these lines of observations are put together, they suggest strongly (maybe decisively) to some that there *are* no common or universal or objective values and that morality is *relative*.

Such a position is not without its problems. For one thing, does not the argument for ethical relativism misfire? Surely it does not follow from the fact that one's moral opinions are conditioned or learned that they are therefore merely subjectively or relatively true. We have learned all sorts

---

[4]Ruth Benedict, "Anthropology and the Abnormal," *Journal of General Psychology* 10 (1934), pp. 72–74.

of things which, nonetheless, we believe to be true, and true for *everyone:* In fourteen hundred and ninety-two Columbus sailed the ocean blue; $2 + 2 = 4$; it is wrong to beat your spouse, starve your children, and torture your pets; etc. And how do disagreements about morality destroy its objectivity? We may disagree also about the nature of the universe, but we would hardly conclude from that that the universe *has* no nature! On the contrary, what is the point of disagreeing at all, unless we believe there is some real *truth* involved? It is important, then, to distinguish between our *opinions* of morality and *morality itself.* Certainly our opinions about morality differ, and certainly they are conditioned by and relative to all sorts of things. But in no other sphere would we so simple-mindedly confuse our opinions of the truth with the truth itself. Why here, where the implications are far more consequential?

Furthermore, and similar to a criticism leveled against emotivism, if the individual is the basis of moral truth, then none of us could ever be mistaken in our moral opinions, for whatever we believe must be true. Or, on the larger interpretation of "individual," such as an individual group, morality would reduce to what happened to be believed by the largest number of people. Both of these seem to many to be necessary but absurd implications of the relativist or subjectivist position.

Some have even charged that ethical relativism not only misfires but *backfires* inasmuch as it involves a sort of *practical contradiction.* It is the contradiction between saying one thing and living another. You may know someone who *claims* to be an ethical relativist, but do you know anyone who *lives* as one? Do we not all, in one way or another, impose our ideas of morality on others? Do we not hold others responsible for their actions? Do we not judge others as morally wrong or reprehensible? Do we not vote, crusade for causes, and make sacrifices for various ideals? But clearly all such actions are meaningful (here, *existentially* meaningful) only on the assumption of an *objective* and *common* morality. In a word, this objection charges that there is really no such thing as a consistent subjectivist.

It should be noted, finally, that *if,* unlike the emotivists, you believe that moral propositions are cognitively significant, that is, that they are either true or false, and *if* you accept the above criticisms of ethical relativism, then you *must* be an ethical objectivist or absolutist. For either ethical relativism is true or ethical absolutism is true; there is no third alternative. If ethical relativism is false, then ethical absolutism must be true. Or, at least, so it seems to many. How does it seem to you?

THE CHALLENGE OF EXISTENTIALISM

We have already encountered the philosophy known as *existentialism:* It was mentioned in Chapter 1, in contrast to both speculative and analytic philosophy, and Albert Camus was cited in Chapter 11 as responding in an existentialist way to the problem of evil. It is difficult to say just what existentialism is, because the existentialists are so varied in their points of view. But that they represent, in different ways, challenges to traditional morality is evident.

For example, the Danish philosopher Søren Kierkegaard (1813–1855) taught the "teleological suspension of the ethical," according to which the individual is enabled to transcend ordinary ethical norms and receive his or her commandments immediately from God. The German Friedrich Nietzsche (1844–1900) rejected Christianity as involving a "slave-morality" and called for a "transvaluation of values" according to which "the will to power" as the basic principle of life will lead to the development of a higher type of humanity. Surely the best-known existentialist is the contemporary French writer and philosopher Jean-Paul Sartre. In addition to authoring works with ponderous titles such as *Being and Nothingness,* he wrote an essay entitled, simply, "Existentialism." This little work is often regarded as the best introduction to existentialism, and certainly it represents yet another existentialist's challenge to traditional morality.

According to Sartre, existentialism turns on its head any philosophy (think especially of Plato) which teaches that everything is what it is by virtue of a transcendent essence: *Essence precedes existence.* No, says Sartre. We begin with the *individual,* the concretely existing human being, the subject. The central tenet of existentialism, in any of its forms, is that *existence precedes essence.* What is first given is the existence of a particular thing; only *after* that does its essence appear. Or, to say it another way, *subjectivity must be the starting point.* However, in its atheistic form, which Sartre himself espouses, existentialism finds nothing outside, above, or beyond the individual to which the individual can leap for its essence, definition, or meaning. God is dead, all objective and transcendent values have disappeared with him, and the individual is alone. This is the meaning of Sartre's famous pronouncement that we are "condemned to be free." Here, to be "free" means to be unconditioned by any moral law or eternal values.

What then do we do? Answer: We must accept the full burden of our freedom and through our choices and commitments contribute to the evolving essence of humanity. What we choose for ourselves, that we become. And what we become, that we contribute to the definition or essence of humanity, for each of us is part of humanity. If, then, we care about the essence of humanity—what it is and will become—we must have a care about our own individual commitments. This sense of aloneness and personal responsibility is the source of the emphasis by Sartre and other existentialists on the anxiety, dread, and despair of the "conscious" individual, the individual who knows the score.

You may be tempted to see here just another version of subjectivism, but there is a difference. In its crassest form, subjectivism denies that any value or idea is any better than another. Clearly Sartre is not saying this. It is true that there is no divine or transcendent foundation of values, and that is precisely why Sartre shifts the responsibility to individuals. Human beings in their freedom (in Sartre's existentialist sense) are themselves the basis of values, and in this sense values are real—evolving, developing, on the move, but *real*. In place of God or a transcendent source of values, ideals, meaning, etc., this philosophy is truly *humanistic*, in that humanity stands center-stage as the criterion of all meaning and value. It is important to see how this differs from the sort of relativism or subjectivism we considered in the last section. That philosophy denied any objective or common values, locating them instead in *individuals*. This philosophy, on the other hand, affirms objective values, but locates them in *humanity*. The difference between subjectivism and humanism is caught by the two claims,

- A man is the measure of all things.
- Man is the measure of all things.

In the following, from his essay "Existentialism," Sartre explains the general nature of this philosophy, and the moral implications of his version of it.

What is meant by the term "existentialism"?

Most people who use the word would be rather embarrassed if they had to explain it, since, now that the word is all the rage, even the work of a musician or painter is being called existentialist. A gossip columnist in *Clartés* signs himself *The Existentialist*, so that by this time the word has been so stretched and has taken on so broad a meaning, that it no longer means anything at all. It seems that for want of an advance-guard doctrine analogous to surrealism, the kind of people who are eager for scandal and flurry turn to this philosophy which in other respects does not at all serve their purposes in this sphere.

Actually, it is the least scandalous, the most austere of doctrines. It is intended strictly for specialists and philosophers. Yet it can be defined easily. What complicates matters is that there are two kinds of existentialist; first, those who are Christian, among whom I would include Jaspers and Gabriel Marcel, both Catholic; and on the other hand the atheistic existentialists, among whom I class Heidegger, and then the French existentialists and myself. What they have in common is that they think that existence precedes essence, or, if you prefer, that subjectivity must be the starting point.

The French writer and thinker Jean-Paul Sartre is probably the best-known existentialist. He was the author of numerous novels (including one entitled *Nausea*), plays, and political and philosophical works. A Marxist and atheist, Sartre locates the full responsibility for human meaning in the commitments and choices of individuals themselves.

Just what does that mean? Let us consider some object that is manufactured, for example, a book or a paper-cutter: here is an object which has been made by an artisan whose inspiration came from a concept. He referred to the concept of what a paper-cutter is and likewise to a known method of production, which is part of the concept, something which is, by and large, a routine. Thus, the paper-cutter is at once an object produced in a certain way and, on the other hand, one having a specific use; and one can not postulate a man who produces a paper-cutter but does not know what it is used for. Therefore, let us say that, for the paper-cutter, essence—that is, the ensemble of both the production routines and the properties which enable it to be both produced and defined—precedes existence. Thus, the presence of the paper-cutter or book in front of me is determined. Therefore, we have here a technical view of the world whereby it can be said that production precedes existence.

When we conceive God as the Creator, He is generally thought of as a superior sort of artisan. Whatever doctrine we may be considering, whether one like that of Descartes or that of Leibnitz, we always grant that will more or less follows understanding or, at the very least, accompanies it, and that when God creates He knows exactly what He is creating. Thus, the concept of man in the mind of God is comparable to the concept of paper-cutter in the mind of the manufacturer, and, following certain techniques and a conception, God produces man, just as the artisan, following a definition and a technique, makes a paper-cutter. Thus, the individual man is the realization of a certain concept in the divine intelligence.

In the eighteenth century, the atheism of the *philosophes* discarded the idea of God, but not so much for the notion that essence precedes existence. To a certain extent, this idea is found everywhere; we find it in Diderot, in Voltaire, and even in Kant. Man has a human nature; this human nature, which is the concept of the human, is found in all men, which means that each man is a particular example of a universal concept, man. In Kant, the result of this universality is that the wildman, the natural man, as well as the bourgeois, are circumscribed by the same definition and have the same basic qualities. Thus, here too the essence of man precedes the historical existence that we find in nature.

Atheistic existentialism, which I represent, is more coherent. It states that if God does not exist, there is at least one being in whom existence precedes essence, a being who exists before he can be defined by any concept, and that this being is man, or, as Heidegger says, human reality. What is meant here by saying that existence precedes essence? It means that, first of all, man exists, turns up, appears on the scene, and, only afterwards, defines himself. If man, as the existentialist conceives him, is indefinable, it is because at first he is nothing. Only afterward will he be something, and he himself will have made what he will be. Thus, there is no human nature, since there is no God to conceive it. Not only is man what he conceives himself to be, but he is also only what he wills himself to be after this thrust toward existence.

Man is nothing else but what he makes of himself. Such is the first principle of existentialism. It is also what is called subjectivity, the name we are labeled with when charges are brought against us. But what do we mean by this, if not that man has a greater dignity than a stone or table? For we mean that man first exists, that is, that man first of all is the being who hurls himself toward a future and who is conscious of imagining himself as being in the future. Man is at the start a plan which is aware of itself, rather than a patch of moss, a piece of garbage, or a cauliflower; nothing exists prior to this plan; there is nothing in heaven; man will be what he will have planned to be. Not what he will want to be. Because by the word "will" we generally mean a conscious decision, which is subsequent to what we have already made of ourselves. I may want to belong to a political party, write a book, get married; but all that is only a manifestation of an earlier, more spontaneous choice that is called "will." But if existence really does precede essence, man is responsible for what he is. Thus, existentialism's first move is to make every man aware of what he is and to make the full responsibility of his existence rest on him. And when we say that a man is responsible for himself, we do not only mean that he is responsible for his own individuality, but that he is responsible for all men.

The word subjectivism has two meanings, and our opponents play on the two. Subjectivism means, on the one hand, that an individual chooses and makes himself; and, on the other, that it is impossible for man to transcend human subjectivity. The second of these is the essential meaning of existentialism. When we say that man chooses his own self, we mean that every one of us does likewise; but we also mean by that that in making this choice he also chooses all men. In fact, in creating the man that we want to be, there is not a single one of our acts which does not at the same time create an image of man as we think he ought to be. To choose to be this or that is to affirm at the same time the value of what we choose, because we can never choose evil. We always choose the good, and nothing can be good for us without being good for all.

If, on the other hand, existence precedes essence, and if we grant that we exist and fashion our image at one and the same time, the image is valid for everybody and for our whole age. Thus, our responsibility is much greater than we might have supposed, because it involves all mankind. If I am a workingman and choose to join a Christian trade-union rather than be a communist, and if by being a member I want to show that the best thing for man is resignation, that the kingdom of man is not of this world, I am not only involving my own case—I want to be resigned for everyone. As a result, my action has involved all humanity. To take a more individual matter, if I want to marry, to have children; even if this marriage depends solely on my own circumstances or passion or wish, I am involving all humanity in monogamy and not merely myself. Therefore, I am responsible for myself and for everyone else. I am creating a certain image of man of my own choosing. In choosing myself, I choose man.

This helps us understand what the actual content is of such rather grandiloquent words as anguish, forlornness, despair. As you will see, it's all quite simple. . . .

When we speak of forlornness, a term Heidegger was fond of, we mean only that God does not exist and that we have to face all the consequences of this. The existentialist is strongly opposed to a certain kind of secular ethics which would like to abolish God with the least possible expense. About 1880, some French teachers tried to set up a secular ethics which went something like this: God is a useless and costly hypothesis; we are discarding it; but, meanwhile, in order for there to be an ethics, a society, a civilization, it is essential that certain values be taken seriously and that they be considered as having an *a priori* existence. It must be obligatory, *a priori*, to be honest, not to lie, not to beat your wife, to have children, etc., etc. So we're going to try a little device which will make it possible to show what values exist all the same, inscribed in a heaven of ideas, though otherwise God does not exist. In other words—and this, I believe, is the tendency of everything called reformism in France—nothing will be changed if God does not exist. We shall find ourselves with the same norms of honesty, progress, and humanism, and we shall have made of God an outdated hypothesis which will peacefully die off by itself.

The existentialist, on the contrary, thinks it very distressing that God does not exist, because all possibility of finding values in a heaven of ideas disappears along with Him; there can no longer be an *a priori* Good, since there is no infinite and perfect consciousness to think it. Nowhere is it written that the Good exists, that we must be honest, that we must not lie; because the fact is we are on a plane where there are only men. Dostoievsky said, "If God didn't exist, everything would be possible." That is the very starting point of existentialism. Indeed, everything is permissible if God does not exist, and as a result man is forlorn, because neither within him nor without does he find anything to cling to. He can't start making excuses for himself.

If existence really does precede essence, there is no explaining things away by reference to a fixed and given human nature. In other words, there is no determinism, man is free, man is freedom. On the other hand, if God does not exist, we find no values or commands to turn to which legitimize our conduct. So, in the bright realm of values, we have no excuse behind us, nor justification before us. We are alone, with no excuses.

That is the idea I shall try to convey when I say that man is condemned to be free. Condemned, because he did not create himself, yet, in other respects is free; because, once thrown into the world, he is responsible for everything he does.[5]

Simone de Beauvoir[6] was a colleague and companion of Sartre. She was a major contributor to the Sartrean strain of contemporary existentialism,

---

[5]Jean-Paul Sartre, "Existentialism," tr. Bernard Frechtman, in *Existentialism and Human Emotions* (New York: Citadel Press, 1957), pp. 12–18, 21–23.
[6]Pronounced *Bow-vwar'*.

but was in her own right an original philosopher and a founding contributor to a major social and intellectual movement—feminism. Certainly the most famous and influential of her works is the landmark book *The Second Sex*, first published in French in 1949 (two volumes). *A propos* of recent and continuing feminist concerns, the extract below displays an application of her ideas to a concrete situation.

Special attention should be given to the French expression *en soi*, which, along with *pour soi*, occurs often in Sartrean literature. In fact, they are fundamental to the whole perspective. *En soi* means, literally, "in itself," and in Sartrean contexts has reference to nonconscious being; this is contrasted with *pour soi*, literally, "for itself," which has reference to conscious being along with the taking of responsibility for one's choices. In respect of the situation of women specifically, de Beauvoir's thought is this. We need the other's "look" on us to know ourselves. But the other's "look" can also objectify us, in the sense of reducing us to *things*, stultifying our freedom to project our own possibilities, thus confining us to the state of *en-soi*. The "look" of the patriarchy (our male-dominated tradition) on woman has projected her as an object (note the reference to "the brutish life of subjection to given conditions"), thus denying her own transcendence, or *pour-soi*. In *The Second Sex*, de Beauvoir is recalling women to their existence as free projections of possibilities—called here "transcendence." It should be apparent that in all of this we are still talking about what we earlier called "existential freedom."

> . . . those who are condemned to stagnation are often pronounced
> happy on the pretext that happiness consists in being at rest. This
> notion we reject, for our perspective is that of existentialist ethics.
> Every subject plays his part as such specifically through exploits or
> projects that serve as a mode of transcendence; he achieves liberty
> only through a continual reaching out toward other liberties. There
> is no justification for present existence other than its expansion into
> an indefinitely open future. Every time transcendence falls back into
> immanence, stagnation, there is a degradation of existence into the
> "*en-soi*"—the brutish life of subjection to given conditions—and of
> liberty into constraint and contingence. This downfall represents a
> moral fault if the subject consents to it; if it is inflicted upon him, it
> spells frustration and oppression. In both cases it is an absolute evil.
> Every individual concerned to justify his existence feels that his existence involves an undefined need to transcend himself, to engage in
> freely chosen projects.

Simone de Beauvoir, who is often called
the "mother of modern feminism," applied
existentialist ideas to the situation of
contemporary women.

Now, what peculiarly signalizes the situation of woman is that
she—a free and autonomous being like all human creatures—
nevertheless finds herself living in a world where men compel her
to assume the status of the Other. They propose to stabilize her as
object and to doom her to immanence since her transcendence is to
be overshadowed and forever transcended by another ego (*conscience*) which is essential and sovereign. The drama of woman lies
in this conflict between the fundamental aspirations of every subject (ego)—who always regards the self as the essential—and the
compulsions of a situation in which she is the inessential. How can
a human being in woman's situation attain fulfillment? What roads
are open to her? Which are blocked? How can independence be
recovered in a state of dependency? What circumstances limit
woman's liberty and how can they be overcome? These are the fundamental questions on which I would fain throw some light. This

EXISTENTIALISM

The philosophy that emphasizes the existing individual, as opposed to abstractions or principles, as the point of departure for authentic philosophizing. Two existentialist slogans from Sartre:

- Existence precedes essence.
- Subjectivity must be the starting point.

means that I am interested in the fortunes of the individual as defined not in terms of happiness but in terms of liberty.[7]

We have already distinguished Sartre's humanistic existentialism from subjectivism. Nonetheless, Sartre's position has been attacked with criticisms similar to those which we saw in the last section leveled against subjectivism. After all, if individual existence precedes the essence of humanity, and nothing at all precedes or conditions the individual's choices, then what is to prevent those choices from being purely arbitrary and, thus, the evolving essence of man as well? That is, if you don't begin with any meaning, how can you end with any?

This is the point of one of Sartre's loudest critics, Gabriel Marcel (1889–1973), whom Sartre mentioned as a Christian existentialist in the above selection. (That Marcel is called an existentialist by Sartre himself, and yet attacked the very basis of Sartre's philosophy, reminds us of what a variety there is among existentialists.) Marcel represents the way in which one might be faithful to the existentialist thesis that subjectivity must be the starting point but, beginning with subjectivity or the concreteness of personal existence, might move to a theistic or transcendent basis of value and meaning. This, says Marcel, is exactly what we must do, for values are not chosen but *discovered*. They are *given*. They are *objective*. According to Marcel, the Sartrean approach bogs down in a hopeless contradiction: It

---

[7]Simone de Beauvoir, *The Second Sex*, tr. and ed. H. M. Parshley (New York: Vintage Books, 1952), pp. xxxiii-xxxiv.

claims that outside our own commitments there is no basis for moral choices, but then turns right around and insists that some choices are better than others. You cannot have it both ways, and you cannot give up (can you?) the view that some choices are better than others. We must, says Marcel, grant the *givenness* of values and meaning. And given by whom, except *God?* From Marcel's *The Philosophy of Existentialism:*

> From [Sartre's] standpoint, values cannot be anything but the result of the initial choice made by each human being; in other words, they can never be "recognised" or "discovered." "My freedom," he states expressly, "is the unique foundation of values. And since I am the being by virtue of whom values exist, nothing—absolutely nothing— can justify me in adopting this or that value or scale of values. As the unique basis of the existence of values, I am totally unjustifiable. And my freedom is in anguish at finding that it is the baseless basis of values." Nothing could be more explicit; but the question is whether Sartre does not here go counter to the exigencies of that human reality which he claims, after all, not to invent but to reveal.
>
> Not to deal exclusively in abstractions, let us take a concrete case. Sartre has announced that the third volume of his *Les Chemins de la Liberté [The Ways of Freedom]* is to be devoted to the praise of the heroes of Resistance. Now I ask you in the name of what principle, having first denied the existence of values or at least of their objective basis, can he establish any appreciable difference between those utterly misguided but undoubtedly courageous men who joined voluntarily the [Nazi] Anti-Bolshevik Legion, on the one hand, and the heroes of the Resistance movement, on the other? I can see no way of establishing this difference without admitting that causes have their intrinsic value and, consequently, that values are real. I have no doubt that Sartre's ingenuity will find a way out of this dilemma; in fact, he quite often uses the words "good" and "bad," but what can these words possibly mean in the context of his philosophy?
>
> The truth is that, if I examine myself honestly and without reference to any preconceived body of ideas, I find that I do not "choose" my values at all, but that I *recognise* them and then posit my actions in accordance or in contradiction with these values, not, however, without being painfully aware of this contradiction . . . It should perhaps be asked at this point if it is not Nietzsche who, with his theory of

the creation of values, is responsible for the deathly principle of error which has crept into speculation on this subject. But although I am the last to underrate the objections to Nietzsche's doctrine, I am inclined to think that his view is less untenable than that of Sartre, for it escapes that depth of rationalism and materialism which is discernible, to me as to others, in the mind of the author of *L'Etre et le Néant* [*Being and Nothingness*].

I would suggest in conclusion that existentialism stands to-day at a parting of the ways: it is, in the last analysis, obliged either to deny or to transcend itself. It denies itself quite simply when it falls to the level of infra-dialectical materialism. It transcends itself, or it tends to transcend itself, when it opens itself out to the experience of the suprahuman, an experience which can hardly be ours in a genuine and lasting way this side of death, but of which the reality is attested by mystics, and of which the possibility is warranted by any philosophy which refuses to be immured in the postulate of absolute immanence or to subscribe in advance to the denial of the beyond and of the unique and veritable transcendence.[8]

THE CHALLENGE OF DETERMINISM

Another difficulty for morality is posed by the *determinist.* In fact, some would say that determinism renders morality (as most of us understand the word) impossible. We saw in an earlier discussion (in Chapter 5) that determinism is the view that all things are causally conditioned such that they could not be otherwise. We also considered some of the problematical implications of this view, though we must now consider more adequately its implications for morality.

What are these implications? Well, if it is true that all things are causally determined, then this must apply also to our willing and choosing. And this means the *denial of free will.* And *this* means the *end of morality.* At least according to many. For is it not clear, they would insist, that morality *presupposes free will?* that *ought* implies *can?* What sense is there in praise and blame and talk of moral responsibility if one could not have done otherwise? if one does not choose and act *freely?* Is it not always relevant, when

---

[8]Gabriel Marcel, *The Philosophy of Existentialism,* tr. Manya Harari (New York: Citadel Press, 1956), pp. 86–88.

trying to establish blame or guilt or responsibility on the part of someone, to ascertain whether that person was forced, drugged, or suffering from some compulsion? Thus free will has seemed to many to be a condition for responsible, moral action.

Your decision between determinism, or the belief that everything, including your will, is causally determined, and indeterminism, the belief that some things, and therefore possibly the will, are not determined, may be a crucial one. And you cannot have it both ways. Either determinism or indeterminism.

But we must not move too fast here. Determinism itself must be viewed in two lights: *hard*-determinism and *soft*-determinism.

The hard-determinist believes not only that all things are determined, but that they are determined ultimately by purely *external* factors, factors outside yourself and over which you have no control. Why did you choose X? *Ultimately* because of things like the circumstances of your birth, upbringing, education, environment, genetic structure—in a word because of everything that has contributed in any way to the shaping and placing of your person and those of all of your ancestors. To say it another way, you chose X because _____ : Fill in here the uncountable causes which, extending as it were from the infinite past, converge at this moment on the movement of your will in favor of X.

Is hard-determinism compatible with morality? According to the hard-determinists themselves, the answer is both Yes and No. On the yes side, the hard-determinist, no less than anyone else, decries murder, theft, and the torturing of starving children. The fact that people have no control over their actions, whether good or evil, has no bearing on those actions being, nevertheless, good or evil. The desire to torture starving children, like cancer, is an evil to be recognized as such and to be dealt with—as you would deal with cancer. Now you do not punish a cancer; you try to *treat* it and *heal* it. (Echoes of Skinner?) But this brings us to the no side of the answer. If morality implies the possibility of praise, blame, and punishment, then the hard-determinist can scarcely accommodate morality. Certainly there is little room for praise, blame, and punishment, in a view of things

---

". . . it is certain that if there is no free will there can be no morality."
—W. T. Stace

according to which no one is responsible for his or her condition in general, which means also his or her moral condition in specific. One is not *responsible*, period.

It is precisely to the issue of *responsibility* that *soft*-determinism speaks. The soft-determinist is, of course, a determinist, and holds, like the hard-determinist, that because of antecedent causes our choices could not be otherwise. But in contrast to the hard-determinist, the soft-determinist shifts our whole attention to the causes which lie *within* the individual. Our actions and choices *are* determined—by our desires, inclinations, attitudes, or, in a word, our *character*.

In this way, the soft-determinists see determinism not only as compatible with morality but as *necessary* for morality. For, they say, your choices or actions can be judged moral or immoral, or you can be held accountable for them, only if they actually reflect your intentions, desires, attitudes, and

---

The famous attorney Clarence Darrow to the prisoners of the Cook County Jail:

> There is no such thing as a crime as the word is generally understood. I do not believe there is any sort of distinction between the real moral conditions of the people in and out of jail. One is just as good as the other. The people here can no more help being here than the people outside can avoid being outside. I do not believe that people are in jail because they deserve to be. They are in jail simply because they cannot avoid it on account of circumstances which are entirely beyond their control and for which they are in no way responsible . . . There are people who think that everything in this world is an accident. But really there is no such thing as an accident . . . There are a great many people here who have done some of these things (murder, theft, etc.) who really do not know themselves why they did them. It looked to you at the time as if you had a chance to do them or not, as you saw fit; but still, after all you had no choice . . . If you look at the question deeply enough and carefully enough you will see that there were circumstances that drove you to do exactly the thing which you did. You could not help it any more than we outside can help taking the positions that we take.

so on. Would you hold someone responsible for an action that did not really spring from his or her character? Would you hold me morally accountable for hitting you in the face if it was the result of a sudden and uncontrollable muscle spasm? If, however, my hitting you in the face was the result of (or was *caused by*) my attitude toward you and my intention to cause you pain, well, isn't that a quite different situation? a situation in which I am *responsible* for my action? a *moral* situation? How then can there be moral behavior and moral judgment without determinism—character-determinism or *self*-determinism, as the position is also called?

David Hume provides a good statement of how praise and blame are possible only if the deeds that are praised or blamed are rooted in, or *caused* by, the doer's character. From the *Enquiry Concerning Human Understanding:*

> The only proper object of hatred or vengeance is a person or creature, endowed with thought and consciousness; and when any criminal or injurious actions excite that passion, it is only by their relation to the person, or connexion with him. Actions are, by their very

---

THE PROBLEM OF FREE WILL AND DETERMINISM

Determinism
The view that all things, including the will, are causally determined.

Indeterminism
The view that some things, and therefore possibly the will, are free of causal determination.

(a) *hard-determinism*
The will is determined ultimately by exterior factors beyond the responsibility of the individual.

(b) *soft-determinism*
The will is determined by the character of the individual, and thus individuals are responsible for their choices.

---

nature, temporary and perishing; and where they proceed not from some *cause* in the character and disposition of the person who performed them, they can neither redound to his honour, if good; nor infamy, if evil. The actions themselves may be blameable; they may be contrary to all the rules of morality and religion: But the person is not answerable for them; and as they proceed from nothing in him that is durable and constant, and leave nothing of that nature behind them, it is impossible he can, upon their account, become the object of punishment or vengeance. According to the principle, therefore, which denies necessity, and consequently causes, a man is as pure and untainted, after having committed the most horrid crime, as at the first moment of his birth, nor is his character anywise concerned in his actions, since they are not derived from it, and the wickedness of the one can never be used as a proof of the depravity of the other.

Men are not blamed for such actions as they perform ignorantly and casually, whatever may be the consequences. Why? but because the principles of these actions are only momentary, and terminate in them alone. Men are less blamed for such actions as they perform hastily and unpremeditately than for such as proceed from deliberation. For what reason? but because a hasty temper, though a constant cause or principle in the mind, operates only by intervals, and infects not the whole character. Again, repentance wipes off every crime, if attended with a reformation of life and manners. How is this to be accounted for? but by asserting that actions render a person criminal merely as they are proofs of criminal principles in the mind; and when, by an alteration of these principles, they cease to be just proofs, they likewise cease to be criminal. But, except upon the doctrine of necessity, they never were just proofs, and consequently never were criminal.

It will be equally easy to prove, and from the same arguments, that *liberty* . . . is also essential to morality, and that no human actions, where it is wanting, are susceptible of any moral qualities, or can be the objects either of approbation or dislike. For as actions are objects of our moral sentiment, so far only as they are indications of the internal character, passions, and affections; it is impossible that they can give rise either to praise or blame, where they proceed not from these principles, but are derived altogether from external violence.[9]

---

[9]David Hume, *An Enquiry Concerning Human Understanding*, in *Hume's Enquiries*, 2nd ed., ed. L. A. Selby-Bigge (Oxford: Clarendon Press, 1902), pp. 98–99.

But the indeterminists, or free-willists, are still unsatisfied. They raise an obvious question: It may be that my choice or action is determined by my own character, but how did I acquire this character—these particular attitudes, inclinations, desires, likes, and dislikes? Is not my character ultimately determined, again, by factors outside me, antecedent to me, and quite beyond my control? Does not soft-determinism have to give way, finally, to hard-determinism with its denial of moral responsibility? As far as *responsibility* goes, is there really any final difference between soft- and hard-determinism? A clearer reduction of soft-determinism to hard-determinism could hardly be found than that of Baron D'Holbach (1723–1789), an atheistic and mechanistic materialist. In the following, from *The System of Nature*, Holbach applies his mechanistic principle specifically to the question of morality, and concludes that all of our moral dispositions, no less than anything else about us, reduce, finally, to necessary determinations.

The *ambitious man* cries out: you will have me resist passions; but have they not unceasingly repeated to me that rank, honours, power, are the most desirable advantages in life? Have I not seen my fellow citizens envy them, the nobles of my country sacrifice every thing to obtain them? In the society in which I live, am I not obliged to feel, that if I am deprived of these advantages, I must expect to anguish in contempt; to cringe under the rod of oppression?

The *miser* says: you forbid me to love money, to seek after the means of acquiring it: alas! does not every thing tell me that, in this world, money is the greatest blessing; that it is amply sufficient to render me happy? In the country I inhabit, do I not see all my fellow citizens covetous of riches? but do I not also witness that they are little scrupulous in the means of obtaining wealth? As soon as they are enriched by the means which you censure, are they not cherished, considered and respected? By what authority, then, do you defend me from amassing treasure? What right have you to prevent my using means, which, although you call them sordid and criminal, I see approved by the sovereign? Will you have me renounce my happiness?

The *voluptuary* argues: you pretend that I should resist my desires; but was I the maker of my own temperament, which unceasingly invites me to pleasure? You call my pleasures disgraceful; but in the country in which I live, do I not witness the most dissipated men enjoying the most distinguished rank? Do I not behold that no one is ashamed of adultery but the husband it has outraged? Do not I see men making trophies of their debaucheries, boasting of their libertinism, rewarded with applause?

The *choleric man* vociferates: you advise me to put a curb on my passions, and to resist the desire of avenging myself: but can I conquer my nature? Can I alter the received opinions of the world? Shall I not be forever disgraced, infallibly dishonoured in society, if I do not wash out in the blood of my fellow creatures the injuries I have received?

The *zealous enthusiast* exclaims: you recommend me mildness; you advise me to be tolerant; to be indulgent to the opinions of my fellow men; but is not my temperament violent? Do I not ardently love my God? Do they not assure me, that zeal is pleasing to him; that sanguinary inhuman persecutors have been his friends? As I wish to render myself acceptable in his sight, I therefore adopt the same means.

In short, the actions of man are never free; they are always the necessary consequence of his temperament, of the received ideas, and of the notions, either true or false, which he has formed to himself of happiness; of his opinions, strengthened by example, by education, and by daily experience. . . .

If he understood the play of his organs, if he were able to recall to himself all the impulsions they have received, all the modifications they have undergone, all the effects they have produced, he would perceive that all his actions are submitted to that *fatality*, which regulates his own particular system, as it does the entire system of the universe: no one effect in him, any more than in nature, produces itself by *chance;* this, as has been before proved, is word void of sense. All that passes in him; all that is done by him; as well as all that happens in nature, or that is attributed to her, is derived from necessary causes, which act according to necessary laws, and which produce necessary effects, from whence necessarily flow others.

Fatality, is the eternal, the immutable, the necessary order, established in nature; or the indispensable connexion of causes that act, with the effects they operate.[10]

---

[10]Baron D'Holbach, *The System of Nature,* tr. H. D. Robinson (Boston: Mendum, 1869), pp. 94–95, 102.

The indeterminist agrees with this but draws the opposite conclusion: not that there is no basis for praise, blame, responsibility, and virtuous conduct, but that determinism must be false! That is, the indeterminist can simply turn the tables: If someone says that since our wills are determined there can be no morality, the indeterminist may answer that inasmuch as morality is a fact our wills must *not* be determined! And, of course, the indeterminists have it in their favor that, as a matter of fact, we *do*—all of us, always, and unavoidably—live our lives on the assumption that there is free will and that people are *responsible*. Thus, according to the indeterminists, the determinists are a little like the relativists, who, as we saw in the last section, might *claim* their position to be true, but cannot *live* as if it were true. In fact, determinists turn out so much to be free-willists that W. T. Stace has concluded that the determinism–free-will problem can hardly be a real problem at all; rather, it must simply involve a misunderstanding in our philosophical language:

> It is to be observed that those learned professors of philosophy or psychology who deny the existence of free will do so only in their professional moments and in their studies and lecture rooms. For when it comes to doing anything practical, even of the most trivial kind, they invariably behave as if they and others were free. They inquire from you at dinner whether you will choose this dish or that dish. They will ask a child why he told a lie, and will punish him for not having chosen the way of truthfulness. All of which is inconsistent with a disbelief in free will. This should cause us to suspect that the problem is not a real one; and this, I believe, is the case. The dispute is merely verbal, and is due to nothing but a confusion about the meanings of words. It is what is now fashionably called a semantic problem.[11]

It must be admitted, though, that the indeterminists are in an awkward spot too. They deny determinism as being incompatible with morality. But what do they replace it with? Actions and choices that are *un*caused? But this would seem to make our actions and choices utterly spontaneous, capricious, irrational, and arbitrary. And certainly this is just as in-

---

[11]W. T. Stace, *Religion and the Modern Mind* (Philadelphia: Lippincott, 1952), pp. 279–80.

compatible with morality and responsibility as is determinism. Something is beyond one's control, and therefore not an object of praise or blame, as much whether it happened by pure chance as whether it was completely necessitated. But what, then, lies in this mysterious zone between pure chance and pure necessity? What might the indeterminist or free-willist *mean* by "uncaused" choices or "free" will? Some indeterminists or free-willists would withdraw at this point with a quiet, "I really don't know. But there must be some such. For it is certainly a bigger problem to reject morality than not to have a clear and coherent idea of free will. Take your choice. *But do you really have one?*"

Others, of a somewhat more analytic strain, have sought for clarification of our terms. We have seen that the whole determinism–free-will controversy is bound up with talk about causality, the principle that every event must have a cause. But is an act of the will really an "act" in any obvious or clear sense? And is a decision really an "event"? It has been suggested, not without merit, that maybe the language in which the whole problem has been posed is inappropriate from the start. Has it been something like a category mistake again? In any event, William K. Frankena's exhortation is well-taken:

> . . . I think that moral philosophers cannot insist too much on the importance of actual knowledge and conceptual clarity for the solution of moral and social problems. The two besetting sins in our prevailing habits of ethical thinking are our ready acquiescence in unclarity and our complacence in ignorance—the very sins that Socrates died combatting over two thousand years ago.[12]

When someone says, "Everything is determined by antecedent causes and could not have been otherwise," is that statement *itself* determined? Do you usually pay much attention to utterances that could not have been different, such as that of someone acting out a post-hypnotic suggestion?

---

[12]William K. Frankena, *Ethics,* 2nd ed. (Englewood Cliffs, NJ: Prentice Hall, 1973), p. 13.

CHAPTER 12 IN REVIEW

Summary

In this chapter we have considered four basic questions which may be thought of as threatening or undermining the very idea of morality:

- Are moral claims meaningful propositions?
- Is morality purely relative?
- Do values originate in human experience?
- Are moral actions determined?

It has seemed to some that if the answer to any of these is Yes, then morality, at least in a more or less traditional sense, is rendered impossible from the very start.

Emotivism charges that moral statements turn out to hold no cognitive significance at all; that is, they are neither true nor false, and are therefore quite literally senseless. On the contrary, they are merely emotional expressions of approval or disapproval: "That is good" = "Ahhh!" Such a view has its roots in the philosophy known as logical positivism and, more specifically, the verification principle with its superempirical criterion of meaningfulness. Aside from the charge that the verification principle is self-refuting, some critics complain this whole approach commits us to a narrow and dogmatic conception of language. Others insist that it also would make nonsense of our practical lives, which are pervaded every day by the necessity of taking values seriously as having their own status, quite independently of our individual emotional responses.

This last point is a relevant objection also to the relativist's challenge: Values are purely relative, possessing no objective or absolute or *real* status beyond the individual's own notions. (Remember that "individual" may mean an individual person or an individual group.) The objectivist freely grants that, of course, our views or *opinions* about morality are largely relative (to circumstances of birth, upbringing, education, etc.), but that morality *itself* is the unconditioned reality that lies behind and makes ultimate sense of our moral quests and even our moral disputes.

Closely related but different is the challenge delivered by existentialism. Here we have looked specifically at the perspective of Jean-Paul Sartre. Sartre summarizes all existential philosophies as teaching that existence precedes essence. According to Sartre's own atheistic view, there is no value, meaning, or definition of humanity apart from that which human beings themselves inject into the picture. Here, "Man is the measure of all things," and it *matters* what we choose and what we thereby make of humanity. On the other hand, this is just what bothers the critics: How *can* it matter if there is no justification *outside us* for our acts and commitments?

Another threat is posed by the determinist, who says that since everything is predetermined, so are our own moral choices and decisions. The soft-determinist seeks to soften this blow with the explanation that our choices are determined, but by our own character, and that that is exactly why we are responsible for them. It is important to ask whether this does not lead right back to hard-determinism, inasmuch as our character has been shaped largely beyond our own control (or has it?). In any event, the free-willist is often fond of turning the whole challenge on its head: Since morality is a nonnegotiable fact of our experience, and since it is unintelligible apart from free will, the will must be (in whatever obscure way) free.

It *is* interesting, isn't it, that while none of these challenges is particularly new, the actual give-and-take world of morality goes right on as if nothing happened? Does morality ever actually succumb to any of these (largely theoretical) challenges?

Basic Ideas

- Cognitive meaning/existential meaning
- The verification principle
- Emotivism
- Problems with the verification principle
- Emotivism as impractical
- Relativism or subjectivism
- Absolutism or objectivism
- Cultural relativism
- Relativism as impractical
- Sartre: Existentialism
    Existence precedes essence
    Subjectivity
    Freedom as the basis of values
- "In itself"/"for itself"
- Marcel's critique of Sartre
- Determinism

- Hard-determinism
- Soft-determinism (self-determinism)
- Indeterminism
- The obscurity of "free will"
- Determinism as impractical

Questions for Reflection

- In the section on logical positivism a piece was quoted from Blanshard's article "The New Subjectivism in Ethics." In light of this whole chapter, do you think it is correct to represent emotivism as "subjectivism"? If not, what is the big difference between emotivism and true subjectivism (or relativism)? And why is Sartre's doctrine of freedom as the baseless basis of value not strictly subjectivism?

- Do you believe that the determinist's challenge to traditional morality is successful? If so, your problem is to give a coherent account of morality that can accommodate at the same time the denial of free will. If you don't think the challenge is successful, your problem is to give a coherent account of free will itself: It's easy to say what it isn't, but what *is* it? Is it necessary, for the sake of morality, simply to postulate an unknown something? Would that be so bad?

- Can you give a good account of the difference between Sartre's idea of freedom and the idea of freedom involved in the debate between free will and determinism?

For Further Reading

Hazel Barnes. *Sartre*. London: Quarlet Books, 1973. A compact introduction to the philosophical-literary contribution of Sartre, by a leading authority.

Richard B. Brandt, *Ethical Theory: The Problems of Normative and Critical Ethics*. Englewood Cliffs, NJ: Prentice Hall, 1959. Chs. 9, 11, and 20. Textbook discussions of emotivism, relativism, and determinism.

Frederick Copleston. *Contemporary Philosophy: Studies of Logical Positivism and Existentialism*. Paramus, NJ: Newman Press, 1956. Extended readable discussions of these two dominating philosophical perspectives, by a noted historian of philosophy.

Frederick Copleston. *A History of Philosophy.* Baltimore: Newman Press, 1946–1974. IX, Chs. 16–17. An overview of Sartre's existentialist philosophy with special reference to freedom as the basis of value.

Gerald Dworkin (ed.). *Determinism, Free Will, and Moral Responsibility.* Englewood Cliffs, NJ: Prentice Hall, 1970. A collection of twelve essays, traditional and contemporary, on various aspects of the free will/moral responsibility issue.

A. C. Ewing. *Ethics.* New York: Free Press, 1953. Chs. 7–8. Beginning but insightful treatments of various forms of subjectivism and the problems of morality and free will.

Jonathan Glover. *Responsibility.* London: Routledge & Kegan Paul, 1970. A full discussion of the problem of free will and moral responsibility, with special reference to the criminal responsibility of the mentally ill.

John Macquarrie. *Existentialism.* New York: World, 1972. An excellent introduction to existentialist philosophy, with numerous references to Satre.

Paul Taylor (ed.). *Problems of Moral Philosophy: An Introduction to Ethics.* Belmont, CA: Dickenson, 1967. Chs. 2 and 6. Traditional and contemporary readings on relativism and moral responsibility in relation to free will.

J. O. Urmson. *The Emotive Theory of Ethics.* London: Hutchinson, 1968. A full, critical treatment, focusing generally on the version advocated by C. L. Stevenson, by a nonadherent.

W. H. Werkmeister. *Theories of Ethics: A Study in Moral Obligation.* Lincoln, NE: Johnsen, 1961. Chs. 1–2. A closely documented account and critique of the two main forms of emotivism.

Bernard Williams. *Morality: An Introduction to Ethics.* Cambridge, England: Cambridge University Press, 1972. An intelligent and concise discussion of relativism and amoralism.

In addition, see the relevant articles ("Ethical Relativism," "Emotive Theory of Ethics," "Determinism," "Sartre, Jean-Paul," etc.) in *The Encyclopedia of Philosophy*, ed. Paul Edwards. New York: Macmillan, 1967.

Utilitarianism

W HAT IS more natural, when confronted with a moral dilemma, than to ask something like: "What should I do to bring about the most happiness to the most people?" Whenever this has been your criterion of behavior, you have been a practicing *utilitarian*.

The actual application of the utilitarian criterion is, however, often a difficult and sometimes a dramatic affair. A true scene:

> He saw a lifeboat sitting about three hundred yards off. It was a small craft, manned by half a dozen sailors. They were scanning the ship carefully.
>
> "Help!" Hudson cried out, "Help me. Over here."
>
> A flashlight winked. Its beam played along the stern of the *Andrea Doria*. Guided by Hudson's screams, the light focused on the desperate sailor clinging to the net.

372

"Help me!" Hudson yelled again. "Quickly. Hurry."

Hudson waited for the men to clasp their oars. He fought against the swift current, energized now by the sight of his rescuers.

But the lifeboat did not move.

"Help!" Hudson called once more. "Hurry. Please!"

Still the lifeboat lay quietly in the water. The flashlight again blinked in Hudson's eyes. They saw him. They heard him. Why would they not come? *My God!* Hudson realized, *the ship is going down . . . now!* In his merchant marine training Hudson had been taught that a lifeboat must sit off at least three hundred yards to avoid being pulled under by a sinking ship. That was where the lifeboat lay. . . .

He lay silent for a time, riding the swells, waiting for the end. An orange globe of sun rose behind him, the fresh beginning of the day mocking the tragedy it revealed. The *Andrea Doria* lay more horizontal than vertical. Deck chairs, suitcases, random bits of clothing, and splintered wood swayed in the waves. Hudson climbed one notch higher on the net as it slowly sank lower into the sea.

His will returned. "Help!" he screamed. "Please come get me. You can't let me die."

He could see the men watching him from the lifeboat. But they did not reach for their oars.

The desperate man resorted to cursing once more. Then he prayed, not to God but to the men in the lifeboat. He cried. He begged.[1]

It's a simple problem: Should the lives of several be jeopardized in order possibly to save one more? Is it *really* a simple problem?

WHAT IS UTILITARIANISM?

We can get at the real nature of utilitarianism in three stages. *First,* at the heart of utilitarianism lies the Principle of Utility. The word "utility" simply means "usefulness," but the utilitarians employ it to mean

---

[1] William Hoffer, *Saved! The Story of the "Andrea Doria"—The Greatest Sea Rescue in History* (New York: Summit Books, 1979), pp. 180–82.

that which promoted the greatest balance of good over evil. Thus utilitarianism is:

1. The doctrine that we ought to act so as to promote the greatest balance of good over evil.

But there must be more, for we have not yet been told what the good *is*. In fact, *second*, utilitarianism has always gone hand in hand with hedonism, which certainly does specify the nature of the good—it is *pleasure*. Thus, utilitarianism is:

2. The doctrine that we ought to act so as to promote the greatest balance of pleasure over pain.

But there is more, for we have not yet been told *whose* pleasure is to be maximized. In fact, *third*, utilitarianism (as the word is usually used) has always gone hand in hand specifically with *social* hedonism, and indeed may be regarded as identical with social hedonism. But here we must slow down a bit.

Like any hedonism, social hedonism or utilitarianism holds to a *teleological* or consequentialist conception of right action: It judges the rightness of an action by its *consequences*. And, like any hedonism, social hedonism or utilitarianism judges the rightness of an action by its production of *pleasurable* consequences. But whereas the egoistic hedonist is motivated out of *self*-interest and aims at *self*-satisfaction, the social hedonist or utilitarian is motivated out of an interest for the greatest possible number of persons and aims at *their* satisfaction. In place of the egoism of egoistic hedonism, social hedonism or utilitarianism substitutes the Benevolence Principle: Happiness is to be distributed as widely and as equally as possible among all people. Thus, utilitarianism is, finally,

3. The doctrine that we ought to act so as to promote the greatest happiness for the greatest number.

Utilitarianism is, obviously, a political perspective as well as a philosophical one. As a democratic point of view it has often been, over the years, the basis of legislative and judicial advances, social reforms, welfare movements, and egalitarian ideals. Not surprisingly, then, the most famous of the utilitarian philosophers have also usually been deeply involved in social and political issues—on the liberal side, naturally.

BENTHAM'S VERSION: QUANTITY OVER QUALITY

Historically, social hedonism or social utilitarianism is identified with the English philosophers Jeremy Bentham and John Stuart Mill. (We realize that we are dealing here with remarkable men when we learn that Bentham was studying Latin when he was 8, and Mill was studying Greek at 3!) These two thinkers, however, represent two different forms of utilitarianism, though the difference reduces to a matter of emphasis: in the one case an emphasis on *quantity* of happiness, and in the other an emphasis on *quality* of happiness.

The founder of modern utilitarianism was Jeremy Bentham (1748–1832).

For Bentham, the process of making moral decisions is really quite simple. All you do is this. First, consider the various courses of action open to you; then, taking into account all the persons affected, and counting yourself as only one of them, calculate the pleasures and pains involved; then, choose that course of action which will result in the greatest balance of pleasure over pain.

As already indicated, when Bentham presses for the greatest balance of pleasure over pain, his idea of pleasure is a purely quantitative one. The *greatest* pleasure for the greatest number means for Bentham the *most* pleasure. That Bentham's really is a purely quantitative notion of pleasure is apparent from his well-known statement that

> Prejudice apart, the game of push-pin is of equal value with the arts and sciences of music and poetry. If the game of push-pin furnish more pleasure, it is more valuable than either.[2]

How do we determine the *most* pleasure? Answer: By means of calculating pleasures and pains. Though this idea goes back a long way, it was

---

Hedonism + Benevolence Principle = social hedonism or utilitarianism

---

[2]Jeremy Bentham, *The Rationale of Reward*, in *The Works of Jeremy Bentham* (Edinburgh: Tait, 1838–43), II, pp. i, 253.

Jeremy Bentham (shown here as a
youth), a utilitarian philosopher who
stressed the quantity over the quality
of happiness

formulated most explicitly in Bentham's idea of a *hedonic calculus*. According to Bentham, in attempting to calculate a pleasure we must, as it were, measure or weigh it in seven ways, taking into account its

1. *intensity*, or how strong it is
2. *duration*, how long it will last
3. *certainty*, how likely it is to occur
4. *propinquity*, how near at hand it is
5. *fecundity*, its ability to produce still further pleasures
6. *purity*, its freedom from ensuing pains
7. *extent*, the number of people affected by it.

Bentham suggested the following verse as a prod to "lodging more effectively, in the memory, these points, on which the whole fabric of morals and legislation may be seen to rest":

> Intense, long, certain, speedy, fruitful, pure—
> Such marks in pleasures and in pains endure.
> Such pleasures seek, if private be thy end:

If it be public, wide let them extend.
Such pains avoid, whichever be thy view:
If pains must come, let them extend to few.[3]

By applying these seven criteria—someone has likened them to a moral thermometer—we ought to be able to grind out, like a machine, what course of action would deliver the most pleasure. Bentham himself speaks of "summing up all the values of all the pleasures." Not that we always would, could, or should indulge in this kind of precise hedonistic arithmetic. On the other hand, do not all of us in fact employ some such method, however roughly, every time we consider and weigh the pleasurable and painful consequences of a projected act?

A further note: Bentham realized that there is a difference between *knowing* what we ought to do and *doing* it. This is especially true in those situations where the happiness of others means self-sacrifice and pain for *you*. (To use our earlier terms, Bentham was a psychological egoist, though not an ethical egoist.) Here Bentham's doctrine of the *Four Sanctions* is relevant: nature, law, opinion, and God. By "sanctions" Bentham means something like binding forces or threats, but it will do to think of these four sanctions as *motivations* for ethical behavior. If in fact, we fail to do what we should, well, natural laws, civil laws, public or personal opinion, and God himself will make it unpleasant for us—either in this life or the next, or in both! Nature, law, opinion, and God "persuade" us to overcome our perverse inclinations and to act in accordance with social utility. Bentham also labeled the Four Sanctions as the physical, the political, the moral, and the religious. But he provided an example which, in any case, makes his meaning clear:

A man's goods, or his person, are consumed by fire. If this happened to him by what is called an accident, it was a *calamity;* if by reason of his own imprudence (for instance, from his neglecting to put his candle out) it may be styled a punishment of the *physical* sanction; if it happened to him by the sentence of the political magistrate, a punishment belonging to the *political* sanction; that is, what is commonly called a *punishment;* if for want of any assistance which his *neighbour* withheld from him out of some dislike to his *moral* character, a punishment of the *moral* sanction; if by an immediate act of

---

[3]Jeremy Bentham, *An Introduction to the Principles of Morals and Legislation,* ed. J. H. Burns and H. L. A. Hart (London: Athlone, 1970), p. 38.

God's displeasure, manifested on account of some *sin* committed by him or through any distraction of mind, occasioned by the dread of such displeasure, a punishment of the *religious* sanction.

As to such of the pleasures and pains belonging to the religious sanction, as regard a future life, of what kind these may be we cannot know. These lie not open to our observation.[4]

MILL'S VERSION: QUALITY OVER QUANTITY

Though Bentham was the founder of modern utilitarianism, his successor was certainly the most famous utilitarian of all: John Stuart Mill (1806–1873).

Mill's little volume with the simple title *Utilitarianism* is a classic of philosophical literature. Furthermore, a clearer expression of the philosophy of the greatest happiness for the greatest number could hardly be imagined. Consider his statement of its *hedonistic* nature:

> The creed which accepts as the foundation of morals "utility" or the "greatest happiness principle" holds that actions are right in proportion as they tend to promote happiness; wrong as they tend to produce the reverse of happiness. By happiness is intended pleasure and the absence of pain; by unhappiness, pain and the privation of pleasure. To give a clear view of the moral standard set up by the theory, much more requires to be said; in particular, what things it includes in the ideas of pain and pleasure, and to what extent this is left an open question. But these supplementary explanations do not affect the theory of life on which this theory of morality is grounded— namely, that pleasure and freedom from pain are the only things desirable as ends; and that all desirable things (which are as numerous in the utilitarian as in any other scheme) are desirable either for pleasure inherent in themselves or as means to the promotion of pleasure and the prevention of pain.[5]

---

[4]Ibid., p. 36.

[5]John Stuart Mill, *Utilitarianism*, ed. Oskar Piest (Indianapolis: Bobbs-Merrill, 1957), pp. 10–11.

And consider his statement of its *socialistic* nature:

> I must again repeat what the assailants of utilitarianism seldom have the justice to acknowledge, that the happiness which forms the utilitarian standard of what is right in conduct is not the agent's own happiness but that of all concerned. As between his own happiness and that of others, utilitarianism requires him to be as strictly impartial as a disinterested and benevolent spectator. In the golden rule of Jesus of Nazareth, we read the complete spirit of the ethics of utility. "To do as you would be done by," and "to love your neighbor as yourself," constitute the ideal perfection of utilitarian morality. As the means of making the nearest approach to this ideal, utility would enjoin, first, that laws and social arrangements should place the happiness or (as, speaking practically, it may be called) the interest of every individual as nearly as possible in harmony with the interest of the whole; and, secondly, that education and opinion, which have so vast a power over human character, should so use that power as to establish in the mind of every individual an indissoluble association between his own happiness and the good of the whole, especially between his own happiness and the practice of such modes of conduct, negative and positive, as regard for the universal happiness prescribes; so that not only he may be unable to conceive the possibility of happiness to himself, consistently with conduct opposed to the general good, but also that a direct impulse to promote the general good may be in every individual one of the habitual motives of action, and the sentiments connected therewith may fill a large and prominent place in every human being's sentient existence.[6]

Bentham and Mill stand together on the Principle of Utility as augmented by the Principle of Benevolence: Actions are right actions if, and only if, they produce pleasure or happiness or satisfaction of needs, and this pleasure or happiness or satisfaction is to be distributed among as many people as possible. With Bentham, Mill agreed also that the basic principles of social utilitarianism cannot be proved, at least not in the usual sense:

> . . . questions of ultimate ends do not admit of proof, in the ordinary acceptance of the term. To be incapable of proof by reasoning is

---

[6]Ibid., pp. 22–23.

common to all first principles, to the first premise of our knowledge, as well as to those of our conduct.[7]

In another sense, though, there *is* a proof:

> The only proof capable of being given that an object is visible is that people actually see it. The only proof that a sound is audible is that people hear it, and so of the other sources of our experience. In like manner, I apprehend, the sole evidence it is possible to produce that anything is desirable is that people do actually desire it.[8]

On the basis of the above quotation, some readers might think that Mill lapses after all into ethical subjectivism: If someone did *not* desire happiness, wouldn't this mean that for him, at least, happiness is not desirable? It should be clear that Mill would answer with another question: If someone did not see an object, would it mean that the object is invisible? Goodness is experienced as happiness, but it hardly follows that goodness has no objective reality apart from the experience of it. Emphatically, Mill, as well as Bentham and all other hedonists, is an objectivist in ethics. The real problem in the above quotation lies elsewhere, as we will see.

Where Mill really split with Bentham was over Bentham's purely *quantitative* view of pleasure. Without denying that quantity is *a* consideration in the calculation of pleasure, it is not as important as the consideration of *quality*.

> Now such a theory of life excites in many minds, and among them in some of the most estimable in feeling and purpose, inveterate dislike. To suppose that life has (as they express it) no higher end than pleasure—no better and nobler object of desire and pursuit—they designate as utterly mean and groveling, as a doctrine worthy only of swine, to whom the followers of Epicurus were, at a very early period, contemptuously likened; and modern holders of the doctrine are occasionally made the subject of equally polite comparisons by its German, French, and English assailants.

---

[7]Ibid., p. 44.
[8]Ibid., pp. 44–45.

When thus attacked, the Epicureans have always answered that it is not they, but their accusers, who represent human nature in a degrading light, since the accusation supposes human beings to be capable of no pleasures except those of which swine are capable. If this supposition were true, the charge could not be gainsaid, but would then be no longer an imputation; for if the sources of pleasure were precisely the same to human beings and to swine, the rule of life which is good enough for the one would be good enough for the other. The comparison of the Epicurean life to that of beasts is felt as degrading, precisely because a beast's pleasures do not satisfy a human being's conceptions of happiness. Human beings have faculties more elevated than the animal appetites and, when once made conscious of them, do not regard anything as happiness which does not include their gratification. I do not, indeed, consider the Epicureans to have been by any means faultless in drawing out their scheme of consequences from the utilitarian principle. To do this in any sufficient manner, many Stoic, as well as Christian, elements require to be included. But there is no known Epicurean theory of life which does not assign to the pleasures of the intellect, of the feelings and imagination, and of the moral sentiments a much higher value as pleasures than to those of mere sensation. It must be admitted, however, that utilitarian writers in general have placed the superiority of mental over bodily pleasures chiefly in the greater permanency, safety, uncostliness, etc., of the former—that is, in their circumstantial advantages rather than in their intrinsic nature. And on all these points utilitarians have fully proved their case; but they might have taken the other and, as it may be called, higher ground with entire consistency. It is quite compatible with the principle of utility to recognize the fact that some kinds of pleasure are more desirable and more valuable than others. It would be absurd that, while in estimating all other things quality is considered as well as quantity, the estimation of pleasure should be supposed to depend on quantity alone.[9]

For Mill, as for most, it hardly needs arguing that although push-pin may be more fun than poetry, it yields an inferior happiness. And can the joy of sex really compare with the joy of the intellect? (The answer is No.) Or to

---

[9]Ibid., pp. 11–12.

John Stuart Mill

John Stuart Mill was born in London in 1806. Although he never attended school, his education was among the most remarkable ever. He was instructed entirely by his father, James Mill, who had him learning Greek at the age of 3 and Latin at 8. By the time he was 14 he had read most of the Greek and Latin classics (in the original languages), and had become expert in widely differing fields, such as history and mathematics. His social and political liberalism had also been shaped at an early age under the influence of his father and his father's associate, Jeremy Bentham. Regarding his reading of Bentham, Mill said: ". . . the feeling rushed upon me, that all previous moralists were superceded, and that here indeed was the commencement of a new era of thought."

In 1823, Mill became a clerk for the East India Company where his father was also employed. He remained with the company until 1858, eventually advancing to a high position. In 1826, Mill fell into a deep depression which, in his autobiography, he likened to the lines of Coleridge:

(continued on next page)

use Mill's language, wouldn't you rather be a dissatisfied human than a satisfied pig, or a dissatisfied Socrates than a satisfied fool? For Mill, as for Bentham, the action is to be pursued which makes for the greatest happiness for the greatest number. But whereas for Bentham "greatest" meant *most*, for Mill it meant *best*.

Granted that two pleasures may differ in quality, who is to say which is the best? Mill answers that the decision must rest with those who have experienced both.

A grief without a pang, void, dark and drear,
A drowsy, stifled, unimpassioned grief,
Which finds no natural outlet or relief
In word, or sigh, or tear.

After many months he rallied from this depression, aided by his own insight, "Ask yourself whether you are happy, and you will cease to be so," and by the poetry of Wordsworth.

The woman in Mill's life was Mrs. Harriet Taylor, whom he met when he was 25. They sustained a Platonic relationship for twenty years. Three years after her husband's death, Mill married her, and when, in 1858 while they were touring France together, she herself died, Mill bought a house in Avignon in order to be near her grave. Mill called her, "the most admirable person I have ever known," and referred to his relation to her as "the honor and chief blessing of my existence." He also attributed to her much of the inspiration and content of his writings.

Although Mill never held an academic position, over many years he frequently contributed articles to journals and magazines and produced many volumes. His philosophical magnum opus was the *System of Logic*, published in 1843. A great champion of liberal causes and representative government, Mill was encouraged in 1865 to stand for election to Parliament. He refused to campaign, contribute to expenses, or defend his views, and *won*. He was defeated in the next election, 1868, and thereupon spent his time either in London or in Avignon, something of a recluse, and cared for by his wife's daughter, Helen. After a brief illness, he died in 1873.

Some of Mill's more important works: *System of Logic, Utilitarianism, Subjection of Women, Principles of Political Economy, On Liberty, Utility of Religion, Autobiography.*

If I am asked what I mean by difference of quality in pleasures, or what makes one pleasure more valuable than another, merely as a pleasure, except its being greater in amount, there is but one possible answer. Of two pleasures, if there be one to which all or almost all who have experience of both give a decided preference, irrespective of any feeling of moral obligation to prefer it, that is the more desirable pleasure. If one of the two is, by those who are competently

PLEASURE: QUANTITY OR QUALITY?

- *Bentham:* "If the game of push-pin furnish more pleasure, it is more valuable."
- *Mill:* "It is better to be a human being dissatisfied than a pig satisfied."

acquainted with both, placed so far above the other that they prefer it, even though knowing it to be attended with a greater amount of discontent, and would not resign it for any quantity of the other pleasure which their nature is capable of, we are justified in ascribing to the preferred enjoyment a superiority in quality so far outweighing quantity as to render it, in comparison, of small account.[10]

And those who have experienced both invariably opt for the higher or more qualitative pleasures.

Now it is an unquestionable fact that those who are equally acquainted with and equally capable of appreciating and enjoying both do give a most marked preference to the manner of existence which employs their higher faculties. Few human creatures would consent to be changed into any of the lower animals for a promise of the fullest allowance of a beast's pleasures; no intelligent human being would consent to be a fool, no instructed person would be an ignoramus, no person of feeling and conscience would be selfish and base, even though they should be persuaded that the fool, the dunce, or the rascal is better satisfied with his lot than they are with theirs. They would not resign what they possess more than he for the most complete satisfaction of all the desires which they have in common with him. If they ever fancy they would, it is only in cases of unhappiness so extreme that to escape from it they would exchange their lot for almost any other, however undesirable in their own eyes. A

---

[10]Ibid., p. 12.

being of higher faculties requires more to make him happy, is capable probably of more acute suffering, and certainly accessible to it at more points, than one of an inferior type; but in spite of these liabilities, he can never really wish to sink into what he feels to be a lower grade of existence. . . . It is better to be a human being dissatisfied than a pig satisfied; better to be Socrates dissatisfied than a fool satisfied. And if the fool, or the pig, are of a different opinion, it is because they only know their own side of the question. The other party to the comparison knows both sides.[11]

Presumably, however, Mill is not inviting us to sample all possible pleasures!

Mill also differed somewhat with Bentham on the matter of moral sanctions. He did not deny Bentham's "external" sanctions of nature, law, opinion, and God—motivations *outside ourselves* for certain behavior. Indeed, he claimed that there is no reason why, for example, "hope of favor and the fear of displeasure from our fellow creatures or from the Ruler of the universe," and any other motivations for moral behavior, should not buttress utilitarian action as well as other kinds of action. He adds, however, an "internal" sanction, a motivation *inside ourselves* to behave in certain ways. Mill calls this "a subjective feeling in our own minds" but it might just as easily be called *conscience*. He also calls it the "ultimate" sanction or motivation of all moral behavior.

> The ultimate sanction, therefore, of all morality (external motives apart) being a subjective feeling in our own minds, I see nothing embarrassing to those whose standard is utility in the question, What is the sanction of that particular standard? We may answer, the same as of all other moral standards—the conscientious feelings of mankind. Undoubtedly this sanction has no binding efficacy on those who do not possess the feelings it appeals to; but neither will these persons be more obedient to any other moral principle than to the utilitarian one. On them morality of any kind has no hold but through the external sanctions. Meanwhile the feelings exist, a fact in human nature, the reality of which, and the great power with which they are capable of acting on those in whom they have been duly cultivated,

---

[11]Ibid., pp. 12–14.

THE FIRST PARAGRAPH IN MILL'S SUBJECTION OF WOMEN:

"The object of this Essay is to explain as clearly as I am able, the grounds of an opinion which I have held from the very earliest period when I had formed any opinions at all on social or political matters, and which, instead of being weakened or modified, has been constantly growing stronger by the progress of reflection and the experience of life: That the principle which regulates the existing social relations between the two sexes—the legal subordination of one sex to the other—is wrong in itself, and now one of the chief hindrances to human improvement; and that it ought to be replaced by a principle of perfect equality, admitting no power or privilege on the one side, nor disability on the other."

are proved by experience. No reason has ever been shown why they may not be cultivated to as great intensity in connection with the utilitarian as with any other rule of morals.[12]

Where does this internal sanction, this "feeling in our minds," come from? Even though Mill has just spoken of it as a fact of human nature, he believes that it is not innate, but acquired and cultivated. On the other hand, this makes it no less natural. As he himself says, we also speak, reason, build cities, and cultivate the ground—activities natural to humans but certainly acquired.

In discussions of morality, the distinction between *what actually results* from one's actions and *why one did it* is often and rightly raised. In the first edition of *Utilitarianism* Mill took a fairly stark position: The moral rightness of an action is independent of the motive behind it. He was severely criticized for this, and in the second edition he added a footnote defending and further explaining himself.

He who saves a fellow creature from drowning does what is morally right, whether his motive be duty or the hope of being paid for his

---

[12]Ibid., p. 37.

"Mill's Logic, or Franchise for Females"

Mill was a great champion of what in his day were radical causes, including women's rights and the abolition of child labor and slavery. This cartoon (published in *Punch*, March 30, 1867) suggests that Mill's work on logic leads to women's liberation.

trouble; he who betrays the friend that trusts him is guilty of a crime, even if his object be to serve another friend to whom he is under greater obligations.*

*An opponent whose intellectual and moral fairness it is a pleasure to acknowledge (the Rev. J. Llewellyn Davies), has objected to this passage, saying, "Surely the rightness or wrongness of saving a man from drowning does depend very much upon the motive with which it is done. Suppose that a tyrant, when his enemy jumped into the sea to escape from him, saved him from drowning simply in order that he might inflict upon him more exquisite tortures, would it tend to clearness to speak of that rescue as 'a morally right action'? Or suppose again, according to one of the stock illustrations of ethical inquiries, that a man betrayed a trust received from a friend, because the discharge of it would fatally injure that friend himself or someone belonging to him, would utilitarianism compel one to call the betrayal 'a crime' as much as if it had been done from the meanest motive?"

I submit that he who saves another from drowning in order to kill him by torture afterwards does not differ only in motive from him who does the same thing for duty or benevolence; the act itself is different. The rescue of the man is, in the case supposed, only the necessary first step of an act far more atrocious than leaving him to drown would have been. Had Mr. Davies said, "The rightness or wrongness of saving a man from drowning does depend very much"—not upon the motive, but—"upon the *intention*," no utilitarian would have differed from him.

Dr. Davies, by an oversight too common not to be quite venial, has in this case confounded the very different ideas of Motive and Intention. There is no point which utilitarian thinkers (and Bentham preeminently) have taken more pains to illustrate than this. The morality of the action depends entirely upon the intention—that is, upon what the agent *wills* to do. But the motive, that is, the feeling which makes him will so to do, if it makes no difference in the act, makes none in the morality: though it makes a great difference in our moral estimation of the agent, especially if it indicates a good or a bad habitual disposition—a bent of character from which useful, or from which hurtful actions are likely to arise.[13]

Is Mill playing with words? Squirming out of a legitimate criticism? Or is his distinction between *motives* and *intentions* valid and important?

ACT-UTILITARIANISM/ RULE-UTILITARIANISM

The utilitarian idea of moral action may be refined further. Philosophers these days are fond of distinguishing between *act-utilitarianism* and *rule-utilitarianism*. Actually, this is a useful and important distinction and may be applied, as we will see later, to other moral philosophies as well.

---

[13]Ibid., p. 24.

An obvious clue to what this distinction implies is contained in the words "act" and "rule." When you hear or see the word "act" you think immediately of something particular: a *particular* deed done in *this* situation. On the other hand, the word "rule" brings to mind something general: *types* of deeds to be done in *every* situation. For the act-utilitarian the question is, What particular action should be done in this situation to bring about the greatest happiness for the greatest number? For the rule-utilitarian the question is, What rule should be followed in this situation to bring about the greatest happiness for the greatest number?

The following summary by William K. Frankena, a well-known ethicist, may help.

ACT-UTILITARIANISM

First, then, there is act-utilitarianism (AU). Act-utilitarians hold that in general or at least where it is practicable, one is to tell what is right or obligatory by appealing directly to the principle of utility or, in other words, by trying to see which of the actions open to him will or is likely to produce the greatest balance of good over evil in the universe. One must ask "What effect will *my* doing *this* act in *this* situation have on the general balance of good over evil?", not "What effect will *everyone's* doing this *kind* of act in this *kind* of situation have on the general balance of good over evil?" Generalizations like "Telling the truth is probably always for the greatest general good" or "Telling the truth is generally for the greatest general good" may be useful as guides based on past experience; but the crucial question is always whether telling the truth in *this* case is for the greatest general good or not. It can never be right to act on the rule of telling the truth if we have good independent grounds for thinking that it would be for the greatest general good not to tell the truth in a particular case, any more than it can be correct to say that all crows are black in the presence of one that is not. Bentham and G. E. Moore probably held such a view, perhaps even Mill; today it is held, among others, by J. J. C. Smart and Joseph Fletcher, though the latter prefers to call it "situation ethics," of which it is one kind.

It should be observed that, for AU, one must include among the effects of an action any influence it may have, by way of setting an example or otherwise, on the actions or practices of others or on their obedience to prevailing rules. For example, if I propose to cross a park lawn or to break a promise, I must consider the effects my doing so may have on other walkers or on people's tendency to keep promises. After all, even if these are thought of as "indirect" effects of my action, they are still among its effects. . . .

Rule-Utilitarianism

Rule-utilitarianism (RU) is a rather different view, which has also been attributed to Mill and has been finding favor recently. . . . it emphasizes the centrality of rules in morality and insists that we are generally, if not always, to tell what to do in particular situations by appeal to a rule like that of truth-telling rather than be asking what particular action will have the best consequences in the situation in question. But, unlike deontologism, it adds that we are always to determine our rules by asking which rules will promote the greatest general good for everyone. That is, the question is not which *action* has the greatest utility, but which *rule* has. The principle of utility comes in, normally at least, not in determining what particular action to perform (this is normally determined by the rules), but in determining what the rules shall be. Rules must be selected, maintained, revised, and replaced on the basis of their utility and not on any other basis. The principle of utility is still the ultimate standard, but it is to be appealed to at the level of rules rather than at the level of particular judgments. This view has been advocated by a number of writers from Bishop Berkeley to R. B. Brandt.

The AU may allow rules to be used; but if he does, he must conceive of a rule like "Tell the truth" as follows: "Telling the truth is *generally* for the greatest general good." By contrast, the RU must conceive of it thus: "Our *always* telling the truth is for the greatest general good." Or thus: "It is for the greatest good if we *always* tell the truth."

This means that for the RU it may be right to obey a rule like telling the truth simply because it is so useful to have the rule, even when, in the particular case in question, telling the truth does not lead to the best consequences.

An analogy may help here. On a particular occasion, I might ask which side of the street I should drive on, the right or the left. To find the answer, I would not try to see which alternative is for the greatest general good; instead, I would ask or try to determine what the law is. The law says that we are always to drive down the right side of the street (with exceptions in the case of passing, one-way streets, and so forth). The reason for the law is that it is for the greatest general good that we *always* drive down a certain side of the street instead of driving, on each occasion, down the side it seems to us most useful to drive on on that occasion. Here, for the greatest general good, we must have a rule of the always-acting kind (with the exceptions built into the rule, hence not really exceptions). If we suppose that for some reason there are special difficulties about our driving on the left, it will follow on utilitarian grounds that we should have a law telling us always to drive on the right. This, although the example comes from law, illustrates the RU conception of how we are to determine what is the morally right or obligatory thing to do.

If we ask why we should be RUs rather than AUs, the RU may answer, as Berkeley did, by pointing to the difficulties (difficulties due to ignorance, bias, passion, carelessness, lack of time, etc.) that would arise if, on each occasion of action, everyone were permitted to decide for himself what he should do, even if he had the help of such rules of thumb as the modified AU offers. The RU may then argue that it is for the greatest general good to have everyone acting wholly or at least largely on rules of the always-acting type instead of always making decisions on an AU basis. This would be a utilitarian argument for RU; and, as an argument, it has some plausibility.[14]

A concrete example may also help. The Gestapo is pounding on the door demanding to know whether Jews are hidden in the attic. We know that Jews *are* hidden in the attic, and we also know their fate—and maybe ours too—if this should be found out. The question is whether or not to tell the truth. Act-utilitarians will ask themselves, What *particular action* in this situation will produce the greatest happiness for the greatest number? And they may well decide to lie in order to save the Jews and thwart the Gestapo's evil intent. Rule-utilitarians, on the other hand, will ask, What *general rule* applied here will produce the greatest happiness for the greatest number? And they might well decide to tell the truth, persuaded that in spite of the unfortunate consequences in this particular situation, truthfulness on the whole or *generally* makes for the greatest happiness.

---

[14]William K. Frankena, *Ethics*, 2nd ed. (Englewood Cliffs, NJ: Prentice Hall, 1973), pp. 35–36, 39–40.

In the case of the classic utilitarians, such as Bentham and Mill, philosophers are not agreed whether they were act- or rule-utilitarians. This may only show that the distinction, though useful in theory, is difficult to apply in practice, at least in an either/or manner. Mill, in fact, seems to have espoused both act- and rule-utilitarianism, though at different levels, which, after all, is probably a rather commonsensical position. We cannot live without rules of conduct, and such rules have been distilled through the experience and wisdom of the ages—they should probably be honored as making for the greatest happiness for the greatest number. On the other hand, some situations are so singular and exceptional (or at least may seem to be at the time) as not to fall into any general category or under any general rule. In such situations we may be forced to act on the basis of what we see dictated *there* as fostering the greatest happiness—though, admittedly, threats and the brandishing of guns and passionate embraces in the backseat of a car may not make for the most objective moral judgments.

Now apply this twofold principle (the role of rules *and* the role of particular actions) to the situation involving the Jews and the Gestapo. Does it help?

SOME OBJECTIONS

We mention here some of the objections made against utilitarianism specifically, and in the next section some objections to hedonism in all of its forms.

In *Utilitarianism*, Mill himself answers a whole string of rather obvious charges against utilitarianism. For example: Utilitarianism is a pig-philosophy which encourages the pursuit of base pleasures; it is a godless philosophy which establishes a criterion of morality independent of the question of God's will; it is such a "calculating" philosophy as to chill our human feelings for one another; it focuses attention on the consequences of actions to the exclusion of their motives; it asks us to do the impossible, namely, to anticipate endless chains of consequences from our actions. If you can't see how Mill would have answered such charges, well, the second chapter of *Utilitarianism* makes good philosophical reading.

But some other problems may be mentioned.

First, it should be evident that utilitarianism sidesteps *to some degree* the charge that it is egoistic. On the other hand, neither is it purely altruistic. Though it tells us to distribute happiness among as many people as possi-

How might a utilitarian reason about the rightness or wrongness of

- capital punishment?
- abortion?
- war?
- minority rights?
- euthanasia?
- genetic engineering?

ble, it also tells us never to forget that each of us is *one* of those people. Whether or not this is a problem depends on how strenuously you take the ideal of altruism. Perhaps social hedonism goes far enough in its concern for the interests of others. But maybe not. Did Jesus, Socrates, or St. Francis count himself even as *one?*

Second, we have seen that all forms of hedonism, but especially Bentham's, employ some type of hedonic calculus, or computation of pleasures. Now this may look good on paper, but how practical is it? Is it really possible to measure and compare, say, the *intensity* of different pleasures in different people? Or even the same pleasure in the same person? Try it. Further, the hedonic calculus is geared to produce certain sorts of results. But though we *may* be able to foresee *some* of the consequences of our actions, who can really foresee all of them, to say nothing of the consequences of the consequences, and so on? We may grant that in certain very general cases the implications of our actions are fairly obvious, but even if we were utilitarians, it is not in *these* situations that we would look for moral guidance, is it? It's when we *aren't* clear about the consequences that we need help.

Third, social hedonism results in some rather awkward puzzles. For example, we are told to act so as to promote the greatest happiness for the greatest number. But is not ten parts of happiness distributed over two people—five parts of happiness each—as much the greatest happiness for the greatest number as ten parts of happiness distributed evenly to ten people? It may be answered that this is where the *Justice Principle* comes in with the idea that happiness is to be spread over as many people as possible. But then we have to ask constantly, Who has how much pleasure? And, as one philosopher has observed, is it really meaningful to say that person A is three-and-a-half times as happy as person B? And in any event, would you be willing to dispatch someone to burn in hell forever even if you could thereby secure the eternal happiness of *every other person in the world?* Clearly, the utilitarian's numbers game is a difficult one to play.

Fourth, it is often objected that utilitarianism (or, for that matter, hedonism in general) is incompatible with the standards of morality that we actually employ. We recognize, for example, the *intrinsic* rightness (that is, rightness for its own sake and apart from its consequences) of acting fairly, telling the truth, and keeping promises. Could you break a promise *without batting an eye*, even if you knew it would promote happiness in general? And what about the possible conflict between the claims of utility and the claims of *justice?* Would you be willing to frame an innocent person if doing so would maximize utility? If a utilitarian argument in favor of reinstating slavery succeeded in showing that the greatest happiness of the greatest number would be thus served, would we feel obligated to do so? Surely we do not really believe that it is right to pursue pleasure and happiness, even of the greatest number, *no matter what*. In the end, our pursuit of the general welfare appears to be conditioned by other and even more basic ideals.

Finally, *fifth*, we must raise the problem of grounding ethics in nature. Like any other form of hedonism, utilitarianism is a *naturalistic* ethic—it takes its clue from nature, or from what *is*. Consider Bentham's claim that

> Nature has placed mankind under the governance of two sovereign masters, *pain* and *pleasure*. It is for them alone to point out what we ought to do.[15]

And Mill's claim that

> The only proof capable of being given that an object is visible is that people actually see it. . . . In like manner, I apprehend, the sole evidence it is possible to produce that anything is desirable is that people do actually desire it. . . . If the opinion which I have now stated is psychologically true—if human nature is so constituted as to desire nothing which is not either a part of happiness or a means of happiness—we can have no other proof, and we require no other, that these are the only things desirable.[16]

---

[15]Bentham, *An Introduction to the Principles of Morals and Legislation*, p. 11.

[16]Mill, *Utilitarianism*, pp. 44, 48–49.

What's Wrong with This Picture?

In the following scenario, Bernard Williams throws into clear relief what—in an admittedly bizarre situation—would be expected of Jim if he were a consistent utilitarian. At the same time, it will be clear to many that what is required on utilitarian grounds is utterly unacceptable. Or is it? What would *you* do if you were Jim?

Jim finds himself in the central square of a small South American town. Tied up against the wall are a row of twenty Indians, most terrified, a few defiant, in front of them several armed men in uniform. A heavy man in a sweat-stained khaki shirt turns out to be the captain in charge and, after a good deal of questioning of Jim which establishes that he got there by accident while on a botanical expedition, explains that the Indians are a random group of the inhabitants who, after recent acts of protest against the government, are just about to be killed to remind other possible protestors of the advantages of not protesting. However, since Jim is an honoured visitor from another land, the captain is happy to offer him a guest's privilege of killing one of the Indians himself. If Jim accepts, then as a special mark of the occasion, the other Indians will be let off. Of course, if Jim refuses, then there is no special occasion, and Pedro here will do what he was about to do when Jim arrived, and kill them all. Jim, with some desperate recollection of schoolboy fiction, wonders whether if he got hold of a gun, he could hold the captain, Pedro and the rest of the soldiers to threat, but it is quite clear from the set-up that nothing of that kind is going to work: any attempt at that sort of thing will mean that all the Indians will be killed, and himself. The men against the wall, and the other villagers, understand the situation, and are obviously begging him to accept. What should he do?*

---

*Bernard Williams, "A Critique of Utilitarianism," in J. J. C. Smart and Bernard Williams, *Utilitarianism: For and Against* (Cambridge, England: Cambridge University Press), pp. 98f.

It is often pointed out that the following statement by Mill (in *Utilitarianism*) involves a simple logical fallacy. What is it?

". . . each person's happiness is a good to that person, and the general happiness, therefore, a good to the aggregate of all persons."

Now aside from the insane person who derives the most exquisite happiness from torturing starving children, such talk is open to the charge of the Naturalistic Fallacy. These utilitarian thinkers, no less than other hedonists, try to derive an *ought* from an *is*. Look at the two quotations above. Don't *factual* judgments seem to be mixed up with *value* judgments again? What have our "natural masters," pain and pleasure, got to do with "what we ought to do"? And although what is psychologically true might have something to do with what is actually desired, what has it got to do with what is *desirable*, or *worthy* of desire, or *right?* This is exactly how G. E. Moore attacked this very passage in Mill.

Well, the fallacy in this step is so obvious, that it is quite wonderful how Mill failed to see it. The fact is that "desirable" does not mean "able to be desired" as "visible" means "able to be seen." The desirable means simply what ought to be desired or deserves to be desired; just as the detestable means not what can be but what ought to be detested and the damnable what deserves to be damned. Mill has, then, smuggled in, under cover of the word "desirable," the very notion about which he ought to be quite clear. "Desirable" does indeed mean "what it is good to desire"; but when this is understood it is no longer plausible to say that our only test of *that*, is what is actually desired. Is it merely a tautology when the Prayer Book talks of *good* desires? Are not *bad* desires also possible?[17]

And philosophers have been attacking him in the same way ever since.

---

[17]George Edward Moore, *Principia Ethica* (Cambridge: Cambridge University Press, 1903), p. 67.

CHAPTER 13 IN REVIEW

Summary

As with egoistic hedonism, utilitarianism is a teleological ethic, emphasizing the consequences of actions as the criteria of their moral worth. Also with egoistic hedonism, it identifies pleasure or happiness as the specific consequence to be attained. It differs, however, in shifting our attention from the pleasure or happiness of the individual to that of society: the greatest happiness for the greatest number.

Bentham and Mill are, historically, the best representatives of the utilitarian position. Bentham pressed for a quantitative interpretation of the "greatest" happiness, and propounded a hedonic calculus to assist in its determination. Mill pressed for a qualitative interpretation of the "greatest" happiness and urged that it is only the widely experienced individual who is in a position to extol the superiority of the qualitative pleasures, for example, the pleasures of the mind.

A contemporary refinement of utilitarianism distinguishes between act-utilitarianism and rule-utilitarianism. The former focuses on particular situations and asks what specific act in that situation would be conducive to the general welfare. The rule-utilitarian, on the other hand, urges the adoption of rules which, applied and practiced in all situations, would result in the general welfare.

Although utilitarianism escapes the charge of egoism, it is subject to many of the complaints leveled against any hedonistic philosophy. Most notably, utilitarianism is, finally, in some sense a naturalistic ethic, finding its basis in what individuals actually, and naturally, desire and strive for. As such it is an obvious target for critics who distinguish *ought* from *is*.

Basic Ideas

- Teleological ethics
- The Principle of Utility
- The Benevolence Principle
- Utilitarianism as social hedonism
- Bentham's version of utilitarianism
- The hedonic calculus: Seven criteria of the greatest pleasure

- Bentham's Four Sanctions
  Nature
  Civil law
  Opinion
  God
- Mill's version of utilitarianism
- The Principle of Utility as unprovable . . .
- . . . and provable
- Mill's criterion of the best pleasures
- Mill's internal sanction
- Mill on the difference between motives and intentions
- Act-utilitarianism
- Rule-utilitarianism
- The Justice Principle
- The Naturalistic Fallacy

Questions for Reflection

- What do you think of Mill's justification of utilitarianism? What about the Naturalistic Fallacy? Are there values to which even the greatest happiness for the greatest number might be sacrificed? What is to say that the greatest happiness for the whole human race is the highest good? If the whole human race were suddenly to disappear, by virtue of what could it *then* be said: "That's too bad"?
- We have encountered the distinction between "higher" and "lower" pleasures. What do you make of Mill's evidence for the qualitative superiority of the higher pleasures? Would *you* rather be an unsatisfied Socrates than a satisfied pig? Why?
- Are you a utilitarian? If so, an act- or rule-utilitarian? In any event, any form of utilitarianism asserts that the morality of any action is determined by the (intended) consequences. Is that *your* belief?

For Further Reading

Michael D. Bayles (ed.). *Contemporary Utilitarianism*. Garden City, NY: Anchor Books, 1968. A collection of ten essays, evaluating utilitarianism from the standpoint of contemporary issues and perspectives.

Richard B. Brandt, *Ethical Theory: The Problems of Normative and Critical Ethics.* Englewood Cliffs, NJ: Prentice Hall, 1959. Ch. 15. A discussion of "Moral Obligation and General Welfare," with special treatment of act- and rule-utilitarianism.

Frederick Copleston. *A History of Philosophy.* Baltimore: Newman Press, 1946–1974. VIII, Chs. 1–2. Chapters on "The Utilitarian Movement," with special treatment of Bentham's and Mill's ethical doctrines, by a noted historian of philosophy.

A. C. Ewing. *Ethics.* New York: Free Press, 1953. Ch. 3. An introductory and unsympathetic treatment of "The Pursuit of General Happiness."

W. D. Hudson (ed.). *The Is-Ought Question: A Collection of Papers on the Central Problem in Moral Philosophy.* London: Macmillan, 1969. Twenty-two essays by well-known thinkers on all aspects of the is-ought relation, with a helpful introduction by the editor.

Philip Blair Rice. *On the Knowledge of Good and Evil.* New York: Random House, 1955. Ch. 5. A chapter on Moore's criticism of Mill (Naturalistic Fallacy), somewhat sympathetic to the naturalist stance.

Henry Sidgwick. *The Method of Ethics.* London: Macmillan, 1907. An old but enduring sophisticated and systematic defense of a version of utilitarianism.

J. J. C. Smart and Bernard Williams. *Utilitarianism: For and Against.* Cambridge, England: Cambridge University Press, 1973. A defense by Smart and an especially compelling critique by Williams of act-utilitarianism.

W. H. Werkmeister. *Theories of Ethics: A Study in Moral Obligation.* Lincoln, NE: Johnsen, 1961. Ch. 5. A closely documented critical account of "universalistic hedonism," concentrating on Bentham's and Mill's versions.

*In addition, see the relevant articles ("Utilitarianism," "Mill, John Stuart," etc.) in *The Encyclopedia of Philosophy*, ed. Paul Edwards. New York: Macmillan, 1967.

The
Role
of
Duty

E | VEN ASIDE from the objections mentioned, it has been charged
that there is something basically wrong with the preceding theories. Something important has been left out. Aren't some things just right
or wrong *no matter what?* Isn't there such a thing as unconditional obligation? duty? To be sure, it is precisely in its exaltation of *duty*, pure and
simple, as the foundation of moral actions, that the theory in the present
chapter is radically different from that of the last chapter.

MORALITY AS UNCONDITIONAL

We saw at the beginning of Chapter 13 that a teleological theory of
morality is one which emphasizes the intended consequences or results of
actions as the criteria of their rightness. And we considered what is probably the best example of this sort of ethical theory: utilitarianism, which

seeks to promote the general welfare. But however it may conceive the "good results," any teleological theory says, "Such-and-such is the right action because it produces such-and-such results." A theory like this is clear, straightforward, and commonsensical.

How odd it might sound, therefore, for someone to say, "The consequences or results of your actions have nothing at all to do with their rightness or wrongness!" This is a *deontological* conception of morality. A deontological theory is one that sets up as the criterion of moral behavior not what might or might not happen—or be intended to happen—as a result of one's actions, but rather the intent to perform one's *duty* through a certain action.

This was exactly the thesis of Immanuel Kant, who, by the way, didn't think it a bid odd. In fact, he regarded it as the only *possible* way to conceive of genuine moral behavior. Why? Kant's answer is found, for the most part, in his *Foundations of the Metaphysics of Morals.* It is a small book, but, as the Kant scholar H. J. Paton says, "one of the small books which are truly great: it has exercised on human thought an influence almost ludicrously disproportionate to its size."[1]

For Kant, morality is a matter of *ought*, or *obligation.* Doesn't any moral theory tell us what we *ought* to do? This is not the problem. The problem is that a distinction is not usually drawn between the conditional *ought* and the *un*conditional *ought*. A conditional *ought*, says, "You ought to do X if you want something-or-other to happen." The *ought* is conditioned by something-or-other. But the unconditional *ought* says, "You ought to do X, period." For Kant, only the unconditional *ought* is the *moral* ought. Why? Because, as we all recognize—don't we?—morality must be *necessary* and *universal;* that is, it must be absolutely binding, and absolutely binding on everyone alike: Whoever you are, whatever your situation, you ought to do X. But the conditional *ought* involves "ifs" and "in-order-thats" and therefore gets mixed up with all sorts of particular circumstances, changing desires, personal inclinations, and so on. Any "morality" (Kant would put it in quotation marks) founded on the conditioned *ought* ("Do X, if . . ." or "Do X, in order that . . .") will therefore be relative and particular rather than necessary and universal—but then it is not real morality, is it?

---

[1]H. J. Paton, in the Preface to his translation of Immanuel Kant, *Foundations of the Metaphysics of Morals*, published as *Kant's Groundwork of the Metaphysic of Morals* (New York: Harper & Row, 1964), p. 8.

This is not to say that in deciding what we ought to do—how to fulfill our duty—we should never take the consequences of our actions into account. Often it is necessary to consider the results of an action in order to perceive whether it is our duty. But it is out of *duty* that we should act, not for the sake of the consequences. Stay with this until it is clear to you, or maybe consider an example. We borrow the following from yet another Kant scholar, Lewis White Beck.

> Imagine two soldiers who volunteer for a dangerous mission; because they see a task they ought to undertake, they voluntarily assume the responsibility for it. Certainly their act will have consequences; equally certain is the fact that they desire certain consequences for their act. The most careful consideration of these consequences, calculation as to how to achieve some desirable consequences and avoid others less desirable, and an ardent desire to attain the goal do not in the least detract from the morality of the men's action if they are indeed acting on the conviction that it is their duty to do these acts; their concern with the consequences may be an essential part of their conduct, necessary for the fulfillment of the obligation they have placed upon themselves. Now imagine that one of the men is killed before reaching his destination, while the other is successful; what moral judgment do we pass upon them? So far as we judge that their motives were equally good (and of course, as Kant repeatedly says, we cannot be sure what anyone's motives really are), we judge them in the same way. Their acts are judged to be equally moral, in spite of the fact that one succeeded and the other failed. Each did his "best," and what he earnestly attempted and the motives which led him to do what he did are the proper objects of moral judgment; what he accomplishes lies to a large extent beyond his control.[2]

Do you see that even with its possible interest in consequences this position is quite unlike, say, utilitarianism? There the question was, Did you act for the sake of promoting the general welfare? But here the question is, Aside from what you accomplish or even tried to accomplish, did you act out of duty?

---

[2]Lewis White Beck, in the Preface to his translation of Immanuel Kant, *Foundations of the Metaphysics of Morals* (Indianapolis: Bobbs-Merrill, 1959), p. ix.

Kant objects to:

- Any teleological conception of moral action
- Any naturalistic basis of moral action

But back to the main point. Another way Kant expresses his rejection of *conditioned* morality is by his rejection of any and all *naturalistic* ethics. As we explained earlier, a naturalistic ethics is one which bases its *ought* in some way on nature, say by an appeal to the physical world, or to psychology, or to human nature, or to history. But such an ethics would be based on what *happens* to be, or *might* be, or *could* be, whereas genuine morality is, again, a matter of *necessity* and *universality*. Do you see that happiness, for example, must for Kant be an impossible basis for moral laws?

This section is entitled, "Morality as Unconditional." Is it clear that for Kant morality is not conditioned by (that is, not defined by, not bound by, not relative to, not based on) anything outside the morality of the act itself? Is it clear how, for Kant, the introduction of the empirical categories of consequences and nature not only clouds but absolutely distorts the idea of morality?

In the following, from the *Foundations of the Metaphysics of Morals*, Kant emphasizes with a vengeance the absolute necessity of separating genuine morality from all empirical considerations, and the necessity, instead, of deriving it *a priori* from pure reason. (By "anthropology," Kant means what can be known empirically about human nature.)

Since my purpose here is directed to moral philosophy, I narrow the proposed question to this: Is it not the utmost necessity to construct a pure moral philosophy which is completely freed from everything which may be only empirical and thus belong to anthropology? That there must be such a philosophy is self-evident from the common idea of duty and moral laws. Everyone must admit that a law, if it is to hold morally, i.e., as a ground of obligation, must imply absolute necessity; he must admit that the command, "Thou shalt not lie," does not apply to men only, as if other rational beings had no need to observe it. The same is true for all other moral laws properly so called. He must concede that the ground of obligation here must not be sought in the nature of man or in the circumstances in which he is

Immanuel Kant

The historian of philosophy Frederick Copleston has described Kant's life as "singularly uneventful and devoid of dramatic incident."

Immanuel Kant was born in 1724 in Königsberg, East Prussia (now Russia), on the Baltic Sea. Kant's father, who immigrated from Scotland (and changed the family name from Cant to Kant), was a saddler. The family was large, poor, and religious. They were Pietists (something like Prussian Puritans), and the continuous round of prayers, religious instruction, and observances is no doubt why Kant in his adult years never attended public worship except on extraordinary occasions. On the other hand, he embraced to the end the ethical principles of his early religious upbringing.

In 1740, he entered the University of Königsberg where he drank in a broad survey of many fields: metaphysics, physics, algebra, geometry, psychology, astronomy, and logic. At the conclusion of his studies he earned a sparse livelihood by becoming a tutor to the Prussian gentry. It was during this time that he was introduced to high society, though he soon withdrew

(continued on next page)

placed, but sought a priori solely in the concepts of pure reason, and that every other precept which rests on principles of mere experience, even a precept which is in certain respects universal, so far as it leans in the least on empirical grounds (perhaps only in regard to the motive involved), may be called a practical rule but never a moral law. . . .

into the ivory tower of academic life. In 1755, he took what we would call a doctoral degree and became a lecturer at the university. In 1770, he was made professor. He taught and published first in science, anticipating Laplace's nebular hypothesis concerning the origin of the universe and Darwin's theory of evolution. But he turned gradually to metaphysics. Kant's lectures were said to be lively and even humorous—though one would never guess this from most of his writings.

In 1781, at the ripe age of 57, he published the monumental *Critique of Pure Reason*. This was followed by the *Critique of Practical Reason* and the *Critique of Judgment*. According to the German writer Herder, Kant spoke "the profoundest language that ever came from the lips of man." Profound perhaps, but perhaps also the most exasperating. He gave the manuscript of his first *Critique* to a colleague, Marcus Herz. Herz returned it half-read, with the explanation: "If I finish it, I am afraid I shall go mad!"

Kant lectured at the university for over forty years. In all this time he never traveled more than 60 miles from Königsberg, and for forty years he did not spend so much as a single night outside that city. Kant was a small man (about five feet tall), extremely frail, and somewhat distorted in his frame. He was meticulous about his health, verging on the neurotic. His daily routine was extremely fixed, beginning every morning at 4:55. It is reported that his daily walk was so regular that he strolled for exactly one hour, eight times up and down the Linden Allee (which came to be nicknamed "The Philosopher's Walk") and so punctual that the townspeople set their clocks by it. He never married, and was, in fact, something of a misogynist. He died in senile dementia on February 12, 1804.

Kant's most important philosophical works include: *Critique of Pure Reason, Critique of Practical Reason, Critique of Judgment, Prolegomena to any Future Metaphysics, Foundations of the Metaphysics of Morals, Metaphysical First Principles of Natural Science, Religion within the Bounds of Reason Alone,* and *On Perpetual Peace.*

But a completely isolated metaphysics of morals, mixed with no anthropology, no theology, no physics or hyperphysics, and even less with occult qualities (which might be called hypophysical), is not only an indispensable substrate of all theoretically sound and definite knowledge of duties; it is also a desideratum of the highest importance to the actual fulfillment of its precepts. For the pure conception

of duty and of the moral law generally, with no admixture of empirical inducements, has an influence on the human heart so much more
powerful than all other incentives which may be derived from the
empirical field that reason, in the consciousness of its dignity, despises
them and gradually becomes master over them. It has this influence
only through reason, which thereby first realizes that it can of itself
be practical. A mixed theory of morals which is put together both
from incentives of feelings and inclinations and from rational concepts must, on the other hand, make the mind vacillate between motives which cannot be brought under any principle and which can
lead only accidentally to the good and often to the bad.

From what has been said it is clear that all moral concepts have their
seat and origin entirely a priori in reason. This is just as much the
case in the most ordinary reason as in reason which is speculative to
the highest degree. It is obvious that they cannot be abstracted from
any empirical and hence merely contingent cognitions. In the purity
of their origin lies their worthiness to serve us as supreme practical
principles, and to the extent that something empirical is added to
them just this much is subtracted from their genuine influence and
from the unqualified worth of actions.[3]

THE GOOD WILL

In this way, Kant eliminates from the start the least suggestion that morality can be based on our natural states and inclinations. He does not be-
grudge us, say, pleasure and happiness, but wants us to see that such "gifts
of nature" cannot be the *foundation* of morality as rationally conceived.

Consider, for example, what we might call the innate gifts of intelligence, wit, and courage, or the accidental gifts of power, wealth, and
honor. Does it take any great insight to see that these are not *absolute*
goods? That they have no *intrinsic* or *unconditional* value? To see that this
is so, just notice how any one of them could be corrupted or turned into
an evil. Well, then, is there anything more basic than these which is absolutely and unconditionally good? Kant says Yes. And it is, in fact, the
very thing that these other things depend on for their goodness, and without which they would become corrupted and turned into evil. What is this

---

[3]Ibid., pp. 5, 27–28.

absolute good, the necessary and sufficient condition for all right action, the foundation of rational morality? The *good will*.

One of the most quoted passages in all philosophical literature is the opening sentence of the first section of the *Foundations:*

Nothing in the world—indeed nothing even beyond the world—can possibly be conceived which could be called good without qualification except a *good will*.

He goes on immediately to show how the good will underlies any possible goodness of our natural gifts:

Intelligence, wit, judgment, and the other talents of the mind, however they may be named, or courage, resoluteness, and perseverance as qualities of temperament, are doubtless in many respects good and desirable. But they can become extremely bad and harmful if the will, which is to make use of these gifts of nature and which in its special constitution is called character, is not good. It is the same with the gifts of fortune. Power, riches, honor, even health, general well-being, and the contentment with one's condition which is called happiness, make for pride and even arrogance if there is not a good will to correct their influence on the mind and on its principles of action so as to make it universally conformable to its end. It need hardly be mentioned that the sight of a being adorned with no feature of a pure and good will, yet enjoying uninterrupted prosperity, can never give pleasure to a rational impartial observer. Thus the good will seems to constitute the indispensable condition even of worthiness to be happy.

Some qualities seem to be conducive to this good will and can facilitate its action, but, in spite of that, they have no intrinsic unconditional worth. They rather presuppose a good will, which limits the high esteem which one otherwise rightly has for them and prevents their being held to be absolutely good. Moderation in emotions and passions, self-control, and calm deliberation not only are good in many respects but even seem to constitute a part of the inner worth of the person. But however unconditionally they were esteemed by the ancients, they are far from being good without qualification. For without the principle of a good will they can become extremely bad, and the coolness of a villain makes him not only far more dangerous but also more directly abominable in our eyes than he would have seemed without it.

The good will is not good because of what it effects or accomplishes or because of its adequacy to achieve some proposed end; it is good only because of its willing, i.e., it is good of itself. And, regarded for itself, it is to be esteemed incomparably higher than anything which could be brought about by it in favor of any inclination or even of the sum total of all inclinations. Even if it should happen that, by a particularly unfortunate fate or by the niggardly provision of a stepmotherly nature, this will should be wholly lacking in power to accomplish its purpose, and if even the greatest effort should not avail it to achieve anything of its end, and if there remained only the good will (not as a mere wish but as the summoning of all the means in our power), it would sparkle like a jewel in its own right, as something that had its full worth in itself. Usefulness or fruitlessness can neither diminish nor augment this worth. Its usefulness would be only its setting, as it were, so as to enable us to handle it more conveniently in commerce or to attract the attention of those who are not yet connoisseurs, but not to recommend it to those who are experts or to determine its worth.[4]

Pore over the above paragraphs until they are digested. Still, even though Kant here uses the phrase "good will" repeatedly, he does not say exactly what it means. If we somehow miss this, then we miss the whole point. For Kant a good will, or a *pure* will, is an intention to act in accordance with moral *law*, and moral law is what it is no matter what anything else is. To act out of a good will is, then, to do X because it is *right* to do X, and for no other reason. This would be *rational* morality.

An important note: Kant stresses the difference between acting "out of" duty and acting "in accordance with" duty. Obviously, we may do something that just happens to accord with what our duty is, but this would hardly make the action moral. In order to be really moral, our action must be done *out* of duty, that is, with a good will or with respect for the moral law.

---

[4]Ibid., pp. 9–10.

KANT'S CATEGORICAL IMPERATIVE

At this point Kant presents us with one of the most famous and important concepts in the history of ethics: the *Categorical Imperative.*

For Kant, the Categorical Imperative is the fundamental principle of morality. More accurately, it is a criterion or *test* by which we can make sure our actions are moral, that is, that they are motivated by a good will or performed out of duty. As Kant states it in its most general form, the Categorical Imperative is this:

> Act only according to that maxim by which you can at the same time will that it should become a universal law.[5]

That is to say, when you are about to do X, ask yourself whether you can will that everyone else act in the same way. If the answer is Yes, then, says Kant, you may be assured that you are acting out of duty or with a good will. Why is this? We will explain in a moment exactly how the Categorical Imperative is a test of right action.

Sometimes the Categorical Imperative is referred to, for short, as the *Principle of Universalizibility,* since it asks us whether we can "universalize" our actions, that is, whether we would demand that everyone else in similar circumstances act in accordance with the same rule as we would. But we must not miss the significance of Kant's own—and more ponderous—expression. What is an *imperative?* It is a *command.* As a command, the Categorical Imperative addresses and constrains our will, which it recognizes might not always (and often enough doesn't!) gladly pursue what it ought. As a command, the Categorical Imperative reckons with our natural perversity; in fact, Kant believed, in his own way, in the traditional Christian doctrine of original sin. But why is this imperative called, further, *categorical?* Here we encounter again the distinction between doing something as a means of *achieving some end* and doing something simply because it's *right.* Kant says that all imperatives are either hypothetical or categorical. A *hypothetical* imperative would command you to do X if you wanted Y (notice the hypothetical form of the statement, "if . . . then"). But a *categorical* imperative would command you to do X inasmuch as X is intrinsically right, that is, right in and of itself, aside from any other considerations—no "ifs," no conditions, no strings attached.

---

[5]Ibid., p. 39.

Kant himself clearly draws the distinction between hypothetical and categorical imperatives:

> All imperatives command either hypothetically or categorically. The former present the practical necessity of a possible action as a means to achieving something else which one desires (or which one may possibly desire). The categorical imperative would be one which presented an action as of itself objectively necessary, without regard to any other end.[6]

And he leaves no doubt as to which of these alone can have any bearing on morality, and why:

> . . . there is one imperative which directly commands a certain conduct without making its condition some purpose to be reached by it. This imperative is categorical. It concerns not the material of the action and its intended result but the form and the principle from which it results. What is essentially good in it consists in the intention, the result being what it may. This imperative may be called the imperative of morality.[7]

It is important to grasp this. A hypothetical imperative is *conditional on* ("if") or *subject to* things, circumstances, goals, and desires; and these, of course, change all the time, are relative to the individual, and so on. But a categorical imperative is *unconditional* (no "ifs") and *independent of* any things, circumstances, goals, or desires. It is for this reason that only a *categorical* imperative can be a *universal* and *binding* law, that is, a *moral* law, valid for all rational beings at all times.

THE TEST OF MORAL ACTIONS

Understandably, the Categorical Imperative, as the fundamental principle of morality, may leave you cold. To be sure, there is no talk here about exciting things like lying, stealing, and adultery. Instead, we are confronted by rather abstract talk about maxims and laws, without any particular

---

[6]Ibid., p. 31.
[7]Ibid., p. 33.

content. It is true. Kant told us above—not in so many words, but at least in these *exact* words—that his Categorical Imperative, the foundation of rational morality, is concerned not with the *matter* but the *form* of morality. On the other hand, its concern for the *form* is precisely for the sake of getting the *matter* right. Let's try to say this in several ways. The Categorical Imperative—

- isn't concerned with *what* you do but *how* you do it, since if the *how* is right the *what* will be right.
- doesn't address specific moral issues but the nature of morality *itself.*
- doesn't prescribe the rightness or wrongness of *particular* actions but what makes *any* action right or wrong.

But, of course, this is largely true of any theory of morality. All right, then, we may state it even more strongly. According to Kant, when we seek to make a moral judgment about a possible course of action, what we primarily need to take into account has nothing to do with pleasure, pain, joy, welfare, happiness, Jews hiding in the attic, threats, or the brandishing of guns. Rather, it has to do with—what must seem exceedingly dull and formal by comparison—the possibility of a *contradiction in our action.*

And this brings us back to the way in which the Categorical Imperative is a *test* of moral actions. When embarking on a certain course of action, I must ask: Does the universalizing of the principle of my action result in a

---

The Categorical Imperative

- It is an *imperative* because it *commands* you to do something.
- It is *categorical* because it commands you to do something *unconditionally*, that is, without regard to consequences or personal desires.

What the Categorical Imperative unconditionally commands is that in situation X you act in such a way as you could will everyone in situation X to act. If you can do that, then you stand a chance of acting from *duty* or out of a concern for what is right.

---

contradiction? If so, the action fails the test and must be rejected as immoral. But it is important to see what is meant here by "contradiction." It is not a *logical* contradiction as often as a *practical* one. It might help to think of the latter sort of self-contradictory action as a *self-stultifying* or *self-defeating* one.

Kant himself provides some concrete examples of how the application of the Categorical Imperative might result in contradiction and backfire.

1. A man who is reduced to despair by a series of evils feels a weariness with life but is still in possession of his reason sufficiently to ask whether it would not be contrary to his duty to himself to take his own life. Now he asks whether the maxim of his action could become a universal law of nature. His maxim, however, is: For love of myself, I make it my principle to shorten my life when by a longer duration it threatens more evil than satisfaction. But it is questionable whether this principle of self-love could become a universal law of nature. One immediately sees a contradiction in a system of nature whose law would be to destroy life by the feeling whose special office is to impel the improvement of life. In this case it would not exist as nature; hence that maxim cannot obtain as a law of nature, and thus it wholly contradicts the supreme principle of all duty.

2. Another man finds himself forced by need to borrow money. He well knows that he will not be able to repay it, but he also sees that nothing will be loaned him if he does not firmly promise to repay it at a certain time. He desires to make such a promise, but he has enough conscience to ask himself whether it is not improper and opposed to duty to relieve his distress in such a way. Now, assuming he does decide to do so, the maxim of his action would be as follows: When I believe myself to be in need of money, I will borrow money and promise to repay it, although I know I shall never do so. Now this principle of self-love or of his own benefit may very well be compatible with his whole future welfare, but the question is whether it is right. He changes the pretension of self-love into a universal law and then puts the question: How would it be if my maxim became a universal law? He immediately sees that it could never hold as a universal law of nature and be consistent with itself; rather it must necessarily contradict itself. For the universality of a law which says that anyone who believes himself to be in need could

promise what he pleased with the intention of not fulfilling it would make the promise itself and the end to be accomplished by it impossible; no one would believe what was promised to him but would only laugh at any such assertion as vain pretense.

3. A third finds in himself a talent which could, by means of some cultivation, make him in many respects a useful man. But he finds himself in comfortable circumstances and prefers indulgence in pleasure to troubling himself with broadening and improving his fortunate natural gifts. Now, however, let him ask whether his maxim of neglecting his gifts, besides agreeing with his propensity to idle amusement, agrees also with what is called duty. He sees that a system of nature could indeed exist in accordance with such a law, even though man (like the inhabitants of the South Sea Islands) should let his talents rust and resolve to devote his life merely to idleness, indulgence, and propagation—in a word, to pleasure. But he cannot possibly will that this should become a universal law of nature or that it should be implanted in us by a natural instinct. For, as a rational being, he necessarily wills that all his faculties should be developed, inasmuch as they are given to him for all sorts of possible purposes.

4. A fourth man, for whom things are going well, sees that others (whom he could help) have to struggle with great hardships, and he asks, "What concern of mine is it? Let each one be as happy as heaven wills, or as he can make himself; I will not take anything from him or even envy him; but to his welfare or to his assistance in time of need I have no desire to contribute." If such a way of thinking were a universal law of nature, certainly the human race could exist, and without doubt even better than in a state where everyone talks of sympathy and good will, or even exerts himself occasionally to practice them while, on the other hand, he cheats when he can and betrays or otherwise violates the rights of man. Now although it is possible that a universal law of nature according to that maxim could exist, it is nevertheless impossible to will that such a principle should hold everywhere as a law of nature. For a will which resolved this would conflict with itself, since instances can often arise in which he would need the love and sympathy of others, and in which he would have robbed himself, by such a law of nature springing from his own will, of all hope of the aid he desires.

The foregoing are a few of the many actual duties, or at least of duties we hold to be actual, whose derivation from the one stated principle is clear. We must be able to will that a maxim of our action become a universal law; this is the canon of the moral estimation of our action generally. Some actions are of such a nature that their maxim cannot even be *thought* as a universal law of nature without contradiction, far from it being possible that one could will that it should be such. In others this internal impossibility is not found, though it is still impossible to *will* that their maxim should be raised to the universality of a law of nature, because such a will would contradict itself.[8]

To this point, we have spoken in the singular of the Categorical Imperative. Actually, it should be added, Kant provided several formulations of Categorical Imperatives, though these are really best thought of as different versions of the same fundamental principle of morality. Certainly they overlap with one another, and they suggest important and differing ways in which the fundamental principle may be viewed and applied.[9]

1. Act only according to that maxim by which you can at the same time will that it should become a universal law.
2. Act only so that the will through its maxims could regard itself at the same time as making universal laws.
3. Act so that you treat humanity, whether in your own person or in that of another, always as an end and never as a means only.

SOME OBJECTIONS

The first objection might, rather naturally, focus on the moral law itself. Kant assumes throughout that there is a moral law, a sort of moral rhyme and reason to things, a "moral law within" that is just as given as the starry heavens above, and that we can be in harmony with it by obeying the Categorical Imperative. But what if someone were to throw up his or her hands and exclaim, "There is no undergirding and overarching morality—it's all up for grabs!"? Does it not behoove Kant (and most other moral

---

[8]Ibid., pp. 39–42.

[9]I have paraphrased these three formulations and arranged them for our own purposes here. In the *Foundations of the Metaphysics of Morals*, they may be found on pp. 39, 47, 52.

How to "Operationalize" Kant's Test for Moral Action

The issue: Is act *X* morally permissible? And if so, is *X* an obligation?

Stage 1. Ask: "Can I will doing *X* universally, that is, everyone in similar circumstances doing *X?*"

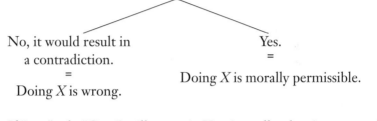

No, it would result in
a contradiction.
=
Doing *X* is wrong.

Yes.
=
Doing *X* is morally permissible.

Stage 2. If "yes," ask: "Can I will to omit *X* universally, that is, no one in similar circumstances doing *X?*"

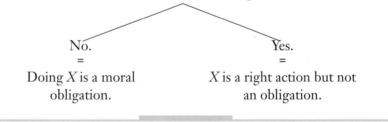

No.
=
Doing *X* is a moral
obligation.

Yes.
=
X is a right action but not
an obligation.

philosophers, as well) to *show* that there is some objective morality that moral philosophy reasons about? How this might be done has been considered in several places already. Do you recall the arguments against nihilism, emotivism, and subjectivism?

Again, if Kant is clear about anything, it is that morality can in no way be based on anything empirical or natural. But why can't one, for instance a *naturalist*, simply turn the tables and say that morality *must* be based on nature, that is, defend naturalistic ethics? You will recall that this was precisely Mill's position, and Mill *followed* Kant, not hesitating to thumb his nose, as it were, at Kant's *a priorism*. Can ethical naturalism be so obviously wrongheaded as Kant made it out to be? But this brings us back to the problems with metaphysical and ethical naturalism themselves.

Closely related, it has been charged that whatever Kant may have *intended*, his radical distinction between the moral world and the natural world may have the *effect* of rendering us morally neutral toward nature. That is, it has the effect of stripping nature of its values and downplaying any moral responsibility we may have toward it. This is an especially big criticism in our day when philosophers have been quickened to the issues of environmental ethics and animal rights.

Another question: Does Kant's theory of morality presuppose a "faculty psychology"? Faculty psychology is the view which divides the person's inner life into distinct and different faculties with their own respective functions and powers. In Kant's theory, desires and inclinations are distinct from and subservient to the will, and the will is something different from and subservient to reason. It is a good question whether the activities of our inner lives can be split apart in this way.

Also, it may be objected to Kant's "universalizing" that every law has some exceptions. But a misunderstanding may be involved here. Kant never gave us any universal laws of action, but universal *maxims* of action. The emphasis is not on the *what* but the *how*. In spite of his own (unfortunate?) example of having to tell the truth irrespective of the consequences, his real point is that whether we tell the truth or not, we must act out of a good will or duty and no exceptions to *that!*

Finally, we come to the problem that you may feel more strongly, and that is probably because it is a more *practical* problem. The strict deontologist has told us, perhaps more times than we care to hear, that consequences (or at least the values of various consequences) are irrelevant for moral decision and action. Is this really practical advice? Who of us,

---

How might a Kantian reason about the rightness or wrongness of

- capital punishment?
- women's rights?
- racial discrimination?
- war?
- the CIA?
- abortion?

knowing full well that, say, telling a lie would result in cruel and innocent suffering, would or could ignore this consequence? And is it not the case that sometimes we *should* wake up in the middle of the night worrying about the consequences of some act or other committed the day before? When the chips are down, in a concrete existential situation, Kant's "formalism" might be too formal for its own good. Man does not live by bare principles alone. Does Kant demand of us that we be more rational than we can possibly be, or even should be?

CHAPTER 14 IN REVIEW

Summary

In Chapter 13 we discussed an ethical theory which was both (1) teleological and (2) naturalistic. In this chapter, we have discussed an ethical perspective which is diametrically opposite in both of these respects.

As we have seen, the best example of such a perspective is found in the moral philosophy of Kant, who emphasized that if morality is to be truly necessary and universal, it cannot be based on accidental and fluctuating *empirical* considerations. That is why the consequences of actions are irrelevant for the morality or immorality of an action, as are considerations such as history, human nature, etc. In the place of any teleological or naturalistic conception of morality, Kant substitutes a completely *a priori* conception: Morality must have a purely *rational* basis. This *a priori* or rational basis of morality is underscored by Kant's well-known pronouncement that only a good will is unconditionally good. That is, it is good in itself. On the other hand, it is a condition for all moral behavior: Without good will anything else, such as power or wealth, would be quickly abused or misappropriated.

What, more exactly, is the good or pure will? It is the intention to act in accordance with moral law, or to act only out of respect for what is right and not for any other reason. Kant formalizes this principle of all morality in the Categorical Imperative: "Act only according to that maxim by which you can at the same time will that it should become a universal law." The ability to universalize (apply to everyone) the rule by which we act in a given situation is a sufficient guarantee of the morality of our action, or that it is being done out of respect for the moral law alone.

As always, this philosophical position too is subject to many criticisms. One of the most common is that it is characterized by a certain abstractness or remoteness. To be sure, it may be difficult to bring to bear a rather lifeless and formal principle like the Categorical Imperative on the concrete and often vivid moral dilemmas we are frequently confronted by. On the other hand, that is just Kant's concern. Do we too easily and quickly decide these issues by obvious and immediate considerations that actually blind us to the real and *rational* basis of moral action?

Basic Ideas

- Deontological ethics
- The conditional vs. the unconditional *ought*
- Kant's rejection of teleological ethics
- Kant's rejection of naturalistic ethics
- The good will, as the basis for morality
- The Categorical Imperative
- Hypothetical vs. categorical imperatives
- Kant's "formalism"
- The Categorical Imperative as a test for moral action
- Three versions of the Categorical Imperative

Questions for Reflection

- What do you think of the effort to establish morality on a purely *a priori* foundation? Do you believe in an objective moral law? Can such a law be dependent on or conditioned by *a posteriori* factors? What *is* its relation to the natural world?
- It is not quite right, is it, to say that for Kant the consideration of consequences is *utterly* irrelevant for the determination of a moral act. Can you explain *both* sides of Kant's view of consequences?

For Further Reading

C. D. Broad. *Five Types of Ethical Theory*. London: Routledge & Kegan Paul, 1930. Ch. 5. An exposition and critique of Kant's moral philosophy, from an old but standard work by a well-known philosopher.

Frederick Copleston. *A History of Philosophy*. Baltimore: Newman Press, 1946–1974. VI, Ch. 14. A clear and authoritative account of the essential points in Kant's moral philosophy.

A. C. Ewing. *Ethics.* New York: Free Press, 1953. Ch. 4. A beginner-oriented chapter on the "Duty for Duty's Sake," a summary and (negative) evaluation of Kant's ethics.

William K. Frankena. *Ethics.* 2nd ed. Englewood Cliffs, NJ: Prentice Hall, 1973. Ch. 2. An elementary discussion of egoistic and deontological theories, with some specific treatment of Kant's ethics.

Justus Hartnack. *Immanuel Kant: An Explanation of His Theory of Knowledge and Moral Philosophy.* Atlantic Highlands. NJ: Humanities Press, 1974. Ch. 3. A brief, clear account of Kant's ethical perspective in relation to his philosophy of religion.

Stephen Körner. *Kant.* Baltimore: Penguin Books, 1955. Ch. 6. A chapter on Kant's moral philosophy, from a standard work on Kant.

H. J. Paton. *The Categorical Imperative: A Study in Kant's Moral Philosophy.* London: Hutchinson, 1946. A complete and authoritative treatment of Kant's moral philosophy, by a foremost Kant scholar.

W. D. Ross. *Kant's Ethical Theory.* London: Oxford University Press, 1954. A full-scale study of Kant's ethical theory.

W. H. Werkmeister. *Theories of Ethics: A Study in Moral Obligation.* Lincoln, NE: Johnsen, 1961. Chs. 8–9. Closely documented and critical studies of the deontological ethics of Kant and some recent revisions of Kantianism.

Robert Paul Wolff (ed.). *Kant: A Collection of Critical Essays.* Garden City, NY: Anchor Books, 1967. Advanced discussions of aspects of Kant's philosophy, including his moral philosophy.

Robert Paul Wolff (ed.). *Kant's Foundations of the Metaphysics of Morals, with Critical Essays.* Indianapolis: Bobbs-Merrill, 1969. A translation of Kant's most important moral work, with worthwhile studies of special issues by nine Kantian scholars.

*In addition, see the relevant articles ("Deontological Ethics," "Kant, Immanuel," etc.) in *The Encyclopedia of Philosophy*, ed. Paul Edwards. New York: Macmillan, 1967.

Glossary

T HE FOLLOWING entries are geared specifically to the present text, though the list is sufficiently comprehensive to assist any philosophy student. The decision to enter noun forms on some occasions and adjectival forms on others has not been arbitrary but determined by the way in which the terms tend to be used in the text. When terms in the entries are themselves in some for separate entries, this is indicated, when appropriate, by the use of **boldface** type.

A posteriori　In **epistemology,** pertaining to knowledge derived from, or posterior to, sense experience.

A priori　In **epistemology,** pertaining to knowledge acquired independently of, or prior to, sense experience.

Absolute　That which is independent of or unconditioned by anything outside itself.

420

Abstraction (abstract idea)   A general idea, an idea from which particularizing features of existing things have been removed (e.g., "table," "dog," or "human") or which results when what a number of particular things have in common is abstracted (e.g., "redness" from various red things).

Accident, Fallacy of   An **informal fallacy** which applies a general rule to a specific situation in which some accidental condition makes it exempted from the rule.

Accidental   In **metaphysics,** a feature or characteristic which does not belong necessarily to the nature of a thing.

Act-utilitarianism   An **ethical** theory which emphasizes particular actions to be taken in particular situations to bring about the greatest benefit.

Actuality   In **scholastic** philosophy, the state of being something in reality as opposed to being something merely **potentially.**

Aesthetics   Philosophy of art, or philosophical reflection on the nature of art and of our experience of beauty.

Alienation   In **Marxism,** the estrangement, induced by **capitalist** exploitation, of the worker from his or her product, self, human nature, and neighbors.

Altruism   The belief that everyone ought as much as possible to seek the good of others.

Analogy, Method of   In **logic,** a form of **inductive reasoning** in which a **conclusion** is drawn about some feature of one member of a class on the basis of a resemblance in some other respect to other members of the class.

Analogy of the Sun   Plato's comparison of the function of the Sun in the visible world to the function of the **Good** in the **intelligible** world: As the Sun illuminates sensible things with light and causes them to exist, so the Good irradiates the **Forms** with truth and causes them to exist.

Analytic philosophy (Linguistic philosophy)   An emphasis in twentieth-century philosophy (largely British) on linguistic analysis, or the analysis of language, as a means of identifying the sources of, and resolving, philosophical problems.

Analytic proposition   A proposition that is true by definition, or **logically** necessary as in "All triangles have three sides."

Anthropomorphism   The representation of something nonhuman, e.g., God, in the likeness of human beings.

Archetype   A model, pattern, or paradigm.

Argument   An attempt to show that some claim is true (the **conclusion**) by providing reasons for it (the **premises**).

Argumentum ad Baculum   "Appeal to force"; an **informal fallacy** which employs intimidation, pressure, etc., as tools of persuasion.

Argumentum ad Hominem   "Appeal to the man"; an **informal fallacy** which irrelevantly attacks the person making a claim rather than attacking the claim itself (abusive form) or seeks to undermine a claim by calling attention to the (irrelevant) circumstances of the one making the claim.

Argumentum ad Ignorantiam   "Appeal to ignorance"; an **informal fallacy** which affirms the truth of something on the basis of the lack of evidence to the contrary.

Argumentum ad Misericordiam   "Appeal to pity"; an **informal fallacy** which directs attention from relevant evidence by arousing pity and sympathy for the plight of someone.

Argumentum ad Populum   "Appeal to the crowd"; an **informal fallacy** which seeks to strengthen a claim by emotional appeal to the passions and prejudices of the listeners.

Argumentum ad Verecundiam   "Appeal to authority"; an **informal fallacy** which appeals to an expert who, though qualified in some other area, is not qualified in the subject area addressed by the claim.

Atman   Sanskrit, "self"; in Hinduism, the self or soul which after enlightenment is understood as being identical with **Brahman,** the source of all reality.

Attribute   Property or characteristic attributed to or **predicated** of something.

Autonomous   The state of being self-controlling, **independent,** or free.

Behaviorism   The school of psychology which by defining psychological terms (e.g., pain) in terms of observable behavior (e.g., sobbing) claims that observable behavior is the proper object of psychological study.

Benevolence Principle   Happiness is to be distributed as widely and as equally as possible among all people.

Big Bang Theory A **cosmological** model according to which the present hypothesized expanding universe has resulted from an explosion of concentrated matter fifteen or twenty billion years ago.

Brahman In Hinduism, the impersonal, supreme reality, the origin and nature of all things.

Categorical Imperative In Kant, the principle of moral conduct: "Act only according to that maxim by which you can at the same time will that it should become a universal law"; more generally, a **moral** command with no "ifs" or "buts."

Category mistake The mistake of employing a concept within a conceptual system to which it is inappropriate (e.g., "I see the carburetor, battery, generator, pistons, etc., but where is the power?").

Causality, Principle of Everything that comes into being is caused, or comes into being by virtue of something outside itself.

Cave, Allegory of the Plato's image whereby he likens the education and ascent of the soul to making one's way out of a darkened cave, which is initially mistaken for reality, into the upper world illuminated by the Sun.

Chōrismos Greek for, "separation" or "gap," applied by Aristotle in criticism of Plato's theory of **Forms** which represented them as **transcendent** and removed from (separated from) the things which they are supposed to be the cause of.

Cogito ergo sum Latin expression employed by Descartes for the **indubitable** starting point of philosophizing: "I think, therefore I am."

Cognitive Pertaining to the act or process of knowing.

Cognitive meaning The status of a claim as being either true or false.

Cognitive science An interdisciplinary (psychology, philosophy, computer sciences, linguistics) exploration of the processes which underlie thinking, utilizing a computational (computerlike) model of mind.

Complex Idea An idea which combines several simple or unanalyzable ideas (e.g., "apple" is compounded out of "red," "sweet," etc.) or other complex ideas (e.g., "typewriter" is composed of keys, carriage, levers, etc.).

Conclusion In an **argument,** the proposition which is supported by the premises.

Conditioned See *Contingent.*

Consequentialism See *Teleological ethics.*

Conservation of Energy, Principle of The amount of energy in any closed system (and therefore the universe) remains constant, i.e., it can be of itself neither created nor destroyed.

Contiguity The state of one thing being in spatial contact with or touching another.

Contingent The state of being dependent for existence on something else.

Converse Accident An **informal fallacy** which generalizes on the basis of an inadequate number of instances or on the basis of atypical instances.

Corporeal Pertaining to what exists as a physical body and is apprehensible by the senses.

Cosmological Argument A **proof** for God's existence: God must exist as the ultimate cause of the **contingent,** physical universe. Also called the **First-Cause Argument.**

Cosmology Study of the origin, nature, and principles constituting the physical universe.

Cosmos From the Greek *kosmos,* "ornament," eventually designating the world or universe.

Cultural relativism The view that **morality** and other values are rooted in the experience, habits, and preferences of a culture.

Deductive reasoning Reasoning in which the **conclusion** follows with logical necessity from the premises.

Deity God, the divinity, the divine nature.

Deontological ethics The view that emphasizes the performance of duty, rather than results, as the sign of right action.

Design Argument See *Teleological Argument.*

Determinism The view that everything that comes into being is caused in such a way that it could not have been otherwise.

Dhyana Meditation methods employed in Hinduism for controlling the mind and attaining detachment from things both external and internal.

Dispositions (mental) Ryle's term for the observable data by which mind is best understood: capacities, proclivities, habits, etc.

Divided Line, the Plato's image of a line bisected above and below to represent, on one side, his conception of degrees of being and, on the other, corresponding degrees of knowledge.

Double-aspect theory In Spinoza, the view that there is only one reality, unknown to us except through its **attributes** of mind and matter, two of the infinite number of aspects of this one reality.

Dualism **Metaphysically,** the view that reality consists ultimately of two fundamentally different entities.

Efficient cause The agent through which something comes into being.

Egoistic hedonism The doctrine that the pursuit and production of one's own pleasure is the highest good and the criterion of right action.

Eidological Argument A proof for God that requires God as the Cause of our idea of perfection.

Eightfold Noble Path, the Principles of living, revealed to the Buddha, which lead to the cessation of desire and thus of suffering.

Emotivism The view, usually associated with **logical positivism,** that **moral** propositions make no claims about reality but, rather, merely express the approval and disapproval of the speaker.

Empiricism The belief that knowledge about existing things is acquired through sense experience.

En soi French, "in itself," used in Sartrean **existentialism** in reference to nonconscious being.

Environmental ethics Application of principles of obligation or right action to issues of the environment, such as pollution, conservatism, treatment of animals, etc.

Epistemological dualism The view that the act of knowing involves primarily two components: the mind that does the knowing and its ideas(s) that are known.

Epistemology The study or theory of knowledge.

Esse Latin, "to be," and hence "being" or "act of being."

Essence The nature or "whatness" of something; that which makes something the kind of thing it is.

Ethical absolutism (Ethical objectivism) The view that **moral** values are independent of human opinion and have a common or universal application.

Ethical relativism (Ethical subjectivism) The denial of any **absolute** or **objective moral** values, and the affirmation of the individual (person, community, culture, etc.) as the source of **morality.**

Ethics   The theory of good and evil as applied to personal actions, decisions, and relations; **moral** values.

Evil, the problem of   See *Theodicy.*

Evolution, theory of   In biology, the theory advanced by Charles Darwin that present life forms have developed gradually from earlier more primitive forms by means of natural selection, which eliminates maladapted forms while new forms are generated by spontaneous mutations.

Ex nihil nihil fit   Latin, **scholastic** expression of the **Principle of Causality:** "From nothing, nothing comes."

Excluded Middle, Law of   Something either is or is not, with nothing in between; a proposition is either true or false.

"Existence precedes essence"   A summary of the (especially atheistic) **existentialist** view that what the human being is, or human **essence,** is created by choices made by existing subjects.

Existential freedom   The denial that values are imposed on humans from without; human **autonomy** in the creation of values.

Existential meaning   The personal importance or relevance of an experience, idea, etc.

Existential proposition   A proposition that affirms or denies the existence of something.

Existentialism   A nineteenth- and twentieth-century philosophical perspective which disdains **abstractions** and focuses on the concrete reality and freedom of the existing individual.

Extension   The property of occupying space.

External sanctions   In Bentham, motivations lying outside us (e.g., law, opinion, God) for behavior of a certain kind.

External world   The objects existing outside and **independently** of our minds.

Factual judgment   A judgment which describes some **empirical** state of affairs.

Faculty   An agent or power by which the mind or soul knows and acts (e.g., memory, will, imagination).

Faculty psychology   An understanding of the mind which distinguishes its several differing capacities and their respectively different functions.

Fallacy   Mistake in reasoning, due to a failure in following the rules for the formal structure of valid arguments (**formal fallacy**) or carelessness regarding relevance and clarity of language (**informal fallacy**).

Fatalism   See *Determinism*.

Final Cause   The end or purpose of a thing.

First-Cause Argument   See *Cosmological Argument*.

Form   In **metaphysics,** the **essence,** nature, or "whatness" of a thing.

Form Philosophy   Any philosophy that posits **Form** or **essence** as a central **metaphysical** category.

Formal Cause   The **essence** or nature of a thing.

Formal fallacy   Mistake in reasoning due to failure in following the rules for the formal structure of **valid arguments.**

Formalism, ethical   A characterization of Kant's criterion of **moral** action, which stresses not the content of the action but the conformity of the will to **moral** principle.

Formalism, mathematical   The view that mathematical study is not about any real entities, either outside the mind (**logicism**) or inside the mind (**intuitionism**).

Forms, theory of   The belief in **transcendent essences** which cause particular things, by **"participation"** or **"imitation,"** to have their general natures.

Fortuitous   Happening accidentally or by chance.

Four Noble Truths, the   Principles revealed to the Buddha concerning the essence of life, based on the belief that it consists of suffering born out of desire.

Free-will Defense   An attempted solution to the problem of **moral evil:** Human beings are endowed with free will by God as a condition for genuine **morality,** trust, love, etc., though it also makes possible the introduction of **moral evil** into the world.

Functionalism   The idea, especially applied to mind, that the nature of something is better understood in light of its function than what it is made of.

Generative grammar   A hypothetical set of rules that will produce all, and only, the grammatical sentences of a language, usually associated with a particular school of linguistics dominated by Chomsky.

Genetic fallacy   An **informal fallacy** which directs attention to the origin or causes (sociological, psychological, etc.) of a belief rather than its **rational** foundation.

Geometrical method   A method for philosophizing modeled on geometrical procedures, most notably **intuition** and **deduction.**

Ghost in the machine, the   Ryle's characterization of Descartes' influential idea that the physical body is inhabited by a spiritual **substance,** mind.

Good, the Form of   In Platonic philosophy, a characterization of the **Form** of Forms, the ultimate principle of all Being and Knowledge.

Hard-behaviorism   The form of **behaviorism** which extends itself beyond the task of describing behavior to the claim that there *is* no "inner person" beyond behavior.

Hard-determinism   The view that the will is **determined** ultimately by factors beyond the responsibility of the individual.

Hedonic calculus   The means of calculating the quantity of a pleasure by applying criteria such as intensity, extent, duration, etc.

Hedonism   The **ethical** doctrine that pleasure is the highest good, and the production of pleasure is the criterion of right action.

Hierarchy   A ranking of things or persons in an ascending order of importance, value, etc.

Humanism   The view that human reality is the highest reality and value.

Hylomorphic Composition   Literally, **matter-form** composition, the view that all natural things require for their existence both passive "stuff" and active, determining **essence.**

Idealism   In **metaphysics,** the theory that all reality consists of mind and its ideas.

Identical judgment   See *Analytic proposition.*

Identity, Law of   A thing is what it is; a true proposition is true.

Identity Thesis   The equation of mental states with brain states.

Imitation, Metaphor of   A metaphor by which Plato attempted to elucidate the relation between sensible things and their **Forms:** Sensible things are mere imitations or copies of their ideal essences.

Immanence   The state of being within or **inherent** in something.

Immanent Forms   An expression of the Aristotelian claim, against Plato's doctrine of the *Separated Forms,* that **Forms** are *in* the sensible things of which they are the **Forms.**

Immutability   The state of being immovable, not subject to change.

Incompatibilism   The belief that genuine free will is logically incompatible with **determinism.**

Independence   In **metaphysics,** existence which is unconditioned by something outside itself.

Indeterminism The view that some things, and therefore possibly the will, are free of **causal** determination.

Indubitable That which is not susceptible to any doubt.

Inductive reasoning Reasoning in which the **conclusion** follows with probability from the **premises.**

Ineffable Inexpressible in language.

Inference The connection by which the **conclusion** of an **argument** follows from the **premises.**

Infinite regress A series of claims, explanations, elements, factors, etc., dependent successively on one another without end.

Informal fallacy Mistake in reasoning due to carelessness regarding relevance and clarity of language.

Inherent Existing in something as an inseparable **quality,** etc.

Innate ideas The view that at least some ideas are inborn, present to the mind at birth.

Inscrutability The state of being incomprehensible or beyond understanding.

Instinct A pattern of behavior that is inborn, invariable, and unique to a particular species.

Intellectual consciousness Awareness of pure (nonsensible) ideas in our minds.

Intelligible Pertaining to, or being of the nature of, thought (as opposed to sense experience).

Intelligible species A **scholastic** way of referring to the general idea of something, **abstracted** from its particular instances of sensible things.

Intentionality The fact, sometimes posed as a problem for physicalists, that mental states (such as beliefs, attitudes, etc.) are directed *toward* or are *about* something or *refer to* things other than themselves.

Interactionism The view that **mind** and **matter,** in spite of their radical difference, stand in a reciprocal **causal** relation.

Internal sanction In Mill, a motivation lying within us (e.g., feeling or conscience) for behavior of a certain kind.

Intrinsic Belonging properly or naturally to a thing.

Intuition The faculty by which truth is apprehended immediately, apart from sense experience or other ideas; in Kant, perceptual awareness of things.

Intuitionism In **epistemology,** the view that we have direct awareness of at least some fundamental ideas about reality as universally and necessarily true.

Intuitionism, mathematical The view that the objects of mathematical study are mind-created mental entities.

Irrational Pertaining to what is incompatible or in tension with the principles of reason itself (strict sense), or with general experience, expectation, etc. (loose sense).

Jainism A sixth-century ascetic **religion** and discipline (fourteen stages of perfection) founded in India in opposition to traditional Hinduism.

Koan A short, inherently paradoxical statement assigned by a **Zen** master to be meditated upon by the disciple seeking ***satori.***

Linguistic universals Innate, fundamental features of structure and organization present to all languages.

Logic The formulation and study of the principles of correct reasoning.

Logical positivism A twentieth-century radically **empiricist** perspective embracing some form of the **Verification Principle.**

Logicism The view that the objects of mathematical study are objective, extra-mental entities.

Mahayana Buddhism Original and atheistic form of Buddhism, whose followers seek *nirvana*, or deliverance, through the cultivation of personal emptiness.

Manichaeism A synthesis of **Zoroastrian** and Christian ideas effected by the Persian prophet Mani (died ca. 275), influential during the third to seventh centuries, characterized by a radical **dualism** of two principles, Good and Evil, conceived as ultimate realities locked in eternal struggle.

Material cause The "stuff" something is made of.

Materialism In **metaphysics,** the view that reality consists only of physical entities with their physical properties.

Matter In Aristotle and St. Thomas, that out of which something is made and which is always potentially something different; in Descartes, a **substance** which is extended or occupies space; in modern philosophy, the **substance** which underlies and upholds **sensible** qualities.

Matters of Fact Ideas which are derived from specific experiences (e.g., "Water freezes at 32 degrees Fahrenheit") and thus bear upon and inform us about the world.

Mechanism   The view which conceives of the universe and everything in it as a machine, that is, as governed by a fixed and finite number of laws.

Medical materialism   A label contemptuously applied to attempts to undermine the religious and spiritual significance of religious experiences by attributing them to disorders of a psychological or even physiological nature.

Metaphysics   The study or theory of reality; sometimes used more narrowly to refer to **transcendent** reality, that is, reality which lies beyond the physical world and cannot therefore be grasped by means of the senses.

Mind   In Descartes, a thinking **substance,** that which underlies and upholds the various intellectual functions.

Mind-body problem   The difficulty of explaining the **causal** relation, supposing there is one, between the **mind** and the body when they are conceived as essentially different **substances.**

Mind-matter dualism   The view that all natural things reduce ultimately to two irreducible and essentially different **substances: mind** and **matter.**

Moral evil   The evil that springs from the human will, such as the Nazi death camps, the Stalin purges, the Manson murders, the Spanish Inquisition, and the Sand Creek Massacre.

Moral law   The **objective** and **absolute moral** principles that are imperfectly expressed in **ethical** codes, legislation, etc.

Moral relativism   See *Ethical relativism.*

Morality   Belief in and conformity to principles of virtuous conduct.

Mysterium tremendum   Latin, "fearful secret."

Mystical ascent   The passage of the soul through successive and purifying stages in preparation for **transcendent** union with God.

Mysticism (classical)   The pursuit of a **transcendent,** unitive experience with the **Absolute** Reality.

Objectivity   In **metaphysics,** existence which is **independent** or unconditioned.

Occasionalism   The view that on the occasion of bodily stimuli or impressions God creates the appropriate idea and response in the mind and vice versa.

Ockham's Razor   An expression for the ideal of **simplicity** or economy in explanation, attributed to the fourteenth-century scholastic William of Ockham: *Entia non sunt multiplicanda praeter necessitatem* ("Entities are not to be multiplied without necessity").

Omnibenevolence   The state, usually attributed to God, of possessing unlimited love or complete benevolence.

Omnipotence   The state, usually attributed to God, of possessing unlimited power.

Omniscience   The state, usually attributed to God, of possessing unlimited knowledge.

Ontological Argument   A **proof** for God's existence: God must exist inasmuch as the attribute of existence (or, in some forms, necessary existence) is part of his nature.

Original sin   The traditional, orthodox Christian doctrine that the universal sinfulness of humans is traceable to Adam's initial sin.

Participation, Metaphor of   A metaphor by which Plato attempted to elucidate the relation between **sensible** things and their **Forms: Sensible** things participate or "share" in their ideal **essences.**

Passivity of perception   The experience in which external, **sensible** realities impose themselves upon us, independently of our desire or will.

Pelagianism   Christian heresy, taught by Pelagius (early fifth century) and combated by St. Augustine, which denied **original sin** with its bondage of the will and stressed human capacity freely to do good.

Petitio Principii   "Begging of the question"; an **informal fallacy** which includes the **conclusion** of an **argument,** usually disguised, in one of its premises; also called circular reasoning.

Phantasm   In **scholastic** terminology, the image, formed in the intellect, of a **sensible** thing.

Phenomenal world   In Kant, the world of things as they appear to us in sense experience, as opposed to how they are in themselves.

Phenomenalism   The view that we have no **rational** knowledge of anything, including the **mind,** beyond what is disclosed in the **phenomena** of perceptions.

Phenomenological fallacy   The confusion of a **sense datum** (e.g., green) with the *experience* of the **sense datum** (which is not a **sense datum**).

Phenomenology   Philosophical perspective that emphasizes what is immediately disclosed in consciousness as the proper object of philosophical reflection.

Phenomenon   Literally, an appearance; usually, an object of sense experience.

Philodoxical   Pertaining to the love of (mere) opinions.

Philosophical theology   See *Natural theology.*

Philosophy   Literally, "the love of wisdom"; the attempt to give a **rational** and coherent account of the most fundamental issues, through an examination and manipulation of relevant concepts.

Physicalism   See *Identity Thesis.*

Pluralism   The view that holds that ultimate reality consists of many things, and that usually emphasizes the disparateness or disconnectedness of things.

Postulate   A principle or reality posited as a condition or explanation for other data.

Potentiality   In **Scholastic** philosophy, the **matter** in a thing by virtue of which it may be changed into something different.

Pour soi   French, "for itself," used in Sartrean **existentialism** in reference to conscious being.

Practical principle   In Kant and some other **moral** philosophers, truth or claim pertaining to **morality.**

Practical reason   In Kant, the reasoning faculty that is inspired by awareness of **moral** duties.

Praeparatio anthropologica   Latin, "preparation for humankind."

Pragmatism (pragmatic theory of truth)   An American philosophy which identifies the meaning of concepts and the truth of propositions with their practical bearing, consequences, results, etc.

Predicate   In grammar, the part of a sentence that attributes a property to the subject; in philosophy, by extension, a property or attribute of something.

Preestablished harmony   The view that bodily and physical states have been preordained by God to correspond at every point with appropriate mental states.

Preexistence   Usually of the soul; the doctrine of an existence prior to embodiment in this world.

Proof See *Argument.*

Properly Basic Belief A belief that is reasonable to accept, though without support from other propositions believed to be true.

Providence (divine) God's general direction over the world and of history; the realization of his purposes.

Psycholinguistics The study of the mental processes underlying the acquisition, production, and comprehension of language.

Psychological egoism The belief that everyone by nature seeks his or her self-interest.

Psychosomatic Pertaining to the mind's ability to induce physiological states.

Quality, sensible A feature or characteristic that is apprehended by the senses (e.g., color).

Quantum mechanics The application of quantum theory (energy and other measurable attributes of **matter** are transmitted in discrete units or quanta) to the interaction of **matter** and energy and to the motions of **atomic** particles.

Raison d'être French, "reason for being."

Rational theology See *Natural theology.*

Rationalism The affirmation of reason in general, with its interest in evidence, examination, and evaluation, as authoritative in all matters of belief and conduct (loose sense); the belief that at least some truths about reality are acquired independently of sense experience, through reason alone (strict sense).

Realism In **metaphysics,** the doctrine that **Forms,** or **essences,** possess **objective** reality.

Recollection, Theory of The theory that essential knowledge, or knowledge of ultimate truths, was acquired in a former existence and is recalled in the present life.

Reformed epistemology An antievidentialist and Calvinist view, according to which belief in God is a **properly basic belief** requiring no **rational** justification.

Relations of ideas In Hume, ideas such that, by virtue of their meanings and relations, one cannot be had without the other, as in the idea of a triangle and the idea of three sides; relations of ideas constitute the basis for **logically** necessary truths, but bear not at all on beliefs or reasoning concerning **matters of fact.**

Relativism See *Ethical relativism.*

Relativity In philosophy, the emphasis on the diversity (and thus non-**absoluteness**) of reason, perceptions, customs, **morality**, etc.

Relativity of perception The inevitable variation in different persons' perceptions of **sensible qualities.**

Religion Usually, a set of beliefs, related rituals, and **ethical** principles, centered on a conception of God, divine reality, or Nature; more fundamentally, the commitment (involving belief and practice) to what is conceived to be highest in worth, power, reality, meaning, etc.

Representative perception The view that our ideas represent or correspond to objects in the **external world.**

Representative theory of ideas See *Representative perception.*

Revealed theology Knowledge of God based on **special revelation,** as in divine self-disclosure in the Bible, Jesus Christ, etc.

Rinzai One of the two main sects of **Zen Buddhism,** introduced into Japan in 1191, and which stresses the sudden illumination of the *satori* experience and the deceptiveness of intellectual knowledge.

Rule-utilitarianism An **ethical** theory which emphasizes rules to be followed in a situation to bring about the greatest benefit.

Saecula saeculorum Latin, "ages of the ages," usually rendered "world without end."

Satori The central experience sought by disciples especially of **Zen Buddhism,** consisting of sudden, inward illumination of the indescribable oneness of everything.

Scholasticism The predominant system or method of theological and philosophical teaching during the Middle Ages, based largely on the Church Fathers and Aristotle.

Science An organized body of knowledge about the natural (i.e., **sensible** or physical) world, together with a model which explains the world on naturalistic principles and which is in principle testable by observation or experiment.

Scientific method The procedure by which **scientific** knowledge of the natural world is acquired: (a) hypothesis or theory building, (b) prediction of observable results, (c) experimental confirmation or falsification, (d) modification of the theory, if required.

Second Law of Thermodynamics The physical principle that entropy, which is a measure of disorder, tends to increase with a result that energy (heat) is being uniformly distributed throughout space.

Second-order studies   Reflection on the history, nature, role, methodology, language, etc., of a discipline or inquiry.

Self-determinism   See *Soft-determinism.*

Self-intuition   The immediate awareness we have of our own selves, consciousness, mental states, etc.

Sense datum   An object of sense-experience as presented to the mind.

Sensible   In epistemology, the quality of being apprehensible by one or more of the five senses.

Sensory consciousness   Awareness of images produced in our minds through sense experience or **sensible** objects in the external world.

Sikhism   Reformed sec of Hinduism, established ca. 1500, which rejected many elements of traditional Hinduism, such as the caste system.

Simple idea   An idea which is unanalyzable into more basic ideas (e.g., red and anger).

Situation ethics   The view that **morally** right action is dictated not by general rules but by immediate circumstances.

Skepticism   A doubting or disbelieving state of mind (loose sense); the philosophical doctrine that absolute knowledge is unattainable (strict sense).

Slave morality   Nietzsche's contemptuous term for traditional Christian **ethics,** with its "weak" virtues and incapacity to affirm life.

Social Hedonism   See *Utilitarianism.*

Socrates   (ca. 470–399 B.C.) Philosophical "gadfly" of Athens, who turned philosophical attention to definitions or the **essences** of things, and to **ethical** and political issues.

Socratic problem   The difficulty of identifying in the Platonic dialogues the authentic teachings of Socrates.

Soft-behaviorism   The form of **behaviorism** which limits itself to the description of observable behavior.

Soft-determinism   The view that the will is determined by the character of the individual, and thus individuals are responsible for their choices.

Sophism   An argument possessing merely the appearance of forcefulness.

Sophist   Literally, "wiseman"; historically, an ancient Greek philosopher particularly adept in manipulative reasoning, sometimes accused of being a philosophical charlatan who "made the weaker argument appear to be the stronger, and the stronger argument to be the weaker."

Sophistical Possessing the mere appearance of argumentative forcefulness.

Sound argument A **deductive argument** that is **valid** and whose premises are true.

Special creation The view that the universe, including humans, was created immediately by God, all at once, in the form in which it now exists.

Special revelation A self-disclosure on the part of God whereby he explicitly reveals himself in a book, person, event, etc.

Species A class or kind of individuals possessing common characteristics or qualities.

Speculative philosophy The attempt to raise and to answer the most ultimate and far-ranging questions and to make sense of reality and experience as a whole.

Speculative principle A truth or claim pertaining to reality.

Steady State Theory The **cosmological** model according to which hydrogen atoms are continually coming into existence to fill the emptiness created by receding galaxies, resulting in a universe that is always in the same state.

Subjectivism See *Ethical relativism.*

Subjectivity In **existentialism,** the concretely existing individual as the point of departure for authentic philosophizing.

Substance Literally, "that which underlies or upholds"; used in modern philosophy to signify the foundation which underlies **sensible qualities** or intellectual activities.

Substantial Form A feature or characteristic which belongs necessarily to the nature of a thing.

Substratum Literally, "that which lies under" (see *Substance*).

Supernaturalism The belief in a reality beyond the natural (space and time) and (usually) upon which the natural is dependent for its existence.

Synthetic *a priori* proposition A proposition in which the predicate adds something to the subject and the truth of which is known independently of sense experiences.

Synthetic proposition A proposition that is not logically necessary, the predicate adding something to the subject.

Systematic doubt The process in which anything susceptible to doubt *is* doubted in the interest of discovering something **indubitable.**

Systematic philosophy A philosophy in which the central idea is worked out for and unifies a broad range or areas such as **metaphysics, ethics, cosmology,** and **aesthetics.**

Tabula rasa Literally, "blank tablet"; used to express the **empiricist** idea that at birth the mind is empty, awaiting the input of sense experiences.

Technology of behavior The use of tools and techniques for the alteration and improvement of behavior.

Teleological Argument A **proof** for God's existence: God, an intelligent being, must exist as the cause of the **teleology** (design, beauty, unity, harmony, etc.) of the physical universe; also called the Design Argument.

Teleological ethics The view that emphasizes the results of actions as the test of their rightness.

Teleological suspension of the ethical Kierkegaard's idea that in an immediate relation with God, universal **moral** principles, or norms, are transcended, and the individual acquires his or her injunction directly from God.

Teleology The study of ends, goals, purposes, often in relation to the physical universe.

Temporal Pertaining to time.

Theism The belief in God; usually one God, transcendent, creator, etc.

Theistic Evolution The belief that God uses natural **evolutionary** processes to bring about his desired effect.

Theodicy From Greek, "justification of God"; the attempt to defend the traditional view of God's existence and nature against the seemingly incompatible existence of evil in the world.

Theology The systematic pursuit of a knowledge of God.

Theoretical reason In Kant, the reasoning faculty that employs and is limited by the *a priori* concepts of the understanding.

Third-Man Argument A criticism of the doctrine of Plato's separated, **transcendent Forms** as leading to an **infinite regress** of explanatory **Forms.**

Thomistic Pertaining to the philosophy of St. Thomas Aquinas.

Transcendence Existence beyond, and thus unconditioned by, space and time.

Transcendental In Kant, pertaining to knowledge or thinking that is conditioned by the mind's *a priori* concepts.

Transformational grammar An early version of Chomsky's **generative grammar** which attempted to account for the underlying relatedness of certain types of sentences (e.g., active and passive) by proposing that all sentences have an underlying abstract grammatical representation, or deep structure, from which various structures are derived through a series of transformations.

Uncertainty Principle It is not possible in principle to know beyond a degree of precision both the position and momentum (or any other pair of observables similarly related) of atomic and subatomic particles.

Universal idea An idea which expresses the common nature or **essence** of things included in a class (e.g., table, dog, human).

Universalizability, Principle of See *Categorical Imperative.*

Unmoved Mover, Doctrine of The belief that an ultimate and **immutable** source of motion is **rationally** required.

Utilitarianism The **ethical** doctrine that an action is right if, and only if, it promotes the greatest happiness for the greatest number of people.

Utility, Principle of We are obligated to act so as to promote the greatest balance of good over evil.

Value judgment A judgment which evaluates something or judges its worth.

Value-theory The study of value in all of its manifestations.

Veridical Corresponding to reality; true, genuine.

Verification Principle A proposition is **cognitively meaningful** if and only if it is either **analytic** or in principle **empirically** verifiable.

Watch analogy An analogy introduced by Paley in evidence of God's existence: There must be a God who is to the universe as a watchmaker is to a watch.

Will to power The central idea of Nietzsche's **ethics,** in which the "overman" transcends traditional, conventional values, regarded as weak and life-denying, and celebrates creative and life-affirming values.

Zen Buddhism Branch of **Mahayana Buddhism,** originating in the seventh century, and emphasizing especially meditation exercises ("zen") leading to *satori* or sudden enlightenment.

Zoroastrianism Iranian religion, supposedly founded by the sixth-century B.C. Zoroaster (also called Zarathustra), marked by a strong **ethical** and **cosmological dualism** (Good vs. Evil, Light vs. Darkness) demanding a decision and an alignment on the part of humans.

Acknowledgments

TEXT ACKNOWLEDGMENTS

St. Thomas Aquinas: Excerpts from *Summa Theologiae* in *Basic Writings of St. Thomas Aquinas*, edited by Anton C. Pegis. Reprinted by permission of Richard J. Pegis.

Aristotle: Excerpts from *Poetics*, translated by Ingram Bywater; *Posterior Analytics*, translated by G. R. G. Mure; and *Metaphysics*, translated by W. D. Ross. Reprinted by permission of Oxford University Press.

St. Augustine: Excerpts from *Against the Academicians, III*, translated by Sister Mary Patricia Garvey, 1957. Reprinted by permission of Marquette University Press. Excerpts from *The Enchiridion on Faith, Hope, and Love*, translated by J. F. Shaw, edited by Henry Paolucci, Washington, DC: Regnery Gateway, Inc., 1961, pp. 12–13. Used with permission. Excerpts from *On Free Choice of the Will*, translated by Anna S. Benjamin and L. H. Hackstaff, The Bobbs-Merrill Company, 1964. Reprinted by permission.

A. J. Ayer: Excerpts from *Language, Truth and Logic*, Victor Gollancz Ltd., 1946. Reprinted by permission.

Basho: Haiku from *An Introduction to Haiku* by Harold G. Henderson. Copyright © 1958 by Harold G. Henderson. Used by permission of Doubleday, a division of Bantam Doubleday Dell Publishing Group, Inc.

Simone de Beauvoir: Excerpts from *The Second Sex* by Simone de Beauvoir, translated by H. M. Parshley. Copyright © 1952 by Alfred A. Knopf, Inc. Reprinted by permission of Alfred A. Knopf, Inc.

Ruth Benedict: Excerpt from "Anthropology and the Abnormal" in the *Journal of General Psychology* 10, 1934, pp. 72–74. Reprinted with permission of the Helen Dwight Reid Educational Foundation. Published by Heldref Publications, 4000 Albemarle St., N.W., Washington, DC, 20016. Copyright 1934.

Albert Camus: Excerpts from *The Myth of Sisyphus and Other Essays* by Albert Camus, trans., J. O'Brien. Copyright © 1955 by Alfred A. Knopf, Inc. Reprinted by permission of the publisher.

Noam Chomsky: Excerpts from "Language and the Mind," in *Readings in Psychology Today*. Copyright © 1969. Reprinted by permission of McGraw-Hill, Inc., 1969.

Paul Churchland: Excerpts from *Matter and Consciousness* by Paul Churchland. Copyright © 1984. Reprinted by permission of MIT Press.

C. L. Ducasse: Excerpt from "The Guide of Life," in *The Key Reporter*, Vol. XIII, No. 2, January 1958. Reprinted by permission of the Phi Beta Kappa Foundation.

William Frankena: Excerpts from William Frankena, *Ethics*, Second Edition, © 1973, pp. 13, 35–36, 39–40. Prentice Hall, Englewood Cliffs, N.J. Reprinted by permission.

Sigmund Freud: Excerpt from *The Future of an Illusion* from Volume 21 of *The Standard Edition of the Complete Psychological Works of Sigmund Freud*, translated by W. D. Robson-Scott, revised and edited by James Strachey. Reprinted by permission of Liveright Publishing Corporation and Sigmund Freud Copyrights Ltd., The Institute of Psycho-analysis, and the Hogarth Press Ltd.

Francis Fukuyama: "The End of History?" in *The National Interest*, Summer 1989. Copyright © 1989 by Francis Fukuyama. Reprinted by permission of International Creative Management.

Stanley J. Grenz: Excerpt from "Star Trek and the Next Generation: Postmodernism and the Future of Evangelical Theology," in *CRUX* 30 (March 1994), pp. 24–32.

John Hick: Excerpts from *Evil and the God of Love* by John Hick. Copyright © 1966, 1977 by John Hick. Reprinted by permission of HarperCollins Publishers.

John Hospers: Excerpt from "Free Enterprise as the Embodiment of Justice" by JohnHospers, from *Ethics, Free Enterprise, and Public Policy: Original Essays on Moral Issues in Business*, edited by Richard T. DeGeorge and Joseph A. Pichler. Copyright © 1978 by Oxford University Press, Inc. Reprinted by permission.

Aldous Huxley: Excerpts from *The Doors of Perception* by Aldous Huxley. Copyright 1954 by Aldous Huxley. Reprinted by permission of HarperCollins Publishers, Mrs. Laura Huxley, and Chatto & Windus, Ltd.

Irenaeus: Excerpt from *Against Heresies*, translated by Alexander Roberts and James Donaldson, in *The Ante-Nicene Fathers*, William B. Eerdmans Publishing Co., 1979. Reprinted by permission.

Isaiah: Excerpt from 55:8–9. Scripture quotation is from the *New Revised Standard Version Bible*, copyright 1989 by the Division of Christian Education of the National Council of the Churches of Christ in the USA. Used by permission.

Alison Jaggar: Excerpt from "How Can Philosophy Be Feminist?" in *American Philosophical Association Newsletter on Feminism and Philosophy*, April 1988. Copyright © American Philosophical Association 1988. Reprinted with permission.

Robert Jastrow: Excerpts from *God and the Astronomers* by Robert Jastrow, Warner Books, Inc., 1978. Reprinted by permission of the author.

St. John of the Cross: Excerpts from *The Dark Night of the Soul* by St. John of the Cross, Frederick Ungar Publishing Co., Inc., 1957. Reprinted by permission.

Immanuel Kant: Excerpts from *Critique of Pure Reason*, translated by F. Max Muller, Macmillan Press, London, and Basingstoke, 1960. Excerpts from *Foundations of the Metaphysics of Morals* reprinted with the permission of The Library of Liberal Arts, an imprint of Macmillan Publishing Company, Inc., translated by Lewis White Beck. Copyright © 1959 by Macmillan Publishing Company. Excerpts from *Prolegomena to Any Future Metaphysics*, translated by Lewis W. Beck, The Bobbs-Merrill Company, Inc., 1950. Reprinted by permission.

Lau-tzu: Poem from *Tao Te Ching* by Lau-tzu, Gia-Fu Feng and Jane English, translators. Copyright © 1972 by Gia-Fu Feng and Jane English. Reprinted by permission of Alfred A. Knopf, Inc.

Lucretius: Reprinted from *The Nature of Things* by Lucretius, translated by Frank O. Copley, with the permission of W. W. Norton & Company, Inc. Copyright © 1977 by W. W. Norton & Company, Inc.

Gabriel Marcel: Excerpt from *The Philosophy of Existentialism* by Gabriel Marcel, translated by Manya Harari. Copyright © 1956 Citadel Press. Published by arrangement with Carol Publishing Group.

Herbert Marcuse: Excerpt from *One Dimensional Man* by Herbert Marcuse. Copyright © 1964 by Herbert Marcuse. Reprinted by permission of Beacon Press.

Karl Marx: Excerpts from *Early Writings*, translated and edited by T. B. Bottomore. Copyright 1964. Reprinted by permission of McGraw-Hill, Inc.

Rudolf Otto: Excerpts from *The Idea of the Holy*, Second Edition, by Rudolf Otto, translated by John W. Harvey, 1950. Reprinted by permission Oxford University Press.

William Paley: Excerpts from *Natural Theology: Selections*, edited by Frederick Ferre, Bobbs-Merrill Publishing Co., 1963. Reprinted by permission of Frederick Ferre.

Alvin Plantinga: Excerpt from *God, Freedom, and Evil* by Alvin Plantinga. Copyright © 1974 by Alvin Plantinga. Used by permission of the publisher, William B. Eerdmans, Grand Rapids, MI.

Plato: Excerpts from *Apology* and *Phaedo*, translated by Hugh Tredennick, and from *Euthyphro*, translated by Lane Cooper from *The Collected Dialogues of Plato*, edited by Edith Hamilton and Huntington Cairns, Bollingen Series LXXI. Copyright © 1961, renewed 1989 by Princeton University Press. Reprinted by permission of Princeton University Press. Excerpts reprinted from *The Republic of Plato*, translated by Francis MacDonald Cornford, 1941, by permission of Oxford University Press.

Gilbert Ryle: Excerpts from The Concept of Mind by Gilbert Ryle. Copyright 1949 by Gilbert Ryle. Reprinted by permission of HarperCollins Publishers and the Principal and Fellows of Hertford College, Oxford.

Jean-Paul Sartre: Excerpt from "Existentialism," translated by Bernard Frechtman, from *Existentialism and Human Emotions* by Jean-Paul Sartre. Copyright © 1957, 1985 by Philosophical Library, Inc. Published by arrangement with Carol Publishing Group.

John R. Searle: Excerpt reprinted by permission of the publishers from *Minds, Brains, and Science* by John R. Searle, Cambridge, MA: Harvard University Press, Copyright © 1984 by John R. Searle.

B. F. Skinner: Excerpts from *Beyond Freedom and Dignity* by B. F. Skinner. Copyright © 1971 by B. F. Skinner. Reprinted by permission of Alfred A. Knopf, Inc.

J. J. C. Smart: Excerpt from "Materialism," in *The Journal of Philosophy*, October 24, 1963. Reprinted by permission of The Journal of Philosophy and the author.

Excerpt from *The Song of God: Bhagavad-Gita*, translated by Swami Prabhavananda and Christopher Isherwood, Vedanta Press, 1951. Reprinted by permission of the Vedanta Society of Southern California.

Daisetz Teitaro Suzuki: Excerpts from *Essays in Zen Buddhism* (First Series). Reprinted by permission of Hutchinson Publishing Ltd.

Richard Taylor: Excerpt from Richard Taylor, *Metaphysics*, 2nd Ed., © 1974, pp. 13–15. Reprinted by permission of Prentice Hall, Englewood Cliffs, N.J.

F. R. Tennant: Excerpt from *Philosophical Theology* by F. R. Tennant, Cambridge University Press, 1930. Reprinted by permission.

Mark B. Woodhouse: Excerpt from *A Preface to Philosophy*. Second Edition, by Mark B. Woodhouse, © 1980 by Wadsworth, Inc. Reprinted by permission of the publisher.

PHOTO ACKNOWLEDGMENTS

Page 8, The Bettmann Archive; *p. 48*, Culver; *p. 69*, Alinari/Art Resource; *p. 82*, New York Public Library, Astor, Lenox and Tilden Foundations; *p. 110*, National Portrait Gallery, London; *p. 112*, National Portrait Gallery, London; *p. 129*, Christopher S. Johnson/Stock Boston; *p. 149*, Metropolitan Museum of Art, Wolfe Fund, 1931; *p. 160*, courtesy Noam Chomsky; *p. 186*, New York Public Library, Astor, Lenox and Tilden Foundations; *p. 220*, Time Inc., © 1966 Time Inc. All rights reserved. Reprinted by permission from Time; *p. 232*, The Bettman Archive; *p. 232*, National Portrait Gallery, London; *p. 235*, The Bettman Archive; *p. 244*, New York Public Library, Astor, Lenox and Tilden Foundations; *p. 273*, Culver; *p. 284*, The Seattle Art Museum, from the Eugene Fuller Memorial Collection, 50.120; *p. 291*, Culver; *p. 314*, photo courtesy Courier, Claremont, CA; *p. 327*, UPI/Bettman Newsphotos; *p. 350*, Culver; *p. 356*, Gisele Freund/Photo Researchers; *p. 376*, National Portrait Gallery, London; *p. 382*, National Portrait Gallery, London; *p. 404*, Archiv für Kunst und Geschichte, Berlin; *p. 387*, New York Public Library, Astor, Lenox and Tilden Foundations.

INDEX